LA Freeway System

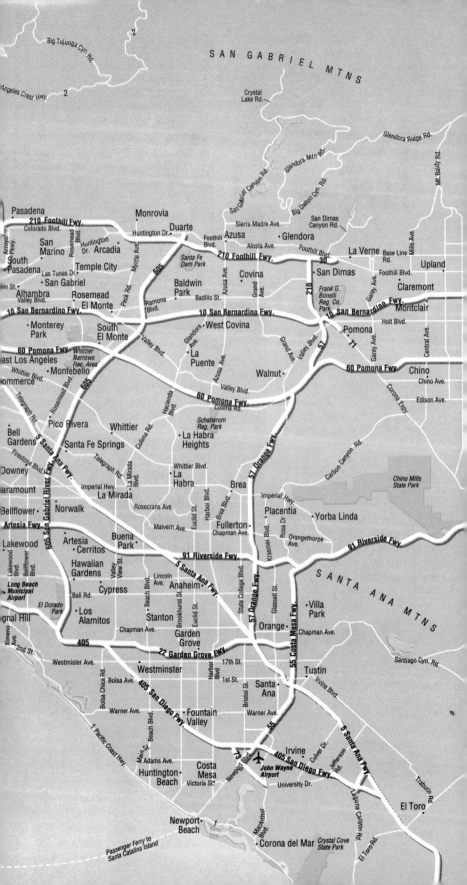

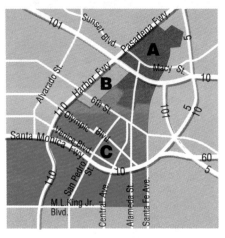

Downtown

Downtown Los Angeles is a surprisingly large and rich area, considering that many have doubted such a thing existed. To make it easier to explore, we have divided it into 3 areas, much of which—another great surprise—can be explored on foot:

A. Historic Core (El Pueblo, site of the first settlement; City Hall; Chinatown; and Little Tokyo);

B. Business and Financial (a corridor of recent high-rise offices to the east of the Harbor Freeway);

C. Commercial and Exposition Park (LA's classic commercial buildings, movie palaces, and markets, south to USC and the museums).

Throughout downtown, the streets are crowded and active by day, often deserted at night. Most stores close just as office workers head home. Over 210,000 workers commute to downtown every day, and daily traffic is more than 350,000 cars. The resident population declined to below 20,000, but is now slowly increasing. From the airport, there is frequent coach service to the major hotels. Driving downtown is a penance: streets are clogged with traffic or construction crews, the one-way system is confusing, and parking garages charge extortionate rates. If you arrive by car, it is best to leave it in your hotel garage. Cruising cabs are rare; call ahead for service. The best ways to get around during the day are on foot and by **DASH** shuttle, a minibus that runs every 6-15 minutes weekdays 6:30AM-6:30PM and Saturdays 10AM-5PM. It only costs a quarter for each of 2 loops that, together, stop at most of the major landmarks. Route A runs from Little Tokyo west to the business corridor, south on Flower to Wilshire, and east to the Garment District. Route B crosses the Harbor Freeway to Library Square, heads north on Grand to the Civic Center, and north again to El Pueblo and Chinatown. Information: 800/8-SHUTTLE. Work has begun on the Metro Rail subway and, if funds don't run out, a 4-mile stretch to mid-Wilshire will be completed in the next few years; eventually, the first line may extend through Hollywood and into the San Fernando Valley.

A. Downtown/Historic Core

This is where LA began; ever since the founding of the city by a handful of Spanish settlers on 4 September 1781, the central core has remained close to its origins around **El Pueblo**. Within a short walk of **City Hall**, you can explore 200 years of history and an extraordinary ethnic and economic diversity. Los Angeles became a Mexican city in 1822, after Mexico won its independence from Spain. In 1847, the Stars and Stripes was raised, and a small stream of Yankee immigrants began arriving. Local boosters roamed the nation singing the praises of a promised land. When, in 1887, 2 competing railroads established links to the midwest, and the fare briefly dropped to a dollar, the trickle became a flood. Immigrants slept in tents and bathtubs. There was a land boom that quickly went bust, leaving downtown with twice as many permanent residents; a third of the newly planted communities also survived.

The more affluent residents began to relocate to the west of downtown, leaving the center and east to new arrivals. Over the years, the influx took its toll, and the area around City Hall became a civic embarrassment. Urban renewal began in the 1930s, with the creation of **Olvera Street** as a symbol of the original Spanish pueblo. In the late '40s, the city created the **Community Redevelopment Agency (CRA)**, which began to acquire properties for renovation and renewal, notably in **Little Tokyo, Chinatown,** and **El Pueblo de Los Angeles**. Ethnic traditions flourish as strongly as ever, here and in surrounding neighborhoods, and you can enjoy the culture and cuisine of almost every country in Latin America and along the Pacific Rim. Los Angeles is home to 750,000 Hispanics, making it one of the largest Spanish-speaking cities in the United States. There are 2 centers of Latino activity downtown: Olvera Street for tourists, and **Broadway** (in Area 1C) for locals.

1 El Pueblo de Los Angeles Historic Park and Olvera Street Bounded by Sunset Blvd, Spring, Arcadia, and Alameda streets. The founding site of the City of Los Angeles, comprising the Plaza, Olvera Street, and several historic or architecturally significant buildings. The City has recently taken over responsibility from the State and is pondering a major redevelopment of the surrounding area. Revitalization of the park is already under way. Olvera Street is named for **Augustin Olvera**, a Los Angeles County judge and supervisor, and was rebuilt in 1930 in the style of a Mexican marketplace. The brick-paved block is lined with shops and *puestos* (stalls), which sell Mexican handicrafts and confections. Food is served at a number of stands and cafés along the street. For dessert, go to the Plaza, where a fruit vendor sells peeled mangos, papayas, and other tropical fruit. The confectioners at the center of Olvera St carry Mexican sweets such as candied squash or brown sugar cones. Delicious Mexican *churros* (donuts) can be found at the bakery near the north-center side of the street. ♦ Daily 10AM-7 or 8PM

2 La Luz del Dia $ You can watch women skilled in the fast-disappearing art of making tortillas by hand. ♦ Mexican ♦ Tu-Su 11AM-10PM. 107 Paseo de la Plaza. 628.7495

2 Sepulveda House (1887) Red-brick business block and boardinghouse, built by **Eliosa Martinez de Sepulveda**. It now houses a **Visitor Information Center**. ♦ M-F 10AM-3PM; Sa 10AM-5:30PM. 624 N. Main St. 628.1274

3 Pelanconi House (1855) One of the first brick buildings in Los Angeles. The 2-story balconied structure was built as a residence with a large wine cellar. It is named for its second owner, **Antonio Pelanconi**. Private residence. ♦ 17 W. Olvera St

Within the Pelanconi House:

Casa La Golondrina $$ Mariachis and dancers entertain while you enjoy Mexican food. ♦ Mexican ♦ Daily 10AM-9PM; closed Wednesday in winter. 628.4349

3 Artes de Mexico Taxco silver jewelry and Guatemalan fabrics. ♦ Daily 9AM-8PM. 19 Olvera St. 620.9782

3 Casa de Sousa Mexican and Central American folk art. ♦ Daily 10AM-8PM. 634 N. Main St. 626.7076

4 Zanja Madre (1783) A fragment of the city's original irrigation ditch, built to carry water from the LA River near Elysian Park.

5 Avila Adobe (1818) LA's oldest adobe, built by **Don Francisco Avila**, one-time mayor of the pueblo. Parts of the original 2-foot-thick walls survive. The simple one-story structure is of characteristic Mexican design, with a garden patio in the rear. Inside are furnishings typical of an early California family of wealth, c. 1840. ♦ Free. Tu-F 10AM-3PM; Sa-Su 10AM-4PM. 10 Olvera St. 628.7164

6 Old Plaza The center of **El Pueblo Historic Park** and the hub of community life through the 1870s. It is now the setting for public festivals that bring back the spirit of the Mexican era. Most notable are **Cinco de Mayo** (5 May, a Mexican holiday), the **Blessing of the Animals** (the Saturday before Easter), and **Las Posadas** (the week before Christmas). At the center of the plaza is the **Kiosko**, a hexagonal bandstand with filigree ironwork. ♦ SE end of Olvera St

7 Old Plaza Firehouse (1884) A castellated brick structure, now a museum containing early firefighting equipment and photographs of 19th-century fire stations. Free guided tours of the area leave from the **Docent Center** next door. ♦ Free. Tu-F 10AM-3PM; Sa-Su 10AM-4:30PM. Tours Tu-Sa 10AM, noon

8 Garnier Block (1890) Built by **Philippe Garnier** as commercial stores and apartments for the city's Chinese businessmen. It is constructed of buff brick with sandstone trim and has an unusual cornice of Victorian Romanesque design. ♦ 415 N. Los Angeles St

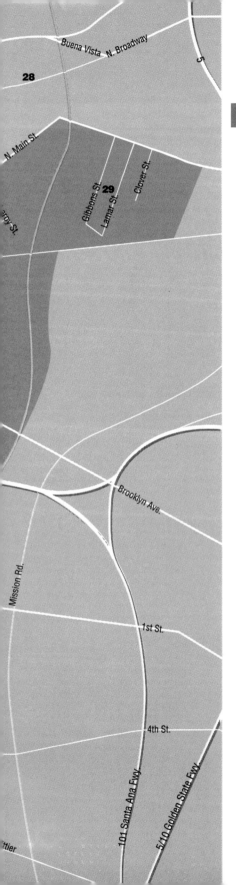

9 Masonic Hall (1858) The city's first lodge, a 2-story Italian Renaissance structure with a cast-iron balcony and 3 arched openings on each floor. Call for group tours. ♦ Free. Tu-F 10AM-3PM. 416 N. Main St. 626.4933

10 Merced Theatre (1870, Ezra F. Kysor) A 400-seat auditorium, with a ground-floor retail store. ♦ 420 N. Main St

11 Pico House (1870, Ezra F. Kysor) A 3-story Italian palazzo built by **Pio Pico**, the last Mexican governor of California. During its heyday the Pico House was the finest hotel in California south of San Francisco. ♦ 430 N. Main St

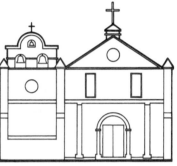

12 Plaza Church (Church of Our Lady the Queen of the Angels) Restored, enlarged, and remodeled several times, the Old Plaza Church was originally a simple adobe built by Franciscan padres and local Indians between 1818-1822. The first structure to be built in the pueblo was the jail, and it was rushed to completion. However, it took the town 40 years to build the church. It is the oldest religious structure in Los Angeles. ♦ 24 hours. 535 N. Main St

13 Union Passenger Station (1939, **John & Donald Parkinson**) One of LA's greatest, least appreciated architectural treasures, and the last of the grand railroad passenger terminals, built jointly by the Southern Pacific, Union Pacific, and Santa Fe. It is a free interpretation of Spanish Mission architecture, combining enormous scale with moderne and Moorish details. The wood-beamed ceiling of the waiting room is 52 feet high, the floors are of marble, and deep scalloped archways lead to 2 atmospheric patios. **Harvey's** restaurant is shuttered, but there are daily departures of the *Desert Wind* to Las Vegas and Chicago, and the *Coast Starlite* to Seattle, plus busy commuter runs to San Diego. As the conductor calls *all aboard*, the ghosts of past glories stir. ♦ 800 N. Alameda St. 683.6875, schedule and ticket information 800/USA-RAIL

14 City Archives Treasury of maps, papers, photos, and council records documenting LA since 1827. Almost unknown, except to city officials, but anyone can make an appointment to do research. One-half mile east of Union Station. ◆ M-F 8AM-5PM. 555 Ramirez St. 485.3512

Downtown Historic Core

15 Main Post Office (Terminal Annex) LA's main mail distribution center is scheduled to move from this handsome building, with its 1930s **Works Progress Administration (WPA)** murals by **Boris Deutsch** depicting the history of communication. The new post office will be located at 7001 S. Central St. 586.1723. ◆ Counter service M-F 7AM-9PM. 900 N. Alameda St. 617.4641

16 Philippe's Original Sandwich Shop $ Legend has it that the French-dip sandwich was invented here in 1908. Since then, the faithful have been coming for simple honest food and 10-cent coffee. The crowd, waiting for a seat at the linoleum-topped tables on the sawdusted floor, is a cross section of LA society, from ballplayers to stockbrokers. (Be sure to have your sandwich double-dipped.) Across the street from the Main Post Office. ◆ American ◆ Daily 6AM-10PM. 1001 N. Alameda St. 628.3781

Chinatown

Centered on 700-1000 N. Broadway in an area roughly bordered by Ord, Alameda, Bernard, and Yale streets. The community of 2 Chinese living in Los Angeles in 1850 increased to 2000 by 1900. About 15,000 people now live here, and the area is the cultural center for over 150,000 Chinese Americans living in the Southland. **Chinese New Year** is celebrated in this part of the city with parades, beauty pageants, and lots of holiday food. The date varies from year to year as the Chinese follow a lunar calendar, but it is usually in February or March. The original settlement on Alameda St was moved northwest in the 1930s to clear the site for Union Station. Civic leaders saw the tourist potential in a *New Chinatown*; in 1938 the theme buildings on the 900 block of North Broadway were built in a *Chu Chin Chow* style, with exaggeratedly curved roof lines and abundant ornament. Behind the gaudy facade is a food shopper's paradise. Chickens squawk, ducks quack, fish swim—you know the food is fresh. Spices, noodles, and glazed ducks extend the menu. Gift shops sell everything from Hong Kong kitsch to fine art. Try **Sam Ward Co**, 959 N. Hill St, for chinaware; **Fong's**, 939-43 Chung King Rd, for art; **Suie One Co**, 122 Ord St, for fine antiques and furniture; **Jin Hing & Co**, 412 Bamboo Ln, for jade; **Sincere Importing**, 483 Gin Ling Wy, for baskets; **Chinese Ritual Paper** on Ord St for exquisite gold and figured papers.

17 Mon Kee ★★$$$ Chaotic and crowded, but it still serves the freshest seafood, superbly prepared. Specialties, including whole crab and shrimp in spicy salt, are worth the wait. ◆ Chinese ◆ Daily 11:30AM-9:45PM. 679 N. Spring St. 628.6717

17 Young Sing ★$$ Down the block from Mon Kee, with the same tank-fresh seafood. It lacks the reputation of Mon Kee, and it also lacks the crowds. ◆ Chinese ◆ Daily 11:30AM-1AM. 643 N. Spring St. 623.1724

17 Savoy ★$ International food at budget prices in an elegant setting, with big mirrors, dark-green walls, and fresh flowers. Oxtail soup, curried prawns, and stir-fried filet mignon are recommended, together with the pastas and exciting desserts. ◆ International ◆ Daily 11AM-10PM. 700 N. Spring St. 613.1038

18 ABC Seafood ★★$$ Cantonese seafood served in a bustling dining room. Dim sum are served for lunch, but the best choice is at dinner time: fresh crab, calamari, or your favorite fish in season. ◆ Cantonese ◆ Daily 8AM-9:45PM. 708 New High St. 680.2887

19 Thanh-Vi ★$ Some of the best Vietnamese food in LA is served in this raffish noodle bar, which might have been imported from Saigon. ◆ Vietnamese ◆ Daily 8AM-7PM. 422 Ord St. 687.3522

20 Mandarin Deli ★$ Dumpling heaven: painless on the pocket, but murder on the waistline. Everything is fresh. Branches in the San Fernando Valley. ◆ Chinese ◆ Daily 11AM-9PM. 727 N. Broadway. 623.6054

20 Miriwa ★$$ Huge, frantic, and—for weekend lunches—packed with locals, just like the Hong Kong dim sum restaurants it is modeled on. For variety (of dumplings and teas) and a slice of life, it is worth the struggle. ◆ Dim Sum ◆ Daily 9AM-3PM, 5-9:30PM. 747 N. Broadway. 687.3088

21 Fortune Seafood ★$$ Delicious, original renditions of standard and exotic Cantonese dishes (don't miss the crab in garlicky black bean sauce) served by unusually cheerful waiters in a spare room decorated with fish tanks. Run by a former manager of the Hop Li. ◆ Cantonese ◆ Daily 11:30AM-1AM. 750 N. Hill St. 680.0640

21 Green Jade ★$$ Very hot Hunanese cooking; if you don't want a skin transplant on your throat, ask them to moderate the spices. Hot-and-sour soup and braised shrimp are highly recommended. ◆ Hunanese ◆ M-Th, Su 11:30AM-3PM, 4:30-9PM; F-Sa 11:30AM-3PM, 5-9:30PM. 750 N. Hill St. 680.1528

22 Hop Li ★$$ Good seafood place, one of the many founded by renegade chefs from Mon Kee. Food is similar to Mon Kee's, and less expensive. ◆ Chinese ◆ Daily 11:30AM-10PM. 528 Alpine St. 680.3939

Restaurants/Clubs: Red   Hotels: Blue
Shops/Parks: Green   **Sights/Culture:** Black

One hundred years ago, when LA had boomed to 11,000 people, there were 92 telephones. The train station had the easiest number to remember: 1

23 Yang Chow ★$$ Sensibly priced Szechuan dishes draw crowds to this rather tacky-looking restaurant. Special kudos go to pan-fried dumplings, *kung pao* chicken, Szechuan beef, and slippery shrimp. ♦ Szechuan ♦ M-Th, Su 11:30AM-9:30PM; F-Sa 11:30AM-10:30PM. 819 N. Broadway. 625.0811

24 Won Kok $ A bustling Cantonese restaurant that stays open and busy until the wee hours. Particularly fine after a night of carousing are their noodle dishes or a bowl of *joak*, a bland but wonderfully soothing thick rice porridge. ♦ Cantonese ♦ Daily 11:30AM-3AM. 208 Alpine St. 613.0700

25 Plum Tree Inn ★$$ Peking duck and *kung pao* chicken are specialties of this stylish restaurant. ♦ Chinese ♦ M-Th, Su 11AM-11PM; F-Sa 11AM-1AM. 937 N. Hill St. 613.1819

25 Foo Chow ★$$ Distinctive dishes include braised sea bass in red wine sauce, fried crab with a spicy bean sauce, and deep-fried oysters. ♦ Chinese ♦ M-Th, Su 11AM-11PM; F-Sa 11AM-1AM. 949 N. Hill St. 485.1294

26 Chiu Chow ★$$ The food of a section of Canton called, not surprisingly, Chiu Chow. The tastes are milder and more subtle than most Cantonese cooking. Try the duck or steamed chicken. ♦ Cantonese ♦ Daily 11AM-11PM. 935 Sun Mun Wy. 628.0097

27 Hunan ★$ Another hot spot in terms of the crowds and the spices used in such dishes as Chinese cabbage, *kung pao* chicken, and meatballs. Bring plenty of beer. ♦ Hunanese ♦ M-Th, Su 11:30AM-2:30PM, 5-9:30PM; F-Sa 11:30AM-2:30PM, 5-10PM. 980 N. Broadway. 626.5050

28 Women's Building Imaginative remodeling changed a 3-story brick warehouse into a gallery and cultural center presenting exhibitions of feminist art, classes, lectures, and public seminars. There is a print workshop also. ♦ Admission. W-F noon-6PM; Sa 10AM-4PM. 1727 N. Spring St. 221.6161

29 San Antonio Winery $ A working winery in an old industrial section of town. The 3-acre site includes tasting rooms, a restaurant, and the original buildings made from wooden boxcars in 1917. Italian sandwiches are the restaurant's specialty. ♦ Winery ♦ M-Th 8AM-7PM; F 8AM-8PM; Sa 9AM-7PM; Su 10AM-6PM. 737 Lamar St. 223.1401

30 Civic Center Second largest governmental center in the US after Washington DC. Pompous and lifeless. You look for the sign, "Abandon hope all ye who enter here." ♦ Bounded by Temple, Main, 1st, and Grand Sts

31 Hall of Records (1962, **Richard Neutra**) One of this talented architect's last and slightest works. ♦ M-F 8AM-5PM. 320 W. Temple St. 974.6616

32 Hall of Justice Building (1925, **Allied Architects**) Municipal Court of the Los Angeles Judicial District, County of Los Angeles, and State of California. ♦ M-F 8AM-4:30PM. 210 W. Temple St. 974.6141

33 US Federal Courthouse Building (1940, **Louis Simon & Gilbert Underwood**) The United States District Court is housed in a handsome WPA-style structure. ♦ 312 N. Spring St. 894.3650

34 City Hall (1928, **Austin, Parkinson, Martin & Whittlesey**) A classic monument now undergoing a long overdue face-lift (by **Hardy Holzman Pfeiffer**), which may also bring back nighttime illumination. Until 1957, this was the only exception to the city's 13-story height limit. The stepped-back building with its pyramid-crowned tower is crammed with historical references, but is unmistakeably Jazz Age American in its brash self-confidence. Inside, luxurious marble columns and an inlaid tile dome give the public areas the feel of a cathedral—don't miss the Easter concert of Renaissance choral music, which exploits the rotunda's accoustics to dazzling effect. Another offbeat attraction is the holographic portrait of **Mayor Tom Bradley**. On a clear day you can see forever from the 27th-floor observation deck (M-F 8AM-1PM). A 45-minute escorted tour offers a capsule history of Los Angeles and California. Tours by reservation only; call at least 2 weeks in advance. Changing exhibitions in the Bridge Gallery weekdays 8AM-5PM. ♦ Free. 200 N. Spring St. 485.2121

35 Los Angeles Children's Museum A touch-and-play experience of exceptional quality. Changing exhibitions on the city's streets, African-American roots, and a kids' television station encourage participation. Classes and workshops are regularly scheduled; call the museum for current availability. Labels in Spanish and English. Weekday parking in the Los Angeles Mall garage. ♦ Admission. M-F 11:30AM-5PM; Sa-Su 10AM-5PM. 310 N. Main St. 687.8800 (recording), 687.8801 (office)

36 Parker Center (1955) Headquarters of the Los Angeles Police Department, named for a former chief of police. ♦ 150 N. Los Angeles St. 485.2121

The present sprawling Los Angeles megalopolis was created by 75 years of growth—one of the greatest population migrations in the history of mankind.

37 Los Angeles Times (1935, **Gordon Kaufmann**; 1973 extension, **William Pereira & Associates**) Stodgy moderne block with a steel-and-glass addition. A free tour allows you to see the making of the newspaper from press room to printing. Children must be 10 or over;

Downtown Historic Core

meet guide at the 1st St entrance. ♦ Free. Tours M-F 11:15AM, 3PM. 202 W 1st St. 237.5757

38 St. Vibiana's Cathedral (1876, **Ezra F. Kysor**) Modeled after a Baroque church in Barcelona, the facade's pilasters and volutes are crowned with a tower and cupola. Inside, relics of the Early Christian martyr, St. Vibiana, are preserved in a marble sarcophagus. ♦ Daily 11:30AM-12:30PM. 114 E 2nd St. 624.3941

Little Tokyo

Roughly bounded by 1st and 3rd streets from Main to Alameda, southeast of the Civic Center. Little Tokyo is the heart of Southern California's Japanese-American community of over 110,000. First settled 100 years ago, the community began to flourish after World War I, but was devastated by the forced evacuation of Japanese-Americans from the Pacific Coast during World War II. Little Tokyo has emerged in the past decade as an active and cohesive area, a mix of late 19th-century commercial buildings and modern structures. *Nisei Week*, held in August, is a major community event, with a parade, street dancing, festival food, and public demonstrations of such Japanese arts as flower arranging, *sumi* brush painting, and the tea ceremony. ♦ Bounded by 1st St (San Pedro Blvd-Central Ave)

39 New Otani Hotel $$$ A symbol of the area's vigorous redevelopment since 1977, the hotel features American- and Japanese-style rooms. The *Japanese Experience* is a pricey but memorable night for 2 in a garden suite that has a sitting room with shoji screens, a Japanese bed, and a soaking tub, plus sauna, massage and dinner in **A Thousand Cranes**. A quality shopping arcade includes the **Kinokuniya**

Bookstore (687.4480) for books on Japanese culture, and **Marukyo** (628.4369) for textiles, kimonos, and futons. In the center of the main lobby is the **Canary Garden**, a pleasant luncheon spot. South of the hotel is a 3-level shopping courtyard, whose primary appeal is to the local community. It gives access to a 4th-story Japanese garden, a haven of tranquility with a dramatic backdrop of new office towers. The **Genji Bar** at this level is a lovely place from where to watch twilight deepen. ♦ 1st St at Los Angeles St. 629.1200, 800/273.2294 (CA), 800/421.8795 (US); fax 213/622.0980

Within the New Otani Hotel:

A Thousand Cranes ★★$$$ Stylish hotel restaurant, overlooking the roof garden, with separate rooms for sushi, tempura, and teppan grill. Excellent service. ♦ Japanese ♦ Daily 11:30AM-2PM, 6-10PM. 629.1200

Commodore Perry's ★$$$ The hotel's American restaurant serves steak and prime rib. ♦ American ♦ M-F, Su 5:30-10PM. 629.1200

40 Astronaut Ellison S. Onizuka Street Formerly **Weller Court**, and renamed for a victim of the *Challenger* disaster, this is a handsome pedestrian precinct. The major tenant is **Matsuzakaya**, a branch of Japan's oldest department store. ♦ Weller St at 2nd St

On Astronaut Ellison S. Onizuka Street:

Nanban-Tei $$ Specializes in *yakitori*—savory barbecued meats and vegetables served on skewers. ♦ Japanese ♦ M-Sa 11:30AM-2PM, 6-10PM. 620.8743

Unashin ★$$ An amazing array of eel dishes (where else in Los Angeles can you get eel liver?). ♦ Japanese ♦ M, W-F 11:30AM-2PM, 5-9:30PM; Sa-Su noon-3PM, 5-9PM. 617.1082

41 Horikawa ★★$$$ A favorite with Japanese businessmen for its sushi bar, *teppan-yaki* grill, and handsome dining room. Horikawa's chef, **Tatsuo Tanaka**, worked for 14 years in one of the best *kaiseki* restaurants of Osaka, and he will prepare a 10-course *kaiseki* dinner or 5-course lunch with 2 days' advance notice. Your group should ask for one of the tea house rooms, where the decor is as artfully calculated as each dish. ♦ Japanese ♦ Tu-Th 11:30AM-2PM, 6-10PM; F 11:30AM-2PM, 6-11PM; Sa 5:30-11PM; Su 5:30-9:30PM. 111 S. San Pedro St. 680.9355

42 Tokyo Kaikan ★$$ A re-creation of an old Japanese inn. Excellent sushi bar and teppan grill. ♦ Japanese ♦ M-F 11:30AM-2PM, 6-10:30PM; Sa 6-10:30PM. 225 S. San Pedro St. 489.1333

For 5000 years the smartest, freest, most creative, anarchic, innovative, best-looking, restless people on the planet have been migrating west along the genetic runway—from Egypt, Persia to Athens, Alexandria, to Rome, Paris, London, Boston, New York. And here now on this Pacific Rim, the human imagination is organizing itself for the next big evolutionary lurch.
Timothy Leary

日 米 文 化 会 館

J A C C C

43 The **Japanese American Cultural and Community Center** A major resource for the entire city. Special events and displays are organized in conjunction with annual community festivals, including *Hanamatsuri* (birth of the Buddha) in early April, *Children's Day* in early May, *Obon* (Festival of the Dead) in June and July, *Nisei* in early August, and *Oshogatsu* (New Year's festivities). The center houses many cultural groups and activities. ♦ 244 S. San Pedro St. 628.2725

Within the Japanese American Cultural and Community Center:

George J. Doizaki Gallery Regular exhibitions of historical treasures and new art and graphics. Posters and distinctive crafts on sale. ♦ Tu-Su 11AM-4PM. 628.2725

Franklin D. Murphy Library Japanese magazines and books on Japan and Japanese-Americans. ♦ Tu-F noon-5PM; Sa 10AM-4PM; Su noon-4PM. 628.2725

Japan America Theater Presents the best in traditional and contemporary performing arts from Japan, including the Grand Kabuki, Bugaku, and Noh dramas, Bunraku puppet theater, plus Western dance and chamber music. ♦ Box office M-F 10AM-6PM; Sa-Su noon-5PM. 680.3700

The JACCC Plaza Designed by **Isamu Noguchi**, with a monumental rock sculpture dedicated to the *Issei* (first generation of Japanese immigrants).

James Irvine Garden (*Seiryu-en or Garden of the Clear Stream*) This garden won the prestigious **National Landscape Award** in 1981. It is a fusion of the 2 cultures, a sunken green oasis for strolling and meditation. Call for hours. ♦ 628.2725

44 **Rafu Bussan** An unusually large selection of lacquerware and ceramics. ♦ M-F 9:30AM-6PM; Sa-Su 10:30AM-6PM. 326 E 2nd St. 614.1181

45 **Japanese Village Plaza Mall** (1979) This shopping complex uses white stucco with exposed wood framing to set off the blue sanchu tile roofs, and incorporates a traditional fireman's lookout tower as a marker. Inset stone paths, rocks, and pools give a rural feeling. ♦ Central Ave (1st-2nd Sts) 620.8861

Within the Japanese Village Plaza Mall:

Yagura Ichiban $$ A *robata* bar, in which grilled snacks are served with drinks alongside a conventional dining room. ♦ Japanese ♦ M-F 11AM-2:30PM, 5-10:30PM; Sa-Su noon-11:30PM. 623.4141

Naniwa Sushi $$ One of the better sushi bars in the area; the dining room serves other Japanese dishes. ♦ Japanese ♦ M-Sa 11:30AM-10PM; Su 11:30AM-9PM. 623.3661

46 **Takaya** ★$ The only place in LA for *kamameshi*, a hearty farmhouse dish, in which rice, vegetables, meat, fish, or chicken are cooked together in an iron pot and served with a large wooden spoon. Don't miss the crisp bits at the bottom of the cauldron. ♦ Japanese ♦ M-F 11AM-3PM, 5-10PM; Su noon-8PM. 305 E 1st St. 689.4837

46 **Sushi Imai** ★$$ Japanese feel at home in this tiny bar. The chef doesn't speak much English and won't make California rolls. But his versatility makes this a must for adventurous *gaijin*, who point and marvel at the results. ♦ Japanese ♦ M-Sa 11:30AM-2PM, 5:30-9:30PM. 359 E 1st St. 617.7927

Eating in **Little Tokyo** ranges from simple to elegant. Moderately priced restaurants usually have plastic models of the dishes they serve in the window. If your tongue fails you, take the waiter outside and point. The Southern California sushi craze started here; to understand sushi's popularity as both cuisine and entertainment, a visit to some sushi bars is recommended. Private tatami rooms, where you sit on the floor and dine Japanese style, are available by reservation in many restaurants. Below is a glossary of sushi terms to make ordering easier:

Aji	**Spanish Mackerel**
Anagi	**Sea Eel (broiled)**
Avocado	**California Roll**
Awabi	**Abalone**
Ebi	**Sweet Shrimp**
Hamachi	**Yellow Tail**
Hashiri	**Scallop**
Iki	**Squid**
Ikuru	**Salmon Eggs**
Kaki	**Oyster**
Kani	**King Crab**
Kappa	**Cucumber Roll**
Maguro	**Tuna**
Masagi	**Smelt Eggs**
Mirugai	**Jumbo Clam, Geoduck**
Nizakani	**Cooked Fish**
Sabi	**Mackerel**
Shaki	**Salmon**
Shiromi	**Halibut, Sea Bass**
Taki	**Octopus**
Tamagi	**Egg**
Tekka	**Tuna Roll**
Tori	**Tuna**
Umeshisi	**Plum Roll**
Unagi	**Fresh Water Eel (broiled)**
Unakyi	**Fresh Water Eel**
Uni	**Sea Urchin Paste**
Yakisakani	**Broiled Fish**

Restaurants/Clubs: Red   Hotels: Blue
Shops/Parks: Green   **Sights/Culture:** Black

11

47 Japanese American National Museum
Scheduled to open in late 1990 in the former **Nishi Hongwangi Buddhist Temple**. Through research, exhibitions, and education it will document the Japanese experience in the United States. ♦ 119 N. Central Ave

Downtown Historic Core

48 The Museum of Contemporary Art (MOCA) at the Temporary Contemporary (TC) (1983, **Frank Gehry**) The transformation of 2 city-owned warehouses was intended as a stop-gap while MOCA's new building was being readied, but the 55,000-square-foot loft space has now become a permanent facility, presenting some of the museum's most ambitious exhibitions. Highlights have included *Blueprints for Modern Living* (on the Case Study House program), *The Automobile and Culture*, and *Tokyo: Form and Spirit*. The building would be worth seeing without the art: Gehry has skillfully preserved the raw character of the interiors, adding a steel-and-chain-link canopy over the street to create an outdoor lobby. **Barbara Kruger**'s mural enlivens the south front. Admission fee covers the TC and MOCA on Grand Avenue. Free admission for members, children under 12, and on Thursday 5-8PM. Low cost parking and easy access from **DASH** shuttle. ♦ Admission. Tu-W, F-Su 11AM-6PM; Th 11AM-8PM. 152 N. Central Ave. 626.6222

49 Oiwake $$ A sushi bar with live *minyo*—Japanese country-and-western music. Customers are welcome to come up on stage and sing along with the band, which colors its songs with every instrument from Chinese bells to maracas. ♦ Japanese ♦ Daily 6PM-2AM. 511 E 1st St. 628.2678

50 Avery Services Corporation Equip a restaurant or buy a single chef's pan at this discount emporium. ♦ M-F 8AM-5PM; Sa 8AM-1PM. 905 E. 2nd St (Alameda St) 624.7832, 800/877.0905

51 Yoro-no-Taki ★$ Businesspeople crowd this wood-paneled room—outpost of a Japanese pub chain—and down large quantities of sake and beer as they nibble on grilled fish, pickled vegetables, and *oden*, a fish cake stew. ♦ Japanese ♦ Daily 5PM-1AM. 432 E 2nd St. 626.6055

52 Hana Ichimonme ★$ If you saw the movie *Tampopo* you will know how seriously the Japanese take *ramen*, and here the noodles are fresh and carefully cooked, the broth rich and delicately spiced. ♦ Japanese ♦ Tu-Su 11:30AM-9PM. 333 S. Alameda St. 626.3514

52 Shibucho ★★$$ Very good sushi bar on the 4th, restaurant floor of Little Tokyo Square, a cavernous shopping center. Chef **Shibuya** has been praised for his artistry. ♦ Japanese ♦ M-Sa 11:30AM-2:30PM, 5:30-10:30PM. 333 S. Alameda St. 626.1184

52 Kappo Kyara ★$$ *Kappo* is the Japanese equivalent of tapas: imaginative nibbles to accompany sake and beer. ♦ Japanese ♦ M-Sa 11:30AM-2PM, 5:30-10:30PM. 333 S. Alameda St. 626.5760

52 Issenjoki ★$$ Cozy, family-run, antique-filled restaurant offering colorful specialties as well as fine salads, noodles at lunch, and *kushiyaki* (grilled kebabs) at dinner. ♦ Japanese ♦ M, W-F 11:30AM-3PM; Sa-Su 11:30AM-5PM. 333 S. Alameda St. 680.1703

53 Higashi Hongwangji Buddhist Temple (1976, **Kajima Associates**) A traditional structure, designed for the **Jodo Shinshu Sect**. A broad flight of stairs leads to the entrance; the blue-tile roof is protected by 2 golden dragons. ♦ 505 E 3rd St. 626.4200

54 Cocola ★$ A happening hangout where you are bound to make friends or run into someone you know. The menu runs the gamut, from essential to exotic. The fries are great, the bartenders pour a mean drink, the scene is hot, and the last call is late (for LA). ♦ American ♦ Tu-Su 11:30AM-2:30AM. 410 Boyd St. 680.0756

54 Tasuki ★★$$$ **Mashiko**, one of the top local sushi masters, presents fresh and flavorful sushi as well as other authentic and sometimes unusual dishes. In winter he serves *mushi sushi*, which is sushi warmed. ♦ Japanese ♦ M-F 11:30AM-2PM, 5:30-10PM; Sa 5:30-10PM. 416 Boyd St. 613.0141

LA's Tallest
Nowhere else in the city is there such a concentration of high rises. Despite LA's reputation as a horizontal city, some of the tallest buildings in the world are in this area. Highest is the 73-story First Interstate World Center building, the tallest building west of Chicago.

	Feet
First Interstate World Center *1989*	1017
First Interstate Bank *1973*	858
Security Pacific National Bank *1973*	738
Crocker Bank *1982*	723
Atlantic Richfield Towers *1971*	699
Wells Fargo Bank *1981*	625
Citicorp Center *1976*	560

Restaurants/Clubs: Red   Hotels: Blue
Shops/Parks: Green   **Sights/Culture:** Black

Ken Frank
La Toque

In the last 10 years Los Angeles has emerged as the leading restaurant city of the United States and arguably the whole world. We offer ethnic diversity that is unequaled anywhere on the face of the earth. The truly devoted and resourceful gastronome can find the most exotic spices from almost any cuisine. With Mexico and the Imperial Valley to the south, the Napa Valley and the San Joaquin to the north, we have access to the freshest and the best-quality foods one could ever want. With modern air freight we can literally shop the world. Although I do most of my shopping by phone, there are still things that one must go out and forage for. Probably the best produce market in the city is the **Irvine Ranch Market** in the **Beverly Center**. From there my favorite places to go are straight down Beverly Boulevard to **Little Tokyo**. The selection of fresh Pacific seafood is irresistible and I always find something new that I can use. Not surprisingly, my favorite restaurants are often Japanese. I also have a weakness for good Italian food, and **Rex**, **Valentino**, and **La Scala** are my favorites.

Richard Meier
Architect

Checking in at the **Bel-Air Hotel**, surrounded by what appears to be the world in bloom, particularly after departing New York on a bleak winter's day.

Dinner at **Spago**, a unique restaurant that catches the rhythm of Los Angeles' most interesting inhabitants.

A Sunday stroll on the **Venice Boardwalk**, for the other half of LA's interesting inhabitants!

A visit to **MOCA**, the newest and most beautifully designed museum, with a stop in **Little Tokyo** for sushi.

Huntington Gardens and Museum are another must-see for visitors and certainly more than an annual excursion for locals.

Patio dining at **Michael's** in Santa Monica on a warm summer evening.

A drive up the coast through **Malibu** with a stop off at a seaside restaurant for drinks and an ocean view.

Evan Kleiman
Angeli Caffè/Trattoria Angeli/Angeli Mare

Olvera Street, the oldest street in LA. Latin street festival feeling. Best place to eat here is **La Luz del Dia**. Get the carnitas and great handmade corn tortillas. Or if you're just in the mood for a snack, go to the little stand in the plaza that serves cucumber or jicama with lime juice and hot chile peppers. If you feel a little more adventurous, go to **El Mercado** at Lorena and 1st. Line up at the stand with the longest line and eat what everybody else is eating—most likely it's a *gordita* stuffed with anything you can imagine! If you feel like eating good, old-fashioned, LA-style Mexican, go to **Barragan's** on Sunset near Echo Park. Order the *arroz con pollo* or the *ropa vieja* or the *sopas*. If you want to grab something on the run, get one of the best burritos or soft tacos in the city at **Yuca's** on Hillhurst.

When I want something simple and historical, I go to **Musso and Franks** on Hollywood Blvd and sit at the counter. Order the grilled lamb chops and creamed spinach with a chiffonade salad and tons of that great bread.

Griffith Park—take a picnic and lay on the grass near the merry-go-round and feel modern life ebb a little.

I guess the major thing that has always held my interest in LA is the fact that it's many mini-cities, so many cultures expressed, and of course, food is the easiest expression to tap into. There are so many great Latin places to try—sometimes its overwhelming. Mexican, El Salvadorean, Nicaraguan, Guatemalan, Peruvian, Chilean, and Cuban.

There are times when I want to tap into the new LA, so I go to **Border Grill** on Melrose for tasty modern Mexican, order Eulalia's chips, *sabana*, or the grilled turkey. For Chinese I go to the **Mandarette** on Beverly Blvd and order everything. When I feel like I need a break from all the insanity of my business, I go to **The Grill** in Beverly Hills for great American classics, Cobb salad, barley-bean soup, short ribs, the best onion rings, rice pudding, and New York-style cheesecake.

Mary Sue Milliken and Susan Feniger
City Restaurant/Border Grill

Bangkok Market on Melrose near the 101 Freeway—great for Oriental vegetables, great curry pastes, and all the Thai ingredients that you could ever need.

Bezjians for wonderful Indian and Armenian selections—especially spices.

Central Market on Broadway downtown—good fresh juice drinks and Mexican specialties like *chipolte* chiles.

Anzen Hardware on 1st and Weller in Little Tokyo—great for Japanese knives, garden tools, and odd hardware.

Book Soup and **Tower Records** on Sunset—great because they're open until midnight so that even night-owl restaurateurs can catch up on their reading, music, and videos.

Analcy's Carnita Stand on Melrose near Wilton.

Pub Mitsuki on Western Avenue between 1st and 3rd—monkfish livers and spicy codfish eggs.

Katsu—impeccable sushi.

Addis Ababa. Ethiopian. The vegetarian platter is A-OK!

Farmers Market at Plummer Park on Mondays—great stuff, great prices.

El Cid on Sunset to watch Flamenco dancers.

Shatto 39 Lanes—pack a picnic and eat with beers while bowling. Open 24 hours.

Neptune's Net—at sunset with loads of friends and piles of shellfish. Bring along wine, eat outside.

Frank Gehry
Architect

I go to **Firenze Kitchens** on North La Brea because my cousin owns it.

B. Downtown/ Business and Financial

High-rise banks and corporate offices rise from a now-flattened **Bunker Hill** and along a narrow corridor flanking the Harbor Freeway. The architecture is generally undistinguished and little has been done to make the pedestrian feel welcome. It is a monument to local boosters who confuse growth with greatness. Massive urban redevelopment has obliterated neighborhoods and landmarks. It began in the 1960s, and the latest installment, **California Plaza**, is only marginally better than what went before.

At the turn of the century, Bunker Hill was the most desirable residential neighborhood in the city, its Victorian gingerbread mansions looking down on what was even then the city's business district. Over the years the neighborhood fell into disrepair. In 1959, the **Community Redevelopment Agency** proposed that the dilapidated Victorian structures, many of which

had been converted into seedy boardinghouses, be demolished, and the top of the hill be leveled (no thought of rehabilitation or adaptive re-use back then!). The resulting open space, plus the elimination in 1957 of the 13-story height limitation on buildings, enticed several major corporations to relocate, thus creating the present cluster of sleek towers.

Flower Street is the main avenue of this burgeoning financial district. The boom has been fueled by the widespread popularity of branch banking in Southern California and the emergence of Los Angeles as the American capital of the Pacific Rim. Of the 6 largest banks in California, 4 have built high-rise headquarters in LA, while the other 2 maintain their Southern California headquarters here. Overseas companies have invested heavily in downtown, for real estate here is a fraction of the cost of Tokyo and Hong Kong.

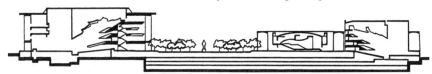

1 The Music Center (1969, Welton Becket & Associates) A white marble acropolis for the performing arts, the West Coast equivalent of New York's Lincoln Center. Nothing better dramatizes LA's growing sophistication in the visual arts than the plans for **Disney Hall**, a 100-million-dollar concert hall, which is soon to be built on the block to the south. The original Music Center was designed by one of LA's big corporate firms—with no public debate—and is as life-enhancing as a mausoleum. Disney Hall—the future home of the LA Philharmonic—was the subject of a widely publicized international architectural competition, won by **Frank Gehry** with a design that soars. The old center is defensive and bleak; the new hall will reach out to the street through a wall of glass. ◆ 135 N. Grand Ave. 972.7211

Within the Music Center:

Dorothy Chandler Pavilion When **Esa Pekka Salonen** or a celebrated guest is conducting the **LA Philharmonic**, when the **LA Opera** is presenting one of its landmark productions, or the **Joffrey Ballet** is at the top of its form, this big barn can be the most exciting place in the city. ◆ Seats 3197. LA Philharmonic 480.3232; LA Opera 972.7211; Joffrey Ballet 972.7611

Mark Taper Forum For 20 years, **Gordon Davidson** has made this one of America's most adventurous theaters, beginning with a production of *Devils*, which was denounced by **Cardinal McIntyre** and provoked a walk-out by **Governor Reagan**—as auspicious a send-off as being banned in Boston. Since then, the Taper has offered 250 productions, including *The Trial of the Catonsville Nine*, *Zoot Suit*, and *Children of a Lesser God*. The horseshoe-plan Taper with its open stage is the only theater in the Music Center where you can see and hear well from every seat in the house. Readings and a literary cabaret are presented at the **Itchey Foot** restaurant across the street; experimental productions at the **Taper, Too** in the **John Anson Ford Theatre** in Hollywood. ◆ Seats 747. 410.1062

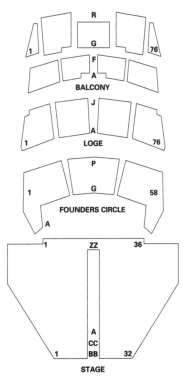

Dorothy Chandler Pavilion

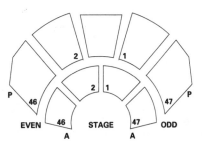

Mark Taper Forum

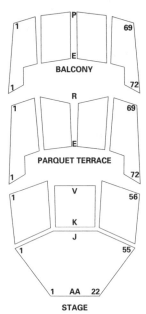

STAGE

Ahmanson Theatre A cavernous house in which the actors sometimes seem to be on a different planet than the audience. Unless you are a faithful subscriber or have lucked into good seats, you had best bring a telescope to see the stars. ◆ Seats 2071. 410.1062

Preconcert Dining Within the Dorothy Chandler Pavilion, at street level, is the **Otto Rothschild Bar & Grill** (972.7322), offering moderately-priced fare. On the 5th floor is the **Pavilion Restaurant** (972.7333), which offers elegant dining and a lavish buffet. It's a good place to know about if you've just won your case at the Federal Courthouse across the street.

Other choices for pretheater dining include **Chinatown, Little Tokyo**, and **Bernard's** in the Biltmore (612.1580). Three blocks south is the **Mandarin Cove** (617.7751), the **California Pizza Kitchen** (626.2616), **Stepps on the Court** (626.0900) in the **Wells Fargo Center, Seventh Street Bistro** (627.1242) in the Fine Arts Building, and **Rex-Il Restaurant** (627.2300) in the Oviatt Building.

2 Department of Water and Power Building (1964, **A.C. Martin & Associates**) West of the Music Center is the headquarters of the largest utility company in the US. The glass-

and-steel building is an elegant stack of horizontal planes that looks its best when lit up at night. ◆ 111 N. Hope St

3 Bunker Hill Towers (1968, **Robert Alexander**) Three high-rise blocks; the first residential structures on redeveloped Bunker Hill. ◆ 800 W 1st St (2nd-Figueroa Sts)

4 California Plaza An 11-acre site, the last open area of Bunker Hill, is now being developed to plans by **Arthur Erickson & Associates**. One office tower is built; to come are more offices and apartments, performance and shopping plazas, the **California Plaza Intercontinental Hotel**, the **Dance Gallery** for the **Bella Lewitsky Dance Company** and visiting companies, and a restored version of **Angel's Flight** (a vintage funicular railway). Architecturally, this is a stiff, conventional scheme that won a limited competition; the runner-up was a marvelously inventive collaboration by architects **Cesar Pelli, Charles Moore, Frank Gehry, Hardy Holzman Pfeiffer**, and others, backed by developer **Robert Maguire**. It would have leavened the dough of downtown LA. However, the city did insist that the developer pay for a new art museum. ◆ Grand-Hill Sts (1st-3rd Sts)

4 Museum of Contemporary Art (MOCA) at California Plaza (1986, **Arata Isozaki**) A dazzling fusion of Western geometry, clad in red sandstone with pyramidal skylights, and the Eastern tradition of solid and void; the first major US building by Japan's leading architect, and one of the city's finest. A sequence of luminous galleries, with exposed vaults, open off a sunken courtyard. Isozaki has even indulged his fascination with **Marilyn Monroe** in the sensuous curve of the parapet overlooking the courtyard.

Under the leadership of director **Richard Koshalek**, MOCA has come far in less than a decade, accumulating a major collection of international scope that includes the works of such artists as **Franz Kline, Claes Oldenberg, Louise Nevelson**, and **Mark Rothko**, and presenting challenging exhibitions that are also presented in the **Temporary Contemporary**, a few blocks away in Little Tokyo.

In the courtyard is a well-stocked shop and **MOCA Café**, an elegant café, both designed by **Brent Saville**. Below the galleries is a steeply raked 162-seat auditorium used for film, video,

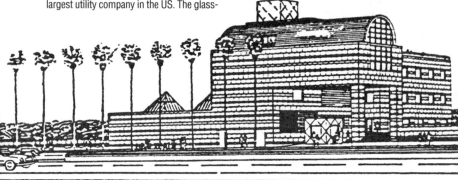

and performing arts. Every Thursday the museum stays open late. There is a bar, free hors d'oeuvres, and (in the summer), live entertainment in the courtyard. Artists, critics, and curators give informative tours of current exhibitions. Parking available at 1st and Grand (lot 16) and the Music Center; rates in the garages below MOCA are astronomical on weekdays before 5PM. MOCA is also served by the DASH shuttle. ♦ Tu-W, F-Su 11AM-6PM; Th 11AM-8PM. 250 S. Grand Ave. 626.6222 (recording), 621.2766 (office)

5 Security Pacific National Bank Headquarters Building and Plaza (1974, **A.C.Martin & Associates**) The well-detailed, 55-story tower is set at an angle to the street and is anchored by the red **Alexander Calder** stabile outside the main entrance. Regular art shows at the northern end of the main lobby. ♦ Gallery: daily 10AM-4:30PM. Building: daily 6AM-7PM. 345 S. Hope St. 345.6211

6 Wells Fargo Center (1983, **Skidmore, Owings & Merrill**) Twin knife-edge towers clad in polished brown granite and tinted glass, developed by **Maguire Thomas Partners**. Between the towers is **The Court**, an exciting glass-walled garden designed by **Lawrence Halprin**, with sculpture by **Jean Dubuffet, Joan Miró, Louise Nevelson**, and **Robert Graham**. More art, by contemporary Californians, is displayed in the upper-level **Court Cafeteria**, a popular lunch spot for office workers. ♦ 350 S. Hope St

Within Wells Fargo Center:

Stepps on the Court ★★$$ Eclectic modern menu—including fresh shellfish, excellent pastas, and salads—served in a cool contemporary setting. A great resource: moderately-priced lunches, drinks at one of the livelier downtown bars, and dinner before or after performances at the Music Center. Validated parking in the Wells Fargo Center. A free shuttle runs every 10 minutes, 7-10:30PM, to the Music Center and the LA Theatre Center. ♦ American ♦ M-F 11AM-3PM, 5-11PM; Sa 4-11PM; Su 4-9:30PM. 626.0900

Fountain Court ★$ Calming courtyard café offers grilled sandwiches, cold poached salmon, and other light fare from Stepps' kitchen. ♦ American ♦ M-F 11:30AM-2PM; Tu-Sa 5:30-9PM. 621.2155

Mandarin Cove ★$$ Excellent Chinese seafood and Western desserts in a stylish peach-and-black room. Espresso bar. ♦ Chinese ♦ M-Th 11AM-9:30PM; F 11AM-10PM; Sa-Su noon-9:30PM. 617.7751

Downtown/Business & Financial

California Pizza Kitchen ★$$ Acclaimed designer pizza (barbecued chicken, roasted garlic shrimp) as well as the basic cheese and tomato; also pastas, salads, and wine. Friendly service and clean, crisp decor. Branches all over LA. ♦ California ♦ M-F 11AM-11PM; Sa noon-11PM; Su noon-9:30PM. 626.2616

McDonald's $ LAPD veteran **Don Bailey** has turned his franchise into a Polo Lounge for the budget-conscious. No anguish here over who gets the power table, just telephone connections to every seat, fresh flowers, and a harpist or flutist to soothe executive stress at lunch on Thursday and Friday. Weight watchers can enjoy a chicken salad instead of the Big Mac and fries. Birthday parties arranged. ♦ American ♦ M-F 5AM-10PM; Sa-Su 8AM-6PM. 626.0709

7 Stuart M. Ketchum Downtown YMCA Sleek coed facility with the latest equipment, Olympic-size pool, running track, and squash and racquetball courts. Membership or daily use fee. ♦ 401 S. Hope St. 624.2348

8 World Trade Center Pedestrian building linked by bridges to the **Bonaventure Hotel** and **Bunker Hill Towers**. A passport office and currency exchange are located in its shopping arcade. ♦ 333 S. Flower St. 489.3337

9 Sheraton Grande Hotel $$$ Shiny luxury hotel beside the freeway with an unusually high level of service and interior design. Lofty atrium lobby and duplex corner suites with huge windows. Complimentary limousine service to the Music Center and Beverly Hills. There is an informal restaurant, the **Back Porch**, as well as **Moody's**, a sophisticated bar. Next door is a cluster of 4 small **Laemmle** movie houses, showing the best new American and foreign films. ♦ 333 S. Figueroa St. 617.1133, 800/325.3535; fax 613.0291

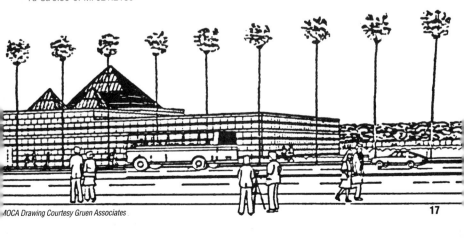

MOCA Drawing Courtesy Gruen Associates.

Within the Sheraton Grande Hotel:

Ravel ★★$$$$ Innovative cuisine from chef **Mark Anderson** in a setting of subdued elegance. Notable attractions are the fine vintage ports served by the glass and live piano music.

Downtown/Business & Financial

♦ California/French ♦ M-F 11:30AM-2PM, 6-10PM; Sa 5:30-9:30PM. 617.1133

10 Original Sonora Cafe ★★$$$ Chef **Felix Salcedo** prepares tasty Southwestern dishes (a lighter, more refined version of Mexican), which include goat-cheese-and-leek quesadilla, duck tamales, and pasta with spicy shrimp. Stunning contemporary New Mexican decor with an exhibition kitchen. Very busy at lunch and at the cocktail hour (order one of their nonslushy adult margaritas). Service can be disorganized. Within the Union Bank Building. ♦ Southwestern ♦ M-F 11AM-2:30PM, 5:30-10PM; F 11AM-2:30PM, 5:30PM-midnight; Sa 5:30-10PM; Su 5-9PM. 445 S. Figueroa St. 624.1800

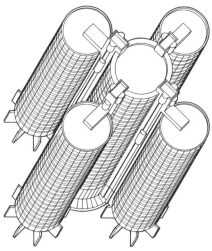

11 The Westin Bonaventure Hotel $$$ (1976, **John Portman**) **Buck Rogers** beside the freeway: 5 mirror-glass silos with glass-bubble elevators and a huge and fanciful atrium. The formula has exhausted its novelty. The hotel is thronged with conventioneers and business travelers who wander around trying to make sense of the 8 levels of shopping, fast food, and restaurants. Among these, the revolving rooftop **Top of the Five** is notable for its 360-degree view; the 4th-floor **Singapore Sate** for its tasty snacks. The lobby is located in the square base of the building, which can be entered from Flower or Figueroa streets. Guests receive complimentary membership in the adjoining **YMCA**. ♦ 404 S. Figueroa St. 624.1000, 800/228.3000; fax 612.4800

Restaurants/Clubs: Red
Shops/Parks: Green
Hotels: Blue
Sights/Culture: Black

Within the Westin Bonaventure Hotel:

Inagiku ★★$$$ Elegant Japanese restaurant specializing in tempura, as well as offering a teppan grill and handsome sushi bar. Tatami rooms are available by reservation. ♦ M-F 11:30AM-2PM; Sa-Su 5:30-10PM. 6th floor. 614.0820

12 444 S. Flower Building An undistinguished corporate tower that replaced the 1935 **Sunkist Building**, with its hanging gardens and statuary. Steps and escalators lead up from a palm-shaded plaza to an upper garden on Hope Street; along the way is a distinguished collection of modern art works by **Mark DiSuvero, Michael Heizer, Frank Stella, Bruce Nauman,** and **Robert Rauschenberg**. Pedestrian bridge over Flower Street to the **Bonaventure Hotel**. ♦ 444 S. Flower St

Within the 444 S. Flower Building:

Wells Fargo History Museum From the company that helped civilize the West: a stagecoach, a 2-pound gold nugget, plus photos and videos recalling 130 years of history. ♦ Open every banking day 9AM-5PM; weekends and evenings by arrangement. ♦ Plaza level. 253.7166

13 First Interstate World Center (1990, **Pei, Cobb, Freed/Harold Fredenburg**) The tallest building in the West: a 1017-foot, 73-story tower, developed by **Maguire Thomas Partners**. The architects have achieved an interplay between orthogonal and circular geometries, which are revealed in the setbacks that lead up to a circular crown. ♦ 633 W 5th St

At First Interstate World Center:

Bunker Hill Steps (1990, **Lawrence Halprin**) A monumental stairway wrapped around the base of the First Interstate tower. Water cascades down from a fountain and restaurants will open off terraces. The steps link Bunker Hill to Hope Street—the 2 vertically separated halves of the business district—and form part of a sequence of landscaped pedestrian areas that Halprin calls *choreography for the urban dance*. To come are his **West Lawn of the Library** and **Hope Street Promenade** leading down to **Grand Hope Park**.

14 Atlantic Richfield Plaza (1972, **A. C. Martin & Associates**) To replace the 1929 **Richfield Building**, a flamboyant black-and-gold Art Deco tower, ARCO commissioned twin 52-story charcoal-gray shafts—the architectural equivalent of a sober business suit—to house its own expanded offices and the **Bank of America**.

Two 20-foot-high bronze doors from the old building are on display in the lobby of the south tower. On the plaza is a striking red helical sculpture, *Double Ascension*, by **Herbert Bayer**, who also designed the executive floors from the carpets on up. Escalators on Flower St lead down to 7 acres of subterranean shopping and eating, plus a church, radio station, and post office. ♦ M-F 10AM-5:30PM; Sa 11AM-4PM. Flower St (5th-6th Sts) 625.2132

Within ARCO Plaza:

Chez François ★★$$$ No view, but the contemporary cuisine is worth the descent into ARCO Plaza. A standard like roast saddle of lamb with rosemary becomes a star atop a fried-potato-and-watercress cake. ♦ French ♦ M-F 11:30AM-2:30PM. Level C. 680.2727

15 The California Club (1930, **Robert D. Farquar**) For years the city was effectively run by members of this private club, a Renaissance-style brick building, and it is still a bastion of power and old money. Worth accepting an invitation; the food is surprisingly good. ♦ 538 S. Flower St. 622.1391

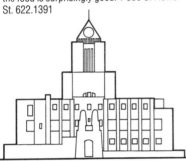

16 Los Angeles Central Library (1926, **Bertram Goodhue** and **Carleton Winslow, Sr.**) One of the great landmarks of downtown was gutted by arson in April 1986, and is now being restored and extended. It combines Beaux-Arts monumentality with touches of Byzantine, Egyptian, and Roman in the surface ornament and incised lettering. There's even a hint of Art Deco. Its interior murals, lawn, and multicolored tiled pyramid peak enrich an increasingly bland neighborhood. Even before the fire, the library was threatened with destruction; it was saved by a transfer of air rights to neighboring plots, which permitted taller towers and a 125-million-dollar contribution by the developer toward an expanded and improved library. **Hardy Holzman Pfeiffer** is currently designing new buildings that will double its capacity. Until their completion in 1993 the library is operating out of temporary premises at 433 S. Spring St. ♦ 612.3200

17 Southern California Gas Center (1991, **Richard Keating/SOM**) A dark gray-and-silver 52-story tower with a distinctive blue glass elliptical crown will be another component of the Library Square development. ♦ 5th St at S. Grand Ave

17 One Bunker Hill (1931, **Allison & Allison**) The former Southern California Edison building is a handsome Art Deco corner block with a lobby mural by **Hugo Ballin**. Handsomely restored. ♦ S. Grand Ave at W 5th St

18 Fountain Pen Shop Classic Waterman, Parker, and Mont Blanc models, plus gold and silver Montegrappas from Italy. Eighth floor of Metropolitan Building. ♦ M-F 8:30AM-12:30PM, 1:30-4PM. 315 W 5th St. 626.9387

19 Caravan Book Store Fine antiquarian bookseller specializing in California history and memorabilia. ♦ M-F 10:30AM-6PM; Sa 11AM-5PM. 550 S. Grand Ave. 626.9944

20 Checkers Hotel $$$$ Small recently opened luxury hotel, a sister of the acclaimed **Campton Place** in San Francisco, created within the shell of the **Mayflower**—itself a luxury hotel when it opened in 1927. Checkers is intended for those who want the best, need

to stay downtown, but cannot stand the huge convention hostelries. The 190 guest rooms and suites are furnished in traditional style with muted colors; niceties include a writing desk and marble bath. Every room has 3 telephones with multiline capability, and the hotel offers its guests a full range of electronic equipment, including personal fax machines, as well as 24-hour room service. There is a rooftop spa with lap pool and several intimate meeting rooms; limousine service and multilingual staff. ♦ 535 S. Grand Ave. 624.0000, 800/628.4900; fax 626.9906

Within Checkers Hotel:

Checkers Restaurant ★★★$$$$ Chef **Jerry Comfort** offers one of the most original menus in town; the room is an oasis of elegance and calm, the service polished. Standout dishes include roast onion with pine-nut aioli, chanterelle soup, house-smoked salmon, exceptional game and desserts. Fine California wine list. Breakfast is worth getting up early for. ♦ California ♦ Daily 6:30AM-10PM. 624.0000

21 Casey's Bar $$ Simple fare served in a setting of white-tile floors, dark paneling, and tin ceilings. This is the most popular after-work meeting place for young downtown office workers. ♦ American ♦ M-F 11AM-11PM. 613 S. Grand Ave. 629.2353

22 Clifton's Silver Spoon Cafeteria $ Occupying a turn-of-the-century building that once housed downtown's most prestigious jeweler, Clifton's is that rare thing: an elegant cafeteria. The basement **Soup Kitchen** serves inventive soups and salads. Also in the basement is the **Meditation Room**, which offers food for thought. ♦ American ♦ M-Sa 7:30AM-3:30PM. 515 W 7th St. 485.1726

23 The Broadway Plaza The Broadway and other stores are ranged around a skylit atrium. ♦ M-Th, Sa 10AM-6PM; F 10AM-7:30PM; Su noon-5PM. 700 W 7th St. 628.9311

Within The Broadway Plaza:

Hyatt Regency $$$ A quality hotel, tastefully decorated. Ask for a room on the **Regency Floor**—it's worth paying a little more for. ♦ 711 S. Hope St. 683.1234, 800/228.9000; fax 629.3230

23 Fowler Bros. Century-old bookstore, run by **Sieg Lindstrom**. Broad stock; children's, travel, and foreign books are specialties. Also office supplies and stationery. ♦ M-F 9AM-5:30PM; Sa 9:30AM-5PM. 717 W 7th St. 627.7846

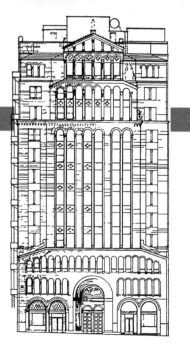

with shrimp, cream, and chives, and risotto with seafood and porcini. ♦ Italian ♦ M-F 11:30AM-2PM, 5-10PM; Sa 6-10:30PM. 227.3464

25 Engine Company No. 28 ★★$$$ This 1912 landmark firehouse has been reborn as a stylish traditional bar and grill. Just the place to unwind with a cocktail and to enjoy comfort food at its best: Cobb salad, grilled fish and garlic chicken, and spicy French fries. Excellent wine list. ♦ American ♦ M-F 11AM-10PM; Sa 5-11PM; Su 4:30-10PM. 644 S. Figueroa St. 624.6996, 800/445.8667

26 Los Angeles Visitors Bureau Maps, fliers, and advice on Southern California's attractions from a helpful and courteous staff who, at last count, were able to deliver it in English, Spanish, Japanese, French, German, Hungarian, and Portuguese. ♦ M-Sa 9AM-5PM. 695 S. Figueroa St. 689.8822

27 Seventh Market Place At the foot of **Citicorp Plaza**, three 42-story towers designed by **Skidmore, Owings & Merrill**, lies this urbane complex, comprising a sunken, palm-shaded patio covered by **Peter Pearce**'s 144-foot space-frame canopy, ringed with 3 levels of specialty stores, **Bullock's**, and **May Co** department stores. Tenants include **Ann Taylor, Johnston and Murphy**, as well as services geared to local office workers. There's a choice of cafés and informal restaurants, or you can brown-bag it on a bench in the leafy, street-level plaza. **The Jerde Partnership** created this people-friendly space in a restrained neo-Victorian style. Validated parking with minimum purchase. ♦ M-F 10AM-7PM; Sa 10AM-6PM; Su noon-5PM. 735 S. Figueroa St. 955.7170

24 Fine Arts Building (1925, **Walker & Eisen**) A splendidly eclectic landmark that was built as a complex of artists' studios enclosing an exhibition hall and was later converted to office space. Developers **Ratkovich and Bowers** commissioned **Brenda Levin & Associates** to restore the Romanesque facade, the high-ceilinged tiled lobby with its gargoyles, fountain, and fanciful murals, and to remodel its interiors. ♦ 811 W 7th St

Within the Fine Arts Building:

Seventh Street Bistro ★★★★$$$$ **Brenda Levin** designed this dramatic room as a cool gray foil to the spectacular cuisine of owner/chef **Laurent Quenioux**. He offers a lunch/dinner menu that changes daily, and three 6-course prix-fixe dinners with wines. A 3-course pretheater dinner is served until 7PM. Innovative dishes have included snapper with a confit of citrus fruits and basil, and salmon wrapped in spinach with lobster sauce. Extensive wine list and a wide choice by the glass. ♦ French ♦ M-F 11:30AM-2:30PM, 5:30-9:30PM; Sa 5:30-10PM. (Off the Fine Arts lobby) 627.1242

25 Los Angeles Hilton $$$ A huge hostelry, popular with business travelers. Amenities include 3 restaurants, a fitness center, and an outdoor pool. ♦ 930 Wilshire Blvd. 629.4321, 800/445.8667; fax 488.9869

Within the Los Angeles Hilton:

City Grill $$$ Grilled fish, salads. ♦ California ♦ Daily 11:30AM-2:30PM. 623.5971

Cardini ★★ $$$$ A stunning Postmodern interior designed by New York architects **Voorzanger and Mills**, in crisp tones of gray and blue and beautifully lit. The space is divided by arches, columns, and open grilles to create a series of intimate enclosures. Standout dishes include an appetizer of thin slices of rare veal with an herb-laden sauce, black ravioli filled

Neon

The first neon signs in America were installed in LA in 1923, over **Earl C. Anthony's Packard** showroom. At that time the **Claude Neon Company** had a worldwide monopoly, but the techniques were soon appropriated by others around the world. Since then the center of action has moved steadily west from Paris to Times Square to LA, and most recently to Hong Kong and Tokyo. Today, LA preserves some of the best vintage neon signs, especially on the rooftops of mid Wilshire Blvd. It has also led its renaissance in the commercial signs on Melrose Avenue, and as an art form whose focus is the downtown **Museum of Neon Art**. MONA (see page 28) runs night tours of LA neon, including some of these highlights:

Golden Pagoda (1938) ♦ 950 Mei Ling Way, Chinatown

Generators of the Cylinder (1982, **Michael Hayden**) ♦ 550 S. Hill St

Felix Chevrolet (1957) ♦ 3330 S. Figueroa St

Mann's Chinese Theatre (1958) ♦ 6925 Hollywood Blvd

Panaieff Ballet Center (1940; unlit) ♦ 150 N. La Brea Blvd

Canter's Bakery (1951) ♦ 419 N. Fairfax Ave

Drive-In (1984, **Lili Lakich**) ♦ Unity Savings, 8501 Wilshire Blvd, Beverly Hills

Clayton's Plumbers (1947) ♦ 2023 Westwood Blvd

Nuart Theatre (1930s) ♦ 11272 Santa Monica Blvd

Richard Koshalek
Director, Museum of Contemporary Art

A weekend visit to the **Museum of Contemporary Art**, which occupies buildings designed by architects Arata Isozaki and Frank Gehry.

An evening at the **Mark Taper Forum** to watch contemporary theater presentations directed over the last 20 years by Gordon Davidson.

Unexpected views, as you travel the freeways of Los Angeles, of the monumental **Hollywood sign** propped up on the side of Mt. Lee.

Lunch or dinner with artists, architects, collectors, and museum curators at **Locanda Veneta, Opera, Indigo,** or **Fennel**.

Visits with my daughter to study the design of private homes by architects, among them, Greene and Greene, Irving Gill, Richard Neutra, Frank Lloyd Wright, Charles Eames, and Frank Gehry.

Any party, such as the annual staff party for the Museum of Contemporary Art at the **Carousel** at **Santa Monica Pier**.

Any New Year's day at the **Rose Bowl** to watch UCLA or USC beat decisively any football team from the Big Ten.

A Sunday afternoon walk through the desert garden at the **Huntington Botanical Gardens** in San Marino.

A trip to the **Watts Towers**, created by Sam Rodia, which is without a doubt the most remarkable work of folk art in the United States.

Gordon Davidson
Director, Mark Taper Forum

Framed view of the ocean through the tunnel at the end of the **Santa Monica Freeway**.

Walking through the back trails of the **Santa Monica Canyon**.

Chaya Brasserie

Sofi Estatorion

Siamese Princess

C'est Fan Fan

Skipping lunch and taking in **MOCA** or **LACMA**.

Huntington Library

Viewing the new fountain through the Robert Graham Door at the **Music Center**.

Trader Joe's, West LA

The Golden Legend Book Shop

Wilder Place

Victor Benes Pastry

Dutton's Bookstore in Brentwood

Stepps Restaurant

Indigo

Off Vine

The bar at **Ma Maison** in the **Sofitel Hotel**.

72 Market Street for brunch.

Franklin Murphy Sculpture Garden at **UCLA** for peace and quiet.

Peter Morton
Morton's

LA County Museum of Art for culture.

Bill White's Foods for health and vegetable burgers.

Coast Highway at dawn or sunset.

Book Soup for magazines and books.

Beverly Hills Hotel Coffee Shop for breakfast.

Locanda Veneta for Italian lunches or dinners.

Michael Roberts
Chef/Restaurateur/Cookbook Author

Tea at **Trumps**—more civilized than shopping and meeting for lunch.

Celebrity Livery—I never drive. Nobody walks in LA. Rent a town car—not limo—by the hour and do shopping with someone else behind the wheel.

Zuma Beach in December—warm sun, cool breeze, no people (hardly).

Topanga Canyon Fish Market—a seafood grill shack; they serve on paper but I arrive with my own tablecloth, napkins, china, and stemware.

Mulholland Highway—best drive in Santa Monica Mountains, from Calabassas to the Ventura County line.

La Plaza—Santa Monica Boulevard—most fun Latin drag show; better than a trip to Tijuana and not as dangerous.

Thursday auctions at **Abel's**.

Laurent Quenioux
Seventh Street Bistro

Driving in Los Angeles at 7AM on Sunday along **Mulholland Drive**.

One of my biggest thrills is to go shopping at **Irvine Market**, located in the **Beverly Center**. You have to watch out or you may end up buying the whole store...or at least groceries for 3 months. The best food market in Southern California.

My favorite restaurant is a tiny place on Sunset Strip called **Talesai**. It is a Thai restaurant and a must-see. It is one of the biggest assets of Los Angeles.

Looking at my restaurant when it is empty because it is so neat and beautiful; but I like it much better when it is full of people, laughing, smoking, grazing on food.

I love my customers talking to me about my cuisine and telling me how wonderful it is. I know the next day they will delight themselves with a fatty hamburger at the stand next door. That's Hollywood!

Staying home and playing the piano is what I enjoy the most in my life, especially after I've worked 7 days in a row from 8AM to 1AM.

When Clark Kent returned to the offices of the *Daily Planet* on Television's *Superman* he was really entering LA's City Hall.

C. Downtown/Commercial and Exposition Park

An area of intriguing complexity. To the north are shops and hotels; to the east commercial, wholesale, manufacturing, and distribution sites. In the south, **Exposition Park** and the **University of Southern California** provide a green oasis amid treeless commercial streets and vintage but dilapidated housing. As with any region of such varied uses, the population is diversified and changes according to the time of day. Most of the area around **Pershing Square** is active during regular business hours, but almost deserted at night. Near the **Coliseum** and **Shrine Auditorium**, nighttime traffic jams occur when football and concert fans collide. The streets of the wholesale distribution centers are quiet until after midnight, then hundreds of trucks fill the roadways. And in the early dawn hours, movie crews are likely to be anywhere downtown filming on the deserted streets.

1 Oviatt Building (1928, **Walker & Eisen**) Formerly an exclusive men's store, built for **James Oviatt**, who had fallen in love with Art Deco on buying trips to Paris. He commissioned the decorative glass from **Rene Lalique**, imported the furnishings from France, and lived in a marvelous zigzag penthouse. In 1976, the building was bought by developer **Wayne Ratkovich**, who hired architect **Brenda Levin** to restore its original glories, and leased the upper floors as offices. You can rent the 13th-floor penthouse for catered parties of up to 50, and dance under the stars on the 1500-square-foot roof (information: 622.6096). ♦ Olive St at 6th St

Within the Oviatt Building:
Rex-II Ristorante ★★★★$$$$ Delicate portions of *nuova cucina* are served in owner **Mauro Vincenti's** imaginative re-creation of the 1930s luxury liner, the *Rex*. This is one of the most exquisite restaurants in the country; the original balconied room, with its dark polished wood and backlit Lalique glass, delights the eye, and chef **Gennaro Villella** dazzles the palate with marvelously full-flavored yet refined dishes that change with the season. The wine list is an education in Italian viniculture. And, for the price of a drink, you can sit in the stylish upstairs bar, and dance on a tiny black marble floor, as a pianist plays Cole Porter. Closed for lunch the first Monday of every month. ♦ Italian ♦ M-F noon-2PM, 6-10PM; Sa 6-10PM. 617 S. Olive St. 627.2300

2 The Biltmore Hotel $$$ (1923, **Schultze & Weaver**) Recently restored at a cost of $40 million, this Italianate Beaux-Arts structure was long a social hub (movie industry leaders met here in 1927 to found the Academy of Motion Picture Arts and Sciences). The palatial decor of the public rooms has been refurbished and regilded by **A.T. Heinsbergen & Co**—which did the splendid Deco murals of the **Cognac Room** in the late 1930s. For the full effect, you should enter through the old portal on Olive Street, facing Pershing Square, and be dazzled by the soaring **Rendezvous Court** (which serves breakfast, tea, and cocktails with piano music). The new entrance turns its back on the square, and is far less distinguished; the recently added office tower is a Postmodern horror. There are 700 traditionally furnished guest rooms and suites, all with **Jim Dine** engravings. The **Presidential Suite** has a private elevator, the **Music Suite** a grand piano. Even those who hate health clubs should check out the music-free exercise rooms and sumptuous Roman bath. The service sometimes leaves much to be desired, especially when the hotel—and its garage—are overtaxed by meetings and receptions. ♦ 506 S. Grand Ave. 624.1011, 800/252.0175 (CA), 800/421.8000 (US); fax 612.1545

Within the Biltmore Hotel:
Bernard's ★★$$$$ Power lunches and romantic dinners in one of the loveliest restaurants in the city—a softly-lit, wood-paneled room with wide-spaced tables and 1920s silverware. The elegant modern menu makes inventive use of the freshest ingredients, especially fish. ♦ French ♦ M-F 11:30AM-2PM, 6-10PM; F 11:30AM-2PM, 6-10:30PM; Sa 6-10:30PM. 612.1580

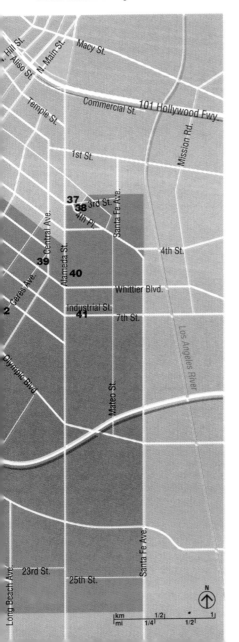

Grand Avenue Bar ★$$$ Italian marble tables and plum-velvet **Mies van der Rohe** chairs, plus exotic plants and works of art that are changed seasonally, form an elegant setting for a delectable lunch buffet, and for vintage wines that are served by the glass.

Downtown/Commercial & Exposition

Evening jazz and complimentary cocktail buffet. ♦ Eclectic ♦ M-F 11:30AM-10PM. 624.1011

3 Pershing Square A blighted space, in urgent need of long-delayed improvements. In 1866, 5 acres of the original pueblo land grant were set aside for public use. The new square supplanted the Old Plaza as the city's center of gravity shifted southwest. In 1918, it was renamed for **Gen. John J. Pershing** Its rich plantings were destroyed in 1951 to construct a multilevel underground parking garage and fallout shelter, whose entry ramps effectively severed the square from the surrounding streets. **SITE Projects**, the New York architects best known for their surreal Best Co stores, won a 1986 competition with a proposal to transform the square into an undulating landscape, containing restaurants and spaces for performing arts. After 2 years of prevarication, this brilliant plan failed to win the financial support of neighboring property owners, who agreed to pay for improvements only if a new design were adopted. Meanwhile, the square has been abandoned to drug dealers and drifters. ♦ Bounded by Olive, 5th, Hill, and 6th Sts

4 Jewelry Mart A papery building that does nothing for Pershing Square. More notable is a 1982 interactive neon art work, *Generators of the Cylinder*, by Canadian-born **Michael Hayden**, which runs the length of the facade. Pedestrians and passing vehicles determine the pattern of flashing lights. The old jewelry district, offering highly competitive prices, extends a block south on Hill Street, between 6th and 7th streets. ♦ 550 S. Hill St

5 Title Guarantee & Trust Building (1930, **John & Donald Parkinson**) Romanticized skyscraper with a gothic crown and zigzag details on the facade and in the lobby. It is designated as a future entry for Metro Rail. ♦ 401 W 5th St

6 Tuttopasta ★$ **Jacques Jordan** operates this no-frills trattoria in an old subway building. The menu is a carbo junkie's fantasy, with stick-to-the-ribs pastas and a few other options. American breakfasts and Italian lunches. ♦ Italian/American ♦ M-F 7AM-2:30PM. 417 S. Hill St. 621.2625

7 Grand Central Public Market An indoor bazaar, frenzied and picturesque, extending from Broadway to Hill Street. **Ira Yellin**—a developer with the vision to see Broadway's potential—commissioned **Brenda Levin** to undertake a major restoration. The stalls sell all types of food, and ready-made Mexican specialties are available for on-premises eating. Plastic wrap is unknown here—butchers use waxed paper—and fruit and vegetable vendors

select your produce from beautiful piles (don't help yourself) and brown bag it. If you're hungry, try a taco or lamb sandwich at stall 43. Thirsty? The juice bar on the Hill St side has 75 kinds. If you're really overwhelmed, have your blood pressure checked at the Health Food counter. ♦ M-Sa 9AM-6PM; Su 10AM-5PM. 317 S. Broadway. 624.2378

8 Broadway The main shopping street for LA's Hispanic community. The crowded sidewalks, exotic sounds, and smells give it an intensely urban quality—much like Upper Broadway in New York, or even Mexico City. But changing tastes, neglect, and the crassest kind of speculative greed threaten the architectural legacy of the prewar years when this was LA's *Great White Way*. Facades have been covered in plastic signs, terrazzo sidewalk ornament is cracked and filthy, and worst of all, the upper stories of several buildings have been lopped off to reduce tax assessments. A few of its monuments have been secured, but the rest of Broadway is in urgent need of enlightened intervention; enjoy its riches while you can.

8 Bradbury Building (1893, **George Wyman**) LA's most extraordinary interior: a Victorian treasure that was, in its time, futuristic. Architectural draftsman **George Wyman** was given the commission and was inspired by a message from his dead brother, received via a Ouija board. Behind the plain brick facade is a skylit interior court that is a marvel of dark foliate grillework, tiled stairs, polished wood, marble, and open-cage elevators. It was used to memorable effect in the movie *Blade Runner* (itself a vision of the future). ♦ Admission. T, Th, Sa 10AM-3PM. 304 S. Broadway. 624.2378

9 Spring Street What was once called the *Wall Street of the West* is slowly coming back from a long period of neglect. This **National Register Historical District** is a treasury of buildings from the first 3 decades of the century. Many have been imaginatively recycled; new structures, including the huge **Ronald Reagan State Office Building** between 3rd and 4th streets, are being added. An **LA Conservancy** flier is a useful guide.

9 Banco Popular (1903) A German immigrant commissioned this Beaux-Arts tower, then considered the city's finest office building. Fine ornament and a marble lobby with a stained-glass dome. ♦ 354 S. Spring St

Movie Palaces

S. Broadway, from 3rd to 9th streets, is the first and largest **Historic Theater District** to be listed on the National Register of Historic Places. The **Los Angeles Conservancy** publishes a flier and offers walking tours. It also organizes **Last Remaining Seats**, an annual series of special events that is held June-July in different theaters. Call 623.2489 for information. Many of these theaters still show movies from noon on, to a predominantly Hispanic audience, and most will let you take a look inside (the **Cameo**, the **Los Angeles**, the **Orpheum**, the **Million Dollar**, the **Arcade**, and the **State**; see these and the rest while you can—many are threatened). **Metropolitan Theaters** operates these bijoux and palaces, but as property values have risen, several of these theaters have been converted to more profitable retail operations. The **Los Angeles**, with one of the city's finest interiors, is dangling by a thread. For information on efforts to preserve these treasures, contact the **LA Historic Theater Foundation** (891.1020).

Broadway's 12 theaters:

Million Dollar (1918) **Sid Grauman** launched his career as a showman in this flamboyant house; it now features lively Latino stage entertainment. **Ira Yellin** plans to restore the theater and make it the centerpiece of his **Central Square** complex—a major boost for Broadway. ♦ 310 S. Broadway

Roxie (1932) Last major theater to be built downtown; zigzag facade. Closed. ♦ 518 S. Broadway

Cameo (1910) Oldest continuously operating movie theater in California, little changed from its original appearance. ♦ 528 S. Broadway

Arcade (1910) Designed in the style of an English music hall as the first Pantages vaudeville house in LA. ♦ 534 S. Broadway

Los Angeles (1931) Architect **S. Charles Lee** created a lobby and auditorium in the style of Versailles in just 3 months. The theater opened with a gala premiere of **Chaplin**'s *City Lights*. ♦ 615 S. Broadway

Palace (1911) Oldest survivor of the Orpheum vaudeville chain; note the terra-cotta reliefs. ♦ 630 S. Broadway

Loew's State (1921) **Judy Garland** (then Frances Gumm) appeared on stage in 1929; the theater was once MGM's downtown showcase. ♦ 703 S. Broadway

Globe (1913) Originally a legitimate theater built for producer **Oliver Morosco**, it later showed newsreels. Original auditorium. Now a popular market. ♦ 744 S. Broadway

Tower (1927) **S. Charles Lee**'s first theater, a 1000-seater on a tiny site. Closed. To reopen soon as a popular market. ♦ 802 S. Broadway

Rialto (1917) Built as a nickelodeon and remodeled for **Sid Grauman**, the theater's best feature is its '30s neon marquee. Closed. ♦ 812 S. Broadway

Orpheum (1926) French Baroque auditorium, opulent marble lobby, fine neon marquee. This vaudeville showcase hosted the 1920s' top talent, including **Pavlova**, **Will Rogers**, and a young **Bob Hope**. Original theater organ. ♦ 842 S. Broadway

United Artists (1926) Spanish Gothic tower designed by **Walker & Eisen**. Within is a cathedral-like theater financed by the original partners of United Artists: **Mary Pickford**, **Douglas Fairbanks**, and **Charlie Chaplin**, who are pictured in the auditorium murals. The interior has been sensitively restored by **Dr. Gene Scott**, who

now uses it as his **University Cathedral**. Two blocks away, at 1038 S. Hill St, is the former **Mayan Theater**, now the **Mayan** nightclub.

Los Angeles Conservancy This preservation society has attracted widespread support, and has begun to effectively combat LA's mania for destroying the best of its past. Members and visitors enjoy a lively program of tours and special events, focusing on the city's rich architectural heritage and diverse neighborhoods. Weekly tours include 4 areas of downtown, including Broadway's theaters; others may include houses of different decades, the Art Deco of **Miracle Mile**, or a film studio usually closed to the public. Call for information on membership, activities, etc. ♦ Recently moved to 727 W 7th St, Suite 955.623.CITY

10 Continental Building (1904, **John Parkinson**) At 175 feet, this was LA's first skyscraper—an ornate pile by an architect who also designed 17 other surviving buildings on the street. ♦ 408 S. Spring St

11 Central Library Pending completion of its new home in 1993, the library has made a wide selection of books available to the public on 6 floors of the 1928 **Design Center**, with its wonderful zigzag lobby and facade. (The building also houses the offices of the **LA Conservancy** and the famed **Aman Folk Dance Ensemble**). ♦ M-F 10AM-8PM; Sa 10AM-5:30PM. 433 S. Spring St

12 The Alexandria Hotel $$ (1906) The best hotel in the city when it opened, welcoming **Theodore Roosevelt, Enrico Caruso, Sarah Bernhardt**, and the first generation of movie makers. The interior has been remodeled, and the stained-glass ceiling of the **Palm Court**, opening off the lobby, has been well restored. ♦ 501 S. Spring St. 626.7484; fax 624.5719

Restaurants/Clubs: Red	Hotels: Blue
Shops/Parks: Green	**Sights/Culture:** Black

12 Broadway Spring Arcade (1923) An enormous skylit space linking Broadway and Spring Street, which an Australian company is trying to turn into a 3-level shopping arcade. The Spanish Renaissance office block is being renovated. ♦ 542 S. Broadway

Downtown/Commercial & Exposition

13 Los Angeles Theatre Center (1916, **John Parkinson**) Opened as a bank, this building was dramatically remodeled and extended by **John Sergio Fisher and Associates** for Artistic Producing Director **Bill Bushnell** and re-opened in 1985 as a complex of 4 small, steeply-raked theaters leading out of the original banking hall. The **Tom Bradley Theater** has an open stage and seats 503; **Theater 2** has a proscenium and seats 296; **Theater 3** has a thrust stage and seats 323; and **Theater 4** is a black box with flexible seating for 99. It is a startling combination of classical and high-tech details, and a shot in the arm for a district that could use more night activity. It's also a critically acclaimed stimulus to LA theater, offering 15 productions a year, ranging from **Shakespeare** and **Oscar Wilde** to new and experimental work and a series of poetry/literary readings. A buffet dinner is served in the lobby before evening performances; sandwiches and salads before weekend matinees. Well-lit parking lot next door. ♦ 514 S. Spring St. 627.6500

14 Finney's Cafeteria (1914) **Ernest Batchelder**'s Craftsman tiles ornament the interior. ♦ 217 W 6th St

15 Story Building & Garage (1916/1934, **Morgan, Walls & Clements**) A Beaux-Arts tower faced in white terra cotta, with superb zigzag garage gates. ♦ Broadway at 6th St

15 Clifton's Brookdale Cafeteria $ Redwood forest interior with waterfall and stuffed moose. On the sidewalk are early 1930s terrazzo roundels of city landmarks. ♦ Cafeteria ♦ Daily 6AM-8PM. 648 S. Broadway. 627.1673

16 Spring Street Towers (1924, **Schultze & Weaver**) Handsome Beaux-Arts bank, recycled as offices, exterior little changed. ♦ 117 W 7th St

17 Cole's Buffet $ Bargain favorite of LA's work force for years. Corned beef, roast beef, pastrami, and French Dip sandwiches. ♦ American ♦ Daily 9AM-midnight. 118 E 6th St. 622.4090

18 Wholesale Flower Market Like the Produce Market, the action here begins at 3AM. The **Flower Market** at 766 Wall Street and the **Growers' Wholesale Florists** at 755 Wall Street are huge halls of flowers reflecting the seasons that Southern California doesn't have. Wholesalers are willing to sell a box to anyone, and Wall Street is lined with smaller merchants who offer potted plants to the public at substantial discounts. The best bargains are to be had after 9AM and on Saturday mornings, when traders are clearing their stocks for the weekend ♦ Wall St (7th-8th Sts) 622.1966

18 Jef's...an Affair with Flowers Unusually fresh, brilliantly arranged flowers—for a big party or an elegant supper. ♦ Daily 6AM-6PM. 744 San Julian Pl. 659.8634

19 Gorky's $ Help yourself to hearty Russian fare—borscht and blinis, chicken with kasha, and piroshki—and home-brewed beer, or come late for live jazz, folk music, and comedy at this lively artists' hangout. ♦ Russian ♦ 24 hours. 536 E 8th St. 627.4060

20 Garment District Los Angeles has been a major center for garment manufacturing since the 1930s. First gaining fame for women's sportswear (Cole of California, Catalina, and Rose Marie Reid transformed the nation's beaches), the current products fit everyone. Jobbers and discount stores offering bargains on everything from children's wear to leather coats line Los Angeles Street from Seventh Street down to Washington Boulevard. A good concentration of retail bargains in women's wear is to be found in the **Cooper Building** (860 S. Los Angeles St, 622.1139). On the 2nd floor is **Fantastic Sportswear** (627.4536) with great buys on Norma Kamali, Anne Klein, and other top labels. On the 4th is the **Linen Room** (622.3320) where bed, bath, and table linens are discounted up to 65 percent. Across the street is **Academy Award Clothes** (811 S. Los Angeles St, 622.9125) with good prices on a huge selection of quality men's suits and formal wear and courteous service.

21 Sam's Fine Foods $ A good Greek salad and a walnut cake that revives flagging energy. ♦ M-Sa 6:30AM-4:30PM. 121 E 9th St. 627.5733

22 The California Mart The southwest corner of 9th and Los Angeles streets houses manufacturers' representatives, most open to the trade only. Currently expanding to the south of Pico Blvd. ♦ 620.0260

23 Lindsey's $ Useful café with pleasant ambiance and nice baked goods. ♦ M-F 8AM-9PM; Sa 9AM-4PM. 112 W 9th St. 624.6684

24 849 (Formerly **Eastern Columbia**) (1929, **Claude Beelman**) Downtown's finest Art Deco building since the Richfield Tower was razed. A 13-story tower faced in turquoise terra cotta with dark-blue-and-gold trim and ornamented with oddly twisted zigzag moldings. Now a wholesale apparel center. **International Food Court** open weekdays for breakfast and lunch. ♦ 849 S. Broadway

25 Gill's Cuisine of India ★$ Luncheon buffet includes good curries and Tandoor specialties. For dinner, try the lamb *Biajia* (with onions) and an unusual sweet carrot dessert, *gajjar halwa*. ♦ Indian ♦ M-Th, Su 11AM-2:30PM, 5:30-9:30PM; F-Sa 11AM-2:30PM, 5:30-10PM. 838 Grand Ave. 623.1050

26 Embassy Auditorium A concert hall with graceful balconies and stained-glass dome, available for rent. (The LA Chamber Orchestra now plays at the Japan-America Theater.) ♦ Seats 1600. 851 S. Grand Ave. 612.6300

Restaurants/Clubs: Red   Hotels: Blue
Shops/Parks: Green   **Sights/Culture:** Black

26 Webster's $$$ (1984, **Charles Moore**) A delightful Postmodern affair; Moore took his inspiration from the ancient ruins of Petra. The front is tiled and has glass walls that can be rolled back for a sidewalk café effect.♦ American ♦ Daily 11:30AM-2:30PM. 851 S. Grand Ave. 743.1572

27 Grand Hope Park (1991, **Lawrence Halprin**) Bureaucratic inertia has stalled construction of this and the landscaped promenade along South Hope Street. The 2-acre park will comprise a series of outdoor rooms created by trellises, fountain, clock tower, and trees, and enhanced by the work of leading local artists. It will be the hub of the planned South Park development, a residential/commercial/office neighborhood bounded by the Santa Monica and Harbor freeways, 8th and Main Streets. ♦ 9th St at Hope St

Drawing Courtesy Jerde Partnership

27 Fashion Institute of Design and Merchandising (1990, **Jerde Partnership**) A fashion museum and gallery, shops and video production facilities, classrooms and offices; a characteristically eclectic design by the Jerde Partnership comprising a 4-story arcade and terrace overlooking Grand Hope Park. ♦ 9th St at Hope St

28 Country Life ★$ Vegetarian restaurant-cum-health food store run by the 7th Day Adventists in a cavernous, rather antiseptic basement. There's a lovely fruit and vegetable salad bar, but it's the creative hot dishes that shine. ♦ Vegetarian ♦ M-Th 11:30AM-2:30PM; F 11:30AM-2:30PM, 5-8PM. 888 S. Figueroa St. 489.4118

29 The Original Pantry ★$ Steaks, coleslaw, remarkable sourdough bread, and the best hash browns in town since 1924. They never close, not even to redecorate. Next door is the Pantry's new **Bake & Sandwich Shoppe**, which serves just what the name promises, daily 6AM-8:30PM. ♦ American ♦ 24 hours. 877 S. Figueroa St. 972.9279

30 Figueroa Hotel $$ Patronized by such touring performers as **The New York City Opera Company** and the **American Ballet Theatre**. The enormous swimming pool has a garden setting and the café is open 6AM-11PM. ♦ 939 S. Figueroa St. 627.8971, 800/331.5151 (CA), 800/421.9092 (US); fax 689.0305

31 Olympic Camera Large stock of cameras, tripods, bags, and film at discount prices. ♦ 828 W. Olympic Blvd. 746.0575

32 Los Angeles Convention Center Holiday Inn $$ Convenient to the commercial centers

Downtown/Commercial & Exposition

of downtown and popular with business travelers. ♦ 1020 S. Figueroa St. 748.1291, 800/863.9418; fax 748.6028

33 Los Angeles Convention Center This municipal facility opened in 1971 and is currently being tripled in size—to 600,000 square feet—to lure major conventions, as well as a varied menu of trade shows and public events. ♦ 1201 S. Figueroa St. 741.1151

34 Transamerica Center This 32-story commercial structure has an observation deck. ♦ Free. M-F 10AM-4PM. 1150 S. Olive St. 742.2111

Within the Transamerica Center:

The Tower Restaurant ★$$$$ Expense-account dining room with good service and a stunning view. A new chef, **Axel Dikkers**, of the Regency Club and Camelions, may restore its former high reputation. ♦ French ♦ M-F 11:30AM-2PM, 6-9:30PM; Sa 6-9:30PM. 1150 S. Olive St. 746.1554

35 Herald Examiner Building (1912, **Julia Morgan**) Morgan, the first woman trained at the Ecole des Beaux-Arts in Paris and the designer of Hearst's San Simeon castle, created a Spanish Mission Revival design inspired by the California Building from the 1893 Chicago World's Fair. The paper is now defunct and the building faces an uncertain future. ♦ 1111 S. Broadway. 744.8000

36 Mayan An upscale nightclub now occupies what was once the **Mayan Theater** (1927, **Morgan, Walls & Clements**). The auditorium that opened with a Gershwin revue, and was long relegated to porn, now contains a 2-level dance floor and bar. A private club, the **Mayan Lounge**, draws stars and top models. Warrior priests glare from the facade; inside is looming statuary and a riot of ornament inspired by a newly excavated Mayan tomb (much as King Tut's launched a fad for ancient Egypt in the early 1920s). Next door is another theater by the same architects, the **Belasco**, now available for rental. Across the street is **Tony's Burger**, a 1932 log cabin, and presiding over the parking lot is **Kent Twitchell**'s 70-foot mural of **Ed Ruscha**. Just a few of LA's surreal juxtapositions. ♦ Building: daily 8AM-5PM; nightclub: daily 9PM-2AM. 1038 S. Hill St. 746.4674

37 Cafe Vignes ★$$ Stylish industrial chic setting for a menu of soups, salads, and steamed entrees. ♦ California ♦ M-F 11AM-7PM. 923 E 3rd St. 687.9709

37 Museum of Neon Art (MONA) Neon artist and graphic designer **Lili Lakich** turned her loft

into one of LA's most vibrant small museums, dedicated to the exhibition and preservation of neon, electric, and kinetic art. Vintage signs are exhibited alongside new work by artists and students. Regular classes and special events for members. Gifts and publications for sale. MONA is currently seeking a larger home. Admission fee for nonmembers over 16. ♦ Tu-Sa 11AM-5PM. 704 Traction Ave. 617.1580 (recording)

42 Wholesale Produce Market A cornucopia of produce, sold by the lug or the bushel only, every weekday from 3AM to noon. The market has 2 main sections: **Produce Court**, off 9th Street just west of Central Avenue; and **Merchants Street**, off 8th Street just west of Central Avenue. **Great Northern Produce** is where top chefs shop for the freshest *haricots verts*, wild mushrooms, mache, and radiccio at wholesale prices. There's a $100 minimum, so put together a group and share the savings. Phone in your order in advance. ♦ 747.0407

42 Vickman's $ A cafeteria-counter restaurant that's been satisfying trenchermen's appetites at bargain prices since 1930. Baked goods are made fresh on the premises. ♦ American ♦ M-F 3AM-3PM; Sa 3AM-1PM; Su 7AM-1PM. 1228 E 8th St. 622.3852

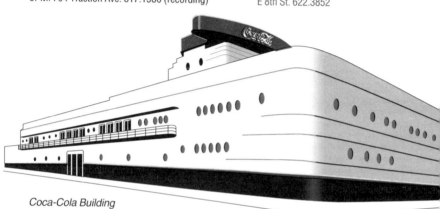

Coca-Cola Building

38 Al's Bar Bohemian hangout that specializes in underground music, performance art, and theater. Crowded, smoky, and raw-edged. ♦ M-F 6PM-2AM; Sa-Su 2PM-2AM. 305 S. Hewitt St. 687.3558

39 American Fish & Seafood Company Chefs shop this market, which sells to the public at wholesale prices. ♦ M-F 7AM-3PM; Sa 7-11AM. 550 Ceres St. 612.0350

39 The Fisherman's Outlet ★$ Buy fish, retail and wholesale, or eat at outdoor tables. A dozen varieties to choose from, in large portions at rock-bottom prices—broiled, deep-fried, or Cajun-style. ♦ Seafood ♦ M-Sa 10AM-3:30PM. 529 S. Central Ave. 627.7231

40 Cirrus Contemporary paintings and fine art prints by Southern Californian artists. ♦ Tu-Sa 11AM-5PM. 542 S. Alameda St. 680.3473

41 LACE (Los Angeles Contemporary Exhibitions) *Eat Your Heart Out*, an annual St. Valentine's Day extravaganza, was founded by this downtown art space, which provides diverse gallery and community art programs. Significant film, video, and audio pieces; performance, music, and installation pieces; as well as sculpture, drawings, and paintings by emerging and well-known regional and nonregional artists have been presented since 1977. The artist-backed organization also has a slide registry for downtown artists and an art periodical library for the public. ♦ Tu-Sa 11AM-5PM; Su noon-5PM. 1804 Industrial St (6th-7th Sts) 624.5650

43 Coca-Cola Building (1937, **Robert V. Derrah**) Five plain industrial buildings disguised as an ocean liner. The streamlined forms, hatch covers, portholes, and flying bridge bring a little salt air to the land of asphalt. Inset at the corners are 2 enormous coke bottles. ♦ 1334 S. Central Ave

44 Second Baptist Church (1925, **Paul Williams**) Lombardian Romanesque church that serves as a center for African-American community activities. ♦ 2412 Griffith Ave. 748.0318

45 Stimson House (1891) Originally designed for prominent lumberman **Douglas Stimson**, the Queen Anne-style house has a tower and a number of medieval fortresslike details. Now occupied by the **Convent of the Infant of Prague** and not open to the public. ♦ 2421 S. Figueroa St

Some people believe that the **Santa Anas**, the hot, dry winds that blow in from the desert, can drive one crazy. **Raymond Chandler**, the mystery writer, wrote of *those hot, dry Santa Anas that come down through the mountain passes and curl your hair and make your nerves jump and your skin itch. On nights like that every booze party ends in a fight. Meek little wives feel the edge of the carving knife and study their husbands' necks. Anything can happen.*

Restaurants/Clubs: Red
Shops/Parks: Green

Hotels: Blue
Sights/Culture: Black

46 Doheny Mansion and Chester Place

Thirteen grand and expensive houses were built here at the turn of the century on one block of a 15-acre residential park. The Doheny Mansion is considered the finest structure on the block. It was designed by **Theodore Eisen** and **Sumner Hunt** for **Oliver Posey** in 1900; shortly after construction, oilman **Edward Doheny** bought the home. Few alterations have been made to the French Gothic château exterior. The house is now owned by the **Sisters of St. Joseph of Carondelet** Open house in mid November. ♦ 8 Chester Pl. 746.0450

46 Chamber Music in Historic Sites

Another annual attraction that makes LA a mecca for music lovers is this series of concerts organized by **Dr. Mary Ann Bonino** for the **Da Camera Society of Mount St. Mary's College**. Many of the performances, by top groups and soloists, are held under the Tiffany glass dome of the Doheny Mansion, the society's home. But that's just for starters. The **Bartok String Quartet** has performed in **Frank Lloyd Wright's Ennis-Brown House**; Prague's **Music da Camera** in the **Grand Salon** of the *Queen Mary*; the **New World Basset Horn Trio** in a former **Masonic Lodge**. Churches, bookstores, a movie palace lobby, and the **Catalina Casino** have also matched architecture with music. ♦ 10 Chester Place. 747.9085

47 St. Vincent de Paul Roman Catholic Church

(1925, Albert C. Martin) Oilman Edward Doheny donated the funds for this church designed in the ornate Spanish style known as *Churrigueresque*, patterned after Baroque scrolled silverwork. The interior is decorated in brightly colored tiles and contains ceiling decorations painted by **Giovanni Smeraldi**. ♦ 621 W. Adams Blvd.

48 Automobile Club of Southern California

(1923) Handsome Mission-revival building with a courtyard where early road signs are displayed. Services offered to members include insurance, towing, travel planning, and maps. Wall maps can be purchased by nonmembers. ♦ M-F 9AM-5PM. 2601 S. Figueroa. 741.3111

49 North University Park

Feisty local preservation groups have protected a concentration of handsome late Victorian houses, laid out after the 1880s population explosion as a prosperous residential neighborhood, linked by streetcar to downtown. Residents have restored several of the finest examples, including the **Bassett House** (2653 S. Hoover St) and the **Miller and Herriott House** (1163 W 27th St). Private residences. ♦ S. Hoover St-Magnolia St (W. Adams Blvd-27th St)

50 Hebrew Union College and Skirball Museum

An institute of Jewish higher learning, opened in 1954. **The Frances-Henry Library of Judaica** contains a special collection of material on the American Jewish experience. **Skirball Museum** has a collection of archeological and

biblical Judaica, including textiles, coins, ritual objects, and marriage contracts. One gallery displays a biblical environment entitled *A Walk Through the Past* that is a delight for children. Changing temporary exhibitions are also offered. ♦ Free. Hebrew Union College: Tu-Th 8:30AM-5PM; F 8:30AM-4:30PM; Su 1-5PM. Skirball Museum: Tu-F 11AM-4PM; Su 10AM-5PM. 3077 University Ave. 749.3424

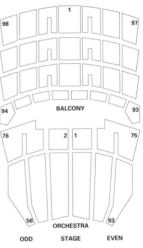

51 Shrine Civic Auditorium

(1926) A movie-set mosque designed for and still used by the Shriners. The cavernous auditorium was neglected after the construction of the Music Center, but has been restored and is making a comeback. Box office at 655 S. Hill St. ♦ Seats 6400. 665 W. Jefferson Blvd. 748.5116

52 The University Hilton

$$$ Located across the street from USC's **Davidson Conference Center**, this comfortable hotel offers a spa, swimming pool, restaurant, and café. ♦ 3540 S. Figueroa St. 748.4141, 800/445.8667; fax 746.3255

53 University of Southern California

Founded in 1880, USC is the oldest major independent coeducational nonsectarian university on the West Coast. The student body has grown from 53 at the founding to the current 31,000. Numbered among the internationally known professional schools are: architecture, law, medicine, dentistry, social work, education, public administration, engineering, gerontology, cinema, performing arts, pharmacology, and international relations. The campus has 191 buildings on 152 acres. Campus open daily year-round; specific buildings open daily 9AM-5PM. Free hour-long walking tours of the campus: ♦ M-F 10AM-2PM. 743.2983. Jefferson Blvd, Exposition, Figueroa, and Vermont streets. 743.2311

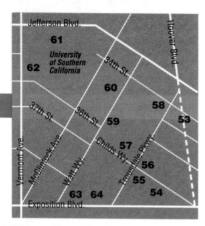

54 Widnezy Alumni House (1880) A 2-story clapboard house, furnished in period style.

55 Hancock Memorial Museum Incorporates historical rooms with original furnishings from a now-demolished mansion. By appointment. ♦ Free. M-F 10AM-4PM. 743.5213

56 Doheny Memorial Library (1932) The principal USC reference library.

57 Bovard Administration Building (1921, John & Donald Parkinson) A Romanesque brick block containing the recently restored 1600-seat Norris Auditorium, which is used for a variety of cultural events.

58 Bing Theater Drama performances are given in this theater. ♦ Seats 589. 743.7923

59 Norris Cinema Theater Film programs in this luxurious theater are open to the public most evenings. ♦ Seats 341. 743.6089

60 Arnold Schoenberg Institute (1978, Adrian Wilson & Associates) A complex, angular structure houses the archive of the great 20th-century composer and a re-creation of the Brentwood studio in which he worked as an exile for the last 17 years of his life. Concerts of contemporary music are given in a small auditorium. ♦ Free. M-F 10AM-4PM. 743.5362

61 McDonald's Olympic Swim Stadium Hosts USC swimming and diving events. ♦ Seats 1500. 743.2222

62 David X. Marks Tennis Stadium Hosts USC tennis matches. ♦ Seats 1000. 743.2222

63 Fisher Gallery Temporary art exhibitions and selections from the **Armand Hammer Collection** of 18th- and 19th-century Dutch painting. ♦ Tu-F noon-5PM; Sa noon-4PM; closed June-August. 743.2799

64 Mudd Hall (1930) An important philosophy library whose building was modeled on a medieval Tuscan monastery.

65 Exposition Park The location of the **Memorial Coliseum, Sports Arena, Museums of Science, Industry, Space,** and **Natural History,** a community clubhouse, and several landscaped areas, including the rose garden. Exposition Park began as a casual open-air market, and in 1872 was formally deeded as an agricultural park for farmers to exhibit their products. Fairs and car-nivals on the grounds were organized by the **Southern California Agricultural Society,** including occasional sponsorship of races on the lot to the rear of the park. The lot was used as a track for horse racing and, on a few occasions, was the site of camel races. Toward the turn of the century it was home to bicycle and automobile competitions. During the park's decline in the early 1890s it became a hangout for society's lower elements and home to 3 saloons. The transformation of the rowdy agricultural park into a major state, county, and city museum center was accomplished by **Judge William Miller Bowen.** The park's romantic attractions made truants of much of Judge Bowen's neighboring Sunday school classes. One Sunday he followed his class to discover their secret destination and utilized his shocking discovery to spearhead a drive to create a landmark of worthwhile cultural significance on the saloon site. By 1910, work on the County Museum of Natural History had begun. ♦ Exposition Blvd-Menlo St (Figueroa St-Martin Luther King, Jr. Blvd)

66 Exposition Park Rose Garden A sunken garden containing over 19,000 rose bushes representing over 190 varieties. At the center are latticework gazebos. When the roses are in bloom, this is the most fragrant spot in town. ♦ Free. Daily 7AM-5PM. Exposition Blvd. Wedding reservations 485.5529

67 California Afro-American Museum A museum dedicated to African-American achievements in politics, education, athletics, and the arts. The front part of the museum is a 13,000-square-foot sculpture court with a sloping space frame ceiling covered with tinted glass. Inside, there is space for changing exhibitions, a research library, a theater, and a gift shop. ♦ Free. Daily 10AM-5PM. 600 State Dr. 744.7432

67 California Aerospace Museum (1984, Frank Gehry) A blank-walled hangar, with echoes of radomes and space-assembly buildings, and an F-104 Starfighter pinned to the facade, seemingly frozen in flight. Inside, open walkways give you close-ups of suspended planes: a 1920 **Wright** glider, a 1927 *Mono Coupe*, a *T-38 Air Force Trainer*, and a *Gemini 11* space capsule. Eventually this building will become a lobby for a much expanded museum in the adjoining red-brick armory, now closed for renovation. ♦ Free. Daily 10AM-5PM. 700 State Dr. 744.7400

67 Mitsubishi Imax Theater Next to the Aerospace Museum is Gehry's octagonal theater, showing different Imax films on a 50- by 70-foot screen. ♦ Seats 430. Admission. Call for schedule. 700 State Dr. 744.2014

68 California State Museum of Science and Industry A great place for kids of all ages, full of exciting new displays alongside old favorites like **Charles Eames' Mathematica,** talking computers, and the **Hall of Health** with *Clearissa* the transparent woman. Innovative exhibitions allow you to check your health, understand electricity and earthquakes, and explore a DC3 and DC8. Gift shop. McDonald's cafeteria. ♦ Free. Daily 10AM-5PM. Exposition Blvd. 744.7400

70 Olympic Arch (1984, **Robert Graham**) This massive sculpture in front of the coliseum is a permanent memento of the 1984 Olympics. It is topped by 2 headless bronze nudes; water polo player **Terry Schroeder** was the model for

the male figure. ♦ Figueroa St and Martin Luther King, Jr. Blvd

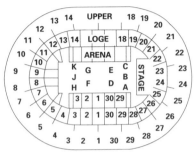

71 Sports Arena (1958) This sister facility to the coliseum is used as a multipurpose indoor sports and entertainment facility. The main auditorium is home to the USC basketball team, as well as host to ice shows, track meets, car shows, concerts, rodeos, and conventions. ♦ Seats 16,000. 3939 S. Figueroa St. 748.6131

Bests

Dr. Craig C. Black
Director, LA County Natural History Museum

The wary wonderment when an 8 year old first sees and hears a **Triceratops** stamping its feet and roaring at a passerby.

The delight of a family as they slowly discover the ferret popping up behind a log in our **Alaskan bear group** or first notice the salmon flopping in a pool under a bear's claw.

Watching the **California Condor** watchers exclaim over the size of the vanishing species.

The incessant quest for more information about **dinosaurs** from visitors of all ages.

The fiery beauty of the Hixon ruby in the **Deutsch Gallery of Gems**.

The **Lando Hall Model of Los Angeles** circa 1940 when we compare it to Los Angeles today.

The **California Museum**'s paintings by **Edwin Deakin**.

The **Parson's Discovery Center**, where children of all ages can handle and learn about the diversity of life on our planet.

The entire **Page Museum**, which is indeed a jewel among natural history museums, at the **Tar Pits**.

Restaurants/Clubs: Red   Hotels: Blue
Shops/Parks: Green   **Sights/Culture:** Black

69 Los Angeles County Museum of Natural History Handsome Spanish Renaissance building, recently restored for the Museum's 75th anniversary. Some of the finest traveling exhibitions in LA, on topics as varied as Hollywood, nomads, volcanoes, and Indonesian court art, are presented here. But the image of the museum is indelibly set by its celebrated collections of reptile and mammal fossils (including several dinosaurs), its innovative **Schreiber Hall of Birds**, minerals, and pre-Columbian artifacts. The **Hall of American History** shows machinery and memorabilia. Native American and Folk Art Festivals are presented every year and the annual *Dinosaur Ball* is a major social event. Children and adults will enjoy the **Discovery Center**, where they learn about nature by handling and working with artifacts. The museum has a bookstore, a fine gift shop, and a cafeteria serving low-priced meals. Bookstore and gift shop. ♦ Admission. Tu-Su 10AM-5PM; free first Tu of every month. 900 Exposition Blvd. 744.3466, 744.3303 (recording)

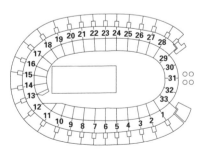

70 Los Angeles Memorial Coliseum (1923) This was the major venue for the 1984 Olympics, as it was for the 1932 Games. Other sports events (including USC football) and concerts are regularly scheduled. ♦ Seats 91,000. 3911 S. Figueroa St. 747.7111

Midtown

The area from downtown to the edge of Beverly Hills and the Westside is a geographical abstraction that includes many distinct neighborhoods. The easternmost section, from the **Harbor Freeway** to **Lafayette Park**, is home to thousands of new immigrants from Central America, Mexico, the Philippines, Southeast Asia, and Korea. West to **La Brea Avenue** is a transitional area, with new and landmark commercial buildings from the 1920s on. **Wilshire Boulevard** from La Brea to **Fairfax Avenue** was developed as Miracle Mile in the 1930s; following a long decline, this strip is being extensively rebuilt. The final section, west to **La Cienega** and **Robertson** boulevards, is a fashionable residential district, studded with design showrooms and art galleries.

Wilshire Boulevard, the spine of this corpulent entity, was originally a path followed by the **Yang-Na Indians** from their Elysian Hills settlement to the tar pits of **Hancock Park**, where they obtained pitch to waterproof their homes. Today's Wilshire runs 16 miles to the ocean, and was named after **H. Gaylord Wilshire** (1861-1927), a rascally entrepreneur from Ohio who made and lost fortunes in orange and walnut farming, gold mining, patent therapeutic electric belts, and real-estate development. The boulevard did not immediately

achieve its present renown. Oil fever captured the city shortly after **Edward Doheny** struck oil near Second Street and Glendale Avenue. (Amazingly, Doheny discovered a small pool of oil with a shovel, 16 feet into the hillside.) By 1905, the neighborhood was dotted with oil wells, and fortunes were made—among them the Hancock family, whose farm included the tar pits near Wilshire and Fairfax. This field was soon exhausted, leaving only the tar pits and a few camouflaged wells as reminders of the boom years.

1 Freeway Overpass Between Figueroa St and Beaudry Ave, Wilshire Blvd passes over the Harbor Freeway. A few blocks north is the stack interchange, where the Hollywood, Harbor/Pasadena, and San Bernardino freeways interlace to form the hub of the Southern California freeway system. Driving north gives you the closest view you will want of a pair of unusually inept buildings—pseudoclassical towers for Coast Savings and Home Savings —which provide 2 more good arguments for winding up the S&L industry.

2 Bob Baker Marionette Theater Since 1963, this has been one of LA's most delightful experiences—for children of all ages. Ticket prices include refreshments and a backstage tour to see how the puppets are made and operated. ♦ Performances Tu-F 10:30AM (except in Sep-Oct); Sa-Su 2:30PM. Reservations required. 1345 W 1st St. 250.9995

3 Pacific Stock Exchange Recently relocated from its landmark building on Spring Street. ♦ Viewing gallery M-F 7:30AM-1:30PM. 233 S. Beaudry Ave. 977.4500

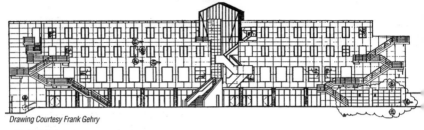

Drawing Courtesy Frank Gehry

Midtown

4 Shangri-La Chinese Seafood ★$$ Shark-fin soup, steamed *tilapia*, braised oysters, and meat-stuffed rice cake have been praised at this large Hong Kong-style restaurant. Dim sum are served at lunch. ♦ Chinese ♦ M-F 11AM-9:30PM; Sa-Su 10AM-9:30PM. 313 S. Boylston St. 250.2288

4 Vertigo A big, fashionable dance club that has relocated from Grand Ave. Many are called, but only a few terminally hip people are chosen from the crowd on the sidewalk and allowed to enter. ♦ Cover. Club: F-Sa 10PM-4AM. Bistro: Tu-Th 11:30AM-2PM; F 11:30AM-2PM, 8:30-11:30PM; Sa 8:30-11:30PM. 333 S. Boylston St. 747.4849

5 Mary Andrews Clark Memorial Residence of the YWCA (1913, **Arthur Benton**) An enormous French château. ♦ 306 Loma Dr

6 Pacific Dining Car ★$$$$ Prime beef aged on the premises, a remarkable wine cellar, and a fine spinach salad. The front dining room was once a railroad car. Good breakfasts. ♦ American ♦ 24 hours. 1310 W 6th St. 483.6000

7 Mayfair Hotel $$$ A vintage hostelry, newly restored. Restaurant and lounge. Free shuttle to downtown. ♦ 1256 W 7th St. 484.9614, 800/874.2642 (CA), 800/821.8682 (US); fax 484.2769

LA Follies

In 1959, **Orson Welles** wrote of LA: *Architectural fantasy is in decline, the cheerful gaudiness is mostly gone, the more high-spirited of the old outrages have been razed or stand in ruins. In the 'better' residential and business districts a kind of official 'good taste' has taken charge. The result is a standardized impeccability, sterile and joyless, but it correctly expresses the community's ardent yearnings towards respectability.* Welles was more prophetic than he knew. The original **Brown Derby** (promoted with the sign '*Eat in the Hat*') is now incongruously placed atop another banal mini-mall and the lumpen **Beverly Center** has displaced a pony ride, and the **Ma Maison-Sofitel Hotel** has replaced a **Tail-o-the-Pup** hot-dog stand. A few programmatic or exotic buildings survive: the **Darkroom** on Miracle Mile and the **Tail-o-the-Pup** hot-dog stand at 329 San Vicente Blvd; in Hollywood, there's **Cross-roads of the World** on Sunset, the **Chinese Theater**, a Moorish house on Sweetzer, and the **Little Red Schoolhouse** on Highland. And Melrose Avenue's windows and storefronts are a joyful anthology of eccentricity. Other attractions are identified in subsequent sections. See them before someone tries to "improve" their sites.

8 Loyola Law School (1981-1987, **Frank Gehry**) An idiosyncratic version of **Thomas Jefferson**'s *Academical Village* has given a new spirit to what was formerly a drab commuter school. Stylized versions of a classical temple and a Romanesque chapel are deployed on a tight-knit campus. Outside stairs create a forced perspective centerpiece on the administration building and encourage social intercourse. The school has established a fine art collection that includes **Claes Oldenburg**'s whimsical construction *Toppling Ladder*. ♦ 1441 Olympic Blvd. 736.1000

9 Paper Source **Wallace** and **Rose Marie Dawes** love paper, and they stock the finest materials for artists, designers, and archivists. This is the place for handmade, marbleized, and gold-leaf sheets; also for weekend workshops. ♦ M-F 9AM-5:30PM; Sa 10AM-4PM. 1506 W 12th St. 387.5820

10 L'Adelita ★$ Multipurpose Mexican and Central American emporium, offering a wide range of baked goods, fresh tortillas, tamales, *pupusas* (Salvadoran cornmeal turnovers), sandwiches, and hot entrees. ♦ Mexican/Central American ♦ Daily 6AM-10PM. 1287 S. Union Ave. 487.0176. Also at: 5812 Santa Monica Blvd, Hollywood. 465.6526

11 Alvarado Terrace A gently curving street laid out in the first decade of the century as a fashionable suburb at the western boundary of the original pueblo of Los Angeles. It's a smorgasbord of eclectic architectural styles, including Queen Anne and Mission Revival, Shingle and English Tudor. **Juan Bautista Alvarado** was the Mexican governor of California, 1836-42. ♦ Pico Blvd (Alvarado-Hoover Sts)

12 Vagabond Inn $$ A small hotel offering budget rates. Continental breakfast. Pool. ♦ 1904 Olympic Blvd. 380.9393, 800/522.1555; fax 487.2662. Also at: 3101 S. Figueroa St. 746.1531

13 New Olympian Hotel $$ An aviary full of exotic birds, tropical foliage, and statuary fills the lobby of this hotel. Pool and free airport shuttle. The lobby was recently renovated. ♦ 1903 W. Olympic Blvd. 385.7141; fax 385.5808

14 South Bonnie Brae Street Westlake (now **MacArthur Park**) was one of LA's first suburbs. Most of it has been rebuilt, but this street survives as a treasury of 1890s houses. Among the standouts are **No. 818**, a regal Queen Anne with an immense veranda, elaborate woodwork, and several types of columns and piers; **No. 824** with its Islamic domed tower; and much of the 1000 block. ♦ 8th St-Olympic Blvd

15 Star 88 ★$ A bright addition to the Thai scene with a striking Postmodern interior. The authentic menu includes such standards as *pad Thai* noodles and exotica like *nai voi* (organ meat soup); *tod mun* (fishcakes) are a must. Food is spiced to order. ♦ Thai ♦ M-F 11AM-3PM, 5-10PM; Sa 5-10PM. 1901 W 8th St. 413.5510

16 Langer's Delicatessen ★$$ One of the few places serving pastrami that a New Yorker would applaud. ♦ Deli ♦ Daily 6:30AM-11PM. 704 S. Alvarado St. 483.8050

17 MacArthur Park Laid out in 1890, it was one of LA's first public gardens, and today provides badly needed recreation space for local immigrant communities. It contains over 80 species of rare plants and trees, a lake with paddleboats for rent, a small band shell for summer entertainment, snack bars, and children's play areas. Over 11 site-specific artworks have been installed in the park as part of a program formerly supervised by **Adolfo Nodal**, now general manager of the city's Department of Cultural Affairs. They include **Judy Simonian**'s *Pyramids* (2 tiled ziggurats linked by a speaking tube), **Eric Orr**'s *Water Spout* (which rises up to 500 feet from the lake), and **George Herm**'s *Clock Tower* (constructed from discarded materials in the spirit of Watts Towers). The neon signs around the park and along Wilshire have been relit to evoke the 1930s; especially notable is the marquee of the **Westlake Theatre**, a handsome 1926 movie palace overlooking the park. The area is currently threatened by drug-related violence. Be aware. ♦ Wilshire Blvd (Alvarado-Park View Sts)

17 Park Plaza Hotel $$ Housed in the landmark 1924 **Elks Building**, a near relation of the Central Library with its grand arches, massive parapet sculptures, and interiors decorated by **Anthony Heinsbergen**. Gym with Olympic pool, squash courts, cocktail lounge, and free parking. ♦ 607 S. Park View St. 384.5281

18 The Otis Art Institute of Parsons School of Design LA's oldest college of art and design, established in 1918, is now a division of the **New School for Social Research** in New York. It offers undergraduate and masters degrees in fine and applied arts, public evening classes, and varied community outreach programs. **Kent Twitchell** has painted one of his best murals, a *Holy Trinity* of soap opera stars, on a wall overlooking Carondelet St. A major extension (**Johnson, Fain, Pereira**) is due for completion by mid-1991. The **Otis/Parsons Art Gallery** presents notable exhibitions. ♦ Free. Tu-Sa 10AM-5PM. 2401 Wilshire Blvd (6th St) 251.0500

It struck me as an odd thing that here, alone of all the cities in America, there was no plausible answer to the question, 'Why did a town spring up here and why has it grown so big?'
Morris Markey, 1932

Wilshire Boulevard was the first street in LA to don parking meters, traffic signals, and Christmas decorations.

18 La Fonda $$ **Los Camperos**, one of the finest mariachi groups anywhere, entertains in this popular spot. The margaritas are especially good and the atmosphere one of the most festive in town. ♦ Mexican ♦ M-F 11AM-2PM, 5:30PM-midnight; Sa 5PM-2AM; Su 5PM-midnight. 2501 Wilshire Blvd. 380.5055

18 Vagabond Theatre One of a fast-shrinking group of repertory revival houses that shows

classic movies the way they were meant to be seen. ♦ 2509 Wilshire Blvd. 387.2171

Drawing Courtesy Carlos Diniz Associates

19 Granada Building (1927) Spanish Colonial architecture combined with Mission-style arches and arcades, designed for architects and artists who wanted courtyard studio offices. ♦ 652 S. Lafayette Park Pl

20 Lafayette Park Another of LA's older public parks, which includes a recreation and senior citizens' center, tennis courts, a picnic area, and a scent garden with numerous fragrant flowers for the blind. ♦ 2800 Wilshire Blvd

20 CNA Building (1972) and the **First Congregational Church** (1932) A mirror glass slab that reflects the sky (actually disappearing at times) and the English Gothic church across the street. ♦ 6th St at Commonwealth St

20 Mi Guatemala $ A storefront restaurant serving local specialties that include *pepian* (a tasty pork stew) and *pan con chile relleno* (a delicious spicy sandwich of shredded beef and pork with green peppers and diced vegetables). ♦ Guatemalan ♦ Daily 11AM-10PM. 695 S. Hoover St. 387.4296

20 Al Fresco $ Owner **Sumol Chomyang** makes this simple café a special place, and offers pizza, pasta, salads, and desserts at budget prices. ♦ Italian ♦ M-F 11:30AM-10PM; Sa 1-10PM. 524 S. Occidental Blvd. 382.8003

21 Brooklyn Bagel Bakery The Big Apple meets the Big Orange. Bagels bring tears to the eyes of expatriates—crisp, shiny crusts garnished with onion. ♦ M-Th 7AM-11:30PM; F 7AM-4AM; Sa 11:30AM-4AM; Su 11:30AM-11:30PM. 2217 Beverly Blvd. 413.4114

22 Tommy's $ Street-side stand serving what its many loyal fans call the best chili burgers in LA. ♦ American ♦ 24 hours. 2575 W. Beverly Blvd 389.9060

Restaurants/Clubs: Red   Hotels: Blue
Shops/Parks: Green   **Sights/Culture:** Black

23 Shibucho ★★$$ Sushi and sashimi of high quality served in a traditional woodsy interior with pebble floors. ♦ Japanese ♦ M-Sa 5:30PM-3AM. 3114 Beverly Blvd. 387.8498

24 Lowenbrau Keller ★$$ Huge helpings at reasonable prices in an elaborate Bavarian setting. Delicious sausages and sauerbraten, with a good choice of local wine and beers. ♦ German ♦ M-F 11:30AM-2:30PM, 6-10PM;

Midtown

Sa 5-10PM. 3211 Beverly Blvd. 480.8462

24 Hamayoshi ★$$ Attractive sushi bar and beautifully appointed back rooms. Private tatami rooms are available by reservation; be sure to be on time. ♦ Japanese ♦ M-Th 11:30AM-2PM, 5PM-midnight; F 11:30AM-2PM, 5PM-2AM; Sa 5PM-1AM; Su 4:30-10PM. 3350 W 1st St. 384.2914

25 Cafe Blanc ★★★$$ In this stark black-and-white shoe box, chef **Tomihisa Harase**, a veteran of **Spago** and **Chinois on Main**, creates Oriental and Occidental food, meshing the techniques of French cuisine with the simple artistry of his native Japan. Intense flavors and inspired combinations characterize the bargain-priced 5-course dinners and simple lunches. ♦ Japanese/California ♦ M-F 11:30AM-3PM, 6-10PM; Sa 6-10PM. 3706 Beverly Blvd. 380.2829

26 Lotus Restaurant ★★$$ Improbably located in the **Midtown Hilton** overlooking the Hollywood Freeway, experts judge this to be one of the best places for Mandarin cuisine this side of Taipei. Specialties include crispy scallops, Shanghai vegetarian goose, jellyfish with candied pine nuts, and pork filet in lotus leaves. ♦ Chinese ♦ M-Th, Su 11:30AM-2:30PM, 5:30-9:45PM; F-Sa 5:30-10:45PM. 400 N. Vermont Ave. 661.8011

27 Casa Carnitas ★$ Kitsch decor, cutesy waitresses, Latino crowds, and Mexican music create an appropriate context for searingly soulful food. Rich Yucatecan specialties include excellent fish and shellfish, pork-and-black-bean stew, and fried plantains. ♦ Mexican ♦ M-Th 11AM-midnight; F-Sa 11AM-1AM. 4067 Beverly Blvd. 667.9953

28 Sheraton Town House $$$ A luxury hotel in the middle of the city with tennis courts, swimming pool, sauna, and gardens. Lanai suites have private patios overlooking the pool and are a good value. ♦ 2961 Wilshire Blvd. 382.7171, 800/325.3535; fax 487.7148

29 I. Magnin Wilshire (1928, **John & Donald Parkinson**) Formerly Bullock's Wilshire. The grandest monument of Art Deco in LA. It was the city's first suburban department store, designed for the automobile rather than the pedestrian, entered from a rear porte-cochere facing over the parking lot. Its proximity to newly fashionable Hancock Park drew traffic away from Broadway, and it set a pattern that was imitated along Wilshire Blvd to the ocean. It's still LA's most handsome store, from its stepped profile to its soaring green-crowned tower; from **Herman Sachs**' portal mural of

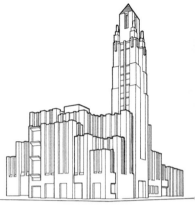

transportation to the miraculously preserved interior design. High-quality merchandise and old-fashioned service. ♦ M-W, F-Sa 10AM-6PM; Th 10AM-8PM; Su noon-5PM. 3050 Wilshire Blvd. 382.6161

Within I. Magnin Wilshire:

The Tea Room $$ Located on the 5th floor, this a genteel period piece that also presents luncheon fashion shows and serves cocktails. ♦ American ♦ M-W, F-Sa 10AM-6PM; Th 10AM-8PM. 382.6161

30 Cassell's Patio Hamburgers ★$ No-frills setting for homemade burgers, potato salad, and fresh-squeezed lemonade. ♦ American ♦ M-Sa 10AM-4PM. 3266 W 6th St. 480.8668

31 Chapman Park Market (1929, **Morgan, Walls & Clements**) The indispensable **Wayne Ratkovich** rehabilitated this vintage shopping center, with its motor court and Churrigueresque facade. It now boasts a quality market and deli, the **Danish Pastry** store, the **Chapman Paper Company**, and 3 restaurants: a yet-to-be-named Mandarin Chinese, the **Clay Pit** (Indian), and **Farfalla** (Italian). Live performances in the courtyard. ♦ W 6th St at Alexandria Ave

32 Hyatt Wilshire Hotel $$$ This luxury hotel has a pool and use of a nearby health club. Two restaurants. Dancing on weekends. ♦ 3515 Wilshire Blvd. 381.7411, 800/228.9000; fax 386.7379

32 St. Basil's Catholic Church (1974, **A.C. Martin & Associates**) Massive modernistic design in reinforced concrete. ♦ Daily 1-4PM. 3611 Wilshire Blvd. 381.6191

33 Ambassador Hotel (1921) Legendary hostelry, home of the **Coconut Grove** nightclub. It was here that **Robert Kennedy** was shot while announcing his victory in the 1968 California primary. Recently purchased by **Donald Trump**, who wishes to convert it to an office building. ♦ 3400 Wilshire Blvd

34 The Windsor $$$$ An institution notable for its huge menu and rich decor. ♦ French ♦ M-F 11:30AM-10:30PM; Sa 4:30-11:30PM. 3198 W 7th St. 382.1261

34 Hotel Chancellor $$ An excellent budget-priced hotel, popular with European and Japanese visitors. Full breakfast and dinners. Pool. ♦ 3191 W 7th St. 383.1183, 800/446.5552 (CA), 800/331.0163 (US); fax 385.6675

35 Taylor's Prime Steaks ★$$$ Everything a good steak house should be: a clubby, wood-paneled space with the finest meat, generous portions, and reasonable prices. Seafood and chops as well as steak. ♦ American ♦ M-F 11AM-10:30PM; Sa 4-11PM; Su 4-10PM. 3361 W 8th St. 382.8449

35 Koreatown One of the city's most dynamic ethnic neighborhoods, roughly bounded by Vermont, Pico, 8th, and Western, but expanding steadily beyond. Rambling old bungalows have been repainted and store fronts provisioned with Korean foodstuffs and identified by distinctive angular calligraphy. The market at the corner of 8th and Normandie is a Technicolor delight, with vividly painted columns, rafters, and trim, a blue-tile roof, and stacks of sacks and bottles.

35 Dong II Jang ★$$ Refined atmosphere of natural wood and subdued lighting. Your order of beef or chicken is cooked on a grill hidden under the removable table top. ♦ Korean ♦ Daily 11AM-10PM. 3455 W 8th St. 383.5757

35 Wilshire Towers Hotel-Apartments $$ Rooms, suites, and apartments in a traditional residential neighborhood. Weekly rates. ♦ 3460 W 7th St. 385.7281; fax 382.1702

36 Ham Hung ★$ The food of the Ham Hung region of Korea, especially *naengmyon* (chilled buckwheat-and-potato-starch noodles with a spicy sauce) is the specialty. ♦ Korean ♦ Daily 11AM-10PM. 809 S. Ardmore Ave. 381.1865

37 Chao Nue ★★$$ Ask for a Thai menu (and its English translation) to enjoy the best northern regional dishes. These tend to be rich and well seasoned—meat-and-vegetable chile, pork curry (*kaeng hung lae*), and catfish with basil steamed in banana leaves (*ap pla*). ♦ Thai ♦ Daily 10:30AM-10PM. 2810 W 9th St. 384.7049, 487.1927

37 Arunee ★$ This is a family-run restaurant with modest decor. But **Trump's** chef **Don Dickman** insists that the crab with cellophane noodles is the best Thai dish in LA. The spicy seafood stew also rates high. ♦ Thai ♦ Daily 11AM-10PM. 853 S. Vermont Ave. 385.6653

38 Korean Gardens ★$$ You can be your own barbecue chef at this lively restaurant, but go prepared for spicy food and clouds of smoke. ♦ Korean ♦ Daily 11AM-11PM. 950 S. Vermont Ave. 388.3042

38 La Plancha ★$$ A gastronomic adventure. Specialties include meats and fish marinated in orange and lime, *empañadas* (a ripe plantain stuffed with cotija cheese), and *nactamals* (delicious giant tamales). Beer, wine, refreshing *cacao* (a chocolate drink), and other drinks made with fruit and corn. Owner **Milton Molina** is your effusive host. ♦ Nicaraguan ♦ M-F 11AM-9:30PM; Sa-Su 9AM-10PM. 2818 W 9th St. 383.1449

39 El Colmao ★$ One of the best Cuban restaurants in town, serving excellent roast pork with black beans and Jerez chicken in a delicious sherry sauce with olives and onions. Very crowded at lunchtime. ♦ Cuban ♦ M, W-F 10AM-9:30PM; Sa-Su noon-9:30PM. 2328 Pico Blvd. 386.6131

40 The Salisbury House $$ Bed-and-breakfast in a restored Craftsman house of 1909 in the historic West Adams district. Antique decor. ♦ 2273 W 20th St. 737.7817

41 West Adams Bed & Breakfast Inn $$ Four guest rooms in an impeccably restored 1913 Craftsman house. Fresh flowers, full breakfast, and reasonable rates. ♦ 1650 Westmoreland Blvd (E of Western Ave at Venice Blvd) 737.5041

Midtown

42 El Cholo $$ **Gable** and **Lombard** used to eat in this 50-year-old Mexican classic. Nostalgia and the atmosphere of a hacienda, plus the whopping margaritas are the primary appeal today. ♦ Mexican ♦ M-Th, Su 11AM-10PM; F-Sa 11AM-11PM. 1121 S. Western Ave. 734.2773. Also at: 840 E. Wooky Blvd, La Habra. 691.4618; Margarita Ryan's Cantina, 4881 Birch St, Newport Beach. 714/955.3868

43 Hang Goo Seafood ★$ Friendly fish place featuring an exceptional young crab soup. The front doors are locked; enter from the back. ♦ Korean ♦ Daily (excluding the 1st Sunday of the month) 11:45AM-midnight. 1106 S. Western Ave. 733.2474

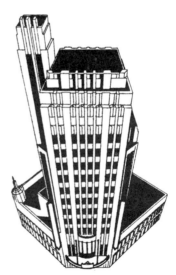

44 The Wiltern Center (1931, **Morgan, Walls & Clements**) Another Art Deco masterpiece, which **Wayne Ratkovich** rescued at the eleventh hour from an insurance company that wanted to clear the site. His gamble proved sound, as it had on the Oviatt and Fine Arts buildings downtown. The corner tower and side wings are clad in green terra cotta; closely-spaced and lively moldings make the tower seem far more imposing than its 12 stories—in contrast to the banal bank towers all around. Architect **Brenda Levin** restored them for lease as offices, stores, and the **Upstage Cafe** (739.9913). Currently on hold is a plan to build a 2-story retail courtyard behind the theater. ♦ 3780 Wilshire Blvd (Western Ave) 489.2626

Within the Wiltern Center:

Wiltern Theatre (1931, **G. Albert Lansburgh**) An imposing marquee and patterned terrazo forecourt lead beneath the tower to a sumptuous movie palace. It was severly vandalized, but has been restored to its former glory by **Brenda Levin** and **Tony Heinsbergen**, son of the original interior designer, for use as a performing arts center. It's a fairyland of Art Deco ornament

Midtown

in pink and green with gold trim; a masterly sequence of spaces that guides the audience into an auditorium whose proscenium is crowned with a sunburst of low-relief skyscrapers. Frequent performances of music, opera, and dance—don't miss the chance to see it. ◆ Seats 2300. 380.5005/5030

Atlas Bar & Grill ★★$$ (1989, **Ron Meyers**) **Mario Tamayo** (who launched **Cha Cha Cha** and **Cafe Mambo**) is the ebullient host in this cavernous space with its wrought-iron screens, splashes of gold, and glitzy lighting. The exotic menu matches the theatrical decor: Brazilian seafood stew, vegetable *tajine*, and black-pepper shrimp are signature dishes; oysters and grills for plainer tastes. The room is jumping but not deafening; there's live entertainment most nights. ◆ Eclectic ◆ M-F 11:30AM-3PM, 6:30PM-midnight; Sa 6:30PM-midnight. 380.8400

The Scene of the Crime A bookstore that might have been described by **Raymond Chandler**, and which features his work alongside 15,000 other mystery and detective titles, including many that are out of print. ◆ M-Sa 10AM-8PM. 487.2583

45 Ginza Sushi-ko ★★★★$$$$ Hidden away in a mini-mall is a branch of a Tokyo sushi bar that's famous for the perfection of its cuisine. Put yourself in the hands of the chef and expect to pay at least $100 a person, for lunch or dinner. Even at these prices it's packed every night, so reserve early for a memorable dining experience. ◆ Japanese ◆ M-F noon-2PM, 6-10PM; Sa 6-10PM. 3959 Wilshire Blvd, No. A 11. 487.2251

46 Former Selig Store (1931) Streamline gem in black-and-gold glazed terra cotta and glass brick. ◆ Western Ave at W 3rd St

47 Kentucky Fried Chicken (1990, **Grinstein-Daniels**) $ A superb piece of innovative design with its curving facade and floating geometric masses. ◆ 340 N. Western Ave

47 Beverly Soon Tofu ★$ Soon is the name and tofu's the game at this simple restaurant specializing in soft bean curd. It comes, spiced to order, with clams, oysters, beef, pork, or seaweed. Don't miss the exotic iced tea made from roasted corn. ◆ Korean ◆ Daily 10AM-10PM. 4653 1/2 Beverly Blvd. 856.0368

The onward march of progress brings many changes and an old resident of the city would be bewildered at the metropolitan appearance of Los Angeles.
LA Star, **4 May 1879**

48 Chan Dara Larchmont ★$$ A slightly sleeker, fancier spin-off of the Thai favorite in Hollywood has been wowing the traditional crowd of Hancock Park. There is a bar as well as a patio that's open for dinner. Specialties include sausage with ginger and lime, stuffed chicken wings, and barbecued beef. The banana fritters are rolled in coconut and sesame seeds before being flamed in rum. ◆ Thai ◆ M-Th 11:30AM-11PM; F 11:30AM-midnight; Sa 5PM-midnight; Su 5-11PM. 310 N. Larchmont Blvd (Beverly Blvd) 467.1052

49 Larchmont Village A shopping street of small town charm and urban sophistication. Nearby is the **Wilton Historic District**, a modest area of California bungalows dating from 1907 to 1925. ◆ Larchmont Blvd (1st St-Beverly Blvd)

49 Louise's Trattoria $$ Large portions of acceptable Italian-American fare, served in a bleached-blond room, have made this restaurant family wildly popular with young pros all over town. ◆ Italian ◆ Daily 11AM-11PM. 232 N. Larchmont Blvd. 962.9510. Also at: 342 N. Beverly Dr. 274.4271; 10645 Pico Blvd. 475.6084; 1008 Montana Ave. 394.8888

49 Prado ★$$ Picture-pretty setting (pale-blue walls, painted angels floating above the chandeliers) for island food. Chef **Javier Prado** is the brother of **Toribio**, who runs **Cha Cha Cha**. Similar menu of exotic dishes that are often over-spiced. No reservations, and the tiny room is sometimes overwhelmed. ◆ Caribbean ◆ M-Sa 11AM-3PM, 6-11PM. 244 N. Larchmont Blvd. 467.3871

50 Day Dreams Country Foods Bakery/deli, with a few tables for eating in. Enjoy sandwiches, soups, salads, and desserts. ◆ M-Sa 5AM-5PM; Su 8AM-2PM. 125 N. Larchmont Blvd. 463.2814

51 Hancock Park/Windsor Square/Wilton Historic District Capt. **G. Allan Hancock**, son of **Henry Hancock**, who bought Rancho La Brea in 1860, began this exclusive residential section in the 1910s. The palatial mansions have been owned by the **Doheny, Huntington, Van Nuys, Janss, Banning, Crocker,** and other notable California families. ◆ Highland-Melrose Aves (Wilshire-Larchmont Blvds)

52 Getty House (1921) English half-timbered house donated to the city by the Getty Oil Company and used as the mayor's official home. Private residence. ◆ 605 S. Irving Blvd

53 Wilshire Ebell Theatre and Club (1924) Renaissance-style buildings popular with movie and television companies. The theater is noted for its cultural and educational programs. ◆ Seats 1270. 4401 W 8th St. 939.1128, 931.1277

54 Fremont Place An elegant residential neighborhood; entry to the privately owned streets is through massive gates on the south side of the 4400-4500 blocks of Wilshire Boulevard. Not open to the public.

Restaurants/Clubs: Red   Hotels: Blue
Shops/Parks: Green   **Sights/Culture:** Black

55 La Cochinita ★$ Cheery Salvadoran restaurant that specializes in *pupusas*, the national dish. These ground corn-pancakes, made to order, are filled with cheese, pork rinds, or meat, and come with a spicy coleslaw. ◆ Salvadoran ◆ Daily noon-midnight. 4367 Pico Blvd. 937.1249

56 La Brea Avenue A hot new location for art galleries, design-oriented stores, and restaurants, notably around the junction with Melrose Avenue, and south to Wilshire Blvd, which are rehabilitating the long-neglected mix of Art Deco and Spanish 1930s buildings. Leading galleries of contemporary art and design include **Jan Baum** (170 S. La Brea, 932.0170), **Ovsey** (126 N. La Brea, 935.1883), **Fahey/Klein Photography** (148 N. La Brea, 934.2250), **Wenger** (828 N. La Brea, 464.4431), **Richard Green** (834 N. La Brea, 460.2924).

56 Louis XIV ★★$$ A French country house-cum-dining club, with a beamed attic upstairs, a cozy room off the downstairs kitchen, wine bar, frescoed burnished ochre walls, candelabras, and a handsome crowd that even jaded New Yorkers talk about. Honest bistro food includes vegetable soup, roasted peppers with anchovies, chicken with mustard sauce, steak *frite*, and lemon tart—as refreshing as the scene. ◆ French ◆ M-Sa 6PM-midnight. 606 N. La Brea Ave. 934.5102

57 LinderDesign Reproductions of classic early modern lamps and furnishings by **Desny, Josef Hoffmann**, and **Otto Wagner**. American classics are available from **Arts & Interiors**, 965.0918. ◆ M-F 10AM-9PM; Sa 10AM-5PM; Su noon-5PM. 440 N. La Brea Ave. 939.4020

57 Rapport Co. Imported contemporary furnishings at affordable prices. ◆ Tu-Sa 9:30AM-5PM. 435 N. La Brea Ave. 930.1500

58 East India Grill ★$$ Friendly bistro, stark decor, and some original dishes—including basil-coconut curries, tandoori ribs, and savory soups. ◆ Indian ◆ M-Th 11:30AM-3PM, 6-10:30PM; F 11:30AM-3PM, 6-11PM; Sa 6-11PM; Su 6-10:30PM. 345 N. La Brea Ave. 936.8844

58 Modern Times Classic American modern furniture and collectibles. ◆ Tu-Sa 11AM-5PM. 338 N. La Brea Ave. 930.1150

59 Samy's Camera A one-stop service station for professionals, with good prices on film and processing, a wide choice of equipment for rent or purchase, and expert service. ◆ M-Sa 9AM-6PM; Su 11AM-4PM. 7122 Beverly Blvd. 938.2420

59 Patina Custom-made hats in felt and straw trimmed with vintage lace, ribbons, and flowers—in period and contemporary styles. Also bridal hats, movie rentals, and architectural details. ◆ W-Sa noon-6PM. 119 N. La Brea Ave. 931.6931

60 Harry *Too much of a good thing can be wonderful*, said **Mae West**, and **Harry Segil** thinks so, too. Here is a dazzling collection of original and recreated '50s furniture, curved and spiked, patterned in lime green and puce, leopard-skin and luminescent vinyl, all refurbished and even jazzier than when they were new. ◆ M-Sa 11AM-6PM; Su noon-5PM. 148 S. La Brea Ave. 938.3344

60 American Rag Company Another retro showroom, where you can buy the gear to wear to Harry's. A few doors up, at **No. 136**, is a similar mix for children. ◆ M-Sa 10:30AM-10:30PM; Su noon-7PM. 150 S. La Brea Ave. 935.3154

60 City Restaurant ★★★$$$ French-trained chefs **Susan Feniger** and **Mary Sue Milliken** range the world in search of inspiration and their eclectic, constantly changing menu makes this one of LA's most exciting restaurants. They also supervise the kitchen of the **Border Grill** on Melrose and in Santa Monica. Sample dishes include Thai duck curry soup, Chinese sausage salad and monkfish, and scallops in coconut broth. **David Kellen** and **Josh Schweitzer** designed this high-tech converted warehouse, which is—intentionally—noisy and upbeat. Snacks only during the afternoon. ◆ Eclectic ◆ M-Sa 11:45AM-11:45PM; Su 5-11PM. 180 S. La Brea Ave. 938.2155

61 Ca' Brea **Antonio Tomasi**, co-owner/chef of **Locanda Veneta**, will prepare Venetian dishes in this big, informal restaurant, which replaces the venerable **Robaire's**. ◆ Italian ◆ M-Sa dinner. 348 S. La Brea Ave

62 Pikme-up Showcase for undiscovered poets; one of the first of LA's bohemian coffeehouses. ◆ American ◆ M-Th, Su noon-2AM; F-Sa noon-3:30AM. 5437 W 6th St (La Brea Ave) 939.9706

63 Campanile ★★★$$$ Old and new combine to form a dramatic sequence of dining areas. **Josh Schweitzer** inserted a glass roof and a concrete frame within the streetfront patio of a Spanish-style building, leaving the pretty tiled fountain and the signature tower, to create one of the most romantic settings in LA. The rustic cuisine, by **Spago** graduates **Mark Peel** and **Nancy Silverton**, draws enthusiastic crowds, sometimes overwhelming the kitchen. Quail is served with wild mushrooms on toasted penne, grilled whole bass on fresh herbs, charred lamb on salad greens, and there's a scrumptious nougat tart with kumquat ice cream. Fans return for a mouthwatering selection of breads at the **La Brea Bakery**, beside the restaurant. ◆ California ◆ Restaurant: M-Sa 6-11PM. Bakery: daily 8AM-4PM. 624 S. La Brea Ave. 938.1447

1860
Attempt made to construct sidewalks out of tar from pits at Rancho la Brea.

64 Miracle Mile In 1920, visionary **A.W. Ross** bought 18 acres of empty land along Wilshire Blvd, from La Brea to Fairfax, and in the late '20s and early '30s developed it as a prestigious business and shopping district. A friend dubbed it *Miracle Mile*. Ross closely supervised the designs of individual buildings and a few relics survive ongoing redevelopment.

Midtown

Security Pacific Bank (1929, **Morgan, Walls & Clements**) A black-and-gold miniature of the Richfield Tower by the same architects. ♦ 5209 Wilshire Blvd

Commercial Building (1930, **Meyer & Holler**) Imposing set-back tower. ♦ 5217-31 Wilshire Blvd

The Dark Room (1938, **Marcus P. Miller**) The facade is a period camera in black vitrolite. ♦ 5370 Wilshire Blvd

Dominguez-Wilshire Building (1930, **Morgan, Walls & Clements**) Finely detailed tower rising above a 2-story retail base. ♦ 5410 Wilshire Blvd

Commercial Building (1927, **Frank M. Tyler**) Twin turrets that look like origami. ♦ 5464 Wilshire Blvd

Desmond's (1928, **Gilbert Stanley Underwood**) Handsome 8-story tower; its low wings have rounded corners. Within is the **Ace Gallery**. **Doug Christmas** shows such artists as **Roger Herman, Bob Zoeli**, and **Pauline Stella Sanchez** (Tu-Sa 10AM-6PM, 935.4411). ♦ 5514 Wilshire Blvd

El Rey (1936, **W. Clifford Balch**) Streamlined movie house, with original marquee, hideously repainted in pink and remodeled inside as the Wall Street nightclub. ♦ 5519 Wilshire Blvd

64 Lew Mitchell's Orient Express ★$$$ Copper and brass accents and modern rattan furniture. A sleek setting for cuisine that runs the gamut from fried calamari to grilled shark. ♦ Chinese ♦ M-F 11:30AM-2PM, 5:30-10PM; Sa 5-10PM. 5400 Wilshire Blvd. 935.6000

65 Miro ★★$$ A modern Korean restaurant, where owner **Dax** (who is also chef, photographer, designer, and artist) has successfully fused tradition and trend. Wonderful dishes such as linguini with shrimps and scallops, delicately fried sea bass, and sweet and spicy beef ribs all come with an unusual beef soup, pungent dipping sauces, and of course, *kim chee*—the garlicky, spicy, fermented pickled cabbage that's a national staple. ♦ Korean. ♦ Tu-Sa 6PM-12:30AM; Su 5-11PM. 809 S. La Brea Ave. 931.9315

66 Adray's Discount electronics and appliances. For service, Circuit City is much better; for the biggest savings, order from 47th Street Photo in New York. ♦ Daily 10AM-8PM. 5575 Wilshire Blvd. 935.8191. Also at: 11201 W. Pico Blvd. 479.0797

67 Prudential Building (1948, **Wurdeman & Becket**) Good example of the dated Gropius version of International Style. ♦ 5757 Wilshire Blvd

68 Wilshire Courtyard (1988, **McLarand & Vasquez**) Sleek stepped-back commercial development, clad in brown marble and handsomely landscaped; a welcome relief from the bland towers and fake-classical boxes that now dominate LA's most prestigious artery. ♦ 5750 Wilshire Blvd. 939.0300

68 Al Amir ★★$$ Authentic middle-Eastern menu that does the standard tabouleh and kebabs exceptionally well, and includes varied treatments of organ meats, *kebey makley* (deep-fried meat balls), delicious salads, and pastries. The polished service and the spacious, elegant interior are a delight. ♦ Lebanese ♦ M-Th 11:30AM-11PM; F 11:30AM-midnight; Sa 5PM-midnight; Su 1:30-10:30PM. 5750 Wilshire Blvd. 931.8740

69 La Brea Tar Pits *La Brea* is Spanish for tar, and the tar that seeps from these pits was used by Indians and early settlers to seal boats and roofs. In 1906, geologists discovered the pits had entrapped 200 varieties of mammals, plants, birds, reptiles, and insects from the Pleistocene Era, and preserved them as fossils. Disneyesque sculptures of doomed mammals add a surreal touch. ♦ Wilshire Blvd (Curson Ave)

At the La Brea Tar Pits:

George C. Page Museum of La Brea Discoveries Established in 1977 within grassy berms topped by a steel-frame canopy. Exhibitions, films, and demonstrations describe the evolution of the pits. Children will revel in the holographic displays that give flesh to the bones of a tiger and a woman excavated here, and a hands-on demonstration of how sticky tar is. Summer visitors can watch paleontologists at work in Pit 91. Gift shop. Free parking in back. ♦ Admission. Tu-Su 10AM-5PM. 5801 Wilshire Blvd. 936.2230

69 Los Angeles County Museum of Art (LACMA) One of the finest, most varied art collections in America. The **Robert O. Anderson Building** (1986, **Hardy Holzman Pfeiffer**) comprises a vast wedge of limestone, glass brick, and green terra cotta that pays homage to the streamline moderne **Coulter's Store** (a former highlight of Miracle Mile). An entry portal of Babylonian proportions frames steps leading up to the original **Ahmanson, Hammer**, and **Bing** pavilions and the courtyard, now roofed over. The sculpture garden has been restored and a formal Japanese garden added.

The **Japanese Pavilion** (1988), overlooking the tar pits, was conceived by the late **Bruce Goff**, and was realized by his protégé, **Bart Prince**. Goff and Prince are true originals, though this gallery reminds some of **Eero Saarinen's** TWA Terminal at New York's Kennedy Airport, while others discover echoes of '50s googie-style coffeehouses. It was designed for **Joe D. Price**, an Oklahoma oil man,

---

Restaurants/Clubs: Red   **Hotels:** Blue
Shops/Parks: Green   **Sights/Culture:** Black

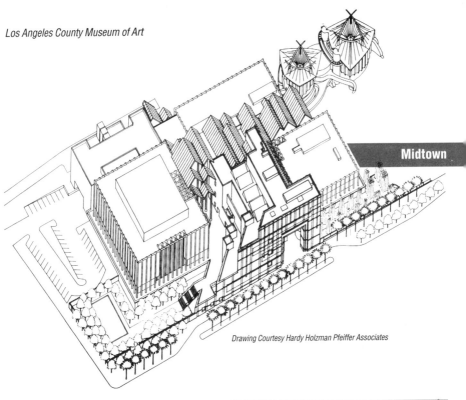

Midtown

Drawing Courtesy Hardy Holzman Pfeiffer Associates

to house his collection of Edo scrolls and screens—which he donated to LACMA in 1982—and to display them in a traditionally Japanese manner. To avoid internal divisions, the building is suspended from a frame of concrete posts and beams and is lit from fiberglass wall panels that evoke shoji screens. Visitors take an elevator to the 3rd floor and walk down a winding ramp through the east wing, past a series of wall niches that frame a constantly changing selection of 30 artworks. The west wing contains *netsuke* and other highlights from LACMA's rich collections, and a book/gift store.

LACMA orginates superb temporary exhibitions. Its permanent collections offer comprehensive coverage of the history of Western Art, in addition to fine holdings of Oriental and Near-Eastern art, costumes, and textiles. The Rifkin Collection of German Expressionism is justly famous. Some of LA's best film series and concerts of contemporary music are regularly presented in the 500-seat auditorium of the **Bing Center**, and there is an outstanding museum store. Jazz concerts are presented in the **Plaza** on Sunday afternoons. Members may rent artworks, and—if they decide to keep them—apply the charges to the purchase price. The new **Plaza Cafe**, with its painterly decor by **David Sheppard**, offers food of a quality far above most museum cafeterias, and is a favorite meeting place for young (art) lovers. Admission fee for nonmembers; free on 2nd Tu of each month. ♦ Tu-F 10AM-5PM; Sa-Su 10AM-6PM. 5905 Wilshire Blvd. 857.6000 (recording)

Museum Bests

Earl A. Powell, III
Director, Los Angeles County Museum of Art

The museum's recently dedicated **B. Gerald Cantor Sculpture Garden** featuring 14 bronzes by the great French master artist Rodin.

The new **Pavilion for Japanese Art**, an international center unique outside that island nation. The renowned Shinen'kan collection of paintings and several hundred extraordinary Netsuke are among the highlights.

The new galleries for ancient art. Now visitors to the Los Angeles County Museum of Art may experience the range of Western art from its foundation in antiquity through medieval period to the late 19th-century with the rich visual heritage seen in the museum's collection.

The remarkable collection of over 200 examples of ancient, Sasanian Islamic, and Indian glass from the 6th century BC to the 18th century AD, a gift of Hans and Varya Cohn.

St. Ignatius Loyola's Vision of Christ and God the Father at La Storta, a masterpiece by the 17th-century Italian painter Domenichino.

Pre-Columbian Mexican sculpture, pottery, and jades.

Sixteenth-century polychromed wood Neapolitan sculpture of Archangel Raphael.

The outstanding **Gilbert collections** of Monumental Silver and Italian Post-Renaissance Mosaics.

Georges de la Tour, *Magdalen with the Smoking Flame.*

Guido Reni, *Portrait of Roberto Ubaldino, Papal Legate to Bologna.*

Rembrandt, *The Raising of Lazarus* and *Portrait of Martin Looten.*

Chardin, *Soap Bubbles.*

Canaletto, *Capriccio: Piazza San Marco Looking South and West.*

Matisse, *Tea.*

Braque, *Still Life with Violin.*

Midtown

Kandinsky, *Untitled (Improvisation).*

George Bellows, *Cliff Dwellers.*

Thomas Cole, *L'Allegro* and *Il Penseroso.*

Sargent, *Mrs. Livingston Davis and Her Son, Edward L. Davis.*

Winslow Homer, *The Cotton Pickers.*

Frank Stella, *St. Michael's Counterguard.*

David Hockney, *Mulholland Drive, the Road to the Studio.*

Giacometti, *Grande Dame IV.*

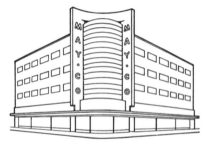

70 **May Co Department Store** (1940, **Albert C. Martin & S.A. Marx**) The immense gilded cylinder set into the southwest corner of this rectangular block is a highlight of Miracle Mile. It is now threatened by redevelopment. ♦ Daily 10AM-9PM. 6067 Wilshire Blvd (Fairfax Ave) 938.4211

Within May Co:

Craft and Folk Art Museum Changing exhibitions of crafts, folk art, and design will be presented on the 4th floor of the May Co store in a 10,000-square-foot gallery designed by **Charles Moore** until the museum's new, greatly expanded quarters (by **Hodgetts** and **Fung**) are completed in 1992. Books and fine crafts available for sale at 5800 Wilshire Blvd. ♦ Tu-Su 10AM-5PM. 937.5544

71 **Loehmann's** This discount clothing store is a woman's best friend, carrying an extensive selection of loungewear, suits, casual and formal wear, and accessories. Quality merchandise discounted 30 percent and more. Haute couture in the **Backroom.** ♦ M-F 10AM-9PM; Sa 10AM-7PM; Su noon-6PM. 6220 W 3rd St. 933.5675. Also at: 19389 Victory Blvd, Reseda. 818/345.7063

72 **Park La Brea Housing and Towers** (1941-48) Large, Regency Moderne complex of low- and high-rise garden apartments in a 176-acre park. ♦ 3rd-Cochran Sts (6th-Fairfax Sts)

73 **The Tennis Place** Sixteen lighted courts open to nonmembers, though most are reserved at peak hours. ♦ Daily 7AM-10PM. 5880 W 3rd St. 931.1715

74 **Turner Dailey Gallery** Fine posters and other 20th-century applied arts. ♦ Tu-F 11AM-6PM; Sa 11AM-5PM. 7220 Beverly Blvd. 931.1185

74 **Fish Grill** ★$ A half-dozen fresh fish are simply grilled in this no-nonsense kosher café that serves a diverse crowd of value-seekers. ♦ Seafood ♦ M-Th, Su 11AM-9PM; F 11AM-2:30PM; Su 10AM-2AM. 7226 Beverly Blvd. 937.7162

74 **Java** ★$ Stylish literary coffeehouse run by UCLA graduates in a converted Art Deco building. Fresh breads, pastries, and light fare sustain those who are reading, playing chess, or listening to the Wednesday and Sunday night readings of poetry and fiction. ♦ American ♦ M-Th 8AM-2AM; F-Sa 10AM-3AM; Su 10AM-2AM. 7286 Beverly Blvd. 931.4943

74 **Tyler Trafficante** Tailored suits and coats for men and women, designed by Australian expatriate **Richard Tyler** with a winning blend of old-world elegance and contemporary theatrics. Housed in a dramatic Art Deco corner building. ♦ M-F 11AM-7PM; Sa noon-6PM. 7290 Beverly Blvd. 931.9678

74 **Muse** ★$$$ A handsome skylit room, compelling modern art, and imaginative, sometimes even inspired cooking. There's a nifty aquarium, and a good bit of fishing, too, at the bar. ♦ California ♦ M-F 11:30AM-2:30PM, 6-10:30PM; Sa 6-11:30PM. 7360 Beverly Blvd. 934.4400

75 **Skank World** It looks like a Goodwill store with punk overtones, but this is the place to find classic '50s furniture at affordable prices, including **Eames'** plywood chairs and the rare example of **Alvar Aalto.** Opens late so the owners can watch *All My Children.* ♦ M-Sa 2:15-6PM. 7205 Beverly Blvd. 939.7858

76 **A.J. Heinsbergen Company** (1925) A tiny medieval brick castle with drawbridge and moat, still occupied by the design company that built it. ♦ 7415 Beverly Blvd. 938.2420

76 **Mario's Cooking for Friends** ★$$ Light, bright dining room and terrace serves good pastas, salads, and poultry dishes from a menu that changes daily. Some dishes are available for takeout in the well-stocked deli that adjoins the restaurant. ♦ Italian ♦ Restaurant: M-Sa 8AM-4PM, 7-10PM. Café: M-Th 8AM-11PM; F-Sa 8AM-midnight. Deli: M-Sa 10AM-10PM. 7475 Beverly Blvd. 931.6342

77 **Pan Pacific Auditorium** (1938) This unique streamline moderne facade was torched by vandals in 1989, and is unlikely to be rebuilt. It was the victim of political timidity and community backlash against overdevelopment. The park doubles as a flood-control basin. ♦ 7600 Beverly Blvd.

Restaurants/Clubs: Red   Hotels: Blue
Shops/Parks: Green   **Sights/Culture: Black**

78 Authentic Cafe ★★$$ Be prepared to stand in line, no matter when you go to this tiny and terminally trendy spot. Rest assured, the generous portions of ethnic fare are worth the wait, are reasonably priced, and are always served with a smile. Bring your own bottle. ♦ Eclectic ♦ M-Th 11:30AM-3:30PM, 5-11PM; F-Sa 11:30AM-3:30PM, 5PM-midnight. 7605 Beverly Blvd. 939.4626

79 CBS Television City (1952, **Pereira & Luckman**; 1976, **Gin Wong Associates**) High-tech boxes containing studios and offices. Free tickets to shows can be picked up at the information window. Some age restrictions. Groups of 20 or more, 852.2455. ♦ Daily 9AM-5PM. 7800 Beverly Blvd. 852.2624

80 Farmer's Market A favorite with locals and tourists, established in 1934 as a cooperative market where local farmers could sell their produce. Today there are over 160 vendors, including 26 stands that offer hot and cold dishes from around the world. Browse, select an appetizer here, an entree there, save room for pastry, and find a seat beneath the umbrellas and awnings. The market section provides fine vegetables, cheeses, meats, pastries, baked goods, and exotic imported foodstuffs. **Mr. K's Gourmet Foods and Coffee** (stall 430) sells hard-to-obtain spices and teas; try **Stone Tropical Fruits** (stall 324) for fruits that you may never even have heard of. Several of the fruit and nut stalls make up and ship gift boxes, as do some of the confectioneries, where you can watch candy being made. ♦ M-Sa 9AM-7PM; Su 10AM-6PM; closed major holidays. 6333 W 3rd St. 933.9211

Within Farmer's Market:

Kokomo ★$ New Age counter offering the best in breakfasts, lunches, and fountain dishes. Great granola, gumbo, and BLTs. ♦ American ♦ M-Sa 8AM-7PM; Su 10AM-7PM. 933.0773

The Gumbo Pot. ★$ Spicy gumbo, fresh oysters, blackened fish, and meat loaf; hearty weekend brunches, too. ♦ Cajun/Creole ♦ M-Sa 9AM-6:30PM; Su 10AM-5PM. 933.0358

Midtown

81 Fairfax Avenue Main Street for the Jewish community of Los Angeles since World War II. Although the majority of Los Angeles Jews currently reside on the West Side and in the San Fernando Valley, the Eastern European Jewish tradition continues as a strong influence in this area. Elderly men congregate on street corners to discuss business and politics; Hassids and a large number of Orthodox Jews walk to the synagogue on Friday night and Saturday; other days women carry shopping bags to the butcher, greengrocer, and bakery.

81 Al's News Newspapers and magazines in profusion. ♦ M-Th 6AM-11PM; F-Sa 6AM-1AM; Su 6AM-10PM. Oakwood Ave at Fairfax Ave. 935.8525

81 Canter's Fairfax Restaurant Delicatessen and Bakery ★$$ The largest and liveliest of the delis on Fairfax. The interior has remained untouched since Doris Day was a girl, and the neon sign on the facade is a classic. Waitresses not only bring your food, they also make sure you eat it. Highly-praised pastrami. ♦ Deli ♦ 24 hours. 419 N. Fairfax Ave. 651.2030

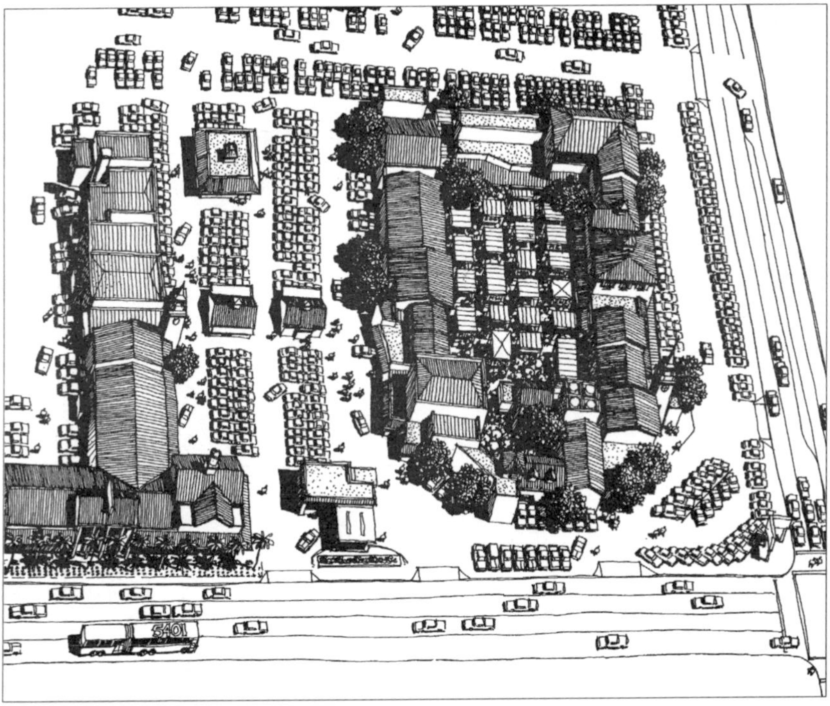

Farmer's Market

81 Cafe Largo $$ **Anna Mariani** and **Jean Pierre Boccara**, who ran the late lamented **Lhasa Club**, have created this restaurant/cabaret that presents nightly comedy, performance art, and rock; poetry on Tuesday. ◆ M-Sa 7PM-closing; Su 6PM-closing. 432 N. Fairfax Ave. 852.1073

82 Nowhere Cafe ★$$ Chicken kabobs with ginger sauce, tofu with ginger-garlic sauce,

Midtown

and whole-wheat pasta with wild mushrooms. ◆ Health food ◆ M-F noon-2:30PM, 6-10PM; Sa-Su 6-10PM. 8009 Beverly Blvd. 655.8895

83 I. Martin Imports Mecca for those in training for the **Tour de France**, or for those who want to race up the side of **Mt. Wilson** on the best bike money can buy. ◆ M-F 10AM-7PM; Sa 9AM-6PM; Su 11AM-5PM. 8330 Beverly Blvd. 653.6900

83 Mandarette ★$$ Eclectic selection of Chinese street food from different regional traditions. The room is simple yet elegant, with high ceilings, white walls, and accents in black and a most calming shade of celadon. ◆ Chinese ◆ M-Th 11:30AM-3PM, 5-10:45PM; F 11:30AM-3PM, 5PM-midnight; Sa 5PM-midnight. 8386 Beverly Blvd. 655.6115

84 Fun Furniture Whimsical architect-designed pieces for kids, including a skyscraper dresser, a taxi toy box, and a fire-engine bed. ◆ M-Sa 10AM-5PM; Su noon-5PM. 8451 Beverly Blvd. 655.2711

84 Coronet Theater Intimate house set back in an almost hidden courtyard. ◆ Seats 280. 366 N. La Cienega Blvd. 659.6415

84 Coronet Bar Small neighborhood place popular with actors, writers, and musicians; a low-key, comfortable place to drink. ◆ M, Sa 5PM-2AM; Tu-F 1PM-2AM. 370 N. La Cienega Blvd. 659.4583

85 Trashy Lingerie Over 8000 items of very intimate apparel in a rainbow of colors. The window displays are a traffic stopper. A membership fee is charged to discourage voyeurs. ◆ M-Sa 10AM-6PM. 402 N. La Cienega Blvd. 652.4543

86 Ma Maison Sofitel Hotel $$$ The exterior beats stiff competition to win the prize for the klutziest-looking building in LA; it even makes the Beverly Center seem tolerable. The interiors of this French chain hotel have a conventional rich look. Nice views north to the Hollywood Hills. Health club and pool. Bargain weekend rates. ◆ 8555 Beverly Blvd. 278.5444, 800/221.4542; fax 657.2816

Within the Ma Maison Sofitel Hotel:

Ma Maison Bistrot ★★$$$ The original Ma Maison on Melrose, whose patio was furnished with plastic chairs and Astroturf, was the in place for food and celebrity glitter. In the 5 years since it closed the stakes have risen, and this reincarnation, still headed by suave **Patrick Terrail**, lacks charisma. But the room is much

prettier, the menu is designed by **David Hockney**, and there are some nice surprises, including snails in a baked potato, fresh mozzarella on an eggplant puree, and cold asparagus with salmon caviar. Stars still come to be pampered and eat well-prepared duck and chicken salads, steak and fries, and chocolate sorbet. ◆ French ◆ M-F 11:30AM-2:30PM, 6-10:30PM; Sa 6-10:30PM. 655.1991

87 Tail-o'-the-Pup (1946) This hot-dog stand is the most celebrated of LA's few remaining programmatic structures. ◆ Hot-dog stand ◆ Daily 6AM-8PM. 329 San Vicente Blvd. 652.4517

88 The Mysterious Bookshop Spies and sleuths, gumshoes and hoods people this store. ◆ M-Sa 10AM-6PM; Su noon-5PM. 8763 Beverly Blvd. 659.2959

89 Madeo ★★$$$$ Chic expense-account dining that's worth the price. Superb veal chops, extraordinary risotto, and delicious desserts. It's a favorite with the ICM agents upstairs and their celebrity clients. It helps to speak Italian. ◆ Italian ◆ M-F 11:30AM-3PM, 6:30-11:30PM; Sa-Su 6:30-11:30PM. 8897 Beverly Blvd. 859.0242. Also at: 295 Whaler's Walk, San Pedro. 831.1199

89 Chasen's $$$$ An institution dating from the time when good food was almost impossible to find in LA. It serves faithful regulars the world's most expensive chili and many other pedestrian dishes in a red-leather-booth-and-knotty-pine decor. To get good service it helps to be a star. ◆ American ◆ Tu-Su 6PM-1AM. 9039 Beverly Blvd. 271.2168

90 Palazzetti Showcase of classic European and American modern furniture, from **Mackintosh** to **Mies**. ◆ M-F 9AM-5:30PM; Sa 11AM-4PM. 9008 Beverly Blvd. 273.2225

90 The Pace Collection Artist-designed furniture. ◆ M-F 9AM-5PM. 8936 Beverly Blvd. 273.5901

90 Pane Caldo Bistrot ★$$ Agents from International Creative Management across the street, dealers, decorators, and shoppers from the surrounding designer's row continue to crowd this plain 2nd-story trattoria. It's hard to miss with a plate of pasta or risotto accompanied by fresh-baked Tuscan bread. ◆ Italian ◆ Daily 11AM-11PM. 8840 Beverly Blvd. 274.0916

90 Kaleido Unique stock of 300 kaleidoscopes, the work of about 90 artists. ◆ M-Sa 11AM-6PM. 8840 Beverly Blvd. 276.6844

90 Diva Offbeat contemporary lighting and furniture. ◆ M-F 9:30AM-6PM; Sa 11AM-5PM. 8818 Beverly Blvd. 274.0650

Early in the century the fertile land of Southern California produced more walnuts, oranges, and avocados than any other part of the nation. This all changed with the post-World War II population boom when land became more valuable for housing than for farming. In the late '50s orange trees were uprooted at the rate of one every 55 seconds. At the peak of this conversion frenzy 3000 acres of orange orchard were destroyed every day.

90 Design Express Contemporary Italian imports and trend-setting California furniture. ♦ M-F 10AM-7PM; Sa 10AM-6PM, Su noon-5PM. 8806 Beverly Blvd. 859.7177. Also at: 3410 S. La Cienega Blvd. 935.9451; 6549 De Soto Ave, Woodland Hills. 818/346.4709

91 Fendi Casa Stylish furniture, lighting, and accessories with a Roman flavor from the prestigious Italian fashion house. ♦ M-F 10:30AM-6PM; Sa noon-6PM. 115 S. Robertson Blvd (3rd St) 285.9931

92 The Ivy ★★$$$ One of the prettiest restaurants in town, a favorite with industry types and the ladies who lunch. It is southwestern in feeling, with adobe walls, open hearths, antiques, and an ivy-strewn terrace. Simple dishes are best; go for the corn chowder and mesquite-grilled shrimp. Save room for the desserts that made the Ivy's reputation, especially the lemon cake topped with white chocolate mousse. And carry some home from **LA Desserts**, which shares space with the restaurant. ♦ American ♦ M-Th 11:30AM-3PM, 6-11PM; F 11:30AM-3PM, 6-11:30PM; Sa 11:30AM-3:15PM, 6-11PM. 113 N. Robertson Blvd. 274.8303

93 Chaya Brasserie ★★★$$$ Marvelous interior by **Elyse Grinstein** and **Jeff Daniels**, who have combined a Japanese esthetic (skylit, pine-framed bamboo grove, and upturned parasol lampshades) with the friendly informality of a Parisian brasserie. Chef **Shigefumi Tachibe** pulls off the same East-meets-West trick in such innovative dishes as tuna tartare and seaweed salad, plus Japanese-accented French and Italian fare. Hot bar scene. ♦ French/Italian ♦ M-Sa 11:30AM-2:30PM, 6PM-12:30AM; Su 6-10PM. 8741 Alden Dr. 859.8833. Also at: 110 Navy St, Venice. 396.1179

93 Cedars Sinai Medical Center Inspiring for the philanthropy that made it possible, but its uninspired gigantism makes it a fit companion for the Beverly Center. A bright spark, architecturally, is the outwardly inconspicuous cancer clinic (1988, **Morphosis**). ♦ 8700 Beverly Blvd. 855.5000

94 Beverly Center This shopping center is comprised of 3 windowless levels of stores, restaurants, and movie theaters atop 4 open decks of parking. The best exterior features are the Beaubourg-inspired glass-enclosed elevators and the tilted Cadillac of the **Hard Rock Cafe**. Boutiques on the upper floors include **By Design, Abercrombie & Fitch, Cacherel, Laise Adzer, Phillipe Salvet** and **Traction Avenue** (for **Michele Lamy**'s cotton sportswear), plus an **American Express** travel office, the usual upscale chains, a **Bullock's**, and a **Broadway**. At the top of the pile are cafés, restaurants (including **La Rotisserie**, a dependable bistro),

and the **Cineplex** movie theaters—14 shoeboxes and 2 comfortable balconied houses. ♦ M-Sa 10AM-9PM; Su 11AM-6PM. Beverly-La Cienega Blvds (San Vicente Blvd-3rd St)

Within the Beverly Center, at street level:

Irvine Ranch Farmers' Market One of our favorites! Chefs have acclaimed this as LA's best retail market—for produce, fish, and meat. Here is where to find the freshest and most ex-

otic—at prices that may diminish your appetite. ♦ M-Sa 9AM-10PM; Su 9AM-9PM. 657.1931

Conran's Habitat An English emporium of well-designed, affordable furnishings for home and office, accessibly displayed and generously stocked. ♦ M-F 10AM-9PM; Sa 11AM-8PM; Su 11AM-6PM. 659.1444

Hard Rock Cafe $$ Owner **Peter Morton** has the Midas touch: from London to LA, these cafés are SRO. Loud music, basic fare, rock 'n' roll memorabilia, and wall-to-wall crowds is the well-tested recipe. An obligatory stop for visiting teenagers, who cheerfully wait in line. ♦ American ♦ Daily 11:30AM-midnight. 276.7605

California Pizza Kitchen ★$ Another branch of this fast expanding chain; the Baskin-Robbins of pizza parlors, whose 18 flavors include Cajun and Peking Duck. The more conventional choices are a better bet. ♦ Pizza ♦ M-Sa 11:30AM-midnight; Su 11:30AM-11PM. 854.6555

95 Organizers Paradise Shelving, wrapping, decorations: one-stop shopping for the habitually untidy and for partygivers. ♦ 100 N. La Cienega Blvd at 3rd St. 657.1884. Also at: 266 N. Beverly Dr, Beverly Hills. 657.1884; 1090 Glendon Ave, Westwood Village. 824.3648

95 New Stone Age Off-the-wall artist-designed objects. For those of more traditional tastes, there's **Freehand**, another fine craft shop, almost next door at 8413 W 3rd St. 655.2607. ♦ M-F 11AM-7PM; Sa 11AM-6PM; Su noon-5PM. 8407 W 3rd St. 658.5969

96 Katsu 3rd ★★$$ A cool, minimalist room, with hand-painted furniture and an atmosphere that might be described as hip zen. Short, innovative menu, a fusion of East and West. Since **Katsu Michite** is the owner, fish is a specialty, but the best bet at lunch is the *bento*, an array of delicious morsels in a lacquered box. More elaborate dishes include a terrine of scallops, halibut and eel, and beef filet stuffed with monkfish mousse. ♦ California/Japanese ♦ M-F 11:30AM-2:30PM, 6-10PM; Sa 6-10PM. 8636 W 3rd St. 273.3605

Beverly Center

96 Locanda Veneta ★★★$$ Host **Jean Louis de Mori** and chef **Antonio Tommasi** have created one of LA's most exciting and authentic trattorias and the crowds have flocked in. Everything on the menu is a winner, but don't miss the handmade mozzarella, duck and chicken dumplings with onion confit, rack of lamb in a mustard-peanut sauce, any of the pastas or risottos, and the vanilla ice cream

Midtown

with chocolate sauce. ♦ Italian ♦ M-F 11:30AM-2:30PM, 5:30-10:30PM; Sa 5:30-10:30PM. 8638 W 3rd St. 274.1893

96 Orso's ★★$$$ The legendary showbiz hangout **Joe Allen's** has been transformed by the same owner into a great looking trattoria with the most seductive patio in town. The bread is fabulous, the hand-painted plates gorgeous, the service friendly, and the cosmopolitan clientele star-studded. The menu is ambitious and appealing, offering such delicacies as veal kidney, tripe, dandelion greens, and Italian cheeses among the pizzas, pastas, and grilled fish. However, some dishes are overpriced and there is some strange house edict that prohibits waiters from pouring wine. ♦ Italian ♦ Daily 11:45AM-11:45PM. 8706 W 3rd St. 274.7144

96 Ma Be ★★$$$ Light and dark wood, aged copper, natural stone, and floral prints are blended to great effect in this multilevel eatery with its cozy bar and airy rooftop terrace. California, French, and Italian cuisines are mixed with flair. Standouts include the sautéed wild mushrooms, salad of crayfish and *haricots verts*, sweetbreads with grapes, and pasta with squab. ♦ California ♦ M-Th, Su 11:30AM-3PM, 6-10:30PM; F-Sa 11:30AM-3PM, 6-11PM. 8722 W 3rd St. 276.6223

97 A Chic Conspiracy Once-worn fashionable attire from movie and television stars, and others who don't need to save their duds. ♦ M-Sa 10AM-6PM; Su noon-6PM. 350 S. La Cienega Blvd. 657.1177

97 Japon ★$$ Sushi master **Koju** has a great sense of humor, entertaining his customers as he performs his craft and switching from classical music to vintage rock. Stylish pastel decor is as fresh as the fish. ♦ Japanese ♦ M 5:30-10:30PM; Tu-Th noon-2:30PM, 5:30-10:30PM; F noon-2:30PM, 5:30-11PM; Sa 5:30-11PM. 8412 W 3rd St. 852.1223

97 Cassis ★$$ Tasteful, comfortable bistro offering contemporary dishes and surprisingly good evening entertainment. ♦ California/French ♦ M-F 11:30AM-3PM, 6PM-midnight; Sa 6PM-midnight. 8450 W 3rd St. 653.1079

98 The Cook's Library **Ellen Rose** turned her hobby into a living when she opened the only LA store that concentrates entirely on cookbooks—new, old, and out-of-print. ♦ Tu-Sa 11AM-6PM. 8373 W 3rd St. 655.3141

99 Beverly Plaza Hotel $$$ Elegant small hotel, popular with solo travelers because of its in-house restaurant and exercise room. Complimentary limousine service. ♦ 8384 W 3rd St. 800/334.6835 (CA), 800/624.6835 (US); fax 653.3464

99 Baby Motives Discount clothes, toys, strollers, and furniture for the very young. ♦ M-F 10AM-5:30PM; Sa 10AM-5PM. 8362 W 3rd St. 658.6015

99 El Mocambo ★$$ Prerevolutionary Havana with a dash of **Carmen Miranda** and *I Love Lucy*. It is flashy and fun, with dangerous tropical drinks, a wild clientele, a beat you can dance to, and some interesting food. Appetizers and pork dishes are good; pass on the desserts, the overpriced coffees, and rum. ♦ Cuban ♦ M, Sa 6-11PM; Tu-F, Su 11:30AM-3PM, 6-11PM. 8338 W 3rd St. 651.2113

100 Indigo ★★$$ Breezy, whimsically decorated, and a little bit wild—with a patio, small singles dining bar, and healthy portions of upscale pastas, pizzas, sandwiches, salads, and grilled meats, all with a Mediterranean or southwest accent. Great rosemary-scented bread. ♦ California ♦ M-W, F 11:30AM-2:30PM, 5:30-10PM; Th 11:30AM-2:30PM, 5:30-11PM; Sa 5:30-11PM. 8222 1/2 W 3rd St. 653.0140

101 Siamese Princess ★★$$ Sedate, regal decor, serious service, a nice wine list, and refined, subtle cooking put this near the top of LA's ubiquitous Thai restaurants. A specialty is *mu sarong*—deep-fried, noodle-wrapped meatballs. ♦ Thai ♦ M-F 11:30AM-2:30PM, 5:30-11PM; Sa-Su 5:30-11:30PM. 8048 W 3rd St. 653.2643

101 Sofi Estiatorion ★$$ Lively family-run restaurant with excellent moussaka and daily specials. Order a glass of the velvety Cypriot dessert wine, *Commanderie 1947*. ♦ Greek ♦ M-Sa 11:30AM-3PM, 6-11AM; Su 6-11PM. 8030 3/4 W 3rd St. 651.0346

102 Mandarin Wilshire ★★$$ Among the 143 offerings of chef **Tony Ngon** are wonderful dumplings, Peking duck, pan-fried noodles, tangerine beef, and flaming bananas. ♦ Chinese ♦ M-Th 11:30AM-10PM; F-Sa 11:30AM-11PM; Su 5-10PM. 8300 Wilshire Blvd. 658.6928

103 Wilshire Crest $$ Small, reasonably-priced hotel. Continental breakfast. ♦ 6301 Orange St. 936.5131; fax 936.2013

104 Caffe Latte ★$$ Friendly neighborhood place with innovative, great-tasting fare, tasteful modern decor, and an interesting crowd; home-baked breads and roasted-on-the-premises coffee beans (which can also be purchased). ♦ American ♦ M 7AM-5PM; Tu-Th 7AM-5PM, 6-10PM; F 7AM-5PM, 6-11PM; Sa 6-11PM. 6254 Wilshire Blvd. 936.5213

105 South Carthay Circle A charming, leafy neighborhood of 1930s stucco cottages that mix Spanish and Art Deco themes. Consistent in style and scale, this historic district is now threatened by predatory developers. Long-gone is a legendary Mission-revival movie palace, the **Carthay Circle**. ♦ E and W of San Vincente Blvd, So of Wilshire Blvd

---

Restaurants/Clubs: Red   Hotels: Blue
Shops/Parks: Green   **Sights/Culture:** Black

106 Rosalind's West African $$ Liberian-born Rosalind and her Peace Corps-vet husband offer an adventurous selection of West African dishes, like ground-nut stew, yam balls, and plantains with ginger and cayenne. ♦ African ♦ Tu-Su 5-10PM. 1044 S. Fairfax Ave. 936.2486

107 Versailles ★★$ Larger version of the original restaurant, serving the same gutsy garlic chicken and pork with black beans, oxtail, and strong coffee. Takeout, too. ♦ Cuban ♦ M-Th, Su 11AM-10PM; F-Sa 11AM-11PM. 1415 S. La Cienega Blvd (So of Pico Blvd) 289.0392. Also at: 10319 Venice Blvd, Culver City. 558.3168

107 Victor's ★$ Exceptional wines (from the next-door store) by the glass and basic food served in a spare room—or to go. ♦ Argentinian ♦ M-Sa 11AM-9:30PM. 8566 W. Pico Blvd. 854.3373. Also at: 3811 Sawtelle Blvd, Culver City. 391.0888

107 Empanada's Place ★$ Authentic Argentinian turnovers stuffed with chicken, beef, sausage, artichoke, and 15 other choices. To eat in or to go. ♦ Argentinian ♦ M-Sa 11AM-9:30PM. 8566 W. Pico Blvd. 854.3373. Also at: 3811 Sawtelle Blvd, Culver City. 391.0888

108 Carl's Bar-B-Q ★★$ Those in the know come from miles around for what experts claim is LA's best East Texas-style barbecue, hickory-smoked and slathered with **Carl Adams**' magical sauce, medium or very hot. With only 3 tables, most of the business is to go. Ribs, chicken, hot links, greens, and dirty rice that is probably the closest thing to heaven you will ever find in a yellow styrofoam takeout box. ♦ American ♦ M-Sa 11:30AM-midnight; Su 2-10PM. 5953 Pico Blvd. No credit cards. 934.0637

108 India's Oven ★★$$ Great tandoori chicken, curries, and *nan* in a fast-food setting. Beer and wine; try the mango *lassi*, a yogurt drink. ♦ Indian ♦ M-Th 11:45AM-4:30PM, 5:30-10:30PM; F-Sa 11:45AM-4:30PM, 5:30-11PM; Su 5-10PM. No credit cards. 5897 W. Pico Blvd. 936.1000

108 Walia ★$ It looks like an African hut, plays hypnotic music, and has beautiful waitresses to serve you soul-searing food—including meat, chicken, and fish stews, such as *doro wot*, and stir-fries such as *yesiga tibs*. Don't ask for cutlery, you can scoop everything up with *injera*, a slightly sour, porous bread. Main dishes come with collard greens, lentils, salad, and yogurt. Frosty Gambian lager is a better bet than the honeyed wine; and do try the coffee. ♦ Ethiopian ♦ Tu-Su 5-11PM. 5881 Pico Blvd. 933.1215

109 Maurice's Snack 'n' Chat ★$$ Popular soul food restaurant serving large platters of meatloaf, short ribs, liver, and onions, accompanied by yams, beets, or black-eyed peas. ♦ Soul food ♦ M-F noon-10PM; Sa 4-11PM; Su 4-9PM. 5549 Pico Blvd. 931.3877

110 Big Easy Cafe $ Good ol' boy food from *Nawleens*—chicken cheese, breaded catfish, barbecued shrimp, sandwiches, peach cobbler, and sweet potato pie. No alcohol. ♦ Cajun ♦ M-Tu 11AM-9PM; W-Sa 11AM-10PM; Su 1-8PM. 2525 S. Robertson Blvd. 837.3626

111 Fred's Bakery Only in LA would bagels aspire to elegance, but these are good enough to lure movie stars. ♦ M-Sa 6AM-6PM; Su 6AM-3PM. 2831 S. Robertson Blvd. 838.1204

111 Homer and Edie's Bistro ★$$$ Authentic Creole cooking: gumbo and catfish and sinfully

rich pecan pie. Homer and Edie want folks to feel like it's Mardi Gras all year round and the live New Orleans jazz played on weekends helps. ♦ Creole ♦ M-F 11:30AM-2:30PM, 6-11PM; Sa 6-11PM. 2839 S. Robertson Blvd. 559.5102

112 St. Elmo's Village Artist **Roderick Sykes** organized friends and neighbors to transform a derelict courtyard into a painted quilt of faces, figures, and inspirational messages, whose verve would have delighted Picasso. ♦ 4836 St. Elmo Dr (La Brea Ave-Venice Blvd) 936.3595

Bests

Piero Selvaggio
Valentino

A Mexican Restaurant: **El Cholo**—on Sunday evening, for margaritas, mariachis, Latin folklore, and people of all races, groups, and looks; a real piece of floating life...with salsa!

An Amphitheater: the **Hollywood Bowl**—the most extravagant picnics, the pops, the stars—rhapsody LA style.

A Charity Event: **Meals on Wheels at Universal Studios**—the greatest chefs of America, the best wineries, a great setting, and a great cause: feeding the hungry poor.

Special Occasion: **Citrus**—the Temple of Michel Richard for incredible food, super desserts...a big man!

A Road: **Pacific Coast Highway**—going back and forth to Malibu, the seabreeze, the beach settings, surfing, racing, thinking.

A Memory: **Rex, Il Ristorante**—because of my wedding, because of Mauro Vincenti, because it's a piece of history, because it's one-of-a kind and...keeps sailing along!

A Free Show: **Venice Beach** on the weekend—maybe the single, most eccentric mixture of show and attractions with people, pets, bikes, waves, freedom, a sketch in the life of a bohemian community.

A Market: **Gelson's** in Pacific Palisades—it is the state-of-the-art supermarket.

With Kids: the **LA Zoo** at Griffith Park—a place for my children with so many activities, animals, people, and space.

Favorite Food Notes: pizza at **Madeo's**, ice cream at **Pazzia**, fun and food at **Emilio's**, plum duck at **Chinois**, steak and fries at **Michael's** in the garden, pasta at **Primi**, fish at **Spago**, something else at **Patina**.

47

Hollywood

Signs reading "No dogs, no actors" greeted the first movie pioneers to arrive in Hollywood, but the marriage of Midwestern farmers and Eastern entertainers overcame its rocky start. Hollywood soon became the symbol of glamour and excitement around the world, a mecca for established talent and unknown hopefuls.

Hollywood is divided economically and geographically into 2 communities: the flatlands and the hills. The flatlands contain the laboratories, stages, and studios in which movies are processed, television taped, and music recorded. Industrial zones are interspersed with bungalows and apartment buildings, many from the 1910s and '20s. Some of them have been restored, others are much decayed. The CRA's Hollywood redevelopment plan is a welcome response to the decline, but it has failed to answer the question: how can the area regain its vitality without losing its character? The old Hollywood had a strong sense of community and this was reflected in its architecture. Too many of the dingbat apartments that have erupted on the side streets, as well

as the new commercial structures along Hollywood, Sunset, and Santa Monica boulevards, are bland or overbearing.

West Hollywood—a pistol-shaped area of these flatlands, formerly administered by LA County—became an independent city in 1984, the 84th in the Greater Los Angeles area. In contrast to old Hollywood, its problem is not decay but excessive growth, and it has wisely applied the brakes. Design showrooms, fashionable shops, restaurants, and hotels abound, and there is a large gay community. Its spine is Santa Monica Boulevard from La Brea Avenue west to Doheny Drive. But its boundaries, from Sunset Strip to Beverly Boulevard in the west, narrowing to a few blocks in the east, are so ragged that it is more practical to describe its attractions together with those of the old Hollywood.

The hills span the rustic charms of **Nichols Canyon** and the raffish counterculture of **Laurel Canyon**. They feature a bizarre mixture of castles and cottages, Spanish haciendas and Moorish temples, winding streets and wild areas

of chaparral. The flatlands of east and central Hollywood have an income half the LA average and a high proportion of recent immigrants, especially from southeast Asia, Latin America, and the Middle East. The hills are more prosperous and settled, appealing to literary and artistic types.

Hollywood was a campground for the **Cahuenga Indians**, and later (because of its proximity to the Cahuenga Pass) a way station on the Camino Real and a major stop on the Butterfield Stage route. When **Harvey Wilcox** registered the subdivision of Hollywood in 1887 it had few residents, and only 165 voters participated in the 1903 vote to incorporate as a city of the sixth class. **Mrs. Wilcox** named the area after the Chicago summer home of a woman she met on the train, and she was its greatest supporter, giving land for churches and schools, keeping demon drink at bay, and welcoming French artist **Paul de Longpre**, whose garden became Hollywood's first tourist attraction. Hollywood surrendered its independence in 1910 to guarantee its access to city water, but it remained a staid farming community of citrus orchards and sheep, with a scatter of houses along unpaved streets lined with pepper trees.

Hollywood

The moviemakers arrived like the Goths in Rome, taking over a saloon on Sunset as the first Hollywood studio, hiring cowboys who rode over front lawns in the excitement of the chase, and greasing intersections to film motorists' skids. The industry soon became prosperous and respectable, and though most of the big companies moved out to Universal City, Burbank, and Culver City in search of cheaper land, their old lots and stages were taken over by independents and are still active. However seedy the reality, the myth endures.

1 Hollywood Boulevard Laid out as Prospect Avenue and lined with ornate mansions, it was rebuilt in the '20s and '30s as the movie colony's Main Street. For a decade or so it boasted fashionable stores, hotels, and restaurants, though the stars came out only at night—for gala premieres at the Chinese and other movie palaces. Forty years of decline have given the boulevard the reputation of a Times Square West, but the architecture has remained almost intact. **Hollywood Heritage**, a lively preservation organization, secured official recognition for the heart of the boulevard as a **National Historic District**—though this may not protect it from massive redevelopment. Look up to enjoy such treasures as the gothic moderne tower of the **Security Pacific Bank** at Highland Ave, and the lively zigzag facades flanking **Frederick's of Hollywood**'s purple tower, the streamlined drugstore on the corner of Cahuenga Blvd, and the 1933 marquee of the **Hollywood Theater** (interior slated to become a Guiness Book of Records museum). Look down for the 1900-plus terrazzo stars of the **Walk of Fame**, commemorating over a thousand entertainment celebrities. You may adopt your favorite star, if you are willing to polish it on the first Saturday of each month. There's a waiting list for **Marilyn Monroe**, but no lack of orphans. **Lupe Velez**, anyone? Call Michael Kellerman at 469.9880

2 Hollywood Roosevelt Hotel $$$ (1927) Restored landmark, site of the first Academy Awards, and former social hub of the movie colony. **Errol Flynn** invented his recipe for gin in a back room of the barber's shop; **Scott Fitzgerald**, **Ernest Hemingway**, and **Salvador Dali** patronized the **Cinegrill** upstairs. **Bill 'Bojangles' Robinson** taught **Shirley Temple** to tap dance up the lobby staircase. Or so the legends go. The 2-story Spanish Colonial lobby with its painted ceiling is worth stopping in to see; **Theodore's** restaurant off the lobby and the Cinegrill (which offers live entertainment nightly) are both sleekly retro in feeling. The Olympic-size pool was painted by **David Hockney**. Memorabilia displayed on mezzanine level. ◆ 7000 Hollywood Blvd. 466.7000, 800/950.7667 (CA), 800/858.2244 (US); fax 462.8056

2 LA Film Permit Office Free daily listings of location filming. ◆ 6922 Hollywood Blvd, suite 602. 485.5324

3 Mann's Chinese Theatre (1927, **Meyer & Holler**) Master showman **Sid Grauman** commissioned this fanciful Chinese temple so that he would have a new stage for his prologues—extravagant spectacles keyed to the movies they accompanied. Legend tells that **Norma Talmadge** accidently stepped into the wet

---

Restaurants/Clubs: Red   Hotels: Blue
Shops/Parks: Green   **Sights/Culture:** Black

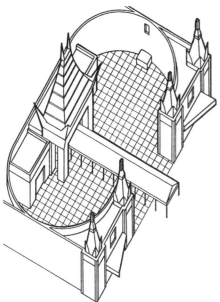

cement of the forecourt, inspiring Sid to round up **Mary Pickford** and **Douglas Fairbanks** to repeat the trick with their hands and feet, and thus inaugurate the world's largest autograph album. He also created the first gala premiere, lining Hollywood Boulevard with klieg lights as the limousines arrived for **De Mille**'s *King of Kings* on opening night, 18 May 1927. The cocoa palms have gone from the forecourt, but the theater is amazingly well preserved, inside and out. ♦ Seats 2200. 6925 Hollywood Blvd. 464.8111

3 Grave Line Tours A treat for lovers of gallows humor. Ex-mortician **Greg Smith** organized this 2-hour tour, in a converted Cadillac hearse, of the homes where stars (from **Sal Mineo** to **Mae West**) met their maker—an improvement on the conventional trips around houses from which stars have long since moved. Tours depart daily at noon from outside Mann's Chinese. ♦ Reservations M-F 1-5PM 876.4286, information 876.0920

3 Hollywood Promenade (scheduled completion 1992, Jerde Partnership) A 150-million-dollar office, hotel, retail, and entertainment complex on a 2-block site that wraps around the Chinese. It is intended to revitalize the street by creating a lively mix of activities, including (if funding can be secured) the **Hollywood Exposition**, an educational museum of the entertainment industries, and **The American Cinematheque**. ♦ Bounded by Hollywood Blvd, Franklin Ave, Highland Ave, and Orange Dr

3 C.C. Brown's $ Vintage ice-cream parlor whose hot-fudge sundae enjoys a legendary reputation. ♦ Ice Cream ♦ M-Th 1-11PM; F-Sa 1-11:30PM. 7007 Hollywood Blvd. 462.9262

4 El Capitan A landmark theater that opened under this name in the 1920s, became the **Paramount** Theater, and has been renovated by **Disney** (scheduled to open in the spring of 1991). ♦ 6835 Hollywood Blvd (Highland Ave)

5 Max Factor Beauty Museum (1931, **S. Charles Lee**) The master of '30s streamline movie theaters created this Regency moderne shrine for the celebrated cosmetics company. Max Factor has vacated the office tower, but has turned its former studio into a fascinating display of how the stars were coiffed and made up. An authentic Hollywood shrine. Cosmetics are on sale at discounts of up to 70 percent next door. ♦ Free. M-Sa 10AM-4PM. 1666 N. Highland Ave. 463.6668

6 B. Dalton Bookseller The largest bookstore on the boulevard; discounted and remaindered

books on the 3rd floor. ♦ M-Th 9AM-10PM; F-Sa 9:30AM-11PM; Su noon-7PM. 6743 Hollywood Blvd. 469.8191

6 Hollywood Wax Museum A melancholy place stuffed with unconvincing replicas of famous stars and assorted celebrities, plus a wax *Last Supper* at which visitors throw coins as though it were a fountain. ♦ Admission. M-Th, Su 10AM-midnight; F-Sa 10AM-2AM. 6767 Hollywood Blvd. 462.8860

7 Egyptian Theatre (1922, **Meyer & Holler**) **Sid Grauman**'s first Off Broadway movie palace was inspired by the newly discovered tomb of King Tut. Gone are the spear carrier who paced the ramparts and the usherettes dressed as Cleopatra's handmaidens. ♦ Seats 1800. 6712 Hollywood Blvd. 467.6167

7 Universal News Agency One of the best sources of hometown (whether Bangor or Bangkok) newspapers and international magazines. ♦ M-Th, Su 7AM-11PM; F-Sa 7AM-midnight. 1655 N. Las Palmas Ave. 467.3850

8 Larry Edmunds Longtime mecca for lovers of film and theater, with a wide selection of books, posters, and stills, but not all it used to be. ♦ M-Sa 10AM-6PM. 6658 Hollywood Blvd. 463.3273

8 Supply Sergeant Survivalists, mercenaries, and bargain hunters can choose from such indispensables as boots, bugles, binoculars, and dummy grenades, plus military surplus clothing and camping gear. ♦ M-Th 10AM-7PM; F-Sa 10AM-9PM; Su 11AM-7PM. 6664 Hollywood Blvd. 463.4730

9 Frederick's of Hollywood (1935, **Frank Falgien** and **Bruce Marteney**) The purple-and-pink Art Deco tower is an appropriate symbol of the flamboyantly sexy apparel. Outlets across America, but this is the original. ♦ M-Th, Sa 10AM-6PM; F 10AM-9PM; Su noon-5PM. 6608 Hollywood Blvd. 466.8506

Walk of Fame

First stars: Joanne Woodward, Ronald Coleman, Burt Lancaster, Louise Fazenda, Olive Borden, Edward Sedgwick, Sr., Ernest Torrence, and Preston Foster.

Started: 1958

Number of stars today: 1922

Most stars: Gene Autry and Tony Martin, with 4 each (radio, TV, movie, recording).

9 **Hollywood Toys and Costumes** LA's largest and best resort for compulsive exhibitionists, renting Halloween costumes year-round, plus masks, wigs, and makeup. ♦ M-Sa 9:30AM-7PM; Su 11AM-6PM. 6562 Hollywood Blvd. 465.3119

10 **Musso and Frank Grill** ★$$ Hollywood's oldest restaurant, open since 1919. Reassuring in its paneled permanence and lack of change, with a comfortable counter for solitary diners. Waiters may be brusque unless they know you. Some rate this restaurant highly, especially for

Hollywood

its martinis, grills, and sourdough bread. ♦ American ♦ M-Sa 11AM-11PM. 6667 Hollywood Blvd. 467.7788

10 **Book City** Huge selection of new and used books on all topics. ♦ M-Sa 10AM-10PM, Su 10AM-8PM. 6627 Hollywood Blvd. 466.2525. Also at: 308 N. Golden Mall, Burbank. 818/848.4417

11 **Janes House** (1903) The last survivor of the mansions that lined the boulevard until the 1920s was a family-run school (1911-26) and is now an official **Visitors Information Center**. The **LA Jazz Society** presents occasional programs at noon in the garden, 469.6800. ♦ M-Sa 9AM-5PM. 6541 Hollywood Blvd. 461.4213

12 **Gorky's** ★$ The late, great **Tick Tock Tearoom** is now an improved outpost of downtown's proletarian cafeteria and brewery. Grab your copy of *The Lower Depths* and your balalaika and join the other sons of toil to enjoy the borscht and kasha *varnishkas* at this hot new hangout. Live evening entertainment. ♦ Russian ♦ 24 hours. 1716 N. Cahuenga Blvd. 463.7576

12 **North Ivar Street** This block of North Ivar above Yucca St still has a lot of '20s and '30s apartment buildings. The **Parva Sed** is where **Nathanael West** lived when he conceived the plan for his scathing Hollywood novella, *Day of the Locust*. He had befriended a lot of the local working girls and would drive them home. In return they sewed his buttons on. Further up the block is the **El Nido**, which was the fictional home for the luckless screenwriter played by **William Holden** in the movie *Sunset Boulevard*.

12 **Joseph's Cafe** $ Long-established favorite serving fabulous gyros, lentil soup, and rice pudding throughout the day. The rock group **U2** eats here. ♦ American/Middle Eastern ♦ M-Sa 7AM-11PM. 1775 N. Ivar St. 462.8697

13 **Greens and Things** ★$ Rib-sticking, fingerlicking good food—short ribs, collard greens, cornbread, and peach pie—served with lemonade in mason jars in a funky dive. ♦ Soul food ♦ Daily 11:30AM-10PM. 6357 Yucca St. 462.7555

13 **Chao Praya** ★$$ To underscore its proximity to the Capitol Records building, the menu is shaped like a record. Service is frequently slow, but the food is good. Low lighting makes

for a romantic late supper. ♦ Thai ♦ M-Th, Su 11:30AM-11:30PM; F-Sa 11:30AM-1AM. 6307 Yucca St. 466.6704

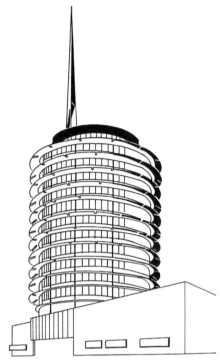

14 **Capitol Records Tower** (1954, **Welton Becket**) Programatic architecture on an epic scale; this tower suggests a stack of records topped by a stylus. In December it is lit to create Hollywood's tallest Christmas tree. ♦ 1750 Vine St

15 **Collector's Book Store** A treasure-trove of movie books, stills, and memorabilia. ♦ Tu-Sa 10AM-5PM. 1708 N. Vine St. 467.3296

16 **Frolic Room** From the expressive neon lettering to the '40s decor, this bar is a hardy survivor. ♦ Daily 10AM-2AM. 6245 Hollywood Blvd. 462.5890

Sunset Strip
Site of the vanished township of Sherman, Sunset Boulevard east to Doheny Drive is now part of recently incorporated West Hollywood. During the century in between, it was administered by LA County. Free of certain legal restrictions enforced in the City of Los Angeles, the Strip has traditionally been a center of nightlife with famous clubs like **Ciro's** and the **Mocambo**. In the '30s and '40s, many Hollywood stars used to stop off here for some relaxation on their way home to Beverly Hills after a day's work at the studios. A steady stream of limousines would drop off glamorous carousers for dining, drinking, and dancing. In the '60s, the Strip was a haven for hipsters and flower children. Rock clubs now predominate. This section of Sunset Boulevard is the art gallery of the entertainment industry. The work of graphic designers and sign painters is constantly displayed on the enormous custom billboards, referred to in the industry as *vanity boards*, elevated above small stucco buildings.

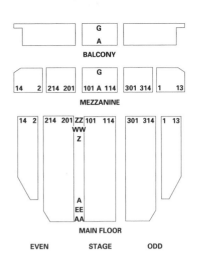

Drawing Courtesy Frank Gehry

16 Pantages Theatre (1929, **B. Marcus Priteca**) A dazzling exemplar of adaptive reuse—movie palace turned showcase for Broadway musicals. Rivals the Wiltern as an anthology of zigzag moderne, from the vaulted lobby guarded by statues of a movie director and an aviatrix, to the amazing fretted ceiling of the auditorium, designed by **Anthony Heinsbergen**. The Academy Awards were presented here in the '50s. ♦ Seats 2900. 6233 Hollywood Blvd. 410.1062

17 Henry Fonda Theatre A brave attempt to bring quality drama to a depressed neighborhood in a conversion of the **Pix** movie house. ♦ Seats 863. 6126 Hollywood Blvd. 410.1062

18 Vine Street Bar & Grill ★$$$ Stylish, intimate club that books the best new and established jazz and blues artists. Good Northern Italian food for pre- and post-theater dining. ♦ M 11AM-3PM; Tu-Su 11AM-3PM, 5PM-2AM. 1610 N. Vine St. 463.4375

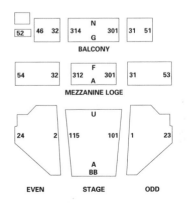

19 James Doolittle Theater One of the best places in LA to enjoy one-person shows and quality drama. ♦ Seats 1038. 1615 N. Vine St. 462.6666

20 Frances Goldwyn Regional Branch Library (1986, **Frank Gehry**) To replace the

Hollywood Library, which was destroyed by arson, Gehry created this cluster of luminous boxes (light is reflected off water in shallow reflecting pools). So outdoorsy is the feel that you hardly notice how well the building is protected ("tighter security than the American Embassy I designed for Damascus," says the architect). A surreal juxtaposition is the **Ivar Burlesque** next door. ♦ M-Th 10AM-8PM; F-Sa 10AM-5:30PM. 1623 Ivar St (Sunset Blvd) 467.1821

20 India Inn ★$ Some of the best *naan*, tandooris, curries, and vegetarian dishes in town. ♦ Indian ♦ Daily noon-3PM, 5-10PM. 1638 N. Cahuenga Blvd. 461.3774

21 Wattles Mansion & Gardens (1905) **Hollywood Heritage** is restoring the house, built as the winter home of an Omaha businessman, and the formal gardens, which were a top tourist attraction in Hollywood's early years. Beyond is a wilderness area that links up to **Runyon Canyon Park**, formerly the **Huntington Hartford Estate**. The Heritage (whose offices are here) gives quarterly tours of neighboring properties, plus walking tours of Hollywood Boulevard, departing from the Capitol Records Tower. ♦ M-F 10AM-4PM; or by appointment. 1824 N. Curson Ave. 874.4005 (or check at the Hollywood Studio Museum)

22 Case Study Apartments (1991, **Adele Naude Santos**) The **Museum of Contemporary Art** commissioned this villagelike cluster of low-income apartments to revive the *Case Study House Program* that *Arts & Architecture* magazine ran from 1945 to 1966. ♦ Franklin Ave at La Brea Ave

23 Yamashiro's Restaurant $$ The oldest building in LA is a 600-year-old pagoda, imported by Oriental art dealers **Adolphe** and **Eugene Bernheimer** as an ornament for the Japanese palace and gardens they built in 1913. It rises high above another landmark, the **Magic Castle** (1925), a French Renaissance château that is now a private club for magicians. The food at Yamashiro's is terrible, but the view at sunset is worth the climb and the price of a drink. Be sure to get a window seat. ♦ Japanese ♦ M-F, Su 5:30-10PM; Sa 5:30-11PM. 1999 N. Sycamore Ave (Franklin Ave) 466.5125

Hollywood is a great place if you're an orange.
Fred Allen

Restaurants/Clubs: Red

Shops/Parks: Green

Hotels: Blue

Sights/Culture: Black

53

24 Freeman House (1924, **Frank Lloyd Wright**) A Mayan-influenced concrete-block structure located in the hills above the Hollywood Bowl, now being restored by USC. To help pay for the restoration, reproductions of Wright's patterned concrete blocks are being made available to donors of $250 or more. ◆ 1962 Glencoe Wy (Hillcrest Blvd) 743.4471

25 Il Vittoriale (1929) The **American Legion Headquarters** have been transformed into an Italian villa for the presentation of *Tamara*, a long-running living movie about Italian poet/

Hollywood

patriot **Gabriele d'Annunzio**. For a stiff fee, you can play voyeur and co-conspirator as the action unfolds in different parts of the house, and enjoy a champagne supper. ◆ Tu-F 8PM; Sa-Su 2:30, 8PM. 2035 Highland Ave. 480.3232

26 The High Tower (1920). A touch of San Gimignano in the Hollywood hills. This campanile, rising sheer from the end of a cul de sac, is an elevator shaft that rises to the streamline villas on either side. Stepped streets reinforce the impression of an Italian hill town. ◆ High Tower Rd

27 Whitley Heights This area was developed in the '20s and '30s by **Hobart J. Whitley**. Like the old Italian villas they were modeled on, these gemlike houses are built into the hillside. **Marion Davies, Gloria Swanson**, and **Ethel Barrymore** are among those who once lived here. Many of the charming houses still have courtyards, fountains, crenelated balconies, and hidden gardens. For private house tours, call 874.6438. ◆ Highland Ave (Franklin Ave)

28 Hollywood Studio Museum **Cecil B. De Mille** rented this horse barn in December 1913, and used it as a set, offices, and changing rooms (alongside the horses) for *The Squaw Man*, the first feature-length movie shot in Hollywood. It stood at Selma and Vine, was trucked to what is now the Paramount lot, and was moved to its present site in 1985, restored by **Hollywood Heritage**, and furnished with stills and other exhibitions. ◆ Admission. Tu-F 11AM-4PM; Sa 10AM-4PM. 2100 N. Highland Ave. 874.2276

29 Loft Towers (1987, **Koning & Eizenberg**) With a nod to neighboring High Tower, these young Australian architects created a pair of suburban lofts, each of which comprises three 20-foot-square rooms for working and living stacked on a double garage, with kitchen and service areas behind. Private residence. ◆ 6949 Camrose Dr

30 Hollywood Bowl A natural amphitheater, originally known as **Daisy Dell**, which was developed in the 1920s as a concert shell, and now hosts the summer season of the **LA Philharmonic**, visiting musicians, and jazz and pop concerts. Popular perennials are the Easter sunrise service and the July 4th and closing night concerts with fireworks. Acoustics are spotty, and only subscribers in their box seats

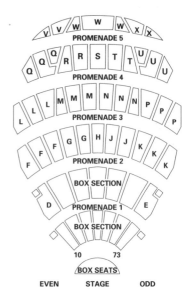

can hear the musicians without amplification, so you may as well sit high up in the cheaper seats and enjoy the view. Dress warmly, bring a cushion, and come early for a picnic—the sylvan glades around the Bowl fill up quickly. There is also a restaurant that serves moderately-priced suppers alfresco on the patio. Parking, in lots along Highland, can be chaotic; a better bet are the 14 park-and-ride buses that serve different parts of LA. On your way in, note **George Stanley**'s moderne statues of music, drama, and dance. Patio restaurant and picnic baskets (to be ordered the previous day, 851.3588). ◆ Seats 17,619. Grounds daily 9AM-dusk, July-Sep. 2301 N. Highland Ave. 850.2000

At the Hollywood Bowl:

Hollywood Bowl Museum Exhibitions on the history of the Bowl include original drawings of concert shell prototypes by **Lloyd Wright** (the son of **Frank**). Visitors may also listen to tapes of memorable Bowl performances in several small listening booths. ◆ Tu-Sa 9:30AM-4:30PM; open until 8:30PM on concert days. Adjacent to the Patio Restaurant. 850.2058

I am a foresighted man, I believe that Los Angeles is destined to become the most important city in this country, if not the world. It can extend in any direction as far as you like; its front door opens on the Pacific, the ocean of the future. The Atlantic is the ocean of the past. Europe can supply her own wants; we shall supply the wants of Asia. There is nothing that cannot be made and few things that will not grow in Southern California. It has the finest climate in the world: extremes of heat and cold are unknown. These are the reasons for its growth.

Henry E. Huntington, 1912

What happens here happens 5 years before anywhere else in America. We send the style to the rest of the country.

Harlan Ellison, 1980

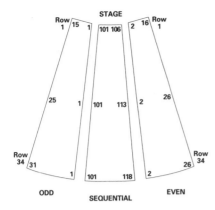

```
                    STAGE
      Row  15  1      101 106   2  16  Row
      1                              1

        25    1      101   113   2      26

      Row  31                          26  Row
      34                                   34
              1      101   118   2

         ODD                      EVEN
                  SEQUENTIAL
```

31 John Anson Ford Theatre Experimental productions by the **Mark Taper Forum** are presented in the **Taper, Too**—under the main stage. ♦ Seats 1300. 2580 Cahuenga Blvd. 972.7211

32 Lake Hollywood A reservoir in the hills offering a splendid view of the Hollywood Sign, a rustic jogging trail, and a sense of what this place looked like a hundred years ago. Climb down to the base of the dam to admire the bear head sculptures. ♦ M-F 6:30-10AM, 2-7:30PM; Sa-Su 6:30AM-7:30PM. Drive north on Cahuenga Blvd across Franklin Ave, right on Dix St, left on Holly Dr, sharp right on Deep Dell Pl, left on Weidlake Dr to lake entrance

33 Hollywood Sign Fifty-foot-high letters near the summit of Mt. Lee, first erected in 1923 to advertise **Hollywoodland**, a residential development on the lower slopes. In 1949, the deteriorating sign and its acreage were deeded to the Hollywood Chamber of Commerce, who took down the -LAND to create a civic advertisement. A new sign costing $250,000 was erected in 1978. ♦ On Mt. Cahuenga above Hollywood

34 Village Coffee Shop $ Homey rendezvous for the area's actors, writers, and singers—the aspirants who live below the Hollywoodland gates, and the more established who live in the hills above. The good food and warm atmosphere make the tables worth waiting for. ♦ American ♦ M-F 8AM-6PM; Sa 8AM-5PM. 2695 Beachwood Dr. 467.5398

35 La Poubelle $$ How to resist a brasserie that calls itself the garbage pail? French waiters shout orders to the kitchen, **Edith Piaf** sings, and owner **Jacqueline Koster** won't let you order anything that doesn't satisfy her. Crêpes,

omelets, and coq au vin are staples. ♦ French ♦ M-Th 5:30-11PM; F-Sa 5:30PM-midnight; Su 11:30AM-10PM. 5909 Franklin Ave. 465.0807

36 Samuels-Navarro House (1928, **Lloyd Wright**) Designed for actor **Ramon Navarro**, this house stretches horizontally along a natural ridge ending with a swimming pool (now enclosed) at one end and a private garden at the other. Pressed copper trims the white stucco surface. Recently remodeled by **Josh Schweitzer**. Private residence. ♦ 5699 Valley Oak Dr

Hollywood

37 American Film Institute Offices of the American Film Institute (AFI) and its Center for Advanced Film Studies now occupy what was once the hillside campus of Immaculate Heart College. **The Louis B. Mayer Library**, open to serious film scholars, has the most extensive collection of movie scripts in the country. The AFI and its **Sony Video Center** present regular public screenings and classes, plus annual film and video festivals. ♦ Seats 135. 2221 N. Western Ave (Franklin Ave) 856.7600

38 5390 Franklin Avenue A flamboyant apartment building, formerly the **Château Elysée**, now owned by the **Church of Scientology**. ♦ Serrano Ave

39 Sowden House (1926, **Lloyd Wright**) This house fuses Mayan and Deco themes, is built around a courtyard, and is entered from within a cavelike opening framed with decorative concrete blocks. Private residence. ♦ 5121 Franklin Ave

40 Onyx Sequel $ Bohemian coffeehouse, featuring the work of local artists. Live music on Sunday afternoon. ♦ American ♦ M-Th, Su 9AM-1AM; F-Sa 9AM-2AM. 1802 N. Vermont Ave. 660.5820

41 Barnsdall Park Located at the top of a hill and ringed by a thick grove of olive trees; a shady oasis and cultural center in the flatlands of eastern Hollywood. Administered by the **City of Los Angeles Department of Cultural Affairs**. ♦ 4800 Hollywood Blvd

---

Hollywood Boulevard: The Golden Road, Hardened Artery, Santa Claus Lane, Main Street in Slacks....
Hedda Hopper, 1941

HOLLYWOOD

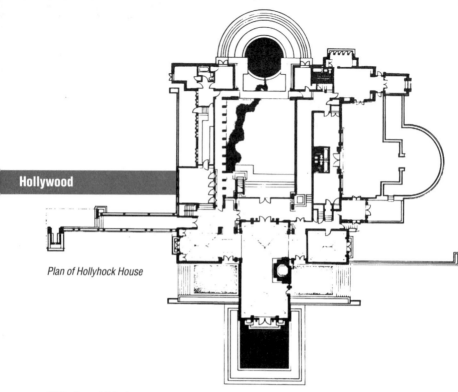

Plan of Hollyhock House

Within Barnsdall Park:

Hollyhock House (1917-20, **Frank Lloyd Wright**) Oil heiress **Aline Barnsdall** commissioned this house—Wright's first in LA—as part of a complex of cultural and residential structures. Named for an abstracted geometric motif based on the flower, it has been restored and includes many of the original Wright furnishings. An interesting guided tour is offered. ♦ Admission. Tours Tu-Th on the hour, 10AM-1PM; Sa and the first 3 Su of each month, on the hour, noon-3PM. 485.4580

Municipal Art Gallery Director **Ed Leffingwell** is exploring the cutting edge of Southern California art. The theater presents a lively and varied bill of films and concerts. Gallery admission charge. ♦ Tu-Su 12:30-5PM. 4804 Hollywood Blvd. Group tours 485.4581

Junior Arts Center An extensive program of sophisticated and innovative studio arts classes for children and young people ages 4-18. The gallery has changing shows designed for a young audience emphasizing participation and activity. ♦ M-F 9AM-5:30PM. Gallery Tu-Su 12:30-5PM. 485.4474

Arts & Crafts Center (1920, **Frank Lloyd Wright**) Arts and crafts classes for adults and older teenagers. Class charge. Class days and times vary. ♦ 485.2116

42 **Brashov's** ★$$ A family-run Rumanian deli/restaurant. You'll find a few tables and plenty of folks from the old country who come to enjoy high-quality, honest food. Good stuffed cabbage, schnitzel, fish borscht, kabobs, and a magnificent chocolate cake. ♦ Rumanian ♦ Daily 11AM-9PM. 1301 N. Vermont Ave. 660.0309

43 **New York George** $$ Homey place with a patio serving good, simple American food (great fries!) at very reasonable prices. ♦ American ♦ Daily 8AM-10PM. 4854 Fountain Ave. 666.910C

44 **Paru's** ★$ Stars of the vegetarian menu include the *masala dosa* (a foot-long lentil flour crêpe filled with potato curry), *samosas* (turnovers), *vada* (lentil donuts served with chutney), and *idli* (rice pancakes with lentil gravy). ♦ Southern Indian ♦ M, W-Su noon-4:30PM, 5-9PM. 5140 Sunset Blvd. 661.7600. Also at: 9340 W. Pico Blvd, 273.8088; 9545 Reseda Blvd, Northridge. 818/349.3546

45 **Jitlada** ★$$ This cozy little treasure, tucked away in a corner mall of no other apparent distinction, serves some of the most delicious Thai food in Los Angeles, and the price is right. Everything is good, but the spicy squid salad is a standout. ♦ Thai ♦ Tu-Sa 11AM-3PM, 5-10PM. 5233 Sunset Blvd. 667.9809

46 **Starsteps** (1981) A 40,000-pound steel sculpture by Chicago artist **John David Mooney** atop the **Metromedia TV** studio. Brightly illuminated at night, it seems to float above the freeway. ♦ Sunset Blvd (Wilton Pl-Hollywood Fwy)

Douglas Fairbanks hosted the premiere Academy Awards show from the Hollywood **Roosevelt Hotel** in 1929.

47 Columbia Bar & Grill ★$$$ Handsome airy brick-and-glass restaurant with a spacious patio, part-owned by **Wayne Rogers** and patronized by entertainment types from CBS and neighboring studios. Salads, crabcakes, and chili are typical of the straightforward menu. ◆ California ◆ M-F 11AM-3:30PM, 5:30-10:30PM; Sa 5:30-10:30PM. 1448 N. Gower St. 461.8800

48 The Hollywood Palladium Famous since 1940, the Palladium has swung to the sounds of the **Dorsey Brothers**, **Glen Miller**, **Stan Kenton**, and **Lawrence Welk**. Current attractions vary from dancing to conventions, but big names still make frequent appearances. Full bar and à la carte dinners offered. ◆ 6215 Sunset Blvd. 466.4311

49 Tasca ★$ Authentic tapas bar serving chilled sherry with such dishes as serrano ham and manchego cheese, shrimp with garlic, fried salt cod fritters, marinated mushrooms, and empanadas. ◆ Spanish ◆ M-Th 11:30AM-11PM; F 11AM-midnight; Sa 1PM-midnight; Su 5-11PM. 6266 ½ Sunset Blvd. 465.7747

49 Off Vine ★$$ A shark juts through the roof of this frame house on a quiet side street—heralding such quirky dishes as New York steak with Jack Daniels sauce, turkeyburgers with 3 sauces, scallops in puff pastry, and blueberry-crumb cake. Show biz clientele. ◆ Eclectic ◆ M-F 11:30AM-3PM, 5:30-11PM; Sa 5:30-11PM. 6263 Leland Wy. 962.1900

50 Cinerama Dome An impressive cellular construction, originally built to accommodate the extra-wide screen of the Cinerama process. The acoustics and sight lines of the theater are remarkably good. ◆ Seats 900. 6360 Sunset Blvd. 466.3401

Chan Dara

51 Chan Dara ★$$ Pioneering Thai restaurant with a large and loyal clientele, so you may have to wait to eat. Wide selection, including *me krob* (sweet fried noodles), *sate*, squid with mint and chili, and wonderfully spicy soups. ◆ Thai ◆ M-F 11AM-1AM; Sa 5PM-midnight; Su 5-11PM. 1511 N. Cahuenga Blvd. 464.8585

51 Martoni's $$ Good bar and hearty food. ◆ Italian ◆ M-F 11:30AM-3PM, 5PM-2AM; Sa 5PM-2AM. 1523 N. Cahuenga Blvd. 466.3441

52 Club Lingerie The best New Wave dance club in town and a lot of fun. There's a no-nonsense minimal interior with a full bar and a spacious dance floor. Live music every night and an aggressively imaginative booking policy featuring rockabilly, punk, R&B, and jazz greats. Good locally famous DJs. Admission charge varies. Must be 21 with ID. ◆ Cover. M-Sa 9PM-2AM. 6507 W. Sunset Blvd. 466.8557

52 Berwin Entertainment Center Handsome Spanish/Deco tower, formerly the **Hollywood Athletic Club**, where **Buster Crabbe** (Olympic gold medallist turned Tarzan) was pool instructor. ◆ 6525 Sunset Blvd

53 Crossroads of the World (1936, **Robert Derrah**) Fantasy architecture in pristine condition: a liner (center buiding) sailing into a foreign port (surrounding English, French, Spanish, and Moorish shops) designed by the architect who did the Coca Cola Building downtown. ◆ 6671 Sunset Blvd

54 Cafe des Artistes ★★$$ You could easily imagine yourself on a back street of Cannes in **Michele Lamy**'s idyllic French bistro. Leafy patio and cool, undecorated dining room, friendly service, and a few delicious *plats du jour*—like the calamari salad, wild mushrooms baked in cream, and steak with *frites*. Good Sunday brunch. ◆ French ◆ M-F noon-2:30PM, 7-11PM; Sa 7-11PM; Su 11:30AM-3PM, 7-11PM. 1534 N. McCadden Pl. 461.6889

54 Stages Trilingual Theatre **Paul Verdier** produces some of LA's most innovative theater—including plays by **Ionesco**, **Marguerite Duras**, and **Ariane Mnouchkine**—in English, French, and Spanish. The space is tiny, so book well ahead. ◆ Seats 300. 1540 N. McCadden Pl. 463.5356, box office 465.1010

55 Hollywood High School (1935) Streamline moderne buildings with decorative reliefs and uplifting inscriptions. Its students are a microcosm of Hollywood's ethnic diversity. ◆ Sunset Blvd at Highland Ave

56 Hampton's ★$$ Great hamburgers made from beef that is ground daily and cooked to order, with exotic toppings and an outstanding salad bar. Rustic setting. ◆ American ◆ M-Th 11AM-10PM; F-Sa 11AM-11PM; Su 10AM-10PM. 1342 N. Highland Ave. 469.1090. Also at: 4301 Riverside Dr. 818/845.3009

57 Little Red Schoolhouse A building that is just what it says. ◆ 1248 N. Highland Ave

58 Arturo's Flowers These people have a goofy genius for oddball promotion, and though the selection is limited, their hours make this place a lifesaver. ◆ Daily 8AM-9PM. 1261 N. La Brea Ave. 876.6482

59 Matuszeks ★★$ The best place this side of an Iowa farm kitchen for hearty food and a welcome that makes you feel like family (remember *Field of Dreams*?). But **Jan** and **Lidia**, a young émigré couple, have their roots in central Europe, and they re-create its old-world flavors and charm. Come hungry and enjoy a feast—from borscht via paprika chicken and the lightest dumplings and sauerkraut to apple raisin strudel with whipped cream. ◆ Czechoslovakian ◆ M-Sa 5-11PM. 7513 Sunset Blvd. 874.0106

West Hollywood became an independent city when its citizens voted for incorporation in November 1984. The city encompasses 1.8 square miles.

Restaurants/Clubs: Red   Hotels: Blue
Shops/Parks: Green   **Sights/Culture:** Black

60 Samuel French Plays, from **Shakespeare** to **Stoppard**, as well as books on theater. ◆ M-F 10AM-6PM; Sa 11AM-5PM. 7623 Sunset Blvd. 876.0570

ꝹAR ꟽAGꞪREB

60 Dar Maghreb ★$$$ Arabian Nights decor and good renditions of the standard dishes. Popular with tour groups. ◆ Moroccan ◆ M-Sa 6-11PM; Su 5:30-10:30PM. 7651 Sunset Blvd. 876.7651

Hollywood

61 Directors Guild of America (1989) A text-book example of how not to build on Sunset. This overpowering curvilinear bronze glass tower is out of scale and character with every-thing around. On the positive side, it has 3 ex-cellent auditoriums, which are currently being used by the **American Cinematheque** for public programs (information: 461.9622). ◆ Seats 600, 143, 46. 7920 Sunset Blvd. 289.2000

61 Gaucho Grill ★$$ The endangered species of meat eaters can indulge themselves at this paradise of the pampas. ◆ Argentine ◆ M-Th, Su 11AM-11PM; F-Sa 11AM-midnight. 7980 Sunset Blvd. 656.4152. Also at: 11838 Ventura Blvd, Studio City. 818/508.1030

62 Villa d'Este Apartments (1928) One of sev-eral lushly planted courtyard apartments that evoke romantic Mediterranean villas. Other cherished examples are located within walking distance at 1400 and 1475 Havenhurst Dr, 8225 Fountain Ave, and 1338 N. Harper Ave. Private residences. ◆ 1355 Laurel Ave

63 Greenblatt's Delicatessen ★$$ Haven for expatriate New Yorkers that became less brusque with the addition of its upstairs dining room. Great pastrami, cheesecake, and wines; full bar; excellent takeout. ◆ Daily 9AM-2AM. 8017 Sun-set Blvd. 656.0606

63 Coconut Teaszer Young, funky rock 'n' roll joint that becomes a madhouse on weekends, with disco dancing, beer, and food included in the cover charge. ◆ Cover. M-Th, Su 8PM-2AM; F-Sa 8PM-4AM. 8117 Sunset Blvd. 654.4773

La Toque

63 La Toque ★★★★$$$$ Chef/owner **Ken Frank** maintains a high level of inventive cuisine. The service and quiet, intimate atmosphere are at-tractive enough, but the kitchen is among the best in LA. Menus change daily, depending on what's available and fresh. The dishes are very French, very expensive, and very good. Superb wine list. The patio is a lovely spot on summer evenings. ◆ French ◆ M-Th noon-2PM, 6:30-10PM; F noon-2PM, 6-10:30PM; Sa 6-10:30PM. 8171 Sunset Blvd. 656.7516

64 Château Marmont Hotel (1927) $$$ A Norman castle, guarding the approach to the Sunset Strip. **Garbo** stayed here; **John Belushi** died here. Its faded elegance has been sensi-tively restored, and its privacy and charm lure movie and music celebrities. Luxury suites with balconies and views, cottages around the pool. ◆ 8221 Marmont Ln. 656.1010, 800/242.8328; fax 655.5311

65 Imperial Gardens ★$$$ You'll find record company execs at the sushi bar, Japanese busi-nessmen in the tatami rooms, and live music in the lounge. Surprisingly authentic food for such a show biz favorite. ◆ Japanese ◆ M-Sa 6-10PM Su 6-9PM. Sushi bar 6-11:30PM. 8225 Sunset Blvd. 656.1750

66 Oscar's Wine Bar ★$$$ A home away from home for Brits. Includes intimate rooms, live jazz, pitchers of Pimm's Cup, steak-and-kidney pie, and cut crystal bowls of trifle. ◆ English ◆ M-Sa 6-11PM. 8210 Sunset Blvd. 654.3457

66 Carlos 'n' Charlie's $$$ One of a chain of flashy restaurants that extends south to Acapulco; notable more for the singles scene than for the food on the whimsically worded menu. Even better action upstairs at **El Privado**. ◆ Mexican ◆ M-F 11AM-2AM; Sa-Su 5PM-2AM. 8240 Sunset Blvd. 656.8830

© St. James's Club

67 St. James's Club $$$$ The former Sunset Tower apartments, a long neglected 1931 Art Deco gem, lovingly restored as a glitzy English-owned residential club. Members are entitled to special upgrades, when available; but if there are rooms, anyone can make a reservation. Ameri-can Express Centurian Club members receive the same services as regular club members. The 12th-floor penthouse, where **John Wayne** once lived, with—legend says—a cow on the balcony, now comprises 2 tiny but opulent suites with great views over the city and hills. Affiliated with clubs in Paris, London, and Antigua. ◆ Deluxe ◆ 8358 Sunset Blvd. 654.7100, 800/225.2637; fax 654.9287

67 Sunset Plaza (1934-36) Genteel stage-set architecture, the centerpiece of a cluster of exclusive stores. ◆ 8400 Sunset Blvd (La Cienega Blvd) 659.0750

67 Butterfield's ★★$$ A leafy patio screened from Sunset's heavy traffic is an idyllic place for lunch on all but the coldest days, and the salads, sandwiches, and daily specials are excellent. Good wines by the glass. ◆ American ◆ M-F 11:30AM-3PM, 6-10PM; Sa 10:30AM-3PM, 6-10:30PM; Su 10:30AM-3PM. 8426 Sunset Blvd. 656.3055

68 The Comedy Store The most important showcase for comedians in the area. The **Main Room** presents established comics; the **Original Room** offers continuous shows of rising new comedians; the **Belly Room** presents female talent. Call for hours. ◆ 8433 Sunset Blvd. 656.6225

69 North Beach Leather You had best have a model's figure not to split the seams of their skintight pants, fitted jackets, and miniskirts. An extrovert's color sensibility also helps. ◆ M-Sa 10AM-6PM; Su noon-5PM. 8500 Sunset Blvd. 652.3224

69 Sunset Marquis $$$$ What a find! An oasis hidden in the midst of Hollywood and *the* place to stay for show and music biz types. Billy Joel, U2, Bruce Springsteen and the like come for such perks as 24-hour security and room service; multi-line phones; workout room with 2 trainers; and MTV station. Accommodations consist of a 106-suite hotel and 12 palatial 1- and 2-bedroom villas which sit on parklike grounds along with 2 pools, a fish pond and exotic birds in cages. The restaurants are for guests and *friends* of the hotel. Complimentary stretch limousine service within 7 miles of the hotel (including downtown LA and Beverly Hills). ◆ Deluxe ◆ 1200 Alta Loma Rd. 657.1333, 800/858.9758; fax 652.5300

70 Chin Chin $$ Dim sum, *potstickers* (pan-fried dumplings), noodles, *mu shu*, and roasted meats served at a counter that rims a frantic open kitchen, and at tables that spill out onto the Sunset Blvd sidewalk. No alcohol. Also in Brentwood, Studio City, Marina del Rey. ◆ Chinese ◆ M-Th, Su 11AM-11PM; F-Sa 11AM-midnight. 8618 Sunset Blvd (Sunset Plaza) 652.1818

70 Le Petit Four ★$ Light meals and sumptuous pâtisserie—also available for takeout, along with delicacies from **Fauchon** in Paris. Eclectic live music. ◆ French ◆ M-Sa 9AM-11PM; Su 9AM-6PM. 8654 Sunset Blvd. 652.3863

71 Dressed to Kill Evening gowns by **Ungaro**, **Givenchy**, **Dior**, and **Patrick Kelly**—for rent. ◆ Tu-F 11AM-7PM; Sa 10AM-6PM; by appointment only. 8762 Holloway Dr. 652.4334

72 Le Dôme ★★★$$$$ Elegant informality with a great view and first-rate bistro food, including black sausage with apples, ham hocks and sauerkraut, roast chicken, and salads. Producers and agents come here for power lunches; you can eat late and there's a lively bar scene. ◆ French ◆ M-F noon-midnight; Sa 7PM-midnight. 8720 Sunset Blvd. 659.6919

72 Nicky Blair's $$$ Noisy, crowded, and glitzy singles bar, which also serves Italian food. Good for star-gazing. ◆ Italian ◆ M-Sa 6PM-2AM. 8730 Sunset Blvd. 659.0929

72 Old World $$ A front patio for people watching. Salads are excellent, as are the Belgian waffles. ◆ Coffeeshop ◆ Daily 8AM-midnight. 8782 Sunset Blvd. 652.2520

73 Gallay Pricey high-style boutique specializing in 4 designers: **Romeo Gigli**, **Azzedine Alaïa**, **Norma Kamali**, and for shoes, **Maud Frizon**.

◆ M-Sa 9:30AM-6PM. 8711 Sunset Blvd. 858.8711

73 Spago ★★★★$$$$ Chef **Wolfgang Puck** is as much a celebrity as any of his glamorous guests. He's often on hand to welcome you, but without neglecting his kitchen. He continues to turn out innovative and delicious pizzas and pastas and mouthwatering Chinese duck, roast salmon with Cabernet sauce, plus terrific desserts, despite the noisy crowds that jam the dining room and patio. Nowhere can you eat so well while gazing at famous faces. Reservations in advance. ◆ California ◆ Daily 6-11:30PM. 1114 Horn Ave. 652.4025

73 Tower Records Bills itself as the largest record store in the world. Across Sunset is an annex selling classical recordings (657.3910) and videos (657.3344). ◆ M-Th, Su 9AM-midnight; F-Sa 9AM-1AM. 8801 Sunset Blvd. 657.7300

74 Chaya Diner ★$ Good Pacific Rim nibbles in a stark setting designed by **Grinstein & Daniels**, enlivened by Oriental banners. You can lunch alone at the sushi-type bar or eat with a group at a long table. ◆ Asian ◆ M-F 11:30AM-3PM, 5-11PM; Sa noon-11PM; Su noon-10PM. 8800 Sunset Blvd. 657.2083

74 Book Soup Marvelous store, which has recently doubled its size and acquired parking in back, specializing in current and classic literature, books on the arts, and a remarkable choice of American and foreign magazines. ◆ Daily 9AM-midnight. 8818 Sunset Blvd. 659.3110

75 Le Bel Age $$$$ Showcase of the **L'Ermitage Hotel Group**—plain on the outside but opulent and refined within. Roomy, well-decorated suites with balconies. Rooftop sports club with sauna, pool, steambath, and a knockout view. ◆ 1020 N. San Vicente Blvd. 854.1111. Reservations: 800/424.4443; fax 854.0926

Within Le Bel Age:

Le Bel Age Restaurant ★★$$$$ Caviar (served with flavored vodkas), *coubiliac* of salmon, chicken Kiev, and quail stuffed with foie gras are among the specialties of this hotel restaurant of Czarist splendor. ♦ Russian ♦ Tu-Sa 6:30-10:30PM. 854.1111

Also in West Hollywood are 5 less expensive all-suite hotels under the same management as Le Bel Age. All are converted from existing apartment buildings and have stylish modern

Hollywood

decor and art works. Reservations for the entire group: 800/424.4443.

Mondrian $$$ A standout (for all the wrong reasons), this hotel's exterior was painted by Israeli artist **Yaakov Agam** in a crude pastiche of the style of the Dutch Modernist. ♦ 8440 Sunset Blvd. 650.8999; fax 650.5212

Le Dufy $$$ 1000 Westmount Dr, south of Holloway Dr. 657.7400; fax 854.6744

Le Parc $$$ 733 West Knoll Dr. 855.8888; fax 659.7812

Le Reve $$ 8822 Cynthia St. 854.1114; fax 657.2623

Le Valadon $$ 900 Hammond St. 855.1115; fax 637.9142

76 Whisky A Go Go Live rock is the specialty here, with a floor up front by the stage for dancing. This has been one of the most popular clubs on the Strip since its opening in 1964. Call for hours. ♦ Cover. 8901 Sunset Blvd. 652.4202

76 Dukes $$ The most popular coffeeshop in West Hollywood. The pace is fast, the food is good, the feel is friendly. They seat you wherever they can at Dukes, which is usually with strangers—but they won't be strangers for long. Customers come in all types, from punk bands to music execs to neighborhood cops. Expect a long wait for brunch on Sunday. ♦ Coffeeshop ♦ M-F 8AM-9PM; Sa-Su 8AM-3:45AM. 8909 Sunset Blvd. No credit cards. 652.9411

77 The Roxy The foremost nightclub in town, decorated in Art Deco style. Rock and jazz performers, already famous or on the right path, are the headliners here. The club is frequently booked by the local music industry to showcase hot new talent. Showtimes vary. Limited menu. ♦ Cover. 9009 Sunset Blvd. 276.2222

77 Gazzarri's The oldest rock club on the Strip boasts 2 stages and dance floors. Local bands. ♦ Cover. W-Su 8PM-2AM. 9039 Sunset Blvd. 273.6606

77 Talesai ★★$$ Chic, upscale Thai restaurant serving some of LA's most distinctive food. Specialties include *hor mok* (shrimp and squid with lemon grass, basil, and coconut), squid sautéed with chile, barbecued chicken, and *masman* lamb (tender lamb cooked with chile-coconut sauce, curry style). ♦ Thai ♦ M-F 11AM-2:30PM, 6-10:30PM; Sa 6-10:30PM. 9043 Sunset Blvd. 275.9724

78 Joss ★★$$$ East meets West in this stunning clean-lined interior with its innovative menu and a good, reasonably priced wine list. Owner **Cecile Tang**, formerly a film director in Hong Kong, has assembled a distinguished cast and offers innovative but often overpriced and modest-size dishes from her home territory. Best bets include sweet-and-sour soup, Mongolian lamb, paper-wrapped spare ribs, and Peking duck. There's a counter for late suppers and a terrace for a lunch of dim sum. The service can be erratic. ♦ Chinese ♦ Daily 11:30AM-11:30PM. 9255 Sunset Blvd. 276.1886

79 Doug Weston's Troubador Long-established rock 'n' roll shrine now specializes in heavy metal bands. ♦ Cover. 9081 Santa Monica Blvd. 276.6168

79 La Masia ★$$$ Versatile restaurant with an upstairs tapas bar, Latin jazz, and salsa downstairs from 9PM. Good paella and other standards. ♦ Spanish ♦ Tu-Th, Su 6PM-midnight; F-Sa 6PM-1AM. 9077 Santa Monica Blvd. 273.7066

79 Dan Tana's ★$$$ An old Hollywood favorite with Chianti-bottle decor, good steaks, and basics like veal, chicken, and linguine with clams. Crowded and pricey; service can be surly. ♦ Italian ♦ Daily 5PM-1AM. 9071 Santa Monica Blvd. 275.9444

79 Palm Restaurant ★★★$$$$ The best steak and lobster in town—also the most expensive. The room is always jammed, the waiters speedy. It's as harried as the New York original. ♦ American ♦ M-F noon-10:30PM; Sa 5-10:30PM; Su 5-9:30PM. 9001 Santa Monica Blvd. 550.8811

79 Greenhouse Aptly-named outlet for some of LA's best flowers. ♦ Daily 8AM-10PM. 8969 Santa Monica Blvd. 273.0977

80 Studio One Backlot Popular club, mostly for gay men, jammed until late with a crowd that watches the shows on stage then creates its own on the floor. Large screen video projections and lighting extravaganzas. Disco, restaurant, and bar. ♦ Cover. Th-Su 9PM-2AM. 652 N. La Peer Dr. 659.0472

80 Rose Tattoo ★$$$ Located behind Studio One disco, this pretty restaurant attracts a gay and straight crowd. Reasonable and usually excellent prix-fixe dinners start with an overflowing basket of crudités and silken sauces for dipping. ♦ Continental ♦ Tu-Su 6:30-11PM; Su brunch 11:30AM-3PM. Cabaret: M-F, Su 5PM-2AM; Sa 7PM-2AM. 665 N. Robertson Blvd. 854.4455

81 Revolver The hottest spot on the boulevard. A video/discotheque extravaganza, packed nightly with a young gay crowd who come to dance the night away. Small espresso bar upstairs. ♦ Cover F-Sa. M-Th 4PM-2AM; F-Sa 4PM-4AM; Su 2PM-2AM. 8851 Santa Monica Blvd. 550.8851

81 Margo Leavin Gallery Claes Oldenburg and **Coosje Van Bruggen** strike again—with a blade slicing through the stucco facade, like a knife through pastry. Just the thing to enliven a side street and win attention for serious offerings of contemporary art, including work by **Dan Flavin** and **Donald Judd.** ♦ Tu-Sa 11AM-5PM. 817 N. Hilldale Ave. Also at: 812 N. Robertson Blvd. 273.0603

82 Ramada West Hollywood $$ Dramatic white and pale gray stucco wings frame an entrance court that blooms with colorful metal flowers by designer **Peter Shire.** The bold facade, sleek lobby, and pleasant guest rooms are meant to entice designers visiting the neighboring showrooms. ♦ 8585 Santa Monica Blvd. 652.6400, 800/228.2828; fax 652.4207

82 EZTV A small upstairs space that showcases independent video tapes. The quality is inconsistent, but some first-rate and often hilarious tapes show up with pleasing regularity. Call for hours. ♦ Admission. 8547 Santa Monica Blvd. 657.1532

83 L'Orangerie ★★★★$$$$ The grandest, most formal of the French restaurants in LA, beautifully furnished and flatteringly lit. High praise for the cassolette of lobster with fennel, the sole with crayfish sauce, the roasted squab stuffed with wild rice and the sinfully rich all-chocolate Dessert du Roy. Now under the exquisite hand of chef **Jean-Claude Parachini** (formerly of the 3-star **L'Ambrosie** in Paris). ♦ French ♦ Daily 6:30-11PM. 903 N. La Cienega Blvd. 652.9770

84 ESPRIT Stylish fashion palace of raw concrete and steel designed by **Joe D'Urso.** Inside are vibrant contemporary fashions in so many tempting colors and styles that management provides shopping carts. ♦ M-F 10AM-8PM; Sa 10AM-6PM; Su 11AM-6PM. 8491 Santa Monica Blvd (La Cienega Blvd) 659.7575

85 Barney's Beanery $$ Immortalized by sculptor **Ed Kienholz** in the '60s, Barney's still offers breakfast, lunch, and dinner with a huge menu, a zillion labels of beer, and a friendly game of pool. ♦ American ♦ Daily 10AM-2AM. 8447 Santa Monica Blvd. 654.2287

85 Globe Theater Charming replica of Shakespeare's wooden **O,** in which the Bard's plays and dramatic readings of his sonnets are presented. ♦ Seats 99. 1107 N. Kings Rd. 654.5623

86 Hugo's ★$$$ Specialty butcher, deli, and restaurant. Excellent pastas, simple entrees, and salads to eat in or to go. Power breakfasts. ♦ Italian ♦ Daily 6AM-11PM. 8401 Santa Monica Blvd. 654.3993

87 Marix Tex-Mex ★$$ Huge margaritas help pass the time while you are waiting for your table in this boisterous Tex-Mex eatery. *Fajitas* and blue-corn tortillas are specialties. ♦ Tex-Mex ♦ M-F 7:30AM-11PM; Sa-Su 8:30AM-11PM. 1108 N. Flores. 656.8800

Hollywood

87 American-European Bookstore Specialties include American literature and history, especially the South and the Civil War and military and European affairs. ♦ Tu-Sa 10AM-10PM. 8273 Santa Monica Blvd. 654.1007

88 Peanuts Gay women predominate at this large and rambunctious dance club. Theme nights and live entertainment. ♦ Cover. Daily 9PM-late. 7969 Santa Monica Blvd. 654.0280

88 Alouette ★$ **Gerard Godineau,** former maître d' at **Bernard's,** and his wife offer generous helpings of coq au vin, grenadine of beef, and other standards at this friendly bistro. ♦ French ♦ M-Sa 5:30-10PM; Su 5-9:30PM. 7929 Santa Monica Blvd. 650.6722

89 Tuttobene ★★$$ **Silvio De Mori** hosts with assurance, and the kitchen is equally steady— from the complimentary *panzanella* (bread, tomato, and garlic salad), by way of pastas and risottos, to the sinful tiramisù. The crowd is always interesting, the service excellent. ♦ Italian ♦ M-F 11AM-2:30PM, 5:30-11PM; Sa 11AM-2:30PM. 945 N. Fairfax Ave. 655.7051

90 The Pleasure Chest A catalog of naughtiness as prosaically displayed as produce in the supermarket. ♦ M-Th, Su 10AM-midnight; F-Sa 10AM-1AM. 7733 Santa Monica Blvd. 659.7970

91 Plummer Park A fragment of the ranch that operated as a truck farm and dairy from 1877 to 1943. The 3-acre park now contains recreational facilities and the original Plummer home (876.1725). A farmers' market is held here every Monday, 10AM-2PM. ♦ 7377 Santa Monica Blvd

91 Studio Grill ★★$$$ Some interesting dishes and superb wines served in a rather drab space. ♦ Eclectic ♦ M-Th noon-3PM, 6-10PM; F noon-3PM, 6-11PM; Sa 6-11PM. 7321 Santa Monica Blvd. 874.9202

92 Port's $$$ Dark and trendy bar that attracts the creative community. Varied menu includes good salads and a long list of nightly specials. Crowded on weekends. Food is served until 1AM. ♦ American ♦ Daily 6PM-2AM. 7205 Santa Monica Blvd (Formosa St) 874.6294

93 Formosa Cafe $ **Philip Marlowe** would have felt at home in this classic Hollywood bar. Stick to the Scotch and skip the Chinese food. ♦ American/Chinese ♦ M-Sa 10AM-10:30PM. 7156 Santa Monica Blvd. 850.9050

94 Burnett Miller Minimalist and conceptual American and European artworks. Installations by **Charles Ray** and **Wolfgang Laib**. ◆ Tu-Sa 10AM-5:30PM. 964 N. La Brea Ave. 874.4757

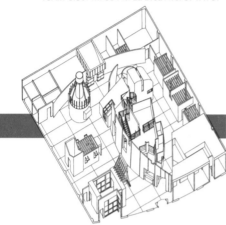

Drawing Courtesy Franklin Israel

95 Propaganda Films (1988, **Franklin Israel**) A brilliant adaptation of an old warehouse; sculptural enclosures within a cavernous space provide offices and meeting rooms for a progressive film production company. ◆ 940 N. Mansfield Ave. 462.6400

96 Maxime's Seafood Restaurant ★$ Great fish at affordable prices, served with a smile. Clam chowder, oysters on the half shell, steamed mussels and clams, and mesquite-grilled fresh fish. ◆ Seafood ◆ M-Sa 11AM-10PM; Su 4-9PM. 6775 Santa Monica Blvd. 461.5644

97 Mignon ★★$ The ex-king of Rumania reportedly had to wait for a table, so you know this Balkan delight is authentic. Carp-roe pâté, white-bean soup, stuffed cabbage rolls, and sour-cherry crêpes are all recommended. ◆ Rumanian ◆ Tu-Th 11:30AM-9:30PM; F-Sa 11:30AM-12:30AM; Su 11:30AM-9:30PM. 1253 N. Vine St. 461.4192

98 Hollywood Memorial Cemetery A 65-acre oasis where a galaxy of top stars found refuge from their fans. **Douglas Fairbanks** has the most elaborate memorial; **Valentino** is in wall crypt 1205, but the lady in black who brought flowers on the anniversary of his death comes no more. Here, too, are **Jesse Lasky** and **Cecil B. De Mille** (who helped establish Paramount Studios, over the garden wall), **Tyrone Power**, **Peter Lorre**, and **Virginia Rappe**, whose unexplained death ruined the career of **Fatty Arbuckle**. Close by is **Beth Olam Cemetery**, where rests mobster **Bugsy Siegel**, a founding father of Las Vegas, who was shot down in his Beverly Hills home in 1947. ◆ M-F 8AM-5PM; Sa-Su 9AM-4PM. 6000 Santa Monica Blvd. 469.1181

99 Don Felipe ★$$ Pining for old Patagonia? Try Don Felipe. Lots of Argentines and good, authentic food seasoned with gusto at a reasonable price. Great mixed grill. ◆ Argentine ◆ Daily 11:30AM-11PM. 1056 N. Western Ave (Santa Monica Blvd) 464.3474

100 Marouch ★$ Delicious Middle Eastern appetizers and roast chicken with garlic in a plain storefront. ◆ Lebanese ◆ Daily 11AM-11PM. 4905 Santa Monica Blvd. 662.9325

101 Bezjian's Grocery Exotic spices and ingredients for Middle Eastern cooking at very low prices. Chutneys and authentic *basmati* rice, imported feta and olives, hummus, and flat breads. ◆ M-Sa 9AM-7PM; Su 10AM-4PM. 4725 Santa Monica Blvd. 663.1503

102 Sompum ★$$ Family-style restaurant serving excellent noodles. Charming patio. ◆ Thai ◆ M, W-Su 11AM-10PM. 4156 Santa Monica Blvd. 669.9906

Melrose Avenue

A cornucopia of adventurous restaurants and fast eateries, radical fashions and used clothing, galleries and design stores lures tourists, trendies, and punks. On weekends, sidewalks are thronged and parking is difficult; in compensation, it's the liveliest scene this side of the Venice boardwalk. Wear comfortable shoes; it's a 3-mile stroll from Highland east to Doheny, though the choicest stretch lies between La Brea and Fairfax. New businesses are pioneering the lower-rent areas to the east, and Melrose trendiness has spilled over onto Beverly Blvd and 3rd St to the south.

103 Cha Cha Cha ★★$$ A huge success from day one, despite its out-of-the-way location and cheerful disregard of production values. What draws the throng is an infectiously friendly spirit, spicy food, and wonderful daily specials. The corn tamale with golden caviar, the giant shrimp in black pepper sauce, and the chicken *poblana* are not to be missed. ◆ Latin/Caribbean ◆ M-F 11:30AM-3PM, 6-10:30PM; Sa-Su 11:30AM-3PM, 5-11:30PM. 656 N. Virgil Ave (Melrose Ave) 664.7723

104 Rincon Chileno ★$$ Chile is a long coastal country and, understandably, much of its best cooking is seafood. Here is a warm, homey spot peopled largely by Chileans where you can sample some authentic dishes. Look for *paila de mariscos* (seafood stew), raw sea urchins, eel, and *pastel de choclo*, an unusual corn casserole. The strong Chilean wines are worth a try, too. Can be crowded on weekends; knowing a bit of Spanish doesn't hurt. ◆ Chilean ◆ T-Th, Su 11:30AM-10PM; F-Sa 11:30AM-11PM. 4352 Melrose Ave. 666.6075

105 Cafe Mambo ★$$ **Mario Tamayo** (of **Cha Cha Cha**) has turned a Victorian house into a funky, colorful Latin/Caribbean restaurant. Actors, artists, screenwriters, lawyers, poseurs, and just about anyone, enjoy such spicy fare as *chilaquiles* (fried tortillas scrambled with eggs and salsa), lobster sandwich with garlic mayonnaise, and tropical chicken with black beans and rice. ◆ Latin/Caribbean ◆ Daily 9AM-3PM, 6-11PM. 707 Heliotrope Dr. 663.5800

105 Modern Objects **Tamayo** switches hats to create clothes for rock stars, including '40s-style draped suits and glitter ties. ◆ M-Sa 11AM-7PM; Su noon-3PM. 4355 Melrose Ave. 669.8309

106 Paramount Studios Last of the major studios in Hollywood; the others departed in search of cheap land. The original entrance gate, through which **Gloria Swanson** was driven by **Erich von Stroheim** in *Sunset Boulevard*, is tucked away at the end of Bronson Ave. There's a new double gate on Melrose. The stages along Gower St were formerly part of the **RKO Studios**; the trademark globe can be seen at the corner. Paramount is closed to the public, but the site is full of atmosphere. Across the street is the **Raleigh** rental studio, which combines new stages with a wood-frame street that seems unchanged from 1915. And 2 blocks east is **Western Costume**, established in 1913, which rents stock clothes to the movies, stage, and Halloween revelers. ♦ 5555 Melrose Ave

106 Orza's ★$$$ A small neighborhood place tucked snugly in the shadow of Paramount Studios. Combination appetizer plates and the mixed grill are suggested for the uninitiated. Stuffed cabbage and grilled sweetbreads are noteworthy. Portions are hearty and generously seasoned. Finish with Turkish coffee. ♦ Rumanian ♦ M-Tu 11AM-3PM; W-F 11AM-3PM, 5-9PM; Sa 5-9PM. 708 N. Valentino Pl. 465.4884

107 A-1 Record Finders Best place for a disc nobody else has; if they don't have it they'll send out a posse. By appointment. ♦ 5639 Melrose Ave. 732.6737

108 Cozmopole A showcase by and of designer **Larry Totah**. New Wave designs (a sofa covered in pink-and-red neoprene, a steel-slab table) are displayed against a backdrop of Pompeian columns and steel columns. By appointment. ♦ 654 N. Larchmont Blvd. 467.2927

108 Elizabeth Marcel's Hat Gallery A millinery shop caught in a '30s time warp, whose owner makes new hats from old blocks and traditional materials. ♦ Tu-Sa 11AM-6PM. 5632 Melrose Ave. 463.3163

109 Zumaya ★★$$ Cozy upscale family-run restaurant with pleasant service and hearty, satisfying food. The fish tacos, special enchiladas, and chicken in spicy sauce are standouts. ♦ Latin ♦ M-Th 11AM-9:30PM; F 11AM-11PM; Sa 5-11PM; Su 5-9:30PM. 5722 Melrose Ave. 464.0624

109 Seafood Village ★$ Popular neighborhood place serving plain fresh seafood from the fish market next door. Reasonable prices. ♦ Daily 11AM-11PM. 5730 Melrose Ave. 463.8090

110 Patina ★★★★$$$ With **Joaquim Splichal** in the kitchen and his wife, **Christine**, to welcome guests, this had to be a hit. The old **Le St. Germain** has been transformed by **Cheryl Brantner**, who has banished the red plush and created an invisible decor of wood, stone, and soft lighting in a succession of intimate dining rooms and a tiny bar. Highlights of the menu include corn blinis with marinated salmon, *mille feuille* of white fish with cabbage and lemon sauce, duck liver with beetroots, and John Dory with calf's feet and oysters—odd combinations that come off with effortless assurance. For lunch, the chicken salad redefines that clichéd dish. There's an exceptional wine list. ♦ Eclectic ♦ M-F 11:30AM-2:30PM, 6-10PM; F-Sa 6-10:30PM; Su 6-9:30PM. 5955 Melrose Ave. 467.1108

111 Emilio's Ristorante ★★$$$ With a central fountain, statuary, and more than its share of Chianti bottles perched on the backs of the red leather booths, Emilio's is more than a little theatrical. The food reflects that same tendency for overabundance; there are a zillion dishes to choose from and lots on the plate. ♦ Italian ♦ M-Tu 11AM-3PM; W-F 11AM-3PM, 5-9PM; Sa 5-9PM. 6602 Melrose Ave. 935.4922

111 Il Piccolino ★★$$ Emilio's wife, **Pauline**, and his son, **Dino Baglioni**, operate this attractive trattoria. Pizza *alla campagniolla* (lots of fresh vegetables on a thin crust) and the *crespelle alla Valdostana* (baked pasta) are good choices, and there's a nice selection of fairly-priced wines. ♦ Italian ♦ Tu-F 11:30AM-3PM, 5-11:30PM; Sa-Su 5-11:30PM. 641 N. Highland Ave. 936.2996

112 New Living Furniture as artwork from the best local and European designers. Competitively-priced reproductions can be custom-made. ♦ M-F 10AM-7PM; Sa 11AM-6PM; Su noon-5PM. 6812 Melrose Ave. 933.5553

113 Citrus ★★★★$$$$ Bernard Zimmerman's airy all-white shed with glass-brick walls enlivened with fresh flowers and colorful paintings is the setting for pastry chef **Michel Richard**'s ambitious restaurant. A fashionable crowd fills every table for lunch and dinner (the leafy patio seems less crammed than the dining room), enjoying dishes that are pretty and tasty. Meltingly soft scallops with crisp-fried Maui onions, oyster custard, and shitake mushrooms *en croute* are good starters; lamb with saffron ravioli, steak in Cabernet sauce, and soy-grilled tuna are fine, but leave room for the desserts. ♦ California ♦ M-Sa noon-2:15PM, 6:30-10:15PM. 6703 Melrose Ave. 857.0034

113 The Rock Store Elvis lives! Memorabilia of the King and the mortal stars who followed. ♦ M-F 11AM-8PM; Sa 11AM-6PM; Su noon-6PM. 6817 Melrose Ave. 930.2980

113 Territory Betty Gold sells Navajo folk art, American Indian jewelry, Pendleton blankets, and other vintage Western and Mexican collectibles. ♦ M-Sa 11AM-6PM. 6907 1/2 Melrose Ave. 937.4006

I should think there is more opportunity for nature-study within the city boundaries of Los Angeles than in any other urban district in the world, and the rabbit shooting must be superb.

R.G. Macdonell, 1935

113 Intermezzo $$ A charming, low-key espresso and pasta bar. The small front room features a bar built around an open kitchen; in the back is a breezy patio with blue and white umbrellas. Homemade pasta to eat in or to go; fresh seafood dishes, soups, sandwiches, and salads. Beer and wine. ♦ Italian ♦ M-Th 11AM-11PM; F 11AM-midnight; Sa-Su 5-11PM. 6919 Melrose Ave. 937.2875

114 Parachute Monochromatic avant-garde chic for men and women in a warehouse that owners **Harry Parnasse** and **Nicola Pelly** have

Hollywood

transformed into an austere concrete cavern. ♦ M-Sa 11AM-7PM. 844 N. La Brea Ave. 461.8822

114 Every Picture Tells a Story Children's books and art for collectors. ♦ Tu-Sa 10AM-5PM; Su noon-5PM. 836 N. La Brea Ave. 962.5420

115 Pink's Famous Chili Dogs $ Hot dogs, hamburgers, and tamales, but the chili dogs are what make it world famous. ♦ American ♦ Daily 7AM-2AM. 711 N. La Brea Ave. 931.4223

115 Danziger Studio (1965, **Frank Gehry**) Minimalist house/studio built for designer **Lou Danziger** that launched Gehry's career. Three blank stucco boxes, adroitly positioned, transform LA's industrial vernacular into high art. Private residence. ♦ 7001 Melrose Ave

116 People **Larry Totah** designed the loftlike space with its wraparound mezzanine to display clothes that range from denim to Dior. ♦ M-Sa 10AM-7PM. 7207 Melrose Ave. 938.1134

116 Cottura Venetian glass, Florentine papers, and rustic hand-painted ceramics. ♦ M-Sa 11AM-6PM; Su noon-5PM. 7215 Melrose Ave. 933.1928

116 Chopstix ★$ High-tech setting (by **David Serrurier**) for a quick lunch, snack, or late dinner within a delightful Art Deco pavilion. Feast on dim sum, great BBQ ribs, and chicken and noodle dishes at prices you won't believe. They deliver—and it even tastes good when cold. ♦ Chinese ♦ M-Th, Su 11:30AM-midnight; F-Sa 11:30AM-1AM. 7229 Melrose Ave. 937.1111. Also at: 14622 Ventura Blvd, Sherman Oaks. 818/783.5834

116 The Bakery on Melrose Scrumptious pastries, and, for your best friend,whole-grain dog biscuits. ♦ Tu-Th 8:30AM-10PM; F-Sa 9AM-1AM; Su 11AM-7PM. 7261 Melrose Ave. 934.4493

116 Nucleus Nuance ★$$$ Late-night dining and dancing to live jazz and swing. Pretty good food and the music can be great. Colorful clientele. ♦ California ♦ M-Sa 6PM-2AM; Su 7PM-2AM. 7267 Melrose Ave. 939.8666

116 Unit 7301 **Klaus Wille** sells authorized reproductions of original Bauhaus furniture. ♦ Tu-Sa noon-6PM. 7301 Melrose Ave. 933.8391

116 A Star is Worn Celebrity wearables and collectibles, contemporary and period. ♦ M-Sa 11AM-7PM; Su noon-5PM. 7303 Melrose Ave. 939.4922

116 Groundlings Theatre A resident company does sleight-of-mouth improvisation using suggestions from the audience. ♦ Seats 99. 7307 Melrose Ave. 934.9700

117 Costumes for Kids Big imaginations in small frames can realize their fantasies of being a fairy princess, a pirate, or a superhero. ♦ M-F 10AM-5PM; Sa 11AM-5PM. 7206 Melrose Ave. 936.5437

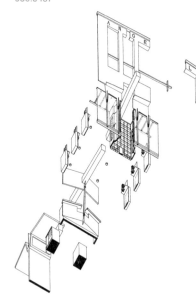

Drawing Courtesy Morphosis

117 Angeli Caffe ★★$$ Chef **Evan Kleiman**'s simple but delicious rustic Italian cooking combined with manager **John Strobel**'s well-selected wine list. Reasonable prices, but Angeli is a victim of its own success; the 2 tiny dining rooms are often uncomfortably crowded and noisy. It is at its most relaxed in late afternoon, when sandwiches and biscotti are served. Takeout a specialty. **Morphosis**, a pace-setting architectural firm, has made the first room a structuralist paraphrase of a Baroque chapel, with wall niches and a pizza oven in place of the altar. The facade comprises a broken arch of rusted steel, glass brick to diffuse the light that floods inside, and a projecting beam (like a toothpick spearing a sandwich). ♦ Italian ♦ M-Sa noon-10:30PM; Su 5-10PM. 7274 Melrose Ave. 936.9086. Also at: 11651 Santa Monica Blvd. 478.1191; 13455 Maxella Ave, Marina del Rey. 822.1984

118 Wound and Wound Clockwork fanatics take note: this is where dreams come true. ♦ M-Th 11AM-10PM; F-Sa 11AM-midnight; Su 11AM-8PM. 7374 Melrose Ave. 653.6703

118 Campo dei Fiori Sensational flower arrangements in a sleek concrete frame with signature vases by **David Hertz**. ♦ M-Th 9AM-9PM; F-Sa 9AM-10PM; Su 10AM-8PM. 646 N. Martel Ave. 655.9966

118 Soap Plant/Wacko Two stores, same management. Together they offer every wonderful little gift or knickknack that you didn't know you needed but suddenly can't live without. There are cards, makeup, fragrant soaps, beach balls that look like globes, plastic dinosaurs, books, and a fine collection of wooden masks. It's the Melrose version of the old general store. ♦ M-W 11AM-11PM; Th-Sa 11AM-midnight; Su noon-8PM. Soap Plant: 7400 Melrose Ave. 651.5587. Wacko: 7402 Melrose Ave. 651.3811

118 ECRU Michele Saee designed this lofty fashion showroom with a facade that frames display windows and spells out the name in huge bronzed letters. The stock includes **Philippe Model** hats, **Robert Clergerie** shoes, and men's and women's European clothes. ♦ M-Sa 11AM-7PM; Su noon-6PM. 7428 Melrose Ave. 653.8761. Also at: 13455 Maxella Ave, Marina del Rey. 821.9962

119 LA Eyeworks Eyeglasses as art; the stark setting and inventive displays rival the best galleries. Classic and outrageous frames of high quality at high prices. ♦ M-F 10AM-noon, 1-7PM; Sa 10AM-noon, 1-6PM. 7407 Melrose Ave. 653.8255

119 Border Grill ★★$$ Refined, innovative variations on Mexican cuisine by **Mary Sue Milliken** and **Susan Feniger**, who divide their time between this storefront, **Border Grill** in Santa Monica, and **City Restaurant**. Delicious food served in a lively setting: sautéed squid with garlic, *sabana* (thin steak wrapped around black beans and grilled scallions), spearfish Veracruza, and steamed *chayote*. ♦ Mexican ♦ M-Sa noon-11PM; Su 11AM-11PM. 7407 1/2 Melrose Ave. 658.7495. Also at: 1445 4th St, Santa Monica. 451.1655

119 Cafe Habana ★$ The pre-Castro spirit animates this storefront café, whose specialty is *El Sandwich Cubano*, a combo of roast pork, ham, Swiss cheese with lettuce, tomatoes, and pickles on a crusty French loaf. Also good are the empanadas and the Spanish bread pudding. Wash it down with a Caribe beer or an exotic soda. ♦ Cuban ♦ M-Th, Su 11AM-11PM; F-Sa 11AM-11:30PM. 7465 Melrose Ave. 655.2822

119 Tommy Tang's ★$$ Good food, fashionable pink-and-gray decor, young, hip clientele. Specialties include Thai toast, barbecue chicken, and Malaysian clams. Dine inside or on a pretty tiled patio. ♦ Thai ♦ M-Th 11:30AM-11:30PM; F-Sa 11:30AM-12:30AM; Su 5-10:30PM. 7473 Melrose Ave. 651.1810

119 Chianti Cucina ★★$$ Splendid pasta and the best breadsticks anywhere from the same kitchen as its parent, **Chianti**, served in a noisy, informal white-tiled room. Thronged with a young, attractive crowd. A good choice for a late-evening dessert and espresso. ♦ Italian ♦ Daily 11:30AM-11:30PM. 7383 Melrose Ave. 653.8333

119 Ristorante Chianti ★★$$$ One of the grande dames of Italian cuisine in Los Angeles.

Etched glass and dark wood booths. Where the tradition of turning amaretto cookie wrappers into flying saucers began. ♦ Italian ♦ Daily 5PM-11:30PM. 7383 Melrose Ave. 653.8333

120 Johnny Rocket's $ This spiffy '50s diner is a popular hangout for kids. Branches all over LA. ♦ American ♦ M-Th, Su 11AM-midnight; F-Sa 11AM-2AM. 7507 Melrose Ave. 651.3361

120 Leathers & Treasures Bruce Springsteen and other rock stars have come here for vintage cowboy boots, bicycle jackets, and other gear. ♦ M-Th 11AM-8PM; F-Sa 11AM-9PM; Su 1-6PM. 7511 Melrose Ave. 655.7541

121 Grau (1989, **Ajax**) Gaudiesque columns frame an organic plywood cave, displaying sophisticated playwear for independent-minded women. Guatemalan weavings and Japanese kimonos inspire the richness of color and texture in **Claudia Grau**'s designs. ♦ Daily 11AM-7PM. 7520 Melrose Ave. 651.0487

122 The Burger that Ate LA $ This is what the street needs—a giant burger emerging hungrily from City Hall. It's vintage California Crazy. ♦ American ♦ M-Th, Su 11:30AM-midnight; F-Sa 11:30AM-1AM. 660 N. Stanley Ave. 653.2647

122 California Beach Rock 'n' Sushi (1989, **Ted Tanaka**) $$ **Godzilla** meets the **Beach Boys**—a 2nd-floor restaurant and sushi bar that looks like the demented vision of how a Japanese who had never left home might imagine Southern California. It's an improved version of an idea born in Newport Beach. ♦ Japanese ♦ M-Th, Su 5:30-11PM; F-Sa 5:30PM-midnight. 7656 Melrose Ave. 655.0123

123 Gelati Per Tutti Corner store designed like a Roman *gelateria* in faux marble serves Italian ices in such flavors as amaretto, zabaglione, and a vanilla that is out of this world. ♦ M-Th, Su 10AM-midnight; F-Sa 10AM-1AM. 7653 Melrose Ave. 653.8970

123 Matrix Theatre Adventurous Equity-waiver playhouse. Artistic Director **Joseph Stern** has presented LA previews of **Harold Pinter**'s *Betrayal*, **Lyle Kessler**'s *Orphans*, and **Simon Gray**'s *The Common Pursuit*, with time out to produce movies. ♦ Seats 99. 7657 Melrose Ave. 852.1445

Restaurants/Clubs: Red   Hotels: Blue
Shops/Parks: Green   **Sights/Culture:** Black

123 Chapo ★★$$ A wonderful neighborhood restaurant with an airy modern decor run by a Belgian family in the friendliest way. Dip bread (from **La Brea Bakery**) into basil-flavored olive oil, or enjoy a sandwich of chicken and prosciutto with goat cheese, red pepper, and rosemary, served with great fries. More substantial fare includes osso buco with ginger risotto, and there's excellent cheesecake. **Sansarra**, a charming New Wave bookstore, occupies the space upstairs. ♦ Mediterranean ♦ M-F 11:30AM-3PM, 6-11:30PM; Sa 6-11:30PM; Su 5-11:30PM. 7661 Melrose Ave. 655.2924

Hollywood

124 Genghis Cohen ★$$$ Upscale Szechuan restaurant serving black-bean crab, crackerjack shrimp, and good *kung pau* to a neighborhood crowd and a smattering of show biz types. The place has a stylish New York feel. ♦ Chinese ♦ M-F noon-3PM, 5-11:30PM; Sa 5-11:30PM; Su 5-10PM. 740 N. Fairfax Ave. 653.0640

125 Thomas Solomon's Garage The son of New York collectors is making waves with short, unadvertised shows—mostly of young Cal-Arts graduates—in a 16-foot-square space. ♦ W-Sa 1-7PM; Su noon-5PM. 822 ½ N. Hayworth Ave. 653.8980

126 Gardel's ★$$$ Terrific Argentinean food in a contemporary, bustling restaurant. There's roast garlic (make sure that everyone at your table eats it or no one does), *boudin noir*, and a wonderful *parillada* (mixed grill) as well as pastas (Argentina was heavily settled by Italians). There's a good selection of Argentinean wines. Gardel was a movie idol and tango dancer *extraordinaire* in Argentina in the '30s. ♦ Argentinean ♦ M-Sa 6-11PM. 7963 Melrose Ave. 655.0891

126 Asiaphile **Noguchi** lamps, Chinese antiques, and Filipino weavings are among the attractions. ♦ M-Sa 11AM-6PM. 7975 Melrose Ave. 653.4744

126 Wilder Place Contemporary hand-crafted pottery and art objects for the home. ♦ M-W, Sa 10AM-6PM; Th-F 11AM-7PM. 7975 ½ Melrose Ave. 655.9072

127 Rondo ★★$$$ Wonderful Tuscan cooking and such specials as a rich *zuppa di pesce*, *tagliata all'erba aromatica* (herb-flavored grilled steak), and great risottos. Handsome contemporary design by **Kellen I. Schweitzer**, but the room can become overcrowded and noisy, like so many fashionable restaurants. ♦ Italian ♦ M-F noon-2:30PM, 6-11PM; Sa 6-11PM. 7966 Melrose Ave. 655.8158

128 Jan Turner Gallery **Tony Delap**, **John Alexander**, and the late **Carlos Almarez** are on the eclectic list of artists shown here; innovative landscapes are a specialty. ♦ M-F 10AM-5:30PM; Sa 11AM-5:30PM. 8000 Melrose Ave. 658.6084

Restaurants/Clubs: Red   **Hotels:** Blue
Shops/Parks: Green   **Sights/Culture:** Black

128 Fantasies Come True Animation cels and character figurines from Disney and the other great movie cartoon familes. ♦ Tu-Sa noon-4PM. 8012 Melrose Ave. 655.2636

129 Modern Living **Terry Phipps** offers modern classics and contemporary furniture by **Philippe Starck**, **Massimo Iosa Ghini**, and **Ettore Sottsass**. ♦ M-F 10AM-7PM; Sa-Su noon-5PM. 8125 Melrose Ave. 655.3899

130 Fred Segal Block-wide complex of youth-oriented stores specializing in nifty T-shirts and sweatshirts, lingerie, luggage, electronic gadgets, cards, kids' stuff, and stationery. In the main store there is a huge selection of the latest (and more traditional) jeans, sportswear, shoes, and clothing that ranges from beach casual to 24-carat chic. Bargains can be found, and the late September sale fills every parking spot for 6 blocks around. Compulsive buyers refuel on chocolate chip cookies and apple pie at the café. ♦ M-Sa 10AM-7PM; Su noon-6PM. 8100 Melrose Ave. 651.4129

130 Improvisation Locals and tourists can be found 2 or 3 deep at the bar on weekends. Catch the best and worst of stand up comedy every night in the back room. Top names sometimes stop in to catch a show or try out new material. Open nightly, call for performance times. ♦ Cover. 8162 Melrose Ave. 651.2583

131 Sonrisa Folk and fine art of unusual quality from Mexico and Central America. ♦ M-F 10AM-5PM; Sa 10AM-6PM. 8214 Melrose Ave. 651.1090

131 William & Victoria Dailey Rare books on art and the sciences, prints, and limited editions. ♦ Tu-F 10AM-6PM; Sa 11AM-5PM. 8216 Melrose Ave. 658.8515

131 Le Chardonnay ★$$$ A *Belle Epoque* Parisian brasserie suffused with a warm glow, as if gaslit. Sinuous tendrils of teak meander around the mirrors that cover the walls. The spaces in between are covered with Art Nouveau tiles; brass fixtures wink and glimmer. The traditional cooking is uneven and the room is excessively noisy. Superb California wine list. ♦ French ♦ M-F noon-2PM, 6-10PM; Sa 6-11PM. 8284 Melrose Ave. 655.8880

132 di-zin High-style Italian furniture and lighting; interior design service. ♦ M-F 10AM-7PM; Sa 10AM-6PM; Su noon-5PM. 8302 Melrose Ave. 651.4400. Also at: 2430 Main St, Santa Monica. 392.9806

132 Kiyo Higashi Austerely handsome space that shows the work of **Larry Bell**, **Penelope Krebs**, and **Guy Williams**. ♦ Tu-Sa 11AM-6PM. 8332 Melrose Ave. 655.2482

132 Tulipe ★★★$$$ **Roland Gilbert** and **Maurice Peguet** are the chefs in this large, brightly-lit bistro. Try the blue-cheese-and pear *pithiviers*, the braised veal shank with vegetables, scallops with caramelized shallots, and the grapefruit mousse and apple tart. ♦ French ♦ M-F 11:30AM-2PM, 6-10PM; Sa 6-10PM. 8360 Melrose Ave. 655.7400

133 Gemini G.E.L. Fine art prints by such artists as **David Hockney, Jasper Johns, Robert Rauschenberg, Jonathan Borofsky,** and **Ellsworth Kelly** in a workshop/gallery designed by **Frank Gehry.** ♦ M-F 9:30AM-5:30PM; Sa 11AM-5PM. 8365 Melrose Ave. 651.0513

133 Sculpture to Wear Jan Ehrenworth sells unusually attractive contemporary jewelry. ♦ M-Sa 11AM-6PM. 8441 Melrose Ave. 651.2205

134 Apartment Building (1925) Come viz me to the Casbah! Private residence. ♦ Sweetzer Ave at Waring Ave

135 Schindler House (1921-22, **Rudolph Schindler**) LA's most innovative house, lovingly restored. Schindler came from Vienna to work with **Frank Lloyd Wright,** and built this house/studio, in which he lived and worked until his death in 1953. Inspired by a desert camp, the architect combined tilt-up concrete slab walls, canvas canopies, and open-air sleeping lofts—techniques and spatial treatments that were novel at the time. **Richard Neutra** lived here in the late '20s, and the house was a meeting place for the avant-garde. ♦ Admission. Sa-Su 1-4PM and by appointment. 833 N. Kings Rd. 651.1510

136 L'Ermitage ★★★★$$$$ Opened in the '70s by chef **Jean Bertranou,** this treasure was given a lighter, brighter character in 1985 by **Dora Fourcade,** a young French-Tahitian entrepreneur. The look is soft and elegant; the cooking of chef **Michel Blanchet** is refined and assured. Don't miss the house-smoked salmon, roast squab with foie gras and rosemary, lobster with scallions, mushrooms, and potato puree, and the celebrated cheese *chariot*. ♦ French ♦ M-Sa 6:30-10PM. 730 N. La Cienega Blvd. 652.5840

137 Pazzia ★★★$$$ It means *craziness* in Italian, but nothing could be saner than this luminous white box and the inventive Northern Italian dishes served at prices half those of **Rex-Il Ristorante,** owner **Mauro Vincenti**'s downtown temple of luxury. The understated decor by **Osvaldo Maiozzi** focuses attention on a spirited futurist painting of racing cyclists and the yellow-shirted waiters whose movements seem choreographed. Chef **Umberto Bombana** brings his refined touch to the freshest seasonal ingredients. Thus the menu is in flux, but dependable staples include the yellow pepper soup and *pappa al pomodoro*, the many pastas, the creamiest ice cream, and strongest espresso. An espresso bar faces the restaurant across a small patio. The **Pazzeria Cafe,** serving pasta and pizza, opened within the restaurant in October 1990. ♦ Italian ♦ M-Sa 11:30AM-2PM, 6:30-10:30PM. 755 N. La Cienega Blvd. 657.9271

137 Akuto Exotic European fashions for men are shown in a dramatic concrete-and-steel set by **Faramaz Matloob.** ♦ M-Sa 10AM-8PM. 755 N. La Cienega Blvd. 657.0430

You can't explain Hollywood, there is no such place. It's just a dream suburb of Los Angeles.
Rachel Fields

137 Clacton & Frinton English-made suits for trend-setting architects and designers, featuring easy cuts and good fabrics. ♦ M-Sa 10AM-6PM. 731 N. La Cienega Blvd. 652.2957

137 Paddington's Tea Room Agatha Christie would have loved this cozy tea shop, which specializes in fresh scones with Devonshire cream and authentically strong tea. ♦ English ♦ M-Sa 10AM-7PM; Su noon-7PM. 729 N. La Cienega Blvd. 652.0624

138 Rosamund Felsen Gallery New and established LA artists, including **Mike Kelley, Chris**

Hollywood

Burden, and **Roy Dowell.** ♦ Tu-Sa 11AM-5PM. 669 N. La Cienega Blvd. 652.9172

138 La Cage Aux Folles $$$$ If you loved the movie, you may enjoy this restaurant/nightclub. Your evening comes complete with pink feathers, quasi-French food, and a drag-queen show. Call for showtimes. ♦ French cabaret ♦ 643 N. La Cienega Blvd. 657.1091

138 Penny Feathers $$ Sandwiches, simple entrees, and breakfast food. Beer and wine. ♦ American ♦ 24 hours. 631 N. La Cienega Blvd. 659.3545

139 Heritage Book Shop Early manuscripts, 17th- to 20th-century first editions, fine bindings, and autographs. ♦ M by appointment only; Tu-F 9:30AM-5:30PM; Sa 10AM-4:30PM. 8540 Melrose Ave. 659.3674

139 Elliott Katt Bookseller Possibly the best LA store for old and new books on film, radio, television, and the performing arts. ♦ M-Sa 11AM-6PM. 8570 ½ Melrose Ave. 652.5178

140 Bodhi Tree Books on Eastern and Western philosophy, health and women's issues, astrology, and religion; also herbs, soaps, tarot cards. ♦ Daily 11AM-11PM. 8585 Melrose Ave. 659.1733

140 Details Upscale architectural accessories by contemporary American and European designers. ♦ M-F 10AM-5PM. 8625 ½ Melrose Ave. 659.1550

141 Du Vin Wine & Spirits Ask **René** for current bargains in French wines and while you're there, pick up some cheese and sandwiches. ♦ M-Sa 10AM-7PM. 540 N. San Vincente Blvd. 855.1161

142 Pacific Design Center (1975/1988, **Cesar Pelli** and **Gruen Associates**) The *Blue Whale* has been joined by a jolly green giant, to further swell the concentration of design showrooms (1.2 million square feet of displays, from the stuffy to the cutting edge) and to cater to a seemingly insatiable demand. You'll need a trade card or a professional designer to get you in to most of them. But you are welcome to eat (or have a drink until 7PM) in the **Melrose Bar & Grill** on the 4th floor of **Center Blue.** It says a lot about the clientele that the 2 most popular dishes are chicken Caesar salad and Cobb salad. On the handsome plaza that separates

Pacific Design Center Drawing Courtesy Carlos Diniz

the center from San Vicente Blvd is the **Murray Feldman Gallery**, which is open to the public and presents high quality architecture and design exhibitions (call for hours). ♦ Pacific Design Center: M-F 9AM-5PM. Restaurant: M-F 11:30AM-3PM. 8687 Melrose Ave. 657.0800

143 Kurland/Summers Gallery Art-glass and clothes-as-art are shown side by side in this loft space. ♦ Tu-Sa 11AM-6PM. 8742A Melrose Ave. 659.7098

Trumps

143 Trumps ★★★$$$ Stark southwestern decor by **Waldo Fernandez**, with square concrete tables, adobe, natural fibers, and contemporary local art on the walls. The regular customers complement the decor; people-watching is a major diversion. Chef **Michael Roberts** helped define California cuisine with inventive combinations of natural ingredients, such as the potato pancake with goat cheese and apples and the steamed salmon with wild rice pancakes. Light lunches, serious dinners, and a surprisingly traditional tea, served with sherry. Takeout and picnics to go. ♦ California ♦ M-Th 11:45AM-10PM; F-Sa 11:45AM-11:45PM; Su 6-9:30PM. 8764 Melrose Ave. 855.1480

143 Morton's ★★$$$ The celebrities who pack this place every night from 9 until late enjoy surprisingly good food and service. If you pass on people-watching and arrive early you'll do even better, though you will miss the essential point of this stylish restaurant, which is so *in* it doesn't need a sign. Lime-grilled chicken and moist rack of lamb are dependable; avoid the more complicated dishes. ♦ American ♦ M-Sa 6PM-midnight. 8800 Melrose Ave. 276.1253

144 Jay Wolf Designer **Waldo Fernandez** added his touch to this collection of sophisticated imported men's wear. ♦ M-Sa 11AM-7PM. 517 N. Robertson Blvd. 273.9893

145 Maxfield Avant-garde couture at drop-dead prices in a spare concrete shell designed by **Larry Totah**. The window display is often worth a detour. ♦ M-Sa 11AM-7PM. 8825 Melrose Ave. 274.8800

145 Asher/Faure Contemporary American and European artists, including **David Reed**, **Jack Goldstein**, and **Llyn Foulkes**. ♦ Tu-Sa 10:30AM-5:30PM. 612 N. Almont Dr. 271.3665

145 Dan Weinberg Young and established New York artists such as **Sol DeWitt** and **Jeff Koons**. ♦ Tu-Sa 11AM-5PM. 619 N. Almont Dr. 453.0180

145 Art Catalogues Museum and exhibition catalogs from the US and abroad. ♦ Tu-Sa 10AM-5PM. 625 N. Almont Dr. 274.0160

146 Cafe Figaro $$ Namesake of the New York coffeehouse, a dark and crowded place that is good for late-night snacks and long discussions about the meaning of life. ♦ American ♦ M-Th 11:30AM-11:30PM; F-Sa 11:30AM-12:30AM; Su 5:30-11:30PM. 9010 Melrose Ave. 274.7664

Bests

Deborah Sussman
Designer, President of Sussman/Prejza Co.

The **Sunset Strip**. You *can* walk in Los Angeles! I love strolling along the little section of Sunset Boulevard around Sunset Plaza Drive. The strip has urbanity, convenience, humane scale, elegance, variety, tradition, and a leisurely pace. It has a real neighborhood plant shop—**Beverly Hills Seed**. Good and unusual clothing stores; Italian and French cafés with crowded tables outdoors—just like in Europe—where you can hear Castilian Spanish, German, Italian, and French simultaneously while sipping good espresso, eating excellent pasta, spearing mediocre but addictive dim sum, and then, of course, low-cholesterol frozen yogurt. Parking is a dream (behind the stores, with a great overlook of the city). Good plays within *walking* distance (at the **Tiffany**)! Having my hair cut at **Yuki's** with sun streaming through the flower-filled shop— views through both ends—then joining the leisurely parade to window shop is like being on holiday.

Fred Segal, Melrose at Crescent Heights. Now an institution, Fred Segal has provided much of my LA wardrobe for several decades. If you can tolerate the hyperactive scene and music (occasionally deafening), you will find an incredibly rich mix of stuff from shoes to T-shirts, silks to jeans, luggage to jewelry. You can also eat (though not too well). It just grew a series of little adjacencies. Preceded "Melrose" by years.

The **Bradbury** building, and all the idiosyncratic buildings of the early, mid, and late 20th century. They are sprinkled throughout the city. Some famous ones include **Union Station**; 1355 N. Laurel, 1920s Italianate courtyard apartments, the most beautiful in LA; **Tail-o-the-Pup; 8806 Beverly Boulevard** (erase what's inside and on the windows, and you will see the former Herman Miller showroom, designed by Charles Eames).

Restaurants that grew out of LA's traditions and location (Pacific basin, Asia, Latin America) including **City** with the most creative cooks I know, and a really sympathetic staff. A brilliant collage of East Indian, Japanese, and Mexican influences plus unexpected original ideas; **Katsu**, at 3 locations; **Michael's.**

Parrots at sunset, flying low, toward the ocean.

Warren Bennis
USC Distinguished Professor of Business

The light. There's no light quite like the light here. It is sometimes golden, sometimes blue, but always illuminating.

72 Market Street. If there is one place that seems now to contain Los Angeles' unique mix of high-speed energy and lackadaisical lazy grace, it's Tony Bill's handsome, easygoing restaurant. The food is superb, the people are good-looking, and there is no pretension in either.

My house. I live almost literally on the Santa Monica beach, on the edge of the Pacific, which I find helps me to keep things in acute perspective.

Los Angeles's Equity Waiver Theaters. There must be 100 of them, and every so often one of them does an exciting new play or revives a vintage Sondheim musical, and there's no such thing as a surfeit of Sondheim.

The surprises. The scruffy restaurant that makes a superb fish stew...the absence of water in the Los Angeles River...the pristine Art Moderne house holding its own among big apartment buildings...the kids on Melrose wearing now what New York designers will "introduce" next year...the gardens in which something is always blooming.

October. The light is high, the air is warm and redolent, the mood is easy, the beach is empty, and one can imagine doing anything.

Mauro Vincenti
Rex, Pazzia, Fennell

Valentino. Piero Selvaggio is probably the smartest Italian restaurateur in LA. For wine, I go to him; for food connections he comes to me.

Mandarin. My favorite Chinese restaurant.

Michael's, for the best steak.

Fennel, for chef Jean-Pierre Bosc.

Citrus, for the cuisine of Michel Richard.

Katsu. Chef Katsu Michite is an artist who converted me to sushi.

Irvine Ranch Market in the **Beverly Center**.

Willette and Manny Klausner
Founding Members, American Institute of Wine & Food

We dine out so frequently, we have many favorite restaurants. Here's a listing of some of our latest choices.

There are no more creative chefs in Los Angeles than

Hollywood

Michel Richard at **Citrus** and Joachim Splichal at **Patina**. These 2 artists always deliver a dazzlingly exciting food experience!

Katsu (on Hillhurst) is one of our favorite neighborhood restaurants. The sushi is fresh, delicious, and spectacularly presented. This is great "diet" food!

Piero Selvaggio makes everyone feel right at home in his smartly redecorated **Valentino**. Let Piero select your menu and recommend an interesting wine from his award-winning cellar.

It's always a special treat for us to dine at **Rex**—with its romantic and elegant setting and Gennaro's creative dishes. For equally inspired Italian dishes in a smart casual setting—with the best gelati in town—**Pazzia** is the place! Both are creations of the visionary restaurateur Mauro Vincenti.

Our normal preference for smaller courses doesn't stop us from going to **Harold & Belle's** (on Jefferson Boulevard) for sumptuous portions of Creole cooking. And we always save room for their best dessert—Harriet's exquisite sweet-potato cheesecake.

Entertaining a group of friends is always a delight at **Joss** on Sunset Boulevard. Innovative Chinese dishes (with spectacular dim sum) and an unusually wide range of wines—with many half-bottles—specially selected to accompany the eclectic cuisine.

We go to **Barragan's** in Echo Park (on Sunset Boulevard) for tasty enchiladas "country style," beef tacos, and *costillas de puerco en salsa chipotle*.

Vegetarian pizza and *scormaza* (warm mozzarella with chopped tomatoes and basil) at **Angeli** on Melrose are personal favorites. We also like the pesto pizza at **Pazzia**, the *fugazza* (with cheese and thinly sliced onions) at **La Strega** on Western, and the special pizzas at **Spago**.

A sunny Sunday afternoon in the garden at **Michael's** eating delectable blueberry pancakes and other treats is California at its best!

Always special for out-of-town foodies, **Chinois-On-Main** in Santa Monica is high-energy and exciting. We like the squab with pan-fried noodles and the lobster *risotto* with fried spinach.

Other longtime favorites include **La Toque, Studio Grill, Celestino, City, Champagne, St. Estephe, Mandarin, Seventh St. Bistro, Langet's** on Alvarado (for the best pastrami sandwich!), and **Yuca's** (on Hillhurst).

Restaurants/Clubs: Red   **Hotels:** Blue
Shops/Parks: Green   **Sights/Culture:** Black

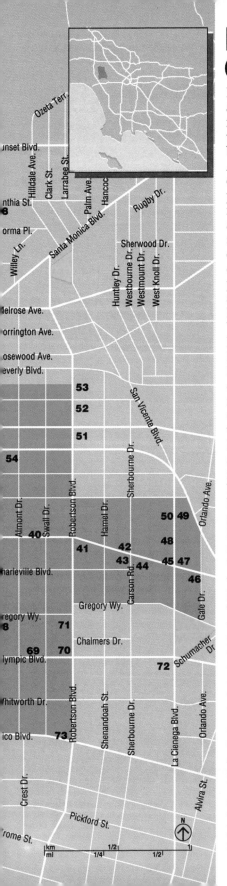

Beverly Hills/ Century City

Beverly Hills is like Disneyland: a place apart from the real world, unnaturally neat and clean, full of expensive adult toy stores and trim rows of old-world buildings. It's the apotheosis of the American dream: a leafy city with low crime, nonpolluting commerce, pretty people, and 2 cars in every garage. The reality comes close to the myth created by journalists, movies, and television. The streets to the north and south of Sunset Boulevard are lined with opulent mansions, with parklike lawns, pools, and tennis courts, though there are simple cottages high up in the hills and modest apartments south of Wilshire Boulevard. Celebrities have lived here since **Mary Pickford** and **Douglas Fairbanks** set up home at Pickfair in 1920. Beverly Hills is narcissistic, and it flaunts its wealth in a manner that has gone out of style elsewhere, but—like Disneyland—it works, and families make sacrifices to live here so that their children can attend some of the best public schools in LA. Most recent developments are bland—commercial clients veer between cast-stone palazzi and black-glass boxes, house designers are still in love with Mount Vernon—but they are pleasingly small-scale. To achieve this paradise, everything is regulated —from the size of signs to overnight parking.

The city got off to a late start—until the 1880s the area was chiefly noted for its fields of lima beans. An attempt to establish the town of Morocco in the land boom of 1887 soon fizzled; the present city was designed by **Wilbur Cook** for the Rodeo Land and Water Company in 1907. Cook laid out the triangular grid of business streets at a 45-degree angle to Wilshire, and the sinuously curving residential streets north to Sunset. The **Olmsted** brothers created the picturesque layout of streets that wind up through the hills above Sunset as though in a landscape park. According to local folklore, founder **Burton Green** picked the original name, **Beverly Farms**, from the place in Massachusetts where President Taft was vacationing. One of the first buildings was the **Beverly Hills Hotel**, begun in 1911, but much of the surrounding area remained undeveloped until long after. As late as 1946, agent **Leland Hayward** was offered a snake-infested tract of hilly land in a prime location at a bargain price. He thought no one would ever want to live there; today it is the affluent **Trousdale Estates**. The residential streets are lushly planted with flowering and shade trees: look for the manicured palms on **Benedict** and **Beverly Canyons**, and the jacarandas that bloom in April and May along **Palm** and **Whittier Drives**. The houses, when they are not obscured by bushes or high walls, display every known architectural style and many hybrids, mirroring the fantasies of immigrants from every corner of the world.

For the visitor, the main attractions are shopping, eating, and looking out for celebrities. The main shopping area—

bounded by Wilshire Blvd, Cañon Drive, and Little Santa Monica Blvd— is known as the *golden triangle*. **Rodeo Drive** is an upstart version of the luxury shopping streets in Europe's capitals. Publicity has made it as celebrated as London's Bond Street, Rome's Via Condotti, and the Rue du Faubourg St Honoré in Paris. LA is too spread out and too recent to achieve a comparable distillation of elegance and prestige, but Rodeo Drive deserves a medal for trying. Many of the top designer labels are represented here, and on the neighboring blocks of Wilshire.

1 Beverly Hills City Hall (1932, **William Gage**) Splendid Spanish Baroque pile, whose scroll ornament and colorful tile dome have been scrubbed in the recent restoration. ♦ 450 N. Crescent Dr (Santa Monica Blvd)

1 Beverly Hills Civic Center (1990, **Charles Moore/A.C. Martin & Associates**) Moore won a competition with his romantic/historical design for a diagonal sequence of 3 landscaped courtyards that would link library, fire and police stations, offices and parking to the remodeled City Hall. The grand vista toward the hills works well and the human scale is pleasing, but the buildings have the insubstantial quality of a movie set—you wonder if they will still be there next week. Repetitive rusticated arches and tile inserts compete with the frilly decoration of the old building. And several of the best features were eliminated to cut costs. ♦ Rexford Dr at Santa Monica Blvd

2 Union 76 Gas Station Extraordinarily daring for this area: a swooping cantilevered concrete canopy of the '50s. ♦ Rexford Dr at Little Santa Monica Blvd

3 Litton Industries (1940, **Paul Williams**) American Federal Revival office building with a grand portico. ♦ 360 N. Crescent Dr

4 Kaktus ★$$ Subdued setting for refined south-of-the border fare. ♦ Mexican ♦ M-Th 11:30AM-3:30PM, 5:30-10PM; F-Sa 11:30AM-11PM. 400 N. Cañon Dr. 271.1856

5 U.S. Post Office (1933, **Ralph Flewelling**) Terra cotta and brick combine with classically framed windows and doors to create a noble structure in the Italian Renaissance style. ♦ 9300 Santa Monica Blvd

6 La Famiglia ★★$$$ Modern, intimate, and friendly restaurant specializing in red and green pasta, and low-cal *nuova cucina*. Patio. Next door, at No. 455, is **Piccola Alley**, a patio restaurant, open weekdays 11:30AM-2PM, 5:30-10PM. ♦ Italian ♦ M-F 11:30AM-2:30PM, 5:30-11PM; Sa 5:30-11PM. 453 N. Cañon Dr. 276.6208

7 Nate 'n' Al ★$$ Big-name stars often come in on weekends to read their Sunday newspapers and talk with friends at this celebrated deli. ♦ Deli ♦ M-F, Su 7:30AM-8:45PM; Sa 7:30AM-9:30PM. 414 N. Beverly Dr. 274.0101

8 The Cheese Store An outstanding selection of imported cheeses. ♦ Daily 9:30AM-6PM. 419 N. Beverly Dr. 278.2855

8 Romeo and Juliet ★★$$$$ Power brokers and rich ladies enjoy good Northern Italian fare in a romantic setting. The pastas, fritto misto, and veal with wild mushrooms have all won acclaim. ♦ Italian ♦ M-F 11:30AM-3PM, 6-11PM. 435 N. Beverly Dr. 273.2292

9 Rangoon Racquet Club ★$$$ Kipling would have felt right at home among the palms and rattan. The menu mixes English with Indian just like the Empire. Friendly and fun. ♦ Anglo-Indian ♦ M-F 11:30AM-11PM; Sa 6-11PM. 9474 Little Santa Monica Blvd. 274.8926

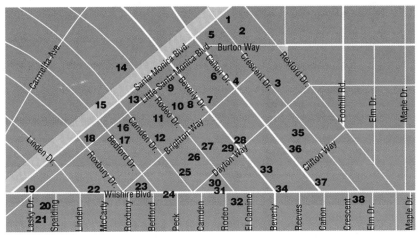

10 Carroll & Co. Men's clothes for the old guard who have included such odd bedfellows as Ronald Reagan, George McGovern, and Gregory Peck. ♦ M-Sa 9:30AM-6PM. 466 N. Rodeo Dr. 273.9060

10 Polo/Ralph Lauren No, you haven't strayed into an English country house—just the latest of Lauren's emporia for visiting squires and anglophiles. If, by some curious mischance, you have no pedigree, Ralph will conceal the fact from your closest friends. ♦ M-Sa 10AM-6PM. 444 N. Rodeo Dr. 281.7200

10 Armani Largest and glitziest of Giorgio Armani's stores; Steven Spielberg and Elton John buy their suits here. ♦ M-Sa 10AM-6PM. 436 N. Rodeo Dr. 271.5555

11 Rodeo Collection A pink marble shopping mall, whose designer boutiques include Gianni Versace, Sonia Rykiel, Fila, and Kenneth Jay Lane. ♦ M-Sa 9AM-6PM. 421 N. Rodeo Dr. 859.8770

11 Frette Exquisite Italian lingerie, table, bath, and bed linens. ♦ M-F 10AM-6PM; Sa 10AM-5:30PM. 449 N. Rodeo Dr. 273.8540

11 Lina Lee Casual, elegant sportswear for men and women. For men, there is suede and leather by La Matta, Brecos, and Ginocchietti; for women a spectrum of 350 new and established designers. ♦ Daily 10AM-6PM. 459 N. Rodeo Dr. 556.2678

12 La Scala ★$$$ An institution that was once known for its celebrities, snooty service, and high prices, has changed its attitude as well as its locations. It is now a kinder, gentler (and more affordable) neighborhood restaurant, serving so-so-food with a smile. Excellent wine list. ♦ Italian ♦ M-F 11:30AM-2:30PM, 5:30-11PM; Sa 5:30-11PM. 410 N. Camden Dr. 275.0579. Also at: 3874 Cross Creek Rd, Malibu. 456.1979

12 Mandarin ★★$$$ Lighter, brighter decor, an expanded menu, and a new manager, Philip Chiang, who took over from his mother. Peking duck, braised lamb, and Beggar's Chicken are key dishes. ♦ Chinese ♦ M-Sa 11:30AM-11PM; Su 5-11PM. 430 N. Camden Dr. 272.0267

13 Standard Cutlery The world's largest selection of cutting implements. ♦ M-Sa 8:30AM-6PM. 9509 Little Santa Monica Blvd. 276.7898

14 O'Neill House (1989, Don Ramos) Antonio Gaudi is alive and well in Beverly Hills! The Catalan architect would be proud of the writhing stucco on this Art Nouveau collector's house—and the still more whimsical guesthouse in the alley behind. Private residence. ♦ 507 N. Rodeo Dr

15 Cactus Garden Cacti and succulents from around the world occupy one section of the most handsome landscaping to be found on any city boulevard. Facing the garden, along the south side, are 6 block-long low-rise parking structures, an exemplary response to the influx of shoppers. ♦ Santa Monica Blvd (Camden St-Bedford Dr)

16 Camp Beverly Hills T-shirts, sweats, and pants for the young California look. ♦ Daily 10AM-6:30PM. 9640 Little Santa Monica Blvd. 274.8317

16 Banana Republic The travel books have gone since this burgeoning chain fell into The Gap, but you can still find the *Out of Africa* look: safari jackets, khaki pants, skirts, and broad-brimmed hats displayed in a movie set interior. Branches all over LA ♦ M-Sa 10AM-6:30PM; Su noon-6PM. 9669 Little Santa Monica Blvd. 858.7900

17 Noa Noa ★★★$$$ (1990, Larry Totah) A stunning interior that is sensual and spiky—Gauguin meets Googie. And chef Ralf Marhencke delights the palate with his sesame-crusted oysters, subtly peppered rack of lamb, and daily specials. The passionfruit soufflé is a standout among the desserts. Kenji Seki is the exuberant owner/host. ♦ Pacific/California ♦ M-F noon-3PM, 6PM-midnight; Sa-Su 6PM-midnight. 464 N. Bedford Dr. 278.1904

Restaurants/Clubs: Red   **Hotels:** Blue
Shops/Parks: Green
Sights/Culture: Black

Rodeo Drive Shopping Map

SANTA MONICA BLVD.

womenswear **Boulmiche Boutique**	474 **Kent and Curwen** traditional menswear
	474 **IXI:Z/Naburd** menswear

LITTLE SANTA MONICA BLVD.

womenswear **Claude Montana** 469	466 **Carroll & Co.** traditional menswear
young casuals **BB1** 465	460 **Celine** Parisian womenswear
womenswear **Lina Lee** 461	458 **Bigi** European & Japanese womenswear
Bottega Veneta 457	456 **Mila Schon** Milanese womenswear
leather handbags & accessories	444 **Polo/Ralph Lauren** classic clothes
womenswear **Theodore** 453	442 **Michael Cromer** luggage
menswear **Theodore Man** 451	436 **Giorgio Armani** designer wear
linens **Frette** 449	430 **Galerie Michael** masterworks
womenswear **Jean Claude Jitrois** 447	428 **Pierre Deux** French home furnishings
decorative arts **Robert Zehil Gallery** 445	420 **Bijan** menswear, by appointment
Rodeo Collection 421	400 **Capital Bank of California**
Gianni Versace, Sonia Rykiel,	
Kenneth Jay Lane and 30 other boutiques	
European art **Mayer Schwarz Gallery** 411	
Bally of Switzerland 409	
women's shoes & accessories	
beauty **Vidal Sassoon** 405	
women's designer wear **Patricia Morange** 403	
jewelry **Fred Joaillier** 401	

RODEO

BRIGHTON WAY

jewelry **Harry Winston** 371	370 **Cartier** jewelry
audio **Bang and Olufsen** 369	366 **Andrea Carrano** handbags/shoes
shoes **A. Testoni** 365	362 **Bernini** menswear
shoes **Ferragamo** 357	360 **Beverly Rodeo Hotel & Cafe**
fashions/accessories **Gucci** 347	346 **Bassini** European menswear
fashions/accessories **Hermés** 343	344 **Benetton** Italian sportswear
art **Dyansen Gallery** 339	342 **Christie's** auction house
menswear **Tommy Hilfiger** 337	340 **Bally of Switzerland**
European menswear **Bardelli** 335	men's shoes & accessories
leathers **Goldfiel** 333	338 **Villeroy & Boch** dinnerware
Designer menswear **Ted Lapidus** 329	332 **Attina** womenswear
perfume/gifts **Giorgio Beverly Hills** 327	332 **Diamonds on Rodeo** jewelry
art **Hanson Galleries** 323	332 **Laise Adzer** hand-dyed womenswear
womenswear **Adrienne Vittadini** 319	320 **David Orgell** jewelry/silver
designer's ready-to-wear **Ungaro** 317	314 **Bowles-Sorokko Gallery**
designer womenswear **Alaia Chez Gallay** 313	312 **Georgette Klinger** beauty
Hammacher Schlemmer 309	310 **Frances Klein Jewels**
adult toy store/gadgets	308 **Sotheby's** auction house
luggage **Louis Vuitton** 307	306 **Battaglia** Italian shoes
womenswear **Chanel Boutique** 301	300 **Van Cleef & Arpels** jewelry

DAYTON WAY

fashion/fragrance **Fred Hayman** 273	**Two Rodeo Dr.** Cartier, Charles Jourdan,
Denmark Jewelers 201	Christian Dior, Valentino, Stringfellows Club,
Alfred Dunhill of London 201	Tiffany's, and other stores
traditional menswear	

RODEO

WILSHIRE BLVD

Beverly Wilshire Hotel 9500	
Buccellati 9500	

18 The Wine Merchant Dennis Overstreet offers classes, tastings, and rental vaults as well as an outstanding selection of rare vintages. ♦ M-Sa 9:30AM-6:30PM. 9701 Little Santa Monica Blvd. 278.7322

19 Creative Artists Associates (1989, **Pei, Cobb, Freed**) As the uncrowned king of the movie business, CAA President **Michael Ovitz** has commissioned an appropriately sleek but understated palace. Its curved marble, steel, and glass facade, circular glass lantern, and precise detailing give an awkward intersection a big lift. ♦ Santa Monica Blvd at Wilshire Blvd

20 Beverly Crest Hotel $$ Conveniently located 54-room hotel, with pool and coffee shop. For the area it's a bargain. ♦ 125 S. Spaulding Dr. Free parking. 274.6801; fax 273.6614

21 Beverly House Hotel $$ A modest and well-run small hotel full of old-fashioned charm. Right on the edge of the shopping district. ♦ 140 S. Lasky Dr. 271.2145

22 Cafe Beverly Hills $$ Home-style cooking around the clock. ♦ American ♦ 24 hours. 9725 Wilshire Blvd. 273.6397

23 Carroll O'Connor's Place ★$$$ A noisy New York-style bar and restaurant where the daily specials are often above-and-beyond the call of duty. ♦ American ♦ M-F 7-10:30AM, 11:30AM-4PM, 5:30-11PM; Sa 11:30AM-4PM, 5:30-11PM. 369 N. Bedford Dr. 273.7585

24 Wilshire Boulevard Wilshire Blvd between Roxbury and Crescent drives is home to some of LA's best department and specialty stores. Handsome older buildings, slick glass high-rises, and lofty palm trees, plus lively pedestrian traffic, give this stretch of LA's Main Street a great sense of style. This is one place smart New Yorkers can enjoy without a car.

Highlights include:

Neiman-Marcus (9700 Wilshire Blvd. 550.5900)

Jaeger (9699 Wilshire Blvd. 276.1062)

Saks Fifth Avenue (9600 Wilshire Blvd. 275.4211)

Charles Jourdan (9654 Wilshire Blvd. 273.3507)

I. Magnin (9634 Wilshire Blvd. 271.2131)

Gump's (9560 Wilshire Blvd. 278.3200)

Buccellati (9500 Wilshire Blvd. 276.7022)

25 Mr. Chow's ★$$$ Glossy black-and-white interior decorated with fine contemporary art. Tame, expensive food that often looks better than it tastes. The chef comes out from the kitchen for a nightly noodle show. ♦ Chinese ♦ M-F noon-2:30PM, 6:30PM-midnight; Sa-Su 6:30PM-midnight. 344 N. Camden Dr. 278.9911

25 Prego ★$$ Tantalizing pizzas are prepared in open wood-burning ovens, but they hardly upstage the carpaccio, gnocchi, pasta, and grilled entrees. Attractive, upbeat, bustling restaurant with a lively bar scene (separated from the dining area by a glass wall) and service that is very congenial if a bit harried. ♦ Italian ♦ M-Sa 11:30AM-midnight; Su 5PM-midnight. 362 N. Camden Dr. 277.7346

26 Giorgio Beverly Hills A celebrated name under new management at a new address, selling its signature scents and casualwear, with a new fashion store to come. ♦ M-Sa 11AM-6PM. 357 N. Rodeo Dr. 274.0200

27 David Orgell Superb jewelry and antique English silver. ♦ M-Sa 10AM-6PM. 320 N. Rodeo Dr. 272.3355

27 Anderton Court (1954, Frank Lloyd Wright) An angular shopping complex with ramps and a jagged tower —one of the master's last and least important works. ♦ 328 N. Rodeo Dr

27 Beverly Rodeo Hotel $$$ A luxury hotel with an intimate, European flavor. Concierge, room service, sundeck, valet parking. Its café serves delicious salads on a terrace overlooking Rodeo, daily 7AM-12:30AM. ♦ 360 N. Rodeo Dr. 273.0300; fax 859.8730

28 The Carnegie Deli ★$$ Woody Allen would choke on his pastrami sandwich, but there's magic in the name, and this designer version (by Pat Kuleto) of the scruffy original packs them in. The decor is a fantasy version of an Art Deco deli. There's valet parking and white bread, but the pastrami is original, the portions huge, and all the basic deli foods are here. ♦ Deli ♦ Tu-Th 7AM-12:30AM; F-Sa 7AM-2AM; Su 7AM-11PM. 300 N. Beverly Dr. 275.DELI

29 Il Fornaio $ Wonderful breads and pizzas; also a café serving pastas and salads. Also in Santa Monica. ♦ Italian ♦ M-F 7:30AM-9PM; Sa-Su 7:30AM-10PM. 301 N. Beverly Dr. 550.8330

Beverly Hills/Century City

29 Graffeo Coffee Roasting Company Just 3 blends—light, dark, and decaf—but they may yield the best cup you've ever savored. ♦ M-Sa 9AM-5:30PM. 315 N. Beverly Dr. 273.4232

30 The Grill ★★★$$$ Chef John Sola has won applause for his assurance with corned beef hash, braised shortribs, and chunky Cobb salad, besides the oak-charcoal grilled fish and meats. This is a place with solid virtues: a warm woodsy setting, professional waiters, and huge helpings at fair prices. ♦ American ♦ M-Sa 11:30AM-11:45PM. 9560 Dayton Wy. 276.0615

31 One Rodeo Drive A whimsical pastiche of Palladio by Johannes Van Tilburg, housing such boutiques as Dunhill, Isis Unlimited, and Denmark Jeweler. Across the street, an even more ambitious development, Two Rodeo Drive, houses the largest Tiffany store outside New York, Christian Dior, Cartier, Valentino, Charles Jourdan, Gianfranco Ferre, Cole Hahn, and Stringfellow's nightclub, with more prestigious tenants to come. ♦ N. Rodeo Dr at Wilshire Blvd

32 Regent Beverly Wilshire Hotel $$$$ (1928, Walker & Eisen) The Regent Group, which owns some of the finest properties around the Pacific, has spent $65 million to restore this grandest of luxury hotels to a level above its former excellence. From the columned gold, cream, and brown marble lobby to the guest rooms (many of which have been doubled in size), the improvements are immediately evident. Exemplary service includes 24-hour concierges and room stewards on every floor. On the ground floor of the Wilshire building is a handsome clubby bar, a drugstore café and the Lobby Lounge, which serves afternoon tea, light meals, and cocktails. ♦ Deluxe ♦ 9500 Wilshire Blvd. 275.5200, 800/545.4000; fax 274.2851

Within the Regent Beverly Wilshire Hotel:

Regent Beverly Wilshire Dining Room
★★★$$$ Surprisingly bold California cuisine in a traditionally elegant setting of polished wood columns, colorful murals, and stunning flower arrangements. Ravioli of smoked chicken, grilled swordfish with sautéed sweet peppers, calf's liver with red wine and shallot sauce, and a garlicky roast chicken are standouts. The smoothly efficient service is equally remarkable, making this a preferred location for power breakfasts and lunches. ♦ California ♦ Daily 7-10:30AM, 11:30AM-3PM, 7-10:30PM. 9500 Wilshire Blvd. 274.8179

33 Tribeca ★$$ Handsome Manhattan-cool, bilevel bar and restaurant offers tasteful busi-

Beverly Hills/Century City

ness lunches and trendy dinners and late-night suppers. The weekend bar crush can be intimidating, but push your way up the stairs to the dining room where the service is smooth and the food sublime. Excellent wines by the glass.
♦ Seafood ♦ M-Th 11:30AM-4PM; F 11:30AM-4PM, 5PM-1AM; Sa 5PM-2AM; Su 5PM-midnight. 242 N. Beverly Dr. 874.2322

34 Sterling Plaza (1929) Gilt-edged refurbishment of a handsome Art Deco office tower built by **Louis B. Mayer** as the MGM Building. Ironically, the much diminished movie company has established its offices a block away behind the blandest of the bland white marble-and-black glass facade. Mayer would not have approved.
♦ Wilshire Blvd at Beverly Dr

34 Israel Discount Bank Odd symbolism: the mosque-like dome originally roofed a theater.
♦ 206 N. Beverly Dr (Wilshire Blvd)

35 Mrs Gooch's Natural Foods Market Organic produce, naturally bred meats without hormones, humanely reared veal, and other goodies. ♦ Daily 9AM-9PM. 239 N. Crescent Dr. 274.3360. Also at: 3476 Centinela Ave, W. LA. 391.5209; 526 Pier Ave, Hermosa Beach. 376.6931

36 The Bistro ★$$$$ A stellar spot for seeing and being seen. Pretty decor; stick to the simpler dishes. ♦ French ♦ M-F noon-3PM (except in summer), 6-10:30PM; Sa 6-10:30PM. 240 N. Cañon Dr. 273.5633

37 Bistro Garden ★$$$$ The prettiest garden—all flowers and white parasols—and one of the most romantic dining rooms. Who cares about the food? Evidently not the well-heeled regulars. ♦ French ♦ M-Sa 11:30AM-11PM; Su 5:30-10:30PM. 176 N. Cañon Dr. 550.3900. Also at: 12950 Ventura Blvd, Sherman Oaks. 818/501.0202

38 Beverly Pavilion Hotel $$$ Sophisticated small European-style hotel with a handsome rusticated stone facade and stylish decor. Complimentary limousine, valet parking, rooftop pool, a spectacular view of the city, and movie channels. ♦ 9360 Wilshire Blvd. 273.1400, 800/441.5050 (CA), 800/421.0545 (US); fax 859.8551

Within the Beverly Pavilion Hotel:

Colette ★★$$$ Leading off the hotel lobby is an intimate and charming French restaurant designed with pleasing understatement by **Brent Saville**. Arched windows overlook Wilshire, but the mood is serene. Chef **Patrick Blobaum**, following in the footsteps of **Patrick Healy** (now running **Champagne**), turns out consistently good modern French food, and mouthwatering desserts. ♦ French ♦ Daily 7-11AM, 11:30AM-2:30PM, 6-10:30PM. 9360 Wilshire Blvd. 273.1400

39 Cafe Connection ★$$ An upscale coffeehouse with a samba beat. Try the *feijoada*, Brazil's national dish (black beans, sausages, and smoked meats), shrimp in coconut milk, or codfish croquettes, washed down with a potent *capirinha*. ♦ Brazilian ♦ M 8:30AM-4PM; Tu-Th 8:30AM-4PM, 6-11PM; F-Sa 8:30AM-4PM, 6PM-2AM. Live music Thursday-Saturday from 8:30PM. 9171 Wilshire Blvd. 271.9545

39 Kate Mantilini ★$$$ (1987, **Morphosis**) One of the most exciting new interiors in LA, as expressive of its period as the Bradbury Building atrium was of the 1890s. Owner **Marilyn Lewis** requested a roadside café, named for a woman boxing promoter of the '40s. What the architects gave her was that and a lot more. Within the shell of a low-rise curtain-wall bank building rises an extraordinarily complex layered space, indirectly lit, with a jagged steel sundial rising from the floor and through the ceiling. Enclosed booths line the 100-foot-long outer wall. Above the open kitchen is a boxing mural by artist

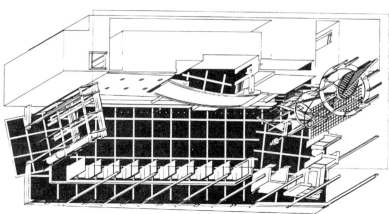

Kate Mantilini Drawing Courtesy Morphosis

John Wehrle. The menu pays homage to **Musso and Frank**, offering hearty servings of meat loaf with crisp kale, roast chicken with mashed potatoes, and a score more basics, plus a wonderful calf's brain omelet. Customers pay for the architecture. ♦ American ♦ M-F 7:30AM-3AM; Sa noon-3AM; Su 10AM-midnight. 9109 Wilshire Blvd. 278.3699

40 Academy of Motion Picture Arts & Sciences Home of Oscar and a lively program of lobby exhibitions, and occasional public screenings in LA's finest 1000-seat theater. ♦ 8949 Wilshire Blvd. 278.8990

41 Wilshire-Robertson Plaza (1990, **Arquitectonica**) This commercial block by the provocative Miami-based firm stands out from the tedious succession of S&L offices. ♦ 8750 Wilshire Blvd

42 The Jewish Quarter A pink stucco block in the style of the rebuilt Jewish Quarter in Jerusalem sells fine and decorative Judaic art in 2 adjoining stores. ♦ M-Th, Su 10AM-6PM; F 10AM-4PM. 8685 Wilshire Blvd. 652.8526

43 Bombay Palace ★$$$ Behind the klutzy pink-and-turquoise facade is a handsome, lofty interior ornamented with tiny gold deities. The Mughal cooking can be excellent, and the weekend brunch is a great bargain. ♦ Indian ♦ Daily 11:30AM-2:30PM, 5:30-10PM. 8690 Wilshire Blvd. 659.9944

44 Hollywood on Location Every weekday at 9:30AM, **Jack Weinberg**, former lawyer and financial consultant, publishes a list of 20 to 30 locations where films, TV shows, and rock videos are being shot. List includes addresses, maps, names of stars and productions, times, and tips for stellar encounters. Friday's list includes some weekend tips. ♦ Fee. M-F 9:30AM-5PM. Pick it up at 8644 Wilshire Blvd. 659.9165

45 Drive-In On the site of **Dolores**, one of LA's original drive-in restaurants, is this dazzling neon mural by **Lili Lakich**, incorporating a tail fin from a '57 Chevy. In the Unity Savings building. ♦ 8501 Wilshire Blvd

45 Goethe Institute Branch of a worldwide organization that promotes German language and culture. Language courses, screenings, exhibitions, and other events, often presented in cooperation with local institutions. ♦ 8501 Wilshire Blvd. Suite 205. 854.0993

46 Wilshire Theatre (1929, **S. Charles Lee**) Stylish zigzag movie house, designed for Fox and restored for use as a stage for musicals and drama. ♦ Seats 1900. 8440 Wilshire Blvd. 642.4242, box office 410.1062

47 Benihana of Tokyo ★$$ Branch of a popular Japanese *teppan* grill chain. ♦ Japanese ♦ M-Th 11:30AM-2PM, 5:30-10PM; F 11:30AM-2PM, 5:30PM-11PM; Sa 5:30-11PM; Su 4:30-10PM. 38 N. La Cienega Blvd. 655.7311

47 Gaylord India Restaurant ★★$$ Local outpost of a high-class chain that began in New Delhi in 1941. The room is understated and beautiful; the food is consistently first-rate. ♦ North Indian ♦ Daily 11:30AM-2:30PM, 5:30-10:30PM. 50 N. La Cienega Blvd. 652.3838

48 Lawry's Prime Rib ★$$ The prime rib and '40s decor are celebrated; you might have to wait for a table. ♦ American ♦ M-Th 5-11PM;

F-Sa 5PM-midnight; Su 3-10PM. 55 N. La Cienega Blvd. 652.2827

49 Ed Debevic's $ Trendy retro coffeeshops and diners open as fast as the originals (like **Ship's** in Westwood) close their doors. This is LA's most ambitious pastiche to date, from the streamline facade to the '50s artifacts within. All it lacks is **Frankie, Annette**, and a gang of crewcut extras doing some soulful rocking. ♦ American ♦ M-Th 11:30AM-midnight; F-Sa 11:30AM-1AM; Su 11:30AM-11PM. 134 N. La Cienega Blvd. 659.1952

50 Matsuhisa ★★★$$$ Storefront restaurant and innovative sushi bar run by a master with 20 years' experience in LA, Lima (Peru), and his native Tokyo. Put yourself in Matsuhisa's hands and prepare to be dazzled by the freshest fish and a poet's skill. ♦ Japanese ♦ F 11:45AM-2:30PM, 5:45-10:30PM; Sa-Su 5:45-10:30PM. 129 N. La Cienega Blvd. 659.9639

51 Michel Richard ★$$ Desserts as art. Tables for *petit déjeuner*, or salad and quiche lunches. A dinner menu is also served. ♦ French ♦ M-Sa 8AM-10PM. 310 S. Robertson Blvd. 275.5707

52 agnès b. Classic French women's linen suits, cotton sweaters, and snap sweatshirts. ♦ M-Sa 11AM-7PM; Su noon-6PM. 100 N. Robertson Blvd. 271.9643

53 Robata ★★★$$$ Authoritative Tokyo restaurant, with a modern decor of granite, glass, and wood. There is a discreet *robata* grill, but the emphasis is on pricey, 12-course *kaiseki* dinners. Master chef **Osamu Miyazama** integrates sushi, country, and contemporary dishes. ♦ Japanese ♦ M-F 11:30AM-2PM, 5:30-11PM; Sa 5:30-11PM. 250 N. Robertson Blvd. 274.5533

54 Il Cielo ★★$$$ Al fresco dining in 2 charming courtyards or a white-walled room with a trompe l'oeil sky. Baked scamorza cheese with eggplant and risotto cooked in black squid's ink are standout dishes. ♦ Italian ♦ M-F 11:30AM-2:30PM, 6:30-10PM; Sa 6:30-10PM. 9018 Burton Wy. 276.9990

Restaurants/Clubs: Red	**Hotels:** Blue
Shops/Parks: Green	**Sights/Culture:** Black

54 Pratesi Hand-embroidered silk sheets, cashmere blankets, and huge fluffy towels for sybaritic millionaires. ◆ M-Sa 9:30AM-6PM. 9024 Burton Wy. 274.7661

55 L'Ermitage Hotel $$$$ Intimate and luxurious—a 120-suite hotel that attempts to capture the European spirit with traditional furnishings,

original artworks, and exemplary service. Rooftop garden, pool, and spa; free chauffered Rolls for excursions within Beverly Hills. **Cafe Russe** serves Russian-accented food exclusively for guests. More reasonably priced is **Le Petit Ermitage** next door. ◆ Deluxe ◆ 9291 Burton Wy. 278.3344, 800/424.4443; fax 278.8247

56 Il Giardino ★★$$$$ In a trellised gardenlike room with small tables set close together, you may feast on a wonderful and varied menu of Tuscan delights, including pasta, risotto, perfectly grilled fish, and herb steak. Food is cooked to order, with the freshest ingredients. The only drawback is the service, which is leisurely at best. ◆ Italian ◆ M-Sa noon-2PM, 6:30-10:30PM. 9235 W 3rd St. 275.5444

57 Maple Drive ★$$$ Large, loud, and fashionable restaurant and nightclub from the team that created **72 Market Street** in Venice—**Tony Bill, Dudley Moore, Julie Stone**, and chef **Leonard Schwartz**. Interior design by **Anthony Greenberg**. There's an oyster and sushi bar, basic food like rotisserie chicken and Caesar salad, and live entertainment. ◆ Eclectic ◆ M-Tu 7:30AM-2:30PM, 6-11PM; W-F 7:30AM-2:30PM, 6PM-midnight; Sa-Su 6-11PM. 345 N. Maple Dr. 274.9800

58 858 N. Doheny Drive (1928, **Lloyd Wright**) Concrete-block house with a dramatic 2-story living room, on a tiny corner lot. The side patio surrounds a spreading tree. Private residence. ◆ Vista Grande St

59 Greystone Park Oil millionaire **Edward L. Doheny** built this 55-room English Tudor mansion for his son in 1928. Long abandoned, it was used as a set for *The Loved One* and later leased by the American Film Institute. The city authorities seem unable to decide what to do with the house, which remains closed. The 16-acre garden, with its balustraded terraces and grassy slopes, is one of LA's loveliest public parks. ◆ Daily 10AM-6PM. 905 Loma Vista Dr. Concert and event information 550.4654

60 Virginia Robinson Gardens Forget the walled-off homes of the stars; by calling a week in advance, you can tour the oldest residence in Beverly Hills, plus 6 acres of lush gardens,

groves of king palms, azaleas, and camellias in the spring. It's a treasury of rarities and specimen trees, including the largest monkey hand tree in California. ◆ Admission. Tours Tu-Th 10AM, 1PM; F 10AM. 1008 Elden Wy. 276.4823

The Beverly Hills Hotel and Bungalows

61 Beverly Hills Hotel $$$$ Nicknamed *the pink palace*, this sprawling Mission-revival hotel (which opened in 1912) has become an unofficial symbol of the city and its hedonistic lifestyle. Sheltered from traffic and prying eyes by dense planting, the hotel has the grace of an earlier era. Embowered in 12 acres of tropical gardens are the legendary pool and the 21 luxurious bungalows where such luminaries as **Chaplin, Garbo, Gable** and **Lombard** stayed. **Howard Hughes**, obsessive about privacy, lived in his 24 hours a day, leaving messages in a tree outside. Formal dining room and acclaimed breakfast counter. Service is the hotel's greatest strength: head concierge **Robert Duncan** claims he got one guest an audience with the Pope, and for another, a game of Scrabble in Russian. ◆ Deluxe ◆ 9641 Sunset Blvd. 276.2251, 800/283.8885; fax 281.2919

Within the Beverly Hills Hotel:

Polo Lounge $$$ Meetings are taken over breakfast and lunch here; deals made on phones at the tables. Not since the fall of Byzantium has the hierarchy of who sits where (or whether) been as solemnly enforced. Don't come unless your status—or self-esteem—is impregnable. Cobb or chicken salad with a glass of Chardonnay in the leafy patio is an affordable treat. ◆ American ◆ Daily 7AM-3PM, 3:30PM-1AM; Su Brunch 11:30AM-3PM. 276.2251

62 Spadena House (1921, **Henry Oliver**) Hansel and Gretel would have lived here if they had made it big with their screenplay. The thatched-roof residence was designed by Oliver as a combined movie set and office. It was moved here from Culver City and may eventually be moved back. Private residence. ◆ Walden Dr at Carmelita Ave

---

Restaurants/Clubs: Red   **Hotels:** Blue
Shops/Parks: Green   **Sights/Culture:** Black

63 Beverly Hilton $$$ Balconied rooms surround the big pool, giving this Hilton the feeling of a resort. Guest and public rooms and the restaurants (among them **Mr. H**, which serves a generous buffet) have been extensively redecorated in lighter, softer colors. Well-equipped fitness center, for guests. ♦ 9876 Wilshire Blvd. 274.7777, 800/HILTONS; fax 859.9011

Within the Beverly Hilton:

L'Escoffier ★★$$$$ The only restaurant in Los Angeles with haute cuisine, dancing, and a great view. Designer **Robert Barry** has given this dowager an elegant new dress, though there was nothing he could do about the low ceiling. A favorite place for anniversary celebrations. ♦ French ♦ M-Th 6:30PM-midnight; F-Sa 6:30PM-1AM. 285.1333

Trader Vic's ★$$$$ Silly rum drinks with little umbrellas and the South Seas setting are the main draws, though the kitchen can produce good appetizers. ♦ Polynesian ♦ Daily 4:30PM-12:30AM. 9876 Wilshire Blvd. 276.6345

64 Jimmy's ★★$$$$ Yet another haunt of the rich and famous, with leisurely service and a rich menu with prices to match. Surprisingly, the food can be quite good and the veal chop is a classic. There is a lively piano bar, which is a nice place for a late-night drink. ♦ French/Seafood ♦ M-F 11:30AM-3PM, 6-11PM; Sa 6-11PM. 201 Moreno Dr. 879.2394

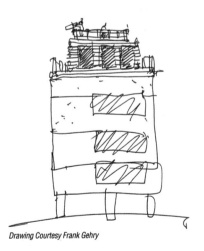

Drawing Courtesy Frank Gehry

65 Wosk Apartment (1983, **Frank Gehry** and **Miriam Wosk**) A surreal penthouse—gold ziggurat, blue dome, black marble arch, and turquoise-tiled walls clustered atop a pink apartment building—juices up an otherwise bland street. Admire it from the tennis courts across the street. Private residence. ♦ 440 S. Roxbury Dr

66 Chez Helene ★$$ Charming homespun bistro with brick-walled patio; specialties include salmon mousse, buttery roast chicken, great *pommes frites*, and raspberry cake with thick cream. ♦ French ♦ Tu-Th 11:30AM-3PM, 6-10PM; F-Sa 11:30AM-3PM, 6-10:30PM; Su 6-10PM. 267 S. Beverly Dr. 276.1558

67 Ruth's Chris Steak House ★★$$$ Acclaimed for what some call the best steaks in town. Traditional menu in a plain brick-and-palm setting. ♦ M-Th 11:30AM-3PM, 5:30-10PM; F 11:30AM-3PM, 5:30-11PM; Sa 5:30-11PM. 224 S. Beverly Dr. 859.8744

67 Celestino ★★★$$$ Chef/owner **Celestino Drago** serves delicious, light dishes in a coolly

elegant setting designed by **Brent Saville**. Wonderful antipasti, pastas, and seafood. Specialties include spaghetti baked in a bag and roast rabbit with olive sauce. ♦ Italian ♦ M-F 11:30AM-2:30PM, 5:30-11PM; Sa-Su 5:30-11PM. 236 S. Beverly Dr. 859.8601

67 Savories ★$ Useful resource for salads, sandwiches, and desserts—to eat in or to go. Order picnic baskets a day ahead. ♦ California ♦ M-F 8AM-8PM; Sa 9AM-6PM. 240 S. Beverly Dr. 276.9481

67 Yank's ★$$ Cajun meat loaf, grilled salmon, and apple pie served in a room that grandmother would enjoy. ♦ American ♦ M-Th noon-3PM, 6-10PM; F noon-3PM, 6-11PM; Sa 5:30-11PM; Su 5-9PM. 262 S. Beverly Dr. 859.2657

68 Four Seasons $$$$ European-style luxury hotel that is elegant and sophisticated like others in this group. The 180 rooms and 106 suites are furnished with antiques. Public areas have marble floors and quality art; fresh flowers are everywhere. Charming garden. Terrace pool with café, sauna, and Jacuzzi. Complimentary limo to Rodeo Drive. ♦ Deluxe ♦ 300 S. Doheny Dr. 273.2222, 800/268.6282; fax 859.3824

Within the Four Seasons:

Garden's ★★$$$ Lovely meals in a pretty setting. The service and wine list are as good as ever. ♦ Eclectic ♦ Daily 11:30AM-2:30PM, 6-10:30PM. 273.2222 ext. 2171

69 Dolores Drive-In $ Original '50s coffeeshop, still in mint condition. Vintage menu of burgers, cherry-lime rookies, and Suzy-Q fries. ♦ American ♦ M-Th, Su 6AM-midnight; F-Sa 24 hours. 8925 W. Olympic Blvd. 657.7455. Also at: 11407 Santa Monica Blvd. 447.1061

70 Christopher Hansen (1990, **Kirkpatrick Associates**) Museumlike setting for custom audio installations and home entertainment centers. Clientele includes top professionals. Sensitive conversion of a former Rolls-Royce dealership. ♦ M-Sa 10AM-6PM. 8822 W. Olympic Blvd (Robertson Blvd) 858.8112

Thank heavens we can escape to Beverly Hills on the weekends. No one in Sacramento can do hair.

Nancy Reagan during Ronald Reagan's term as Governor of California

71 Rosebud Elin Catz is an artist in icing, creating Memphis-inspired white-chocolate cakes and other delectable confections. ◆ T-Sa 10AM-6PM. 311 S. Robertson Blvd. 657.6207

72 Margaret Herrick Library and Film Archive of the Academy of Motion Picture Arts & Sciences Fran Offenhauser and **Michael J. Mekeel** did the imaginative conversion of this 1928 landmark building, which was inspired by Seville's **La Giralda**, but actually housed a water treatment station. The project was a triumph for local preservationists—to offset the loss of the zigzag Beverly Theatre on Wilshire. The **Library**, one of the country's finest collections of film books, magazines, and archival treasures, is open

Beverly Hills/Century City

without charge to serious students of cinema. ◆ M-Tu, Th-F 9AM-4:30PM. 333 S. La Cienega Blvd (Olympic Blvd). 278.4313

Century City

This was once **Twentieth-Century Fox's** back lot, which was sold off in the late '50s and developed by the **Alcoa Corporation**. It is as sterile and unfriendly a place as Brasilia, with no street life, and little good architecture to redeem it. However, it is strategically placed, between Beverly Hills and the booming Westside. It had a slow start, but is now boffo, and new office towers are being constructed to accommodate the influx of lawyers and entertainment executives.

73 Raja ★$$ Kashmiri specialties, tandoori shrimp and chicken, and vegetable dishes at very reasonable prices. All-you-can-eat lunch buffet. ◆ Indian ◆ M-Th, Su 11:30AM-2:30PM, 5:30-10:30PM; F-Sa 11:30AM-2:30PM, 5:30-11PM. 8875 W. Pico Blvd. 550.9176

74 Hymie's Fish Market ★$$$ Top show-biz types come for the excellent lobster bouillabaisse, clams, oysters, etc. A no-nonsense place. Excellent fish market. ◆ Seafood ◆ Restaurant: M-Th 11:30AM-2:30PM, 5:30-10PM; F 11:30AM-2:30PM, 5:30-10:30PM; Sa 6-10:30PM; Su 5-9PM. Fish market: M-F 10AM-10PM; Sa-Su 3-10:30PM. 9228 W. Pico Blvd. 550.0377

74 Beverlywood Bakery Some of the best pumpernickel and rye this side of Central Europe. ◆ M-Sa 6AM-6:30PM; Su 6AM-5:30PM. 9128 W. Pico Blvd. 550.9842

74 Gordon's Fresh Pacific & Eastern Fish Market Whole fish at very reasonable prices, and it's open on Saturday morning when Hymie's is not. ◆ M-Sa 8:30AM-6PM, Su 9-10AM pick-ups only. 9116 W. Pico Blvd. 276.6603

75 Delmonico's ★★$$ When the fad for Cajun-Creole faded, this restaurant switched to seafood. The large airy room with ceiling fans and tables crowded in the center is reminiscent of an old Parisian brasserie and filled with the same fearsome din; to avoid it try for one of the wooden booths that hug the walls. Long, lively bar in front serves oysters and great Bloody Marys. ◆ Seafood ◆ M-F 11:30AM-11PM; Sa-Su 5-11PM. 9320 W. Pico Blvd. 550.7737

76 Osteria Romana Orsini ★★$$$ Perhaps it's the lunching execs from nearby Twentieth Century Fox who give this place such a clubby feel. Well-prepared Italian food, including Roman specialties. The desserts are fine and the bountiful lunchtime antipasto buffet is memorable. There's a club upstairs that persists in such amusingly antediluvian behavior as charging women less for admission than they charge men. ◆ Italian ◆ Restaurant: M-F noon-2:30PM, 6-11PM; Sa 6-11PM. Club: Th-Sa 10PM-2AM. 9575 W. Pico Blvd. 277.6050

77 Twentieth Century Fox Studios No tours, but you can drive up to the gate and glimpse the *Hello Dolly* street, a re-creation of turn-of-the-century New York, with false facades and painted stages. This was Hollywood's first studio planned for sound, created by pioneer **William Fox**, who then lost control of the company he had established. **Darryl Zanuck** ruled here over such eminent subjects as **Shirley Temple, Carmen Miranda**, and director **John Ford**. It was also home to **Marilyn Monroe,** *Cleopatra,* and *M★A★S★H.* Fox has survived more predators than the maiden in a melodrama; currently it's flourishing. ◆ 10201 Pico Blvd. 277.2121

78 JW Marriott Hotel at Century City $$$$ Another chain luxury hotel, but at least it's warmer and more welcoming than the Century Plaza. It's housed in a peach pyramid, and peach is a favorite tone within. There's a Roman-style spa and outdoor pool and a limo to drive you in style the half-mile up the street to the Shubert Theatre. ◆ 2151 Avenue of the Stars. 277.2777, 800/228.9290; fax 277.9438

79 Century Plaza Hotel $$$$ If you are not the president of the United States or a mere CEO arriving by helicopter you may feel intimidated. The scale, from the forecourt to the 8000-square-foot **Plaza Suite** that occupies the 30th floor of the recently added tower, is vast. The original hotel, an elliptical block designed by **Minoru Yamasaki**, opened in 1966 and contains 750 rooms and huge banquet facilities. In back is a 14-acre garden with a large pool. The 30-story 320-room **Tower**, inaugurated by **Ronald Reagan** in 1984, is more intimate and exclusive, handsomely furnished and full of museum-quality artworks. Afternoon tea is served in the **Living Room**, off the lobby. Health club. Restaurants include the informal **Garden Pavilion, Cafe Plaza,** and **Terrace.** ◆ Deluxe ◆ 2025 Avenue of the Stars. 277.2000, 800/228.3000; fax 551.3355

Within the Century Plaza Hotel:

La Chaumière ★★$$$$ Clublike room, paneled in alderwood, with 18th-century French pastoral paintings, serving such dishes as duck liver piccata, seafood with lobster saffron sauce, and calf's livers with a sauce of black currants and dry vermouth. Twenty-three wines are served by the glass. ◆ Eclectic ◆ M-Th 11:45AM-2:45PM, 6-10PM; F 11:45AM-2:45PM, 6-10:30PM; Sa 6-10:30PM; Su 6-10PM. 277.2000

Yamato ★$$$ Japanese food for unadventurous tastes in a serene setting with gracious service; tatami rooms available. ◆ Japanese ◆ M-F 11:30AM-2:30PM, 5-11PM; Sa 5-11PM; Su 4:30-10PM. 277.1840

79 Fox Plaza (1987, **Johnson, Fain & Pereira Associates**) The most dramatic addition to Century City since the original twin towers. This handsome 34-story office tower is faceted like a crystal, banded in salmon granite and gray-tinted glass, and positioned to dominate the sweep of Olympic Blvd and the midtown skyline. A complementary tower is planned. ◆ 2121 Avenue of the Stars

80 The ABC Entertainment Center and Century Plaza Towers (1975, **Minoru Yamasaki**) Yamasaki's silvery triangular towers are an improvement on his World Trade Center in New York. The low-rise offices and theaters, by another architect, are pedestrian. Ramps and escalators lead to an underpass that links the center to the hotel. The street, plaza, and concourse levels include a shopping mall, theaters, and restaurants. ◆ Avenue of the Stars at Constellation Blvd

At the ABC Entertainment Center and Century Plaza towers:

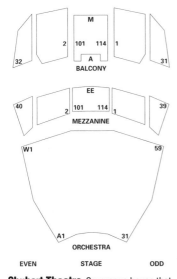

Shubert Theatre Cavernous house that hosts long runs of Broadway spectaculars. ◆ Seats 1829. Box office 201.1500, 800/233.3123

Cineplex Odeon Century Plaza Theaters The 600-seat **Theater Two**, with its big screen and luxurious rocking chairs, is one of the best places in LA to enjoy a first-run movie. But, be warned, the theater does not validate, and parking charges before 5PM on weekdays are exorbitant unless you sneak over from the **Century City Shopping Center**. ◆ 553.4291

LA has ¹/₅ of all swimming pools in the US.

The most American of all American cities.
Hamilton Basso

The Avenue Saloon $$ A New York-style bar with an excellent view. ◆ M-F 11:30AM-3PM, 5-10:30PM; Sa 5-10:30PM. 553.1855

Harry's Bar & American Grill ★★$$$ An oasis in the desert modeled on Harry's Bar in Florence. Harry's sponsors an annual Hemingway write-alike contest. Good carpaccio, veal scallopine, tortellini, and hamburgers with crisp onion rings in a pleasant room. Crowded at lunch. ◆ Italian ◆ M-F 11:30AM-3PM, 5:30-10:30PM; Sa 5:30-10:30PM. 277.2333

Sports Deli $$ Three 25-inch televisions for the sports fans; salt-water aquariums for others. ◆ Deli ◆ M 7:30AM-7:30PM; Tu-F

7:30AM-8:30PM; Sa-Su 10AM-8:30PM. 553.5800

81 Hy's Grill ★★$$$ A well-regarded Canadian steakhouse that also serves grilled fish, chicken, and fine potato pancakes. Live jazz and dancing in the evenings. ◆ American ◆ M-F 11:30AM-2:30PM, 6-11PM; Sa-Su 6-11PM. 10131 Constellation Blvd. 553.6000

82 Century City Shopping Center One of the earliest of LA's malls has been upgraded, with the addition of lively graphics, the **Marketplace** (by **BTA Associates** of Boston), and the **AMC** theaters, a superior multiplex in which the quality of sound, projection, and sightlines is far above average. The center comprises 100 stores on an 18-acre site, with ample free parking below. A major attraction is **Gelson's**, one of LA's top markets (277.4288). The anchor stores are **Bullock's** and **The Broadway**. Other stores include **Crate & Barrel** (well-designed housewares), **Brentano's** (exemplary general bookstore), **Jon Merten** (luxury men's wear), **La Nouvelle** (designer women's wear), **Godiva Chocolatier**, and a well-stocked newsstand. **Heaven** is full of glitzy kitsch and has a malt shop for the kids. The youngsters will also enjoy the **Imaginarium**, a hands-on toy store. ◆ M-F 10AM-6PM; Sa 10AM-9PM; Su noon-6PM. 10250 Little Santa Monica Blvd. 277.3898

At Century City Shopping Center:

Cabo Cabo Cabo $ Great bar. Two-hundred-fifty brands of spirits, 50 beers, and 50 tequilas. ◆ Mexican ◆ M-Th 11AM-10PM; F-Sa 11AM-11PM; Su 7:30-10PM. Century City Shopping Center. 552.2226

82 Stage Deli of New York ★$ Big, brightly lit place, with an authentic New York feel, oversize sandwiches, and egg creams. ◆ M-Th, Su 7:30AM-midnight; F-Sa 10AM-1AM. Century City Marketplace. 553.3354

Los Angeles has more palm trees —approximately 50,000 of them—than any other city in the U.S.

We find ourselves suddenly threatened by hordes of Yankee emigrants, who have already begun to flock into our country, and whose progress we cannot arrest.
Governor Pio Pico, 1846

Westside

In Los Angeles, as in most great cities, wealth and fashion have moved steadily west over the past century. Space, greenery, and hills are obvious attractions; proximity to the ocean brings cleaner air and evening breezes that make air conditioning unnecessary, even at the height of summer. The entire area is primarily residential, but there's a sharp contrast between the modest houses and apartments that predominate south of Wilshire and the lushly planted estates of **Bel Air, Brentwood**, and **Pacific Palisades** to the north of that axis. In this affluent section, private tennis courts and pools, Porsches and Mercedes are almost commonplace, and there are 5 major country clubs—the **Los Angeles, Hillcrest, Brentwood, Bel Air**, and **Riviera**. But in contrast to Beverly Hills, which flaunts its wealth, the golden ghettoes of the **Westside** are outwardly restrained, the homes hidden by trees and high walls, the preferred stores villagelike in their apparent simplicity.

Westwood attracts property speculators as a stray dog collects fleas, and they have trashed what may once have been LA's most charming village. Banal apartment and office towers have turned Wilshire Blvd into a traffic-clogged canyon. The Mediterranean-style shopping village, created by a single visionary developer 60 years ago, has been cheapened by a proliferation of undistinguished

banks, shacks, and fast-food chains. Modestly-scaled houses on leafy side streets are giving way to filing cabinets of stunning mediocrity that strain at the zoning limits and erode the spirit of place. **UCLA**, which might have set a good example, has been among the worst offenders.

The area was originally part of the 1843 land grant of *Rancho San Jose de Buenos Ayres*. The property changed hands many times, becoming the **John Wolfskill** ranch after 1884. In 1919, **Arthur Letts**, founder of **The Broadway** and **Bullock's** department stores, bought the farmland and turned a neat profit by selling it to the **Janss Company**. In 1926 Westwood was annexed to Los Angeles in a civic enlargement that included a large portion of the Santa Monica Mountains, the Pacific Palisades, and Brentwood. In 1929, when UCLA opened its Westwood campus, the Janss Company had already built 2000 houses and a bustling master-planned shopping village. The Westside boom had begun.

Westwood Village was designed for promenades, not cruising, and by the

1960s it was clogged with traffic, a problem that worsened as it succeeded Hollywood as the moviegoing center of LA, with what may be the greatest concentration of first-run theaters in the world. The intersection of Wilshire and Westwood boulevards is now the busiest in the city. But if you are young there is no better place to gather, and the sidewalks are jammed on weekends. High rents have driven out many of the quality stores; fast noshing is the dominant element today. There seems to be a croissant or cookie store on every block, a score of pizza places and ice-cream parlors, plus hamburgers, falafel, and frozen yogurt. Also clothes, from preppy to pop but mostly athletic; banks wooing tomorrow's big spenders; video outlets, and a Bullock's. Several bookstores have closed, but **B. Dalton** (904 Westwood Blvd, 208.7395) hangs on; there's a new independent, **Butler/Gabriel Books** (see below); and of course, the ubiquitous **Crown** discount outlet (10912 Lindbrook Dr, 208.1052). Parking lots fill quickly and on Friday and Saturday nights, it makes sense to leave your car in the large free parking lot behind the **Federal Building** (11000 Wilshire Blvd at Veteran Ave) and take the shuttle into the village. A gray **DASH** minibus runs a loop past all the major theaters every 10-15 minutes Friday 6:30PM-1:30AM, Saturday 11AM-1:30AM.

1 Village Theatre (1931, P.O. Lewis) The marvelous Spanish moderne tower still dominates the village, and the gleaming white stucco moldings, porte-cochere with free-standing box office, and golden flourishes within enhance the street and the pleasure of moviegoing. **Fox Studios** built a chain of Spanish theaters along the West Coast before the Depression put them out of business; the Deco FOX sign that crowns the tower has been refurbished and relit.
♦ 961 Broxton Ave. 208.5576

2 Bruin Theatre (1937, S. Charles Lee) A streamlined bijou with a sensuously curved and neon-lit marquee. Traffic between the Bruin and Village theaters and neighboring stores makes this the liveliest pedestrian crossing in the city.
♦ 948 Broxton Ave. 208.8998

3 Butler/Gabriel Books Personal selection and service; the kind of store that rekindles the joy of reading. ♦ M 10AM-9PM; Tu-Sa 10AM-10PM; Su 11AM-6PM. 919 Westwood Blvd. 208.4424

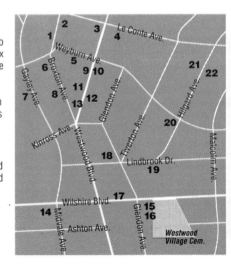

4 Contempo-Westwood Center Restored and refurbished in the 1960s by **A. Quincy Jones** and named for the fine Danish furniture store that occupies the center, this is a pleasant compound of shopping, dining, and theater all together. Ethnic crafts are sold alongside the furniture. The original Mission/Craftsman-style building was by **Stiles and Clements** in 1929. ◆ M-Tu, Th-Sa 10AM-7PM; W 10AM-9PM; Su noon-5PM. 10886 Le Conte Ave. 208.4107

Within the Contempo-Westwood Center:

Stratton's ★$$$ Dine under a canopy of wisteria in the lovely tile-and-stone patio or indoors in the old English-style dining room. The cooking and service have been much criticized of late, but the grilled swordfish with salsa has won acclaim. ◆ Eclectic ◆ Tu-Th, Su 11:30AM-2PM, 5:30-9:30PM; F-Sa 11:30AM-2PM, 5:30-10:30PM. 208.8880. Also at: 16925 Ventura Blvd, Encino. 818/986.2400

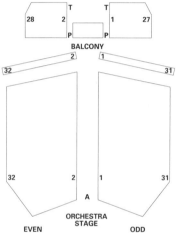

BALCONY

ORCHESTRA
STAGE
EVEN   ODD

Westwood Playhouse A small theater for revues and musicals with good sightlines and a thrust stage. ◆ Seats 498. 208.6500

5 Wilger Co. Traditional men's clothes by **Kilgour, French & Stanbury**, and some sharper Italian styles. ◆ M-W, F-Sa 10AM-6PM; Th 10AM-7:30PM. 10924 Weyburn Ave. 208.4321

6 Mario's $$ Cheerful, unsophisticated Southern Italian restaurant and pizzeria, jammed with students. ◆ Italian ◆ M-F 11:30AM-11:00PM; Sa-Su 4PM-midnight. 1001 Broxton Ave. 208.7077

7 Breadstiks Astonishingly, a full-service independent supermarket, with fresh takeout dishes, has taken on the convenience stores. ◆ M-F 8AM-10PM; Sa-Su 9AM-10PM. 1057 Gayley Ave. 209.1111

7 Videotheque Good stock and a knowledgeable staff. ◆ M-Th, Su 10AM-10PM; F-Sa 10AM-midnight. 1035 Gayley Ave. 824.9922. Also at: 8800 Sunset Blvd, W. Hollywood. 657.8800; 330 N. Beverly Dr, Beverly Hills. 858.7600

8 Stratton's Grill ★$$ Unpretentious, moderately priced saloon/grill that's now a better bet than its parent. Splendid period decor—polished tile, gleaming mahogany, a huge oval bar, and

animal heads on the walls. Chili, mesquite-grilled chicken and fish, and sausages with apples are dependable; desserts, from sundaes to apple and pecan pies, are the real homemade article. Service by clean-cut students is exemplary. Noisy bar scene downstairs; ask for an upstairs booth if you want to converse. ◆ American ◆ M-Th, Su 11AM-11PM; F-Sa 11AM-midnight. 1037 Broxton Ave. 208.0488

9 Bel Air Camera Wide range of camera, audio, and video equipment. Competitive prices and expert service. ◆ M-Sa 9AM-6PM; Su 11AM-4PM. 1025 Westwood Blvd. 208.5150

10 The Good Earth $$ Comfort and quality at reasonable prices; one of a chain of health food restaurants and homespun bakeries. ◆ Organic ◆ M-Th, Su 9AM-11PM; F-Sa 9AM-midnight. 1002 Westwood Blvd. 208.8215

Westside

10 Campbell-Tolstad Stationers Survivor of a more gracious age, selling fine pens and writing papers alongside more prosaic needs. Good old-fashioned service in new premises. ◆ M-Sa 10AM-9PM; Su noon-6PM. 1002 Westwood Blvd. 208.4322

11 Alice's Restaurant $ A favorite with students and moviegoers, serving dependable fare in a friendly and informal setting. ◆ American ◆ Daily 10AM-midnight. 1043 N. Westwood Blvd. 208.3171

12 Yesterday's $ When the day's shopping has you beat, the fresh-fruit daiquiris are heaven-sent. ◆ California ◆ Daily 11:30AM-1:30AM. 1056A Westwood Blvd. 208.8000

13 Contempo Casuals (1929, **Allison & Allison**) First of the Village's Spanish landmarks, this handsome domed structure with its portico and arched windows anchors a major street intersection. **Morphosis** adapted the space for use as a trendy women's clothes store. ◆ M-Sa 10AM-9PM; Su noon-6PM. 1099 Westwood Blvd. 208.8503

Restaurants/Clubs: Red   **Hotels:** Blue
Shops/Parks: Green   **Sights/Culture:** Black

14 The Tower (1988, **Helmut Jahn**) Pretentiousness amid the mediocrity of Westwood's highrises—a striped marble concoction from Chicago's *meister* of slick. ♦ 10940 Wilshire Blvd

15 Westwood Inn Motor Hotel $$ Convenient and budget-priced. ♦ 10820 Wilshire Blvd. 474.1573

16 Westwood Memorial Cemetery The graves of **Marilyn Monroe, Natalie Wood**, and **Peter Lorre** are tucked away behind the Avco Center movie houses. ♦ Daily 8AM-4PM. 1218 Glendon Ave. 272.2484

17 Armand Hammer Museum of Art (1990, **Edward Larabee Barnes**) Hammer broke a pledge to donate his art to LACMA in order to build this monument, which squats, shiny and windowless, like a footstool beneath his corpo-

rate tower. As architecture it's another nail in the coffin of the Village; as an art repository it has been derided by professionals for planning to put profit ahead of curatorial expertise. As a showcase for Hammer's masterpieces and visiting shows, it may surmount these handicaps. ♦ Admission. Daily 11AM-6PM. 10889 Wilshire Blvd. 208.3915

18 Hamlet Gardens ★★$$$ **Marilyn Lewis** of **Hamburger Hamlet** fame opened this crisp and savvy restaurant in a Spanish-style brick rotunda. The salmon tartare, pizzas, salads, and grills justify the high prices. The guacamole is ground at your table with mortar and pestle. ♦ California ♦ M-Th 11:30AM-3PM (pizza 5:30PM), 6-10:30PM; F-Sa 11:30AM-11:30PM. 1139 Glendon Ave. 824.1818

19 Flax Art Supplies An eye-catching red sculpture by **Franco Assetto** wraps the front of this shop, with its 2 floors of brushes and paints, papers and drafting equipment. A valuable resource. ♦ M-F 8AM-5:30PM; Sa 9AM-5PM. 10852 Lindbrook Dr. 208.3529

20 International Student Center $ A multilingual restaurant operated by UCLA. ♦ Daily 11AM-2PM. 1023 Hilgard Ave. 825.3384

21 Hilgard House Hotel $$$ Small, elegant hotel a few minutes from the Village and UCLA. ♦ 927 Hilgard Ave. 208.3945, 800/826.3934; fax 208.1972

22 Westwood Marquis $$$$ An oasis of civility and luxury across the street from UCLA and a short walk from the Village. General manager **Jacques P. Camus** maintains a high standard of service in this medium-size all-suites hotel. The rooms are spacious and well-furnished; there's a leafy garden and pool and 2 restaurants. The **Dynasty Room** offers classic French cuisine in an elegant setting and a special 600-calorie *cuisine minceur* dinner. Formal teas are served in a handsome lounge. There is a concierge, complimentary limousine service, and spas for men and women. ♦ Deluxe ♦ 930 Hilgard Ave. 208.8765, 800/421.2317; fax 824.0355

23 Strathmore Apartments (1937, **Richard Neutra**) When this modern bungalow court rose from a then-empty hillside, its stark lines attracted such tenants as **Orson Welles, Charles** and **Ray Eames** (who experimented with laminated plywood in the bathtub), **Clifford Odets**, and **Luise Rainer**. It remains one of the best preserved of several Neutra apartment buildings in and around the Village. Private residence. ♦ 11005 Strathmore Dr

24 Tischler House (1949, **Rudolph Schindler**) A geometrically sculptured house; one of the architect's last and best works. Private residence. ♦ 175 Greenfield Ave

25 University of California at Los Angeles UCLA is celebrated worldwide, and it has grown to be a city within the city. It began in 1881 as a state normal school, moved to Westwood in 1929, and today has the largest enrollment (33,500 students) of the 9 UC campuses. The first 4 buildings—Italian Romanesque brick palazzos, laid out around a grassy quadrangle—remain the best. Most of the 85-plus that followed are merely dull; some, like the newly-completed **Doris Stein Eye Research Center**, are as inspiring as Mao's tomb in Beijing. The **Ueberroth Building**, facing out to the Village, could be mistaken for a military bunker. Happily, the gardeners make up for the architects' lack of talent. The 411-acre campus is beautifully landscaped with superb trees and exotic plants and provides numerous spots for walking, jogging, or quiet reverie. Perhaps the moral is if you are asked for a donation, make it for a tree or a scholarship, not a building. (This may change—the review process has been upgraded and some reputable architects have been hired.) Major schools include medicine, geology, botany, engineering, geography, and management. The graduate schools are renowned in interdisciplinary areas, such as neurophysiology. Library holdings (5.5 million books) are among the world's largest.

The best way to get to the campus is by bicycle or shuttle bus; cars are restricted to a few ring roads. To park in one of the perimeter structures you should buy a token from one of the information booths located at the main entrances on Sunset Blvd and Hilgard and Le Conte avenues.

At the University of California at Los Angeles:

A Walking tours depart from the **Visitors Center** in Room 1417 of the Ueberroth Building, weekdays 8AM-5PM. Free maps are available in different languages. For group and weekend tours call 206.8147. The free **Campus Express** minibuses circulate from the Village through the campus every 5 minutes, weekdays 7:15AM-6PM. ♦ 10945 Le Conte Ave. 825.4321

The city of Philip Marlowe and Charlie Chaplin, of Mickey Mouse and Frank Lloyd Wright, of weirdos, professors, gangsters, gurus, millionaires and nice ordinary people, a failed Jerusalem, a low-density Babylon.
Mark Girouard *Cities and People* 1985

Royce Hall

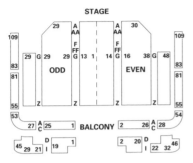

B Royce Hall (1929, **Allison & Allison**) One of the buildings of the original quadrangle, with classrooms, offices, and a public auditorium that presents a concert series featuring world-famous performers during the school year. ◆ Seats 1850. UCLA Central Cultural Events Box Office 825.9261, evening box office 478.7578

C Powell Library (1928) Originally the main library of the campus, it now houses the undergraduate collection. The rotunda and grand staircase are notable. ◆ Reference desk 825.1938

D Haines Hall (1928) Another original building. Located within is the **Museum of Cultural History**, which presents changing anthropological and archeological exhibitions of material and is scheduled to move to the new **Fowler Building**, west of Royce Hall. ◆ Free. W-Su noon-5PM. 825.4361

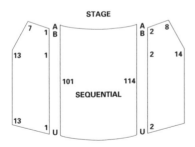

E Schoenberg Hall Named for the composer who lived in Los Angeles between 1933 and 1951 and taught at USC and UCLA. The **School of Music** and **Institute of Ethnomusicology** are located here, as well as a small auditorium that hosts unusual concerts. ◆ Seats 550. UCLA Central Cultural Events Box Office 825.9261

F University Research Library (1964, **A. Quincy Jones**) A superb reference collection; loans available to students, faculty, and anyone who makes a donation to become a *Friend of the Library*. Exhibitions of literary material from the **Department of Special Collections** are dis-

played on the 1st floor. A guide to all of UCLA's specialized libraries is available. For hours call 825.8301. ◆ Reference desk 825.4731

G Dickson Art Center A complex of classrooms, art studios, library, and the **Grunwald Center for the Graphic Arts**, which collects prints, drawings, and illustrated books. The **Belt Library of Vinciana** is open to students by appointment. Most important is the **Frederick S. Wight Art Gallery**—one of the most adventurous and eclectic in LA—which presents exhibitions of contemporary and historical art. The small shop in the gallery sells art books, posters, and crafts. ◆ Free. Tu 11AM-8PM; W-F 11AM-5PM; Sa-Su 1-5PM. Closed July-August. 825.1461

H Melnitz Hall UCLA Film, Radio and Television Archives presents nightly screenings when school is in session. A great place

for archival classics, and series of old and new movies from around the world, plus video treasures. Some are admission-free.
◆ 206.3456 (recording), 206.8013 (office)

I Franklin Murphy Sculpture Garden An idyllic 5-acre greensward that looks its best when the jacaranda trees bloom in April. Major work by **Jean Arp**, **Henri Matisse**, **Joan Miró**, **Henry Moore**, **Auguste Rodin**, **David Smith**, and others.

J North Campus Student Center A popular campus dining spot with the same low prices as all UCLA restaurant facilities. ◆ M-F 7:30AM-10PM; Sa-Su 10AM-5PM. 825.1177

K Kerckhoff Hall Student activity offices and a moderately priced coffeehouse. ◆ M-F 7AM-1AM; Sa-Su 10AM-midnight. 825.0611

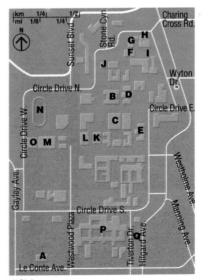

UCLA

Restaurants/Clubs: Red   **Hotels:** Blue
Shops/Parks: Green   **Sights/Culture:** Black

L Ackerman Student Union In the center of campus, housing the student store and the **Tree House Restaurant**. Actually 4 restaurants in one, the Tree House has fresh fruits and salads and a full-meal section, all at very low prices. The student store has a fine selection of academic books and a full range of UCLA-imprinted wares. ◆ M-F 8AM-12:30AM; Sa-Su 11AM-mindight. 825.0611

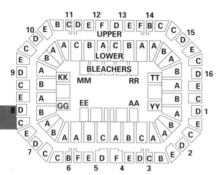

M Pauley Pavilion (1965, **Welton Beckett & Associates**) Home of the UCLA **Bruins** basketball team. Concerts, cultural events, and volleyball games are also held in the arena. ◆ Seats 12,545. UCLA Central Sports Ticket Box Office 825.2101

N Drake Stadium Track and field stadium. ◆ Seats 11,000. Event information 825.4546

O LA Tennis Center Built for the 1984 Olympics ◆ Seats 9500. Event information 825.4546

P Center for Health Sciences The entire southern end of the campus, from Tiverton to Gayley fronting on Le Conte, is occupied by one of the largest medical complexes in the nation. The schools of Medicine, Dentistry, Nursing, and Public Health are located here, as well as 8 research institutes, including the world-famous **Neuropsychiatric Institute** and the **Jules Stein Eye Institute**. The **UCLA Hospital and Clinics**, also located in the complex, operates a 24-hour emergency room, which is reached via an entrance at Tiverton and Le Conte. ◆ Emergency 825.2111, physicians referral 825.0881, 800/825.2631

Q Mathias Botanical Gardens An 8-acre shaded canyon, on the southeast end of campus off Hilgard and Le Conte, planted to create a peaceful, woodsy retreat with mature specimens of unusual size. No restroom facilities. ◆ Free. M-F 8AM-5PM; Sa-Su 8AM-4PM. Garden information 825.3620

26 Century Wilshire Hotel $$ Middling-size hotel with garden patio and fully equipped kitchen units. ◆ 10776 Wilshire Blvd. 474.4506, 800/421.7223; fax 474.2535

27 Del Capri Hotel $$ Most units have kitchens; a Continental breakfast is offered every morning. ◆ 10587 Wilshire Blvd. 474.3511; fax 824.0594

28 The Beverly Hills Comstock $$$ Low-key, reliable hotel in a converted apartment building. There's a homey feeling that makes it popular with those on extended visits; you feel as though you're staying at a friend's garden court condo rather than in a hotel. Each of the 73 suites has a living room, dining area, kitchen, and one or more bedrooms. Courtyard with swimming pool. ◆ 10300 Wilshire Blvd. 275.5575, 800/343.2184; fax 278.3325

29 Lunaria ★★★$$$ **Bernard Jacoupy** has left **Le Meridien** in Newport Beach and has brought **Antoine's** chef, **Dominique Chavanon**, to his new restaurant. It's a treasure: cool, spacious dining room, caring service, good accoustics, and a reasonably priced menu. Standout dishes include seared scallops with green lentils, smoked duck with onion tart, gratin of sea bass with pesto, and mouth-watering desserts. ◆ French ◆ Tu-F 11AM-2PM, 6-11PM; Sa-Su 6-11PM. 10351 Santa Monica Blvd. 282.8870

30 Bel-Air Wine Merchant Broad selection of European and California wines, including many small labels. ◆ M-Sa 10:30AM-7:30PM. 10421 Santa Monica Blvd. 474.9518

31 Champagne ★★★$$$ Chef **Patrick Healy** and his wife, **Sophie**, have opened this elegant auberge on a deserted stretch, and have proved that brilliance outshines location. The service is polished, the atmosphere unpretentious, and the food fantastic. Healy divides his menu into 3 sections—contemporary, rustic, and spa—as a demonstration of his versatility. ◆ French ◆ M-Sa 6-10:30PM. 10506 Santa Monica Blvd. 470.8446

32 Mormon Temple (1955, **Edward Anderson**) The 257-foot tower crowned with a 15-foot gold-leaf statue of the angel Moroni makes this a familiar landmark on the LA skyline. Seen from Santa Monica Blvd it looks like a gigantic '40s cocktail cabinet. This is the largest temple of the Church of Jesus Christ of Latter Day Saints outside of Salt Lake City, and is open only to church members. Visitors may tour the grounds or the **Visitor Information Center**, open daily 9AM-9:30PM. ◆ 10777 Santa Monica Blvd. 474.1549

33 Ramayani ★$ For the hungry and penurious, the rijsttafel (multicourse rice feast) promises a pleasurable orgy of eating. ◆ Indonesian ◆ Tu-Su 11:30AM-9PM. 1777 Westwood Blvd. 477.3315

34 La Bruschetta ★★★$$$ Elegant service and decor; excellent Northern Italian cuisine. Portions are homestyle hearty, and there's a very good wine list. Recommended are the osso buco (veal shank), roasted squab, and any of the pasta dishes. ◆ Italian ◆ M-Th 6-10PM; F-Sa 6-11PM. 1621 Westwood Blvd. 477.1052

35 Westwood Fettucine Bar $$ Tomato, spinach, sage, and basil noodles (to name a few) can be matched with one of over 35 sauces, from marinara to a white-truffle sauce. Wine and beer. ◆ Italian ◆ Tu-Su 5-10PM. 1553 Westwood Blvd. 473.5728

36 Sisterhood Bookstore Books of every kind by and about women; also music and cards. Frequent humanist and feminist readings. ◆ M-F 10AM-8PM; Sa-Su 10AM-6PM. 1351 Westwood Blvd. 477.7300

37 The Spanish Book Store Spanish and Latin American titles. ◆ M-Sa 10AM-6PM. 10977 Santa Monica Blvd. 475.0453

37 Jasmine Tree ★★$$ Upscale Mandarin restaurant on the 2nd level of a mini-mall. The Taiwanese chef prepares excellent mushroom-and-duck soup, pan-fried dumplings, Peking duck, and fiery *kung pao* squid. ◆ Chinese ◆ M-F 11:30AM-10PM; Sa-Su noon-10PM. 11057 Santa Monica Blvd. 444.7171

38 Shamshiry ★$ Popular family restaurant serving huge portions of shish kebab, chicken *faisanjan* (braised in pomegranate sauce), and pilaf in a bare-bones setting at modest prices. This stretch of Westwood has been dubbed *Teherangeles* for its concentration of Iranian bakeries and restaurants ◆ Persian ◆ M-Th, Su noon-10PM; F-Sa noon-11PM. 1916 Westwood Blvd. 474.1410

38 Booksellers Row Along Westwood Blvd between Santa Monica and Pico boulevards are several small specialized bookstores.

38 Technical Book Company Professional and scientific books. ◆ M-Sa 9:30AM-5:30PM. 2056 Westwood Blvd. 475.5711

38 Vagabond Books Modern fiction, movies, and theater. ◆ M-Sa 11AM-6PM; Su noon-5PM. 2076 Westwood Blvd. 475.2700

Koutoubin

39 Koutoubia ★★$$$ Named for a famous mosque in Marrakesh, this desert tent with its hassocks and low brass tables is a showcase of the customs and cuisine of the Magreb. Chef/owner **Michael Ohayon** is a master of couscous and *tajines* (well-done lamb cooked with onion, parsley, cilantro, honey, raisins, and other fruits), but will prepare special treats if you call ahead—fresh brains with coriander sauce, *b'stilla* (flaky pastry stuffed with chicken, cinnamon, and spices) with squab, and sea bass with red chilis, all with delicious anise bread. ◆ Moroccan ◆ Tu-Su 6PM-10PM, sometimes later on weekends. 2116 Westwood Blvd. 475.0729

40 Wally's Liquor and Gourmet Foods A California redwood and high-tech store that offers the best in food and wine. Boutique vineyard labels unavailable elsewhere, plus a cheese department that includes buffalo mozzarella, California goat cheese, pizzas, and chili dogs. Ever-present owner **Steve Wallace** knows everything about California wines. ◆ M-Sa 9AM-9PM; Su 10AM-6PM. 2107 Westwood Blvd. 475.0606

41 Barry Levin Science fiction and fantasy books. By appointment, only. ◆ 2253 Westwood Blvd. 458.6111

42 Patout's ★★★$$$ **André** and **Gigi Patout** have brought to LA the warm hospitality and authentic Cajun cuisine of their 3 restaurants in Louisiana. Leaf-patterned walls, fronds of Spanish moss, and blond wood create a pleasing setting for dishes that change with the seasons and incorporate what's fresh in from Louisiana. Crab, shrimp, and cream, in different combinations, recur throughout the menu, which is rich but not cloying. The shrimp remoulade, chicken-and-sausage gumbo, Lady Fish (grilled redfish topped with crab and shrimp in lemon-butter vermouth sauce), and the chicken Elizabeth are good choices. ◆ Cajun ◆ M-Tu, Sa 6-10PM; W-F 11:30AM-2:30PM, 6-10PM; Su 11:30AM-3PM. 2260 Westwood Blvd. 475.7100

Westside

43 The Apple Pan $ Midwestern basics draw crowds at all hours of day and night to this homely clapboard cottage. ◆ American ◆ M-Th, Su 11AM-midnight; F-Sa 11AM-1AM. 10801 W. Pico Blvd. 475.3585

43 La Cite des Livres Books, maps, and tapes from France. ◆ Tu-Sa 10AM-6PM. 2326 Westwood Blvd. 475.0658

44 Nizam ★★$ A lovely couple runs one of LA's nicest Indian restaurants. Exemplary renditions of standards and such unusual dishes as *dai papri* (fried lentil wafer chips tossed with potatoes, onion, cilantro, and yogurt). ◆ Indian ◆ M-Sa 11:30AM-3PM, 5:30-11PM. 10871 W. Pico Blvd. 470.1441

44 Anna's $$ Sicilian-style thick-crusted or crispy thin-crusted pizza; the sauce is good and the cheese plentiful. Light on toppings. ◆ Pizza ◆ M-Th 11:30AM-11PM; F 11:30AM-midnight; Sa 4PM-midnight; Su 4PM-11PM. 10929 W. Pico Blvd. 474.0102

44 Needham Book Finders Vintage and out-of-print titles. By appointment, only. ◆ 2317 Westwood Blvd. 395.0538

44 Matteo's $$$$ A celebrity hangout for the older generation, especially on Sunday nights. People go to see and be seen, more than to eat. ◆ Italian ◆ Tu-Su 5PM-11PM. 2321 Westwood Blvd. 475.4521

45 C.G. Jung Library, Archive & Bookstore Everything you ever wanted to know about analytical psychology. ◆ M-Sa noon-5PM. 10349 W. Pico Blvd. 556.1193

A trip through a sewer in a glass-bottom boat.
Wilson Milzner

The 1984 Summer Olympics, held in Los Angeles, was the most widely watched ever. 2500 technicians, 56 cameras, 660 miles of cable, and 2 communications satellites brought the Olympics to over 120 nations. 187 1/2 hours of Olympic events were televised, nearly 2 1/2 times as many as the Montreal Games in 1976.

Restaurants/Clubs: Red   Hotels: Blue
Shops/Parks: Green   **Sights/Culture:** Black

un ristorante

46 Primi Plus ★★★$$$ **Piero Selvaggio** of **Valentino** opened Primi for anyone who likes to make a meal from first courses. In fact, the portions are as generous as main courses in more pretentious restaurants. Pastas are the forte; risotto *nero* (cooked in black squid's ink) is one of the stars. The choices range from bread and salami with extra-virgin olive oil to grilled quail and hearty traditional fare. There's

Westside

a choice of ambiance between the shiny high-style dining room and a plainer covered patio. Takeout. ◆ Italian ◆ M-Th, Su 11:30AM-3PM, 5:30-11PM; F-Sa 11:30AM-3PM, 5:30PM-midnight. 10543 Pico Blvd. 474.0632

47 John O'Groats ★$ Great breakfasts and lunches with tartan touches—like biscuits, fish and chips, and shortbread. ◆ Scottish ◆ M-Sa 7AM-3PM. 10628 W. Pico Blvd. 204.0692

48 Westside Pavilion (1987, **Jerde Partnership**) Another indoor shopping mall, with glass-vaulted atrium and trendy paste-on Postmodern design. In form it borrows from 19th-century arcades, but the colors and details are overdone and the free parking is a disaster. **Nordstrom** and **May Co** department stores anchor 3 levels of boutiques. It's a predictable mix of clothes, gifts, fast food, and a GTE phone mart. The **Goldwyn fourplex** often has exclusive runs of the better independent releases. ◆ M-F 10AM-9:30PM; Sa 10AM-7PM; Su 11AM-6PM. 10800 W. Pico Blvd (Westwood Blvd) 474.5940

48 Nordstrom New branch of a Seattle-based chain, whose stock and service are exemplary. Most remarkably, they give the customer the benefit of the doubt. By example, they are forcing improvements on competing stores. Shoes and stylish American clothes are specialties. ◆ M-F 10AM-9:30PM; Sa 10AM-7PM; Su 11AM-6PM. 10800 W. Pico Blvd (Westwood Blvd) 470.6155

48 Sisley ★$$ Dependable pizzas and homemade pastas for exhausted shoppers. ◆ M-Th, Su 11:30AM-10PM; F-Sa 11:30AM-10:30PM. 10800 W. Pico Blvd. 446.3030

49 Bryan's County Saloon ★$ Woodsy Western interior and a finger-licking choice of sliced beef in a spicy sauce, beef hot-links, beans, cornbread, and peach cobbler. ◆ American ◆ M-Th 4-10PM; F-Sa 11AM-11PM; Su 10:30AM-9PM. 10916 W. Pico Blvd. 474.4263

The Bird of Paradise is the official flower of Los Angeles.

50 Disc Connection Original-cast and soundtrack albums are a specialty of this eclectic used record store. ◆ M-Th, Sa 11AM-7PM; F 11AM-9PM; Su noon-6PM. 10970 W. Pico Blvd. 208.7211

51 Petal House Architect **Eric Moss** has taken a modest suburban house and, using the simplest materials, opened it up like a flower. Private residence. ◆ 2828 Midvale Ave

52 Hu's Szechwan Restaurant ★$ Bring your own beer to this bare-bones joint, which is packed with locals digging their chopsticks into the spicy Szechuan specialties. ◆ Chinese ◆ Tu-Sa noon-2:30PM, 5-9:30PM. 10450 National Blvd. 837.0252

53 Trader Joe's Great offers on wine and cheese, coffee and nuts, plus exotica that are wittily described in the monthly catalog. Branches all over town. ◆ Daily 9AM-10PM. 10850 National Blvd. 474.9289

54 Circuit City Part of a national chain that offers electronics and appliances at competitive prices, *and* caring service—a rare combination. ◆ M-F 11AM-9PM; Sa 10AM-7PM; Su 11AM-6PM. 3115 Sepulveda Blvd. 391.3144

55 Orleans ★★$$$ The Cajun-Creole craze has passed as quickly as it came, but this exuberant shoot from the **Paul Prudhomme** tree is still flowering. Gumbo, zesty shrimp creole, blackened prime rib and redfish, and jambalaya are hard to resist—but save room for the bread pudding with Bourbon sauce. ◆ Cajun/Creole ◆ M-Th 11:30AM-2:30PM, 6-10:30PM; F 11:30AM-2:30PM, 5:30-10:30PM; Sa 5:30-10:30PM; Su 5-10:30PM. 11705 National Blvd. 479.4187

56 From Spain ★$ Chef **Juan Rodriguez** prepares such Catalan dishes as grilled fresh sardines with garlic, sautéed *chorizo*, and grilled pork chops with red-pepper sauce. Bread with serrano ham is always a good bet, and don't miss the suckling pig if it's available. ◆ Spanish ◆ M-F 11AM-2:30PM, 5-10PM; Sa 3-10PM. 11510 W. Pico Blvd. 479.6740

57 Chan Dara ★★$$ Third of a family that began in Hollywood and Larchmont Village. **Don Carsten**'s neon-accented interior glows with rich lacquers, and the kitchen also sparkles. The vegetable soup (crammed with goodies), huge and flavorful naked shrimp, broad noodles with chicken, and beef *panang* are stand-outs. ◆ Thai ◆ M-F noon-11PM; Sa 5PM-midnight; Su 5-11PM. 11940 W. Pico Blvd. 479.4461

58 Bellini's Trattoria ★$ Innovative pasta dishes in this modern neighborhood place include *farfalle* with artichoke hearts and walnuts, and saffron linguini with fresh tomato *coulis*. ◆ Italian ◆ M-F 11:30AM-3PM, 5:30-11:30PM; Sa-Su 5:30-11:30PM. 12021 W. Pico Blvd. 477.4057

58 Music Machine Leading rock, blues, and reggae groups perform through the week. Large dance floor and 2 bars. ◆ Cover. Tu-Su call for showtimes. 12220 W. Pico Blvd. 820.5150

58 Rent-A-Wreck Owner **Dave Schwartz** has successfully franchised his idea country-wide, but still manages this, the original facility. Don't say anything rude about the poster over the counter or you may be turned away. If you pass the test, you can choose from hundreds of cars with personality. Vintage Mustang convertibles are a specialty. The scruffy surfaces are deceptive; the cars rarely let you down and will dramatize your disdain of conventional status symbols. In the land of Mercedes, a battered Chevy is king. ◆ M-F 7:30AM-6:30PM; Sa 8AM-4PM; Su 8AM-1PM. 12333 W. Pico Blvd. 478.0676, 478.4393

59 Kirk Paper A paper supermarket; wheel your basket down the aisles and pick up reams of the stuff, plus every kind of office supply, at budget prices. Indifferent service. ◆ M-F 7:30AM-5PM; Sa 8AM-4PM. 11800 Olympic Blvd. 478.4026

60 Eureka Brewery & Restaurant ★★$$ **Wolfgang Puck**'s brewpub features his own beer prepared in glowing copper tanks that also serve as major adornment's in **Barbara Lazaroff**'s neo-industrial interior. The menu includes Spagolike pizza, homemade sausage and salami, Thai *satay*, and salads. Very loud; bring earplugs or exercise your vocal chords. ◆ Eclectic ◆ Daily 11AM-2PM, 6-11PM. 1845 S. Bundy Dr. 207.1000

61 Sawtelle Boulevard Named for a subdivision that didn't take, Sawtelle is now a thriving Japanese/Mexican community of small businesses, most related to the gardening trade. ◆ Santa Monica Blvd-Olympic Blvd

61 Cafe Katsu ★★$$ Japanese-influenced French cooking in a tiny, spare space. Owned by **Katsu Michite**, whose **Los Feliz** restaurant is a sushi shrine. ◆ French ◆ M-Sa 11:30AM-2:30PM, 6PM-10PM. 2117 Sawtelle Blvd. 477.5444

62 Yamaguchi Bonsai Nursery Buy a 100-year-old miniature tree, lotus stock, or leave your bonsai here while you vacation. ◆ M-Sa 7AM-5PM; Su 8:30AM-4PM. 1905 Sawtelle Blvd. 473.5444

63 The Wine House Huge and eclectic stock of wines, beers, and spirits, competitively priced. ◆ M-Sa 10AM-7PM; Su noon-6PM. 2311 Cotner Ave. 479.3731

64 LAX Luggage One of a row of discount stores, LAX has good prices on name-brand bags. ◆ M-Sa 10AM-6PM; Su 11AM-5PM. 2233 Sepulveda Blvd. 478.2661

65 Odyssey Theatre Artistic Director **Ron Sossi** heads this 3-stage avant-garde theater offering plays and performances. Recently moved from its old home at Bundy and Ohio. ◆ Three theaters, each seats 99. 2055 S. Sepulveda Blvd. 477.2055

66 The Sports Club LA In earlier times we built temples to God or Mammon; now it's the body beautiful that's enshrined, and this is St. Peter's. There are 100,000 square feet, marble-paved or carpeted, where subscribers can exercise, work off steam, and save a trip to the singles bar. Members only. ◆ M-F 6AM-11PM, Sa-Su 8AM-7:30PM. 1835 Sepulveda Blvd. 473.1447

67 Nuart Theater One of LA's last surviving movie repertory houses showing adventurous new work, theme series, classics, and camp favorites. Fine streamline neon marquee. ◆ 11272 Santa Monica Blvd. 478.6379

Westside

68 The Isle of California Much-faded classic mural, done in the late '60s by the **LA Fine Arts Squad**, shows the rugged Arizona coastline after the *Big One* has sent California off into the Pacific. ◆ Santa Monica Blvd at Butler Ave

68 Gianfranco ★$ This deli/restaurant is a useful place to go before or after an art film at the neighboring Nuart or Royal theaters. Stick to the antipasti and homemade pastas. ◆ Italian ◆ M-Sa 11AM-3PM, 5:30-11PM. 11363 Santa Monica Blvd. 477.7777

69 Javan ★$ Crisp black-and-white interior, delicious off-beat dishes, and a full license. Specials have included *zereshk polo* (chicken with rice pilaf flavored with dried barberries), *gheymeh* (lamb shank with split yellow peas), and steamed spinach with tart yogurt. ◆ Persian ◆ Daily 11:30AM-11PM. 11600 Santa Monica Blvd. 207.5555

70 Toledo ★$$$ Authentic Castilian cuisine served in 2 dark, cozy rooms. It helps to love garlic. One of the few places to go for real paella. ◆ Spanish ◆ Tu-Th 11:30AM-2PM, 5:30-10:30PM; F 11:30AM-2PM, 5:30-11PM; Sa 5:30-11PM; Su 4:30-10PM. 11613 Santa Monica Blvd. 477.2400

70 Trattoria Angeli ★★★$$$ Ambitious version of the **Angeli Caffe** on Melrose by the same team. Architect **Michele Saee** (formerly with **Morphosis**) has created a dramatic high-ceilinged wood-and-steel structure within an old warehouse, preserving its original bow trusses. Chef **Evan Kleiman** (author of 3 exemplary cookbooks) gives full rein to her passion for rustic regional fare. Manager **John Strobel** runs a tight ship and has assembled one of LA's best Italian and California wine lists. The room can get crowded and noisy, but never like Melrose. Private dining room upstairs. ◆ Italian ◆ M-F 11:30AM-2:30PM, 6PM-late; Sa-Su 5PM-late. 11651 Santa Monica Blvd. 478.1191

Restaurants/Clubs: Red   **Hotels:** Blue
Shops/Parks: Green   **Sights/Culture:** Black

71 Ike Ichi ★$$ LA outpost of a 9-generation-old sushi bar in Osaka. The variety of clams, fish eggs, and unusual fish is astounding. ◆ Japanese ◆ Tu-Th 11:30AM-2:30PM, 5-10PM; F-Sa 11:30AM-2:30PM, 5-11PM. 11951 Santa Monica Blvd. 477.1390

72 Bombay Cafe ★$ Tandoori chicken, samosas, *sev puri* (bread layered with vegetables and chutney), and homemade mango and ginger ice cream are good choices in this simple 2nd-floor mall restaurant. ◆ Indian ◆ Tu-Th 11AM-10PM; F 11AM-11PM; Sa 4-11PM; Su 4-10PM. 12113 Santa Monica Blvd. 820.2070

Brentwood

West of Bel-Air, this exclusive residential area is chic, casual, and countrified. Stucco and clapboard cottages and substantial houses sit

Westside

well back from leafy streets. You could imagine yourself in a small town, but this is high-rent territory, and the condo builders are moving in. The roads that wind up into the hills have an even more rustic feel. Brentwood's main street is San Vicente Boulevard, whose green median is lined with huge coral trees, making it a shady trail for joggers.

73 Bicycle Shop Cafe $$ A bistro-type café offering crêpes, salads, and light dinners amid antique and modern cycling regalia. ◆ French ◆ M-Th, Su 11AM-midnight; F-Sa 11AM-1AM. 12217 Wilshire Blvd. 826.7831

73 Sostanza ★★$$ Dramatically muraled *ristorante* in a new office building offers an innovative selection of delicious food. **Michael Feker**'s specialties include pasta with lentils and porcini, and rack of lamb with peanut sauce. ◆ Italian ◆ M-F, Su 11:30AM-2:30PM, 6-10PM; F-Sa 11:30AM-2:30PM, 6-11PM. 12100 Wilshire Blvd. 207.4273

74 The Junk Store Vintage men's and women's clothes, including silk Hawaiian shirts; all clean and beautiful. ◆ M-F, Su noon-6PM; Sa 11AM-6PM. 11900 Wilshire Blvd. 479.7413

75 Fragrant Vegetable ★$$ Branch of the acclaimed original in Monterey Park. Elegant decor and refined vegetarian dishes, with flavors much blander than the original's. ◆ Chinese ◆ M-Th 11:30AM-11PM; F-Sa 11:30AM-11:30PM. 11859 Wilshire Blvd. 312.1442

76 Aashiana ★$ An elegant 2nd-floor restaurant where the stars are seafood—calamari, fish *tikka*, and fish Goa; also the breads. ◆ Indian ◆ M-F, Su 11:30AM-2:30PM, 5:30-10PM; Sa 5:30-10PM. 11645 Wilshire Blvd. 207.5522

77 Sawtelle Veterans' Chapel (1900, **J. Lee Burton**) White gingerbread chapel. ◆ 11000 Wilshire Blvd

---

Murals Highlights include the redwood forest at the corner of Lincoln Blvd and Ocean Park Blvd and, 8 blocks west, a view of Ocean Park in the '30s, both by **Jane Golden**

77 Wadsworth Theater Near the Veterans' Chapel. Used by UCLA for chamber music, plays, and special film screenings. Free jazz concert on the first Sunday of month. ◆ Seats 1400. Ticket information 825.9261, evenings 478.7578

78 Tutto Pasta/Pasta Maria ★★$$$ **Silvio De Mori** of **Tuttobene** operates this evenings-only restaurant (which by day is an Italian takeout). Carpaccio and Caesar salad, gnocchi and pasta, grilled prawns and veal chop are excellent though pricey. The setting cheerfully casual. ◆ Italian ◆ Pasta Maria: M-Sa 9AM-5PM. Tutto Pasta: M-Sa 6-10PM. 11620 San Vicente Blvd. 207.2833

79 Toscana ★★★$$$ Splendid rustic food served in a bright modern setting, and it hums with a crowd of satisfied diners at lunch and dinner. Standouts from an unchanging menu include the grilled vegetables, pizzas and perfect risottos; the sautéed sea bass and grilled meats (including an authentic *bisteca Fiorentina*) and the tiramisù. ◆ Italian ◆ M-Th 11:30AM-3PM, 5:30-10:30PM; F-Su 11:30AM-2:30PM, 5:30-10:30PM. 11633 San Vicente Blvd. 820.2448

79 Brentwood Bar & Grill ★★$$$ This is the very model of a modern million-dollar restaurant. Handsome room, even handsomer clientele, active bar, exposed kitchen, and an exemplary wine cellar. Don't miss the grilled duck or steak, Pacific oysters, potato-and-onion tart, and the decadent desserts. Excellent service. ◆ California ◆ M-Th 11:30AM-2:30PM, 6-10PM; F-Sa 11:30AM-2:30PM, 6-11PM. 11647 San Vicente Blvd. 820.2121

79 Daily Grill ★$$ Sibling of **The Grill** in Beverly Hills, located upstairs in an upmarket mall. The setting is masculine, the mood fun, and the food dependable. Chicken potpie, Cobb salad, great onion rings, French fries, and rice-pudding pie are favorite choices. If the crowds are too thick, try **What's Up**, an inventive, reasonably priced place on the 3rd floor. ◆ American ◆ M-Th, Su 11AM-11PM; F-Sa 11AM-midnight. 11677 San Vicente Blvd. 442.0044

80 Berty's ★$$$ Leisurely dining in a cool, tranquil environment. Try the blue-crab ravioli and a grilled veal chop before moving on to a tempting dessert. ◆ California ◆ M-F 11:30AM-2:30PM, 6-10PM; Sa 6-10PM. 11712 San Vicente Blvd. 207.6169

80 Chin Chin $ **Brent Saville** designed this offshoot of the popular café on Sunset Strip. Dim sum and other light Chinese dishes in a bright tiled room and on a handsome roof terrace with big white umbrellas. ◆ Chinese ◆ M-Th, Su 11AM-11PM; F-Sa 11AM-midnight. 11740 San Vicente Blvd. 826.2525

80 La Scala Presto $$ Stylish junior version of the Beverly Hills original. Popular with the young for its pastas, pizzas, and antipasti at reasonable prices. ♦ Italian ♦ M-Th 11:30AM-10PM; F-Sa 11:30AM-11PM. 11740 San Vicente Blvd. 826.6100. Also at: 3821 Riverside Dr, Toluca Lake. 818/846.6800; 3874 Cross Creek Rd, Malibu. 456.1979; 410 N. Cannon Dr, Beverly Hills. 275.0579

81 Dutton's This may be the finest bookstore in the city. Three separate rooms are grouped around a courtyard, making it easier to locate your chosen theme. Music and the humanities are Dutton's strong suits, but there's a good choice of new and used books in every major field. Also discs and tapes, readings, and book signings. Friendly, expert service. ♦ M-F 9:30AM-9PM; Sa 9:30AM-6PM; Su 11AM-5PM. 11975 San Vicente Blvd. 476.6263. Also at: 3806 W. Magnolia Blvd. Burbank. 818/840.8003

82 Brentwood Country Mart A red barn houses 26 village shops, including an espresso bar, a fresh juice bar, a deli, and a grocery. Standouts include the **Brentwood Camera Shop** (394.0256), the **Book Nook** (393.7903), and **Gourmet Meats** (394.5279), which also sells fish and barbecued chicken. When the Westside was a refuge for émigrés from Hitler, **Arnold Schoenberg** and **Marta Feuchtwanger** shopped here. Outdoor dining. ♦ 26th St at San Vicente Blvd. 395.6714

83 Will Rogers State Historic Park This 187-acre park was the home of cowboy/humorist/writer/performer Will Rogers between 1924 and 1935. Inside the house are possessions and memorabilia from his busy career. A nearby **Visitor Center** shows a 10-minute film on Rogers' life, narrated by his friends and family, and sells Rogersiana. An avid polo player, Rogers' 900-by-300-foot polo field is the site of polo matches on Saturday 2-4PM and Sunday 10AM-noon, year-round, weather permitting. (Rogers, who was once mayor of Beverly Hills, gave the **Polo Lounge** its name when he and his pals repaired there after a game.) The extensive grounds and the chaparral-covered hills invite hiking and picnicking. This is a fire-hazard area, so no fires are allowed. ♦ Free. Park: daily 8AM-6PM. House: daily 10:30AM-4:30PM. Parking fee. 14235 Sunset Blvd. 454.8212

84 Cliff May Office (1953, **Cliff May**) The architect's wood-paneled studio and, on the 13000 blocks of Riviera Ranch and Old Oak streets, a generous selection of his celebrated ranch houses, immediately recognizable by their broad shingle roofs and stucco walls. ♦ 13151 Sunset Blvd

85 Temple House (1936) As a child, actress **Shirley Temple** (now US Ambassador to Czechoslovakia) lived with her parents in this delightful small-scale European farmhouse. Private residence. ♦ 231 N. Rockingham Ave

86 Maria's Italian Kitchen $ Standout pizza with a delightful crust and a variety of toppings. Mostly takeout. ♦ Pizza ♦ Daily 10AM-10PM. 11723 Barrington Ct. 476.6112

87 Mount Saint Mary's College A small private liberal arts college atop one of the most beautiful view sites in the city. The **J. Paul Getty Center**, to be designed by **Richard Meier** as a showcase for all but the Greek and Roman art now displayed in Malibu, will rise from a neighboring eminence in 1995. ♦ 12001 Chalon Rd. 476.2237

Pacific Palisades
A community founded as a new Chatauqua in

1922 by the Southern Conference of the Methodist Episcopal Church. Made famous by its western border of oceanfront bluffs that frequently crumble down onto Pacific Coast Highway, the Palisades is an upper-class neighborhood with the highest median income of any area in the City of Los Angeles—twice that of most other areas. Many of the streets in the Palisades are named for bishops of the Methodist Church.

88 Marix Tex Mex Playa ★$$ A branch of the rambunctious West Hollywood restaurant. ♦ Mexican ♦ M-Th, Su 11AM-11PM; F-Sa 11AM-midnight. 118 Entrada Dr. 459.8596

89 Case Study Houses Some of LA's most innovative houses were commissioned or brokered by **John Entenza**, owner and editor (1938-62) of the pace-setting *Arts and Architecture Magazine*. He launched the **Case Study House Program** in January 1945 to encourage locally based progressive architects to create affordable prototypes for the postwar house, using the latest materials, techniques, and furnishings. Over the next 20 years, 24 of the 36 houses and apartment buildings published in the magazine were built, all over southern California. Two of the most famous are located here, on a meadow overlooking the ocean: the classic steel-and-glass house/studio that **Charles** and **Ray Eames** built for themselves, and a more conventional house that Eames designed with **Eero Saarinen** for **Entenza**, both in 1949. Also on the site is a small house by **Richard Neutra**. None is visible from the street. Private residences. ♦ Chatauqua Blvd (So of Corona del Mar)

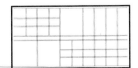

Charles and Ray Eames House

90 Uplifters Club Cabins. In the early 1920s an offshoot group of the **Los Angeles Athletic Club** built cottages in the rustic hills of the Pacific Palisades. Many of the residences were log cabins. Private residences ♦ 1, 3, 18 Latimer Rd, 31, 32, 34, 38 Haldeman Rd

91 Rustic Canyon Recreation Center A quiet sylvan glade for picnics and barbeques. For groups over 20, call 454.5734. ♦ 601 Latimer Rd

91 Kappe House (1968, **Raymond Kappe**) The architect built this expansively scaled concrete-and-wood home for himself. Private residence. ♦ 715 Brooktree Rd

92 Bridges House (1989, **Robert Bridges**) Bridges designed and engineered this woodsy 3-level house/office atop concrete piers. It rises from a precipitous site, 70 feet above the traffic on Sunset Blvd. Private residence. ♦ 820 Chautauqua Blvd

Westside

93 Ristorante Lido ★★$$ Stylish, friendly oasis in a restaurant-poor neighborhood. The gnocchi with gorgonzola sauce, risotto, grilled shrimp, and tiramisù are all wonderful, as is the chewy country bread. An informal spin-off, the **Caffe Lido**, is located at 147 W. Channel Dr, Santa Monica. 459.8823. ♦ Italian ♦ Daily 6-10:30PM. 15200 Sunset Blvd. 459.9214

93 Tivoli Café ★$$ Upscale neighborhood spot specializing in designer pizzas, sandwiches, and tiramisù, plus daily specials. ♦ Italian ♦ M-Sa 11:30AM-11PM; Su 2-10PM. 15306 Sunset Blvd. 459.7685

94 Gelson's Market A cornucopia of fresh produce, specialty meat cuts, and exotica. ♦ Daily 8AM-10PM. 15424 Sunset Blvd. 459.4483

95 Moss House (1979, **Eric Moss**) The architect transformed this '40s house for his family, adding a flying buttress, super graphics, and other witty touches. Private residence. ♦ 708 El Medio Ave

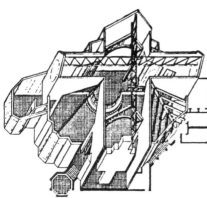

Drawing Courtesy Moore Ruble Yudell

96 St. Matthew's Episcopal Church (1983, **Moore Ruble Yudell**) **Charles Moore** worked closely with the parishioners when designing this replacement for a church destroyed by fire. The result is indisputably modern, but the subtle use of historic design elements, from Renaissance to California Craftsman, ground the building in tradition. Of note are the exposed wooden rafters under a lofty ceiling, inset windows that capture the landscape, and Moore's sensitivity to natural light. ♦ 1030 Bienveneda Ave. 454.1358

97 Self-Realization Fellowship Lake Shrine An open-air temple dedicated to all religions, founded in 1950 by followers of **Paramahansa Yogananda** on what was once a movie set. Ponds, lakes, waterfalls, windmills, and gazebos make this a pleasant place for walking or meditation. ♦ Tu-Su 9AM-4:45PM. 17190 Sunset Blvd. 454.4114

98 Gladstones 4 Fish $$$ Close-up views of the ocean and the sun sinking over Malibu. The banana daiquiris draw crowds, especially on weekends. As for food and service, you'd do better for less with a cold lobster and a bottle of Chardonnay on the beach. ♦ Seafood ♦ Daily 7AM-11PM. 17300 Pacific Coast Hwy. 478.6738

Bel-Air
A posh hillside community, developed by Alphonzo E. Bell in the early '20s, which rapidly became a preferred location for stars and other celebrities who valued the privacy and the views. There's not much for the outsider to see along the winding roads with their Mediterranean names since the best houses are hidden from the street.

99 Bel-Air Sands Hotel $$$ A peaceful exotic hideaway (rattan furniture and jungle prints in the lobby) within a stone's throw of the San Diego freeway. Enjoy **Echo Restaurant**, a sheltered pool, and an air of distinction at a reasonable price. ♦ 11461 Sunset Blvd. 472.2513; fax 471.6310

100 UCLA Hannah Carter Japanese Garden (1961, **Nagao Sakurai**) An enchanted garden amid the private estates, with rocks and wooden structures imported from Japan, and Japanese trees and plants. Behind the teahouse is a Hawaiian garden. Open by reservation ♦ Tu 10AM-1PM; W noon-3PM. 10619 Bellagio Rd. UCLA Visitors Center 825.4574

101 Hotel Bel-Air $$$$ The most exclusive and sybaritic hotel in LA: just 92 exquisitely appointed rooms and suites in rambling Mission-style buildings. Even the setting induces a sense of tranquillity: a wooded canyon 5 minutes north of Sunset but a world away in spirit. Like the Mansion on Turtle Creek in Dallas, it was lovingly made over by **Caroline Hunt Schoellkopf** after her **Rosewood Hotels** group purchased the hotel in 1982. Five designers brought their personal style to guest and public rooms, which are further enhanced by wood-burning fireplaces, natural stone, and masses of fresh flowers. The 11-acre gardens, with their waterfall and swan lake, were further improved. The emphasis, as always, is on seclusion: it is possible to imagine that you are the only guest in residence.

The restaurants are prettier than ever and the cooking, under the direction of executive chef **Peter Rosenberg**, is excellent. There's a choice between a wood-paneled bar, an open-air terrace, and the **Bel Air Dining Room** (★★★$$$$), which imaginatively combines the best of French and new California cuisines. ◆ Deluxe ◆ 701 Stone Canyon Rd. 472.1211, 800/ 648.4097; fax 476.5890

102 Cafe Four Oaks ★★★$$$ This has always been one of the most charming hideaways in town, but the kitchen has seesawed. Currently, it's in the talented hands of chef **Peter Roelant**, who is putting his emphasis on vegetarian dishes, including terrine of eggplant, tomatoes, and fresh basil, and fresh soups and vegetable salads. ◆ California ◆ Daily 11AM-2PM, 6-10PM. 2181 N. Beverly Glen Blvd. 470.2265; fax 476.5890

103 Adriano's Restaurant ★★$$$$ The food, the hilltop, and the personal attention will combine to make you feel transported to Italy. Don't be fooled by the shopping center locale; this elegant spot offers such authentic treats as Genovese minestrone, wonderful risotto and gnocchi, as well as simple grills. ◆ Italian ◆ Tu-Th 11:30AM-3PM, 6-10:30PM; F 11:30AM-3PM, 6-11PM; Sa 6-11PM; Su 6-10PM. 2930 Beverly Glen Circle. 475.9807

103 Shane (hidden on the Glen) ★★$$ Barbara Lazaroff helped transform this tiny shopping center storefront into a colorful southwestern cave—apt decor for a restaurant that marries Santa Fe to Spago. Spicy chicken soup, fried calamari with aioli, pizzas, and pastas are all good bets. ◆ Southwestern ◆ M-Th 11:30AM-2:30PM, 6-10:30PM; F 11:30AM-2:30PM; Sa 6-11PM; Su 5:30-10PM. 2932 Beverly Glen Circle. 470.6223

103 Santo Pietro's Pizza $$ Casual sidewalk café and espresso bar with daily Italian specialties as well as pizza spun in the air by a champion frisbee thrower. ◆ Italian ◆ Daily 11:30AM-midnight. 2954 Beverly Glen Circle. 474.4349. Also at: 1000 Gayley, Westwood Village. 208.5688; 11741 San Vicente Blvd, Brentwood. 826.6788; 12001 Ventura Pl, Studio City. 818/508.1177

Bests

Leon Whiteson
Architecture Critic

A delicious brew of the banal and the bizarre, the sleazy and the sleek, Los Angeles offers its delights to the perceptive eye at every turn. Here are some of my favorite LA details:

The long view down Western Avenue seen from the parking lot of the **Griffith Observatory**, which cuts a clean line to the distant Palos Verdes Peninsula.

Wilshire Boulevard, at right angles to Western, is a 17-mile-long dinosaur spine of mid- and high-rise buildings poking up through the low-lying urban fabric of the city from downtown to Santa Monica.

Evergreen Cemetery in Boyle Heights is a tombstone history of one of LA's oldest districts. Anglos, Latinos, Koreans, and Japanese, segregated in death as in life, fill this pleasant park, encapsulating stories of the city's shifting populations.

The **Mayan Theater** on Hill Street downtown until recently presented the wonderfully bizarre experience of watching a widescreen, hardcore porn movie while Tlaloc and Huitzilpotchli glowered down on you through the erotic gloom.

Crystal Cove near Corona del Mar in Orange County is a hidden coastal village of clapboard houses that looks like a movie set of a New England fishing port.

Unmarked and invisible from the highway, the cove's rocky beach plays host to dolphins and elephant seals as well as humans.

Watts Towers, built by Sam—not Simon—Rodia, is the finest act of visionary architecture in Southern California. Rodia called his creation *Pueblo Nuestro*, Our Town, and meant it as a private work of art transcending the banalities of his failed personal life and the trashy city he saw springing up around his walled towers.

Salisbury House, a Richardsonian Romanesque mansion on West 20th Street now reincarnated as a restaurant and bed-and-breakfast hostelry, is a symbol of the struggle to revive a once-grand section of the inner city now fallen on decay. Sipping wine beside the stone fireplace on a winter's evening while police sirens scream outside provides the rarified frisson of a well-filled belly in the midst of desperate poverty.

The spurting water jets in **Echo Park Lake** come as a surprise to motorists emerging from a tunnel under the Hollywood Freeway. Suddenly, in the midst of urban incoherence, the serene and shaded body of water refreshes the spirit and lifts the soul above the mean streets that seem ready to trap you in their tangled web.

Few Angeleno vistas are free of the massive billboards that often seem more solidly constructed than the city's architecture. The famous **Marlboro Man** on **Sunset Boulevard** is an LA icon, and the marvelously ugly **Toyota** sign that beckons motorists on the **Harbor Freeway** is an urban landmark in a metropolis whose public buildings seldom display the same verve.

Beverly Hills' Trousdale Estates offers a collection of the most vividly vulgar nouveau riche residential extravaganzas to be found anywhere. Ranging in style from ancient Roman to interplanetary, Trousdale houses are unencumbered by taste in the best LA tradition. One mansion's driveway sports a row of little white lions with paws raised to salute the visitor.

Cafe Kafka on Sunset Boulevard in Hollywood is a hole-in-the-wall Formica table eatery that hosts performances of *Metamorphosis* and *The Penal Colony*. There is no rarer pleasure than munching on a health-food salad while watching Gregor Samsa turn into a bug 2 feet from your face.

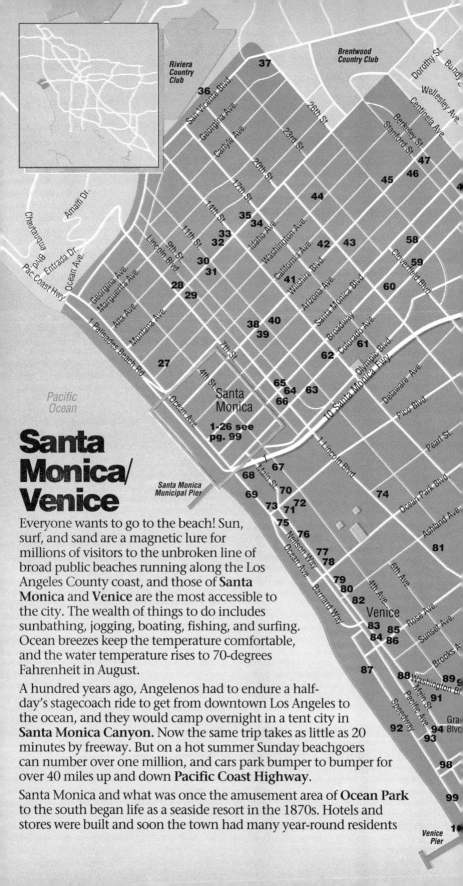

Riviera
Country
Club

Brentwood
Country Club

Santa
Monica/
Venice

Everyone wants to go to the beach! Sun,
surf, and sand are a magnetic lure for
millions of visitors to the unbroken line of
broad public beaches running along the Los
Angeles County coast, and those of **Santa
Monica** and **Venice** are the most accessible to
the city. The wealth of things to do includes
sunbathing, jogging, boating, fishing, and surfing.
Ocean breezes keep the temperature comfortable,
and the water temperature rises to 70-degrees
Fahrenheit in August.

A hundred years ago, Angelenos had to endure a half-
day's stagecoach ride to get from downtown Los Angeles to
the ocean, and they would camp overnight in a tent city in
Santa Monica Canyon. Now the same trip takes as little as 20
minutes by freeway. But on a hot summer Sunday beachgoers
can number over one million, and cars park bumper to bumper for
over 40 miles up and down **Pacific Coast Highway.**

Santa Monica and what was once the amusement area of **Ocean Park**
to the south began life as a seaside resort in the 1870s. Hotels and
stores were built and soon the town had many year-round residents

who voted in 1887 to incorporate as an independent city. In the 1930s, Santa Monica led a dual life as a quiet residential suburb and a haven for offshore gambling ships. It appears in **Raymond Chandler**'s novels as *Bay City*. The opening of the **Santa Monica Freeway** in 1966 permanently altered the town's sleepy tempo.

The northern sector of Santa Monica is wealthy and family-oriented. The central and southern parts of the city have attracted an influx of professionals and young singles drawn to the many apartments and condominiums by the short commute downtown, the temperate weather, clean air, and abundant outdoor recreational facilities. In recent elections, these middle-class tenants rebelled against escalating rents and threats of redevelopment, and voted in a city council that was dubbed the *People's Republic of Santa Monica* by those for whom rent control and curbs on building herald a communist takeover. Passions have since cooled, and the city seems to be sharing in the Westside's building frenzy.

1 Santa Monica Pier The smells of popcorn, cotton candy, and corn dogs, the soft resonance of the boardwalk underfoot, the calliope of the merry-go-round, and the metallic din of the penny arcade make the pier a spot for fun and nostalgia. Two piers were built side by side between 1909 and 1921, were threatened with demolition in 1973, and were badly damaged by storms in 1983. Citizens rallied to save them, and the city now backs the **Pier Restoration Corporation**'s ambitious development plan that will add to and upgrade what has survived. Coming attractions include a parking garage for the cars that now clutter the pier, a museum/library on the pier's history, and a fun zone at the far end. Presently, food services, amusement arcades, and souvenir stores line the pier. Children will love the 70-year-old carousel with its 56 prancing horses, familiar for its supporting role in *The Sting.* Free concerts with dancing under the stars are presented on Thursday night in the summer. At night the long line of white lights strung along the pier's edge create a poetic landmark for those coming down the coast highway from the north. Architects **Moore Ruble Yudell** created **Carousel Park** to the south as a stepped gateway to the pier, an open theater for beach sports, and a children's park— with a dragon of riverwashed granite boulders (entrance at Colorado and Ocean avenues). To the south, the same architects have landscaped a section of **Ocean Park Beach**, and the entire 3-mile stretch of beach is being turned into the **Natural Elements Sculpture Park**. Already installed, across from Pico is **Douglas Hollis**'s *Wind Harp* (singing beach chairs). **Carl Cheng**'s *Santa Monica Art Tool* is a concrete roller that is towed by a tractor to imprint a miniature metropolis on the sand. ◆ Carousel Sa-Su 10AM-5PM. Party rentals 394.7554

1 South Bay Bicycle Trail A beachside trail runs from the pier 19 miles south to the city of Torrance.

2 Santa Monica Freeway *The Christopher Columbus Transcontinental Highway* sweeps through a curved tunnel from the Pacific Coast Highway, setting you on a dramatic new course. It's as exciting a way to begin a cross-country journey as on the long-lamented *Super Chief.*

3 Opera ★★$$ This beautiful beachside brasserie with its stunning ocean view has settled down, curtailed its excesses, and now concentrates on boldly flavored food from the sun belt. Grilled *focaccia* with a wild mushroom-and-walnut topping, lavender chicken, and grilled swordfish are favorite dishes. ◆ California ◆ Tu-Th 6-10PM; F-Sa 6-11PM; Su 11AM-3PM. 1551 Ocean Ave. 393.9224

3 Red Sea ★$$ A fine introduction to the tantalizing cuisine of Ethiopia. Try *doro wat,* a chicken dish with red chiles, ginger, cumin, shallots, and butter; *kifto,* a version of steak tartare; or any of several spicy vegetable dishes. Food is served on a common platter and you scoop it up with *injera,* a spongy flat bread—without knives or forks. ♦ Ethiopian ♦ M-Th, Su 11AM-11PM; F-Sa 11AM-11:30PM. 1551 Ocean Ave. 394.5198

3 Ivy at The Shore ★★$$$ Informal oceanfront version of the more stylish Ivy in West Hollywood. Spacious and airy with big rattan chairs and an outdoor terrace. The menu includes crabcakes, grilled fresh fish, and steaks, pastas, and salads. A good place to show out of town visitors looking for the elusive *LA lifestyle.*
♦ California ♦ M-Th 11:30AM-3:15PM, 5:30-11PM; F 11:30AM-3:15PM, 5:30-11:30PM; Sa-Su 11AM-3:15PM, 5:30-11:30PM. 1541 Ocean Ave. 393.3113

3 Fennel ★★★$$$$ Four French food celebrities fly in from Paris on a rotating basis to work alongside resident French chef **Jean-Pierre Bosc**. Predictably, the concept outruns the reality, but when it works, you can eat as well here as anywhere—on wonderful veal sweetbreads and lobster terrine with caviar chantilly, gigotin of lamb Provençale, and to-die-for desserts. Service can be snooty and there's no place to wait.
♦ French ♦ M 6:30-10PM; Tu-Th noon-2:15PM, 6:30-10PM; F-Sa noon-2:15PM, 6:30-10:30PM; Su noon-2:15PM, 6-9:30PM. 1535 Ocean Ave. 394.2079

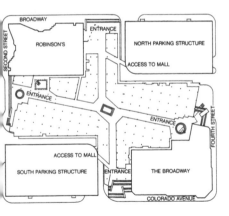

4 Santa Monica Place (1979-81, Frank Gehry) A huge white skylit galleria shopping mall on 3 levels. The cutaway facade with its balcony views of the ocean, the use of supergraphics to animate blank walls, the mesh screen on the parking garage, and the asymmetrical plan show that an architectural intelligence rather than a cookie cutter was involved. **Robinson's** and **The Broadway** anchor the complex, which includes **Karl Logan, Compagnie BX** (**Michael Glasser**'s boutique), **Natural Wonders, Club Monaco** (featuring **Alfred Sung** clothing), and over 150 other small stores. The **USC School of Fine Arts** shows innovative southern California artists in its **Atelier; Heal the Bay Marine Biology Museum** leads the effort to fight the polluters.
♦ M-F 10AM-9PM; Sa 10AM-6PM; Su 11AM-6PM. Bounded by Broadway, Colorado Ave, 2nd, and 4th Sts

5 Carmel Hotel $$ A well-kept economy hotel, close to Santa Monica Place. ♦ 201 Broadway. 451.2469

6 A Change of Hobbit A bookstore dedicated to science fiction and fantasy. ♦ M-Th 10:30AM-8PM; F-Sa 10:30AM-6PM. 1433 2nd St. 473.2873

7 Second City A skit and improvisational troupe from Chicago (whose graduates include **Mike Nichols** and **Elaine May, Bill Murray** and **Dan Aykroyd**) performs in what was formerly the **Mayfair Music Hall**. You can eat before the performance and order drinks at your table—if you can stop laughing long enough to sip.
♦ Admission. Performances Tu-Th 8:30PM; F-Sa 8 and 11PM; Su 7:30PM. 214 Santa Monica Blvd. 451.0621

Santa Monica/Venice

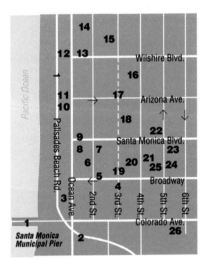

8 Ye Olde King's Head $ Convincing facsimile of an English pub, complete with darts, fish and chips, and warm beer. Popular with the local British colony. ♦ English ♦ M-Sa 11AM-11PM, bar until 1AM; Su noon-11PM. 116 Santa Monica Blvd. 451.1402

9 Bellevue French Restaurant $ A cozy neighborhood spot; try the marine salad or the Friday bouillabaisse. ♦ Seafood ♦ M-Th 11:30AM-9:30PM; F-Sa 11:30AM-10PM; Su 12:30-9:30PM. 101 Santa Monica Blvd. 393.2843

10 Art Safaris Lorel Cornman organizes tours of the best of LA's contemporary art scene. Small groups are escorted by knowledgeable guides in a limo or minivan to selected galleries and studios. Join an existing tour or call in advance for one that is tailored to your special interests.
♦ 1341 Ocean Ave. 458.8028

HOTEL SHANGRI·LA

10 Shangri-la Hotel $$$ Like the monastery in the classic 1937 movie, this is a streamline moderne gem, and —with its view over **Palisades Park** and the ocean —is almost as idyllic. There's no lounge or bar, just a quiet, unassuming lobby. Rooms and suites have been remodeled with a clean-edged '30s look, including Deco posters, grays and pinks, and frosted glass. Most have ocean views, many have sundecks. Prices are very reasonable and it's within walking distance of shops and the beach. ◆ 1301 Ocean Ave. 394.2791

11 Visitor Assistance Stand Free sightseeing maps and bus and tour information. ◆ Daily 10AM-4PM. Ocean Ave at Arizona St. 393.7593

Santa Monica/Venice

11 Camera Obscura Nearby, in the **Senior Recreation Center**, is a quiet upstairs room where startling projections of the outside world appear on a circular white surface. ◆ Daily 10AM-4PM

12 Palisades Park The steep, crumbly cliffs along the edge of the ocean are called the Palisades. A traditional spot for Angelenos to watch the sunset fade over the ocean, the park is one of the oldest and best maintained in the city. Its towering palms and semitropical trees form beautiful bowers for strolling or jogging, as well as a haven for the elderly—who gossip and play chess—and for the homeless. Steps lead down to the beach. ◆ Ocean Ave from Colorado Blvd to Adelaide Dr

Within Palisades Park:

Palisades Park Gates Craftsman-style field stone gates, made in 1912 and decorated with tiles by **Ernest Batchelder** of Pasadena. ◆ Ocean Ave at Wilshire Blvd

13 Sheraton Miramar Hotel $$$ A luxury resort hotel popular with Japanese and European tourists. The enormous **Moreton Bay** fig tree in the center courtyard was planted in the 19th century. **Garbo, Bogart** and others stayed in the bungalows. ◆ 101 Wilshire Blvd. 394.3731, 800/325.3535; fax 458.7912

14 Huntley Hotel $$$ High-rise with upstairs restaurant and great ocean views. ◆ 1111 2nd St. 394.5454, 800/556.4012 (CA), 800/556.4011 (US); fax 458.9776

MICHAEL'S

15 Michael's ★★★★$$$ Michael McCarty's white-on-white restaurant pioneered the new California cuisine; now it has settled down to being an institution. The prices have been lowered and you will probably be seduced by the inventive dishes (such as grilled quail with a confit of Maui onions) made from the freshest ingredients in season—locally or from around the world. The flowery patio with its big white umbrellas (heaven for Sunday brunch) and the dining room that doubles as one of LA's better contemporary art galleries (**David Hockney, Jasper Johns**) are a matchless setting for the rich and beautiful in fashionably casual attire. A meal here is a magical experience. ◆ California ◆ M-F noon-2PM, 6:30-9:45PM; Sa-Su 10:30AM-2PM, 6:30-9:45PM. 1147 3rd St. 451.0843

16 Postively 4th Street ★$ A sweet and sophisticated takeout place with tasty soups, salads, pastas, and desserts. ◆ Takeout ◆ M-Th 7AM-4PM; F 7AM-8PM. 1215 4th St. 393.1464

17 3rd Street Promenade This 3-block pedestrian street with its faded stucco facades has been landscaped (with topiary dinosaurs) and given a major facelift, revealing such architectural gems as the **Keller Building**, restored by **Frank Dimster** (3rd & Broadway), the Europa (3rd & Wilshire), and the **W.T. Grant Building** (1300 block). **Johannes Van Tilburg** designed the block at 3rd and Arizona in the style of the Viennese Werkstatte. Other attractions include 16 movie screens and some of the city's best specialty bookstores: **Arcana Books on the Arts** (No. 1229, 458.1499) as well as 2 rare bookdealers, **Kenneth Karmiole** (No. 1225, 451.4342) and **Krown & Spellman** (No. 1243, 395.0300). On Wednesday the area is animated by a farmers market on the 200-400 blocks of Arizona. ◆ 3rd St (Broadway-Wilshire Blvd)

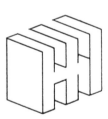

17 Hennessy & Ingall LA's best resource for books and magazines on art, architecture, and design, with a spiky Constructivist facade designed by **Morphosis**. ◆ M-F 10AM-6PM; Sa 10AM-5PM. 1254 3rd St Promenade. 458.9074

17 Krown & Spellman Classic, medieval, and Renaissance books. ◆ M-Sa 10AM-5PM. 1243 3rd St Promenade. 395.0300

18 Midnite Special Bookstore Specializes in politics, sociology, and literature. Call for information on readings. ◆ M-F 10:30AM-6:30PM; Sa 10:30AM-8PM; Su noon-5PM. 1350 3rd St Promenade. 393.2923

Jean Louis Vignes tended some of California's first wine vineyards in the 1820s, and by the middle of that century the LA area sported over 90 different vineyards—the original heart of California wine country.

19 Broadway Deli ★$$ (1990, **Steven Erlich**) Stripped Deco interior of stylish simplicity linking the restaurant with the bar and the shopping area (bakery, grocery, wine shop). Excellent sandwiches and salads, grills and deli basics; good choice of beers and wines by the glass. ♦ American ♦ Restaurant: M-Th, Su 7AM-midnight; F-Sa 7AM-2AM. Stores: M-F 10AM-10PM; Sa 8AM-10PM; Su 8-9PM. 1457 3rd St Promenade. 451.0616

19 Remi ★★★$$$ (1990, **Adam Tihany**) Cool, sophisticated interior and unusually civilized service. Chef **Francesco Antonucci** offers the most authentic Venetian food in LA. *Bigoli* (whole-wheat linguine with red onions and anchovies), squid in its ink with polenta, and sweet-sour duck have been acclaimed. ♦ Italian ♦ Tu-Su 11:30AM-2:30PM, 6-11PM. 1451 3rd St Promenade. 393.6545

19 Broadway Bar & Grill ★★$$ Those who left their heart in San Francisco can reclaim it here. Delightfully old-fashioned food, service, and decor. ♦ American ♦ Daily 10:30AM-11PM. 1460 3rd St (Broadway) 393.4211

20 Border Grill ★★$$ (1990, **Josh Schweitzer**) The decor is half Mexican cantina, half punk nightclub; it vibrates with sound and color. A new showcase for the inventive cuisine of **Mary Sue Miliken** and **Susan Fenniger**. Shrimp ceviche and bread soup, braised duck and lamb tacos are standouts. Communal tables for single diners and those without reservations. ♦ Mexican ♦ M-F 11:30AM-3PM, 5:30-11PM; Sa 11AM-3PM, 5PM-midnight; Su 11AM-3PM. 1445 4th St. 451.1655

21 Fama ★★$$ **Hans and Mary** (Fama) **Rockenwagner** opened this spin-off from their Venice original, and it is a big success. **David Kellen** has opened up the restaurant to the street through a big picture window, creating a stylized forest—a blond plywood version of the Expressionist set for *The Cabinet of Dr. Caligari.* The menu includes such delights as broad noodles with duck confit and shitake mushrooms, roasted pork loin with toasted ricotta ravioli, and walnut plum tart. ♦ Eclectic ♦ M-F 11:30AM-2:30PM, 6-10PM; Sa-Su 5:30-11PM. 1416 4th St. 458.6704

22 James Corcoran Gallery Contemporary Southern California artists, including **Ed Ruscha**, **Joe Goode**, and **Ken Price**. ♦ Tu-F 10AM-6PM; Sa 11AM-5PM. 1327 5th St. 451.4666

23 The British Raaj ★$$$ Mild, creamy food with traditional names—lamb Bombay, chicken Madras—is served in charming surroundings. ♦ British/Indian ♦ M-Th 11:30AM-2PM, 5:30-10PM; F-Sa 11:30AM-2PM, 5:30PM-1AM; Su 5:30-10PM. 504 Santa Monica Blvd. 393.9472

23 Phoenix Bookstore Western and Eastern philosophy, metaphysics, and psychology. A nice place to linger and browse. ♦ M-Sa 10AM-9PM; Su noon-8PM. 524 Santa Monica Blvd. 395.9516

24 Shoshana Wayne Gallery American and international contemporary art; artists represented include **Deborah Remington** and **Fay Jones**, **Michael Schulze** (Germany), and **Aharon Gulska** (Israel). ♦ Tu-F 10AM-5:30PM; Sa 10AM-5PM. 1454 5th St. 451.3733

25 Bikini (1991, **Cheryl Brantner**) **John Sedlar**, executive chef of **St. Estephe**, has moved to this handsome new space and plans to combine French technique and Latin ingredients in such light and colorful dishes as crab-stuffed chiles, shrimp with vanilla, plus *the most unusual fortune cookies you've ever seen.* Brantner promises a *big wave* of wood in a sensual, subdued interior. ♦ Eclectic ♦ M-F 11AM-2PM, 6-10PM; Sa 6-10PM; Su 5:30-9:30PM. 1411 5th St. 395.8611

26 Angels Attic Museum Miniatures, toys, and dolls in a restored Victorian house; tea and cookies served 12:30-3:30PM on the porch. ♦ Admission. Th-Su 12:30-4:30PM. 516 Colorado Ave. 394.8331

Santa Monica/Venice

27 The Sovereign Hotel $$ Designed by **Julia Morgan**, the architect of the Hearst castle in San Simeon, this small Mediterranean-style hotel is a pleasant mixture of old-world charm and modern convenience. ♦ 205 Washington Ave. 395.9921, 800/533.5388 (CA), 800/331.0163 (US); fax 458.3085

Montana Avenue
If the 10 blocks from 7th to 16th streets were to be covered in lava, future archeologists could construe the tastes of the local inhabitants from the evidence they would find. The natives were fond of personal adornment (18 women's clothing stores, 16 hair and beauty shops), cleanliness (11 laundries and cleaners), and eating (7 restaurants, 9 gourmet take-outs, and 11 other food stores). They were a generous people (14 gift boutiques) but worried about their health (12 doctors and 10 dentists). They worshiped children (6 specialty stores), dogs, and cats (1 each). These were probably brought to the Aero, a neighborhood shrine in which rows of seats face a blank white screen. Judging from the contents of the 8 design stores, this region may have been settled by the English. Currently, Montana is a satisfying combination of the useful and the decorative, but the balance may be shifting as whole blocks are slickly redeveloped.

28 Aussie Surf & Sport Beach and surf wear from down under. ♦ M-Sa 10AM-6PM; Su 11AM-4PM. 701 Montana Ave. 395.2205

29 7th Heaven Delectable takeout food—sandwiches to complete meals. They'll even do your Thanksgiving turkey. ♦ M-F 7AM-8PM; Sa-Su 7AM-7PM. 710 Montana Ave. 451.0077. Also at: South Coast Plaza, Costa Mesa. 714/668.9461

29 Le Petit Moulin ★$$$ Homemade pâté, pink rack of lamb, and crisp duck in a traditional setting. ♦ French ♦ M-Sa 5:30-10PM. 714 Montana Ave. 395.6619

30 Imagine Imported toys and gifts for children. ♦ M-Sa 10AM-6PM; Su noon-5PM. 1001 Montana Ave. 395.9553

31 Babalu ★$ Tropical decor, folk art on the walls, and tasty light dishes like crabcakes and shrimp *quesadillas*. ♦ Caribbean/Mexican ♦ Tu-Su 8AM-11PM. 1002 Montana Ave. 395.2500

31 Louise's Trattoria $$ A favorite with the young, who go for the pizzas, calzone, *focaccia* with roasted garlic, and homemade pastas. ♦ Italian ♦ M-Sa 11AM-11PM; Su noon-11PM. 1008 Montana Ave. 394.8888

31 Father's Office Over 20 esoteric brews are on tap in this friendly neighborhood tavern. ♦ M-W 3PM-1:45AM; Th-Su noon-1:45AM. 1018 Montana Ave. 393.2337

31 Legacy One of the many tempting gift stores. This one has the flavor of Greenwich, Connecticut. ♦ M-F 10AM-6:30PM; Sa 10AM-5PM; Su 1-5PM. 1022 Montana Ave. 395.9060

Santa Monica/Venice

32 Weathervane Sophisticated dressers are high on the women's sportswear by Ferretti and others, and shoes by Robert Clergérie. **Weathervane for Men** at 1132 Montana Ave (395.0397). ♦ 1209 Montana Ave. 393.5344

32 Nonesuch Early California paintings, cowboy relics, and santos. ♦ M-Sa 11AM-5:30PM. 1211 Montana Ave. 393.1245

33 Le Marmiton For the most elegant of picnics, or when you would love to eat in a fine French restaurant but can't afford it. ♦ Takeout ♦ Tu-Sa 10AM-7PM. 1327 Montana Ave. 393.7716

34 Artcessories Whimsical and traditional wearable art and accessories. ♦ M-Sa 10AM-6PM; Su noon-5PM. 1426 Montana Ave. 395.8484

34 Archilla Limited edition daywear and sophisticated casuals in quality imported fabrics. ♦ M-Sa 10AM-6PM; Su noon-5PM. 1426 Montana Ave. 395.1013

34 Montana Mercantile In a stark white and glass-brick building are shelves of great kitchen equipment. Cooking classes are given in back. ♦ M-F 10AM-6:30PM; Sa 10AM-6PM. 1500 Montana Ave. 451.1418

34 Federico Native American and Mexican textiles, antiques, and jewelry. ♦ M-Sa 11AM-6:30PM. 1522 Montana Ave. 458.4134

34 Cafe Montana ★$ A local favorite has moved a block to larger, spiffier premises, but has kept the same pleasing menu of soups, salads, and grilled fresh fish. Excellent breakfasts and desserts. ♦ California ♦ Tu-Su 8AM-3PM, 6-10PM. 1534 Montana Ave. 829.3990

35 a.b.s California Casual and career women's wear and costume jewelry. ♦ M-F 11AM-8PM; Sa 10AM-7PM; Su 11AM-5PM. 1533 Montana Ave. 393.8770

35 Brenda Cain Vintage clothes for men and women, including a stash of Hawaiian shirts. ♦ M-Sa 10AM-6PM; Su noon-4PM. 1617 Montana Ave. 393.3298

35 Il Fornaio Seductive country breads, pastries, and pizza to go. Within the store is **Tanaka's**, for quality produce, **Ashford Flowers**, and the **LA Gourmet**. This is one-stop shopping for partygivers. ♦ M-Sa 7AM-6:30PM; Su 8:30AM-2:30PM. 1627 Montana Ave. 458.1562

36 La Mesa Drive Huge Moreton Bay figs canopy this lovely street, which is lined with fine Spanish-Colonial style '20s houses by **John Byers**. Examples are at **Nos. 1923, 2102,** and **2153**. Byer's own home at **No. 1034** is a Monterey Colonial variant with a 2nd-story balcony. Private residences.

37 Camelions ★★$$$ Another **Byers** house has been converted to one of the most enchanting restaurants in LA. Small rooms are ranged around a courtyard fronting a quiet street. Chef **Thomas Hogan** prepares a mixture of old favorites and innovative fare, with a nod to French tradition. ♦ California ♦ Tu-Th 11:30AM-2:30PM, 6-10:30PM; F-Sa 11:30AM-2:30PM, 6-11PM; Su 11AM-2PM, 5:30-10PM. 246 26th St. 395.0746

38 Tampico Tilly's $ A pleasant hybrid of old Mexico and young California. ♦ Mexican ♦ Daily 11:30AM-11PM. 1025 Wilshire Blvd. 451.1769

39 At My Place Eclectic nightclub with restaurant offering jazz, rhythm, and blues. Call for hours, program. ♦ Cover. 1026 Wilshire Blvd. 451.8597

40 The Address Slightly worn designer-label clothes. Make a splash without going broke. ♦ M-Sa 10AM-6PM; Su noon-5PM. 1116 Wilshire Blvd. 394.1406

41 Verdi ★★★$$$ **Bernard** and **Sheila Segal's** *ristorante di musica* combines sophisticated Tuscan food with excerpts from operas, operettas, and Broadway musicals sung by some of the finest young artists in Los Angeles. **Morphosis** converted a historic building whose exterior resembles a toy opera house, creating a marvelous fusion of theater and dining room, and a bar with excellent sightlines where you can enjoy the music for the price of a drink or a

Restaurants/Clubs: Red   Hotels: Blue
Shops/Parks: Green   **Sights/Culture: Black**

dessert. Opera murals by **David Schorr**. You can receive monthly newsletter or check the program when you make your reservation. ♦ Italian ♦ Tu-Su 6PM-2AM. 1519 Wilshire Blvd. 393.0706

42 Chartreuse ★$$ Owner/chef **Bruno Moeckli** has moved here from Pico Blvd, and continues to serve such signature dishes as Roquefort soufflé and roast duck with gooseberries. Good California wine list. ♦ Eclectic ♦ M-F 11:30AM-2:30PM, 6-9:30PM; Sa 6-9:30PM. 1909 Wilshire Blvd. 453.3333

43 Carlos & Pepe's $$ A favorite after-work meeting spot for the young of the Westside. The central bar serves great nachos. ♦ Mexican ♦ M-Th, Su 11:30AM-11PM, bar until 1AM; F-Sa 11:30AM-2AM. 2020 Wilshire Blvd. 828.8903

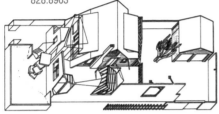

Drawing Courtesy Frank Gehry

44 Gehry House (1978, **Frank Gehry**) A mecca for students of architecture, an outrage to the neighbors. **Gehry** described the original Dutch-gabled cottage as "a dumb little house with charm." Around it he built a carapace of corrugated metal and plywood, chain link and glass, creating a design statement that might have been concocted by a Russian Constructivist of the early '20s. Private residence. ♦ 22nd St at Washington Ave

45 McGinty's Irish Pub $ Cozy haven for traditionalists, with ale, music, dancing, and darts. Curries and other Indian food served at long tables. ♦ Irish/Indian ♦ Daily 10:30AM-11:30PM. 2615 Wilshire Blvd. 828.9839

46 Madame Wong's West Club offering 2 floors of entertainment and a rich selection of name pop bands, Chinese food, and 3 bars. ♦ Cover weekends only. Music 9PM-1AM; F-Sa 9PM-2AM (doors open 5PM). 2900 Wilshire Blvd. 829.7361

47 Wilshire Books A diverse collection of new and used books. ♦ M-Sa noon-7PM; Su noon-5PM. 3018 Wilshire Blvd. 828.3115

48 Marquis West ★$$$ Traditional, rather formal restaurant serving consistent Southern Italian food. Some say the fried calamari are the best in LA. ♦ Italian ♦ M-F 11:30AM-2PM, 5:30-10:30PM; Sa 5:30-10:30PM; Su 4:30PM-9:45PM. 3110 Santa Monica Blvd. 828.4567

In contrast with the rest of the US, where the landscape was formed over hundreds of millions of years, most of the geological processes that created Los Angeles have taken place relatively recently—within the last few million years.

49 Southern California Institute of Architecture (SCI-ARC) A creative design laboratory established by **Ray Kappe** in 1972 and currently headed by **Michael Rotondi**, one of the first graduates, who is also a partner in **Morphosis**. Four hundred students from 50 countries study in a nondescript collection of rented warehouses with a talented and aggressive faculty. Exhibitions and lectures by the world's leading architects are open to the public without charge. SCI-ARC has become a magnet, attracting progressive architects to move their offices to the neighboring lofts. ♦ 1800 Berkeley St. 829.3482

50 Valentino ★★★★$$$$ Sicilian-born owner **Piero Selvaggio** is a magician, pulling truffles from his hat and surprising his devoted clientele with unfamiliar dishes from all over Italy. These have included fried squid and ricotta fritters, lobster cannelloni, and loin of beef in balsamic vinegar. He will be happy to compose a menu for a special dinner. The wine list is one

of the best in America, the service is warm and professional, and the decor combines elegance, comfort, and striking contemporary style. ♦ Italian ♦ M-Th, Sa-Su 5:30-10:45PM; F 11:30AM-2:30PM, 5:30-10:45PM. 3115 W. Pico Blvd. 829.4313

50 McCabe's Guitar Shop Open weekend evenings for intimate cabaret featuring live performances of folk music and blues by well-known performers. Call for performance times. ♦ 3101 W. Pico Blvd. 828.4403

51 California Map Center Sheldon Mars has LA's best stock of maps, local and international. ♦ M-F 8:30AM-5PM; Sa 9AM-4PM. 3211 Pico Blvd. 829.6277

52 Yum Cha $$ Hip fast food in a sophisticated setting. Spit-roasted Hunan chicken, spicy Szechuan noodles, and dim sum are the specialties. ♦ Chinese ♦ M-F 11AM-2PM, 5-9PM; Sa-Su 5-9PM. 3435 Ocean Park Blvd. 450.7000

53 Typhoon (1991, **Grinstein-Daniels**) Dramatic 2-level space in the airport terminal, across the tarmac from DC3. An eclectic, moderately priced menu will be served in a cherry-paneled dining room with a mirror-glass map of the world, and on an observation terrace shaded by pierced metal silhouettes of vintage planes. ♦ Eclectic ♦ 3221 Donald Douglas Loop So (Bundy Dr)

54 Museum of Flying Close-up views of vintage planes, including a 1924 **Douglas World Cruiser** and a **DC3** that were built on this site before Douglas Aircraft merged with McDonnell and moved to Long Beach. Also here are **Spitfires** and **Mustangs**, the workhorse fighters of the second World War. There's a theater, store, and views out over Santa Monica Airport, from which these veterans still fly. ♦ Admission. Tu-Su 10AM-6PM. 2772 Donald Douglas Loop. 392.8822

54 DC3 ★$$$ (1989, **Charles Arnoldi**) Stunning artist-designed interior adjoining the museum and overlooking the airport. The sun-filled room is a delightful setting for lunch, though executive planes taking off are better glimpsed through glass than from the terrace. At night it becomes a singles scene with a lively bar and a lot of table-hopping by the hippest of the hip, which distracts from the long waits and erratic food. There's disco dancing on weekends. ◆ California ◆ Restaurant: M-Th 11:30AM-2:30PM, 6-10PM; F 11:30AM-2:30PM, 6-11PM; Sa 6-11PM; Su 11AM-2:30PM, 6-11PM. Disco and bar: F-Sa 9PM-2AM. 2800 Donald Douglas Loop. 399.2323

55 Il Forno ★$$ Wonderful pizza and pasta served in a noisy, crowded room.◆ Italian ◆ M-Sa 11:30AM-3PM, 5:30-11PM. 2901 Ocean Park Blvd. 450.1241

56 Sun Tech Townhouses (1981, **Urban Forms**) A striking high-tech terrace of condominiums.

Santa Monica/Venice

A similarly-scaled group, with a false classical facade, is located at 2332 28th St. Private residences. ◆ 2433 Pearl St

57 Maryland Crab House ★★$$ Fresh seafood from the East includes spicy steamed crabs (which you crack with a hammer, protected by a bib), bluefish, scrod, oysters, and shad roe in season. ◆ Seafood ◆ Tu-Th noon-2:30PM, 5-9PM; F noon-2:30PM, 4-10PM; Sa noon-10PM; Su noon-9PM. 2424 Pico Blvd. 450.5555

58 Children's Book and Music Center Books, records, musical instruments, and a story hour on the first and third Saturday of each month. ◆ M-Sa 9AM-5:30PM. 2500 Santa Monica Blvd. 829.0215

59 Cutter's $$$ This stylish hangout occupies a corner of the **Colorado Place** atrium and offers an eclectic range of grills, grazing fare (oysters, pizzas, and pastas), and vintage wine by the glass. Colorado Place has been expanded by **Maguire Thomas Partners**, and may soon fulfill its long neglected potential. ◆ California ◆ M-F 11:15AM-3PM, 5-10PM; Sa noon-4PM, 5-11PM; Su 4-9PM. 2425 Colorado Ave. 453.3588

60 Andrea Ross Gallery (1989, **Grinstein/ Daniels**) Inventive design as a setting for contemporary western and southwestern painting and sculpture, with an emphasis on the figurative. One of 3 galleries inventively inserted into the same bow-trussed warehouse. ◆ Tu-Sa 10AM-6PM. 2110 Broadway. 453.6662

60 Meyers/Bloom Gallery (1988, **Frederick Fisher**) Conceptual work by American and European artists, including **Boyd Webb**, **George Stone**, and **Nancy Dwyer**. ◆ Tu-Sa 10AM-5PM. 2112 Broadway. 829.0062

60 Krygier-Landau **Barbara Kasdan**'s extraordinary photos and works by such contemporary painters as **Nancy Rees** and **Richard Sedivy** are shown here. ◆ Tu-Sa 10AM-5PM. 2114 Broadway. 453.0086

61 Richard Kuhlenschmidt Conceptual and post-conceptual American artists, including **Tim Ebner**, **Jim Isermann**, and **Matt Mullican**. ◆ Tu-Sa 11AM-5:30PM. 1634 17th St. 450.2010

62 Santa Monica Seafood One of the largest, freshest selections of fish outside of downtown. ◆ M-Sa 9:30AM-6PM. 1205 Colorado Blvd. 393.5244

63 Pence Gallery Contemporary art by emerging and mid-career artists, including **Cam Slocum**, **Ann Preston**, and **Tom Knechtel**. ◆ Tu-Sa 10AM-5:30PM. 908 Colorado Ave. 393.0069

63 Maloney Gallery Paintings and sculptures by artists from both coasts. ◆ W-Sa 11AM-5PM or by appt. 910 Colorado Ave. 392.2330

63 Fred Hoffman Gallery **Julian Schnabel**, **John McCracken**, **A.R.Penck** and **Vernon Fisher** are among the American and European artists shown here. ◆ Tu-F 9:30AM-5:30PM; Sa 10AM-5PM. 912 Colorado Ave. 394.4199

63 Blum Helman Contemporary art, with an emphasis on New York. Artists include **Ellsworth Kelley**, **Bryan Hunt**, and **Donald Sultan**. ◆ Tu-Sa 10AM-5:30PM; Sa 11AM-5PM. 916 Colorado Ave. 451.0955

63 Linda Cathcart The former director of Houston's Contemporary Art Museum shows **Cindy Sherman**, **Robert Longo**, and **Louise Bourgeois**. ◆ Tu-F 10AM-5:30PM; Sa 11AM-5PM. 924 Colorado Blvd. 451.1121

64 Dorothy Goldeen Gallery Contemporary painting, sculpture, and works on paper by emerging and mature artists, including **Nam June Paik**, **Ed Paschke**, and **Robert Arneson**. ◆ Tu-Sa 10:30AM-5:30PM. 1547 9th St. 395.0222

65 Warszawa ★★$$ Hearty homemade peasant food in warm, friendly surroundings. Bortsch, hunter's stew, and cheesecake are standouts. ◆ Polish ◆ Daily 5:30-10:30PM. 1414 Lincoln Blvd. 393.8831

66 Bay Cities Importing Mediterranean foods, deli counter, sandwiches, pastas, cheeses, wines, and extra-virgin olive oils—even rose and orange water. ◆ M-Sa 8AM-7PM; Su 8AM-6PM. 1517 Lincoln Blvd. 395.8279

67 Guest Quarters $$$ New all-suite hotel, with sweeping views, a terrace restaurant, outdoor pool, and fitness facilities. It's a great buy for families, since the suites sleep 4. ◆ 1707 4th St. 395.3332, 800/424.2900; fax 452.7399

LA has more licensed Rolls-Royces than any other city

68 Loew's Santa Monica Beach Hotel $$$$
A new luxury hotel high above the beach that
looks down on the "cottages" that **Charlie
Chaplin** and **Mary Pickford** built for themselves when this beachfront was deserted.
There are 350 rooms and suites flanking a lofty
glass-roofed atrium, Victorian in inspiration,
out of which flow the restaurants and a half-
covered pool. There's a fitness center and an
array of business facilities and meeting spaces.
The **Coast Cafe** and **Lobby Restaurant** have
ocean views and offer lighter fare all day. **Riva**
is an Italian seafood restaurant with stylish decor whose service and kitchen got off to a
shaky start. ♦ 1700 Ocean Ave. 458.6700,
800/223.0888; fax 458.0020

69 Pacific Shores Hotel $$$ Lodgings with an
ocean view. ♦ 1819 Ocean Ave. 451.8711,
800/241.3848; fax 394.6657

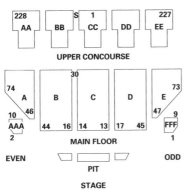

UPPER CONCOURSE

MAIN FLOOR

EVEN   ODD

PIT

STAGE

70 Santa Monica Civic Center The complex
includes the **Santa Monica Civic Auditorium**,
which presents big-name rock and jazz con-
certs, exhibitions, and trade shows. ♦ Seats
3500. 1855 Main St (box office Main St at Pico
Blvd) 393.9961

71 Cafe Beignet ★$ Knowing pastiche of a '50s
coffee shop, with neon accents and *Rock
Around the Clock* on the jukebox. Grab a ham-
burger and a malted milk before you go to the
Bay Shore Bowl (399.7731) next door, or linger
for a substantial meal of gumbo, Southern-
fried chicken, charred pork chops with dirty
rice, or pan-fried oysters. And tell the waitress
if you like to taste the spices—the teenagers
don't. You can reserve the entire restaurant and
bowl for a private party. ♦ American ♦ M-F
7AM-11PM; Sa-Su 8AM-11PM. 234 Pico Blvd.
396.6976

72 Vidiots Independent, foreign, and cult movies
for rent and sale. ♦ M-Th, Su 11AM-11PM; F-
Sa 11AM-midnight. 302 Pico Blvd. 392.8508

73 Park Hyatt on Santa Monica Beach $$$$
One of the Hyatt chain's smaller, more exclu-
sive "Park" hotels, scheduled to open in early
1991. Hyatt is going all out to please upscale
travelers in this 198-room oceanfront hotel,
with accommodations ranging from single
rooms to suites with fireplaces, mini-bars, and
Jacuzzi tubs; a department to assist guests with
business needs; a multilingual staff; a state-of-

the-art health spa; an outdoor pool and Jacuzzi
overlooking the Pacific; restaurants; bars;
meeting rooms; and ballroom. ♦ Deluxe ♦ One
Pico Blvd (Ocean Ave) 392.1234; fax 458.6478

74 Marlow's Books New and used books of all
kinds, sheet music, and magazines. ♦ M-F
10AM-8PM; Sa 10AM-6PM; Su noon-6PM.
2314 Lincoln Blvd. 392.9161

75 Eli Broad Family Foundation (1927/88,
Frederick Fisher) Private art foundation open
by appointment to scholars and curators. It
mounts changing displays of its contemporary
art collection and loans works to traveling exhi-
bitions and museums. Fisher has created a
stunning series of naturally lit galleries on 5
floors of a former telephone exchange. ♦ 3355
Barnard Way. 399.4004

Main Street
Slightly south of Santa Monica proper is **Ocean
Park**, once a seaside resort with thousands of
tiny beach cottages and a large Coney Island-

style amusement park. The neighborhood now
includes a booming shopping and dining area
for several blocks of Main Street—a pleasant
place for walking and browsing. There is a high
concentration of restaurants, most of which
have rear patios.

76 Pioneer Boulangerie and Restaurant $$
Hearty soups and fresh salads at the down-
stairs buffet, a family-style Basque dinner upstairs, or a simple snack or Continental breakfast on the outdoor patio. Built around a bakery—a glassed-in area allows you to see the
cooks at work. ♦ Bakery daily 7AM-9:30PM.
Patio breakfast daily 7AM-noon. Restaurant M-
F 11AM-3PM, 4:30-9:30PM; Sa 10AM-3PM,
4:30-9:30PM; Su 9AM-3PM, 4:30-9:30PM.
2102 Main St. 399.1405

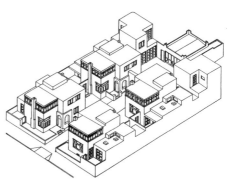

77 Horatio West Court (1919, **Irving Gill**)
Located one block off Ocean Park Boulevard
near Neilson Avenue, these impressively modern 2-story apartments were far ahead of their
time. Private residences. ♦ 140 Hollister Ave

Restaurants/Clubs: Red   Hotels: Blue
Shops/Parks: Green   **Sights/Culture:** Black

77 Gilliland's ★★$$ Very popular for its homey decor and unexpected menu, which ranges from samosas to yellowtail in *tomatillo* sauce to potato pancakes and Irish stew. High tea with harp music on Thursday and Friday afternoons. ♦ Eclectic ♦ M-Th 11:30AM-2:30PM, 6-10:30PM; F 11:30AM-2:30PM, 6-11PM; Sa 6-11PM; Su 5:30-10PM. 2424 Main St. 392.3901

78 Edgemar (1989, **Frank Gehry**) **Abby Sher** commissioned this urban village: a mixed-use development that points up the numbing mediocrity of the mini-malls elsewhere in the city. Gehry has created, not a facade with a car park in front, but a cluster of sculptural forms (high-tech, streamline, minimalist) that relate well to neighboring buildings and define a series of pedestrian spaces. ♦ 2435 Main St

Within Edgemar:

Santa Monica Museum of Art (1989, **Paul Lubowicki** and **Susan Lanier**) An egg-processing plant transformed into a sympathetic show-

Santa Monica/Venice

case for a diversity of contemporary art shows and events. Director **Thomas Rhoads** plans to alternate between LA and European artists, photographers, and performers. ♦ Admission. W-Th 11AM-8PM; F-Su 11AM-6PM. 2437 Main St. 399.2801

Gallery of Functional Art Artist- and architect-designed objects, lighting, and environments. ♦ Tu-Sa noon-9PM; Su noon-7PM. 2429 Main St. 450.2827

78 Highlights Ron Rezek and Lori Thomsen have displayed their choice of the "fifty best lights in the world"—and can order up many more. Call ahead if you are coming at lunchtime. ♦ Tu-F 10AM-6PM; Sa-Su 11AM-6PM. 2447 Main St. 450.5886

78 Art Options Brian Murphy designed a tropical industrial interior for this contemporary crafts store. ♦ M-W, F 10AM-6PM; Th noon-8PM; Su noon-5PM. 2507 Main St. 392.9099

79 Heritage Square Museum (1984, **Sumner P. Hunt**) Period rooms, local archives, and artifacts housed in a restored 19th-century house designed by Hunt for **Roy Jones**, a son of one of the city's founders. ♦ Free. Th-Sa 11AM-4PM; Su noon-4PM. 2612 Main St. 392.8537

79 The Heritage ★$$$ Sophisticated contemporary cuisine in a restored 1906 house that was built for a former mayor of Santa Monica. ♦ American ♦ W-Su 6-11PM; Sa-Su 10AM-3PM, 3-5PM. 2640 Main St. 392.4956

79 Bootz Exotic boots for urban cowboys in any skin you can think of. ♦ M-Sa 10AM-11PM; Su 11AM-7PM. 2654 Main St. 396.2466

80 Merlin McFly Magical Bar and Grill Magic acts every night but Sunday enliven this opulent bar. ♦ Daily 11:30AM-2AM. 2702 Main St. 392.8468

Santa Monica is LA's busiest freeway.

80 Max Studio Leon Max's casuals, suits, and special dresses for trendy 20 year olds. ♦ M-Sa 11AM-7PM; Su 11AM-5PM. 2712 Main St. 396.3963

80 Jadis Art Deco and other vintage furniture and collectibles of the choicest quality. ♦ Daily noon-5PM. 2701 Main St. 396.3477

80 Paris 1900 Sells museum-quality antique clothing, by appointment only. ♦ 2703 Main St. 396.0405

80 Chinois on Main ★★★★$$$$ Noisy, crowded, expensive—and not to be missed by anyone who loves inventive cuisine in the most stylish of settings. **Wolfgang Puck** created this fusion of East and West and—with chef **Kazuto Matsutaka**—has refined and improved the menu. Try the warm curried oysters, Mongolian lamb, or ginger-stuffed whole sizzling catfish with sweet pepper sauce. Desserts are special, the standout being an assortment of 3 *petits crème brûlées*. **Barbara Lazaroff** did the wonderful decor, which incorporates a fine screen by **Miriam Wosk**. Try for a table away from the open kitchen. ♦ French/Chinese ♦ M-Tu, Sa 6-10:30PM; W-F 11:30AM-2PM, 6-10:30PM; Su 5:30-10PM. 2709 Main St. 392.9025, 392.3037

80 Nature's Own Jeffrey Marshall offers eons-old fossils and minerals—mounted in jewelry or in room-size samples. ♦ M-Th, Su 11AM-9PM; F-Sa 11AM-11PM. 2736 Main St. 392.3807

80 Main Street Gallery Japanese antiques, folk art, and **Issey Miyake's Plantation** clothes for women. ♦ Daily 11AM-6PM. 2803 Main St. 399.4161

80 Wildflour Boston Pizza $$ The only pizzeria with whole wheat crust as well as white. And a huge spinach salad loaded with avocado and artichoke hearts. ♦ Pizza ♦ M-Th 11AM-11PM; F-Sa 11AM-midnight; Su noon-10PM. 2807 Main St. 392.3300. Also at: 2616 Lincoln Blvd. 392.8551; 13723 Fiji Wy, Marina del Rey. 821.3666

81 Galaxy Cafe $ Huge portions of hearty food—steamed clams, vermicelli with basil-tomato sauce, and potato pancakes served with exuberance in a streamlined '50s coffee shop. Breakfast available all day. ♦ American ♦ M-F 11:30AM-3PM, 5PM-midnight; Sa-Su 9AM-midnight. 2920 Lincoln Blvd. 392.9436

82 Famous Enterprise Fish Company ★$$ Fresh fish mesquite-grilled for the taste of the great outdoors. ♦ Seafood ♦ M-Th, Su 11:30AM-10PM; F-Sa 11:30AM-11PM. 174 Kinney St (Main St) 392.8366

82 The Buttery Croissants and coffee, brioches, chocolate chip cookies, and pasta. ♦ M 7AM-noon; Tu-Su 7AM-6PM. 2906 Main St. 399.3000

82 Homeworks Novel gifts and housewares. ♦ M-Sa 10AM-7PM; Su 11AM-6PM. 2923 Main St. 396.0101

83 Buon Gusto ★$$ Charming courtyarded café with mouthwatering deserts—*tiramisú*, ricotta cheesecake, and chocolate rum cake. The rest of the food is just OK. ♦ Italian ♦ Tu-Su 11:30AM-3PM, 5:30-11PM. 3110 Main St. 452.4288

Venice

At the turn of the century, tobacco magnate Abbot Kinney tried to create a model community fashioned after Venice, Italy, that would spur Americans to achieve their own cultural renaissance. A network of canals drained the marshy land and fed into the Grand Lagoon; the arcades along Windward Avenue and a few beleagured waterways to the south are all that survive of Kinney's grand design. A 3-day opening celebration, beginning on 4 July 1905, featured gondola and camel rides. The community was briefly self-governing, but the developers concentrated on oil exploitation and honky-tonk entertainment. In 1925, residents voted for annexation by the City of Los Angeles—which soon paved over all but 3 of the original 16 miles of canals and closed the speakeasies and gambling houses that thrived during Prohibition.

But Venice and neighboring Ocean Park continued to flourish as *Coney Island West*, defying the bluenoses and devastation by storm and fire. Flanking the boardwalks and several piers were Arabian bath houses and Egyptian bazaars, roller coasters and freak shows. As the area became more raffish and run-down it lured those who couldn't afford to live—or didn't feel at home—elsewhere. Beats gave way to hippies, Hells Angels to drug gangs; the elderly, artists, urban pioneers, and the adventurous all settled here in a crazy quilt of humanity. The diversity is symbolized in the weekend circus on Ocean Front Walk, during which jocks, executives, panhandlers, hipsters, families, bikini-clad girls, and cops in shorts promenade or roll along the boardwalk on every imaginable wheeled device. It has become a compulsory stop for tourists from Tokyo to Topeka. You can rent skates or bikes and join the scene.

Away from this colorful craziness are the studios of leading artists—many of which can be explored on the annual Art Walk (information: 392.8630)—and a ferment of cultural activity. Some of LA's most adventurous new architecture and restaurants are slotted in amid the peeling stucco and clapboard cottages. The greatest threats today are from crime and gentrification, not physical deterioration. When beach parking is full, you can leave your car in the city lot at Washington and Venice boulevards, and take the Dash Shuttle to the beach, Sunday 9AM-9PM, every 15 minutes.

84 Venice Renaissance (1989, **Johannes Van Tilburg**) Imaginative mixed-use development, with condos over stores, an arcade, and irregular massing that enhance the street and echo the tradition of Venice. ♦ Main St at Navy St

Within Venice Renaissance:

Chaya Venice (1989, **Grinstein/Daniels**) ★★$$$ Stunning new restaurant by the designers and owner of **Chaya Brasserie** in West Hollywood. Bronze and copper, natural woods and stone, and a Japanese ceiling mural achieve a pleasing harmony. Curried-crab soup and tuna spring roll, spicy swordfish and saffron paella are dishes to order. Late supper nightly to 12:30AM. ♦ Eclectic ♦ M-F 11:30AM-2:30PM, 6-10:30PM; Sa 6-11PM; Su 5:30-10PM. 396.1179

Weller   Don Weller

85 Robin Rose Ice Cream A life without chocolate raspberry truffle or white-chocolate ice cream is a life not lived to its fullest. A multicolored neon signboard identifies the other irresistible flavors. Branches are all over town. ♦ M-Th, Su 11AM-11PM; F-Sa 11AM-midnight. 215 Rose Ave. 399.1774

86 The Rose Cafe and Market ★$$ Eclectic modern dishes served in the dining area; lighter fare, including breakfasts and great pastries, can be ordered at the counter, to go or to eat on the patio. ♦ Eclectic ♦ M-Sa 9AM-11PM; Su 9AM-3PM. 220 Rose Ave. 399.0711

86 Gold's Gym This is the original home of the unbelievable well-oiled and rippling bod. There are free weights and Universal and Nautilus equipment. Intermediate bodybuilders work out here as well as pros like **Samir Bannut**, **Mr. Olympia**, and **David** and **Peter Paul**, aka the **Barbarian Brothers**. Facilities for men and women. ♦ M-F 5AM-11:30PM; Sa-Su 7AM-11:30PM. 360 Hampton Dr. 392.6004

87 Land's End $$ Fresh seafood is the thing to order at this popular patio restaurant. ♦ American ♦ M-F 6-10:30PM; Sa-Su 10AM-3PM, 6-10:30PM. 323 Ocean Front Walk. 392.3997

Legend has it that Santa Monica was named by **Father Juan Crespi** who was reminded by the area's spring waters of the tears shed by St. Monica when her son, later known as St. Augustine, turned to Christianity.

87 The Fig Tree $$ Grilled fish and flavorful vegetarian dishes served inside and on a peaceful patio just off the boardwalk. ◆ California ◆ Daily 9AM-10PM. 429 Ocean Front Walk. 392.4937

88 World Gym Joe Gold left his first gym to establish this indoor and outdoor workout space. World's weights produced a long list of champions, among them Arnold Schwarznegger. Men's and women's exercise facilities. ◆ M-Sa 6AM-10PM; Su 6AM-8PM. 812 Main St. 399.9888

RÖCKENWAGNER

89 Röckenwagner ★★★$$$ Wonderfully subtle yet simple cooking using the best meats and the freshest fish. **Hans** and **Mary Röckenwagner** are personally involved, and it shows. The tiny dining rooms, designed by **Kellen/Schweitzer** to give the illusion of spa-

Santa Monica/Venice

ciousness, are among the most relaxed of any top restaurant in LA. Specialties have included loin of veal with mustard wine sauce, veal and sweetbreads with onion and rice mousse, crab soufflé and plum tart. ◆ California ◆ Tu-Th 6-9:30PM; F 6-10PM; Sa-Su 5:30-10PM. 1023 W. Washington Blvd. 399.6504

89 Sabroso ★★$$$ A sweet and gentle place for lunch on the ivy-covered patio or for dinner in the tiny dining room. Sophisticated Mexican cooking, using duck, sausage, and shell fish, handmade tortillas, and a great mole sauce, plus regional specialties. ◆ Mexican ◆ Tu-Su 11AM-2PM, 6-10PM. 1029 W. Washington Blvd. 399.3832

90 Hal's Bar & Grill ★$$ Salads, pastas, and other basic fare in a hang-loose interior. A favorite with local artists. ◆ California ◆ M-Th 11:30AM-3PM, 6-10:30PM; F 11:30AM-3PM, 6-11PM; Sa 9AM-3PM, 6-11PM; Su 9AM-3PM, 6-10:30PM. 1349 W. Washington Blvd. 396.3105

91 Caplin House (1979, **Frederick Fisher**) This quirky, idea-packed house for the editor of *Wet* magazine was a statement of style for architect and client. Private residence. ◆ 229 San Juan Ave

92 Sidewalk Cafe $ A bustling spot for seeing and being seen. ◆ American ◆ M-Th, Su 8AM-midnight; F-Sa 8AM-1AM. 1401 Ocean Front Walk. 399.5547

92 Spiller House (1980, **Frank Gehry**) A pair of houses, each with 2 parking spaces and a garden, shoehorned onto a tiny plot. They combine a corrugated steel exterior with a woodsy interior. An archetypal low-cost Venice landmark. Private residence. ◆ 39 Horizon Ave

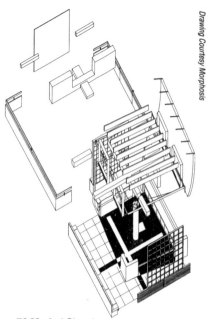

92 72 Market Street ★★★$$$ Actor/director/producer **Tony Bill** teamed up with his chums **Dudley Moore** and **Liza Minelli** to create this hot spot. The classy modern art and the prospect of Moore tickling the ivories draws the show biz and art crowds. **Morphosis** brilliantly remodeled the lofty interior, formerly used as a studio by **Frank Gehry** and **Robert Irwin**, as an airy skylit space, with shutters opening onto the street arcade, a semi-enclosed bar, and a glass-brick wall to enclose the back dining room. Chef **Leonard Schwartz** transforms the most basic dishes, like chili, black-bean soup, meat loaf, and catfish, into irresistible treats, and is just as successful with more innovative dishes. ◆ American ◆ M-Th 11:30AM-2:30PM; F 11:30AM-2:30PM, 6-11:30PM; Sa 6-11:30PM; Su 10AM-2:15PM, 6-10:30PM. 72 Market St. 392.8720

92 Small World Books Broad stock, with a special emphasis on mysteries and poetry. ◆ Daily 10AM-8PM. 1407 Ocean Front Walk. 399.2360

93 Venice Mural Terry Schoonhoven's large, much-faded mural shows a mirror image of the city on a very clear day with the distant mountains in view. Venice is full of murals—French filmmaker **Agnes Varda**, a local resident, did a poetic documentary called *Murs Murs* about them. One of the best is a block north, facing the ocean across a parking lot: **Jon Werhle**'s *The Fall of Icarus*. Another, recently renewed, is **Wallace Cronk**'s *Venice on the Half-Shell*. A local agency, **SPARC**, is commissioning more with city funds. ◆ Windward Ave at the Speedway

94 Windward Circle From 1905-29 this was the **Grand Lagoon**. Architect **Steven Erlich** has tried to awaken its ghosts with 3 complementary buildings that use concrete-filled culvert pipes to suggest Venetian porticoes. The giant **Race Through the Clouds** rollercoaster finds an echo in the neon loop of a retail block; a food market is flanked by metal frames that

---

Restaurants/Clubs: Red   Hotels: Blue

Shops/Parks: Green   **Sights/Culture:** Black

recall the steam-driven dredgers that excavated the canals. A residential block occupies the site of the **Antlers Hotel**, which was demolished in 1960. To the south is a post office, containing **Edward Biberman**'s mural of the history of Venice. ♦ Main St at Windward St

94 Hama Sushi ★$$$ A favorite neighborhood sushi bar. ♦ Japanese ♦ Tu-Th 11:30AM-2PM, 5:30-10:30PM; F 11:30AM-2PM, 5:30-11:30PM; Sa 5:30-11:30PM; Su 5:30-10:30PM. 213 Windward Ave. 396.8783

94 St. Mark's ★★$$$ (1989, **Osvaldo Maiozzi**) Loud, hip jazz club serving food that is sometimes outstanding. Hurried and occasionally obnoxious service. Dramatic granite, stainless-steel, and cobalt blue suede interior by the architect of **Pazzia**. ♦ French/Italian ♦ Cover W-Su. Daily 6PM-2AM. 23 Windward Ave. 452.2222

95 Capri ★★$$$ Serious food in a minimalist setting. Chef **Fabio Flagiello** offers such unexpected treats as polenta with prosciutto, artichokes and wild mushrooms, and swordfish with *focaccia* and red peppers. ♦ Italian ♦ M, W-F noon-2:30PM, 6-10:30PM; Sa-Su 6-10:30PM. 1616 W. Washington Blvd. 392.8777

95 Comeback Inn $ Intimate, rustic club offering vegetarian dishes and live music, ranging from jazz/fusion to avant-garde, from 9PM nightly. ♦ Cover. Restaurant Tu-Sa 6PM-midnight; Su noon-10PM. 1633 W. Washington Blvd. 396.7255

96 Dandelion Cafe $ Alfresco sandwich and salad bar—a peaceful retreat from beach madness. ♦ American ♦ Tu-Su 8AM-5PM. 636 Venice Blvd. 821.4890

96 Beyond Baroque Literary/Arts Center Adventurous readings, lectures, and performances that sustain the bohemian tradition of Venice. **Abbot Kinney** would have approved. In the old City Hall. Call for program. ♦ 681 Venice Blvd. 822.3006

97 DASH Weekend and holiday shuttle bus service. Buses run every 15 minutes 9AM-9PM. ♦ City lot at Washington and Venice Blvds

98 West Beach Cafe ★★$$$ A sleek white skylit box that pioneered the new California cuisine and the practice of exhibiting serious art works on the walls. Bar and restaurant remain favorite hangouts for the local art scene, despite (or perhaps because of) the noise and erratic service. Shrimp and sausage salad, napoleon of salmon, and roast lamb with sage are typical dishes. There's an excellent wine list. Pizza served until late. ♦ California ♦ Tu-F 8AM-2:30PM, 6-10:30PM; Sa-Su 10:30AM-2:30PM, 6-10:30PM. 60 N. Venice Blvd. 823.5396

98 Rebecca's (1987, **Frank Gehry**) ★$$$ A forest of rough wood is juxtaposed with sleek back-lit onyx panels; metal-scaled crocodiles hang from the ceiling, and there's a chandelier in the form of a glass octopus. Few consider the food worth the high prices, but owner **Bruce Marder** has the magic touch and the

place is fashionably jammed (and noisy) every night of the week If you want to hear yourself talk, ask for a booth. Best bets include the chicken *fajitas*, lamb-tongue tacos, grilled shrimp, and meltingly tender leg of lamb *adobada*. The bar is a flourishing singles scene. ♦ Mexican ♦ Daily 6-11PM. 2005 Pacific Ave. 306.6266

98 L.A. Louver Gallery Works by important LA artists, including **David Hockney**, **Ed Moses**, **Tony Berlant**, and **Michael McMillen**. ♦ Tu-Sa noon-5PM. 55 N. Venice Blvd. 822.4955. Also at: 77 Market St. 822.4955

98 Venice canals A frail remnant of Abbot Kinney's vision can be found in a succession of side canals and Venetian bridges. The city would like to fill them in, so catch them while they are still here. ♦ SE of Venice Blvd and Pacific Ave

99 Norton House (1984, **Frank Gehry**) Family house for a Japanese-American artist (note the rough log *torii* over the gate) and her screen-

writer husband (who works inside a lifeguard shelter overlooking the beach). Privacy and complexity on a minuscule site. Private residence. ♦ 2509 Ocean Front Walk

100 The Venice Beach House $$ Bed-and-breakfast in a charming house just off the ocean front in a quieter part of Venice. Each of the 8 rooms is individually decorated. ♦ 15 30th Ave. 823.1966

Bests

Cesar Pelli
Architect

Watts Towers (Rodia)

Bradbury Building (Wyman)

Horatio West Court (Gill)

Lovell House (Neutra)

Gamble House (Greene and Greene)

Eames House (Eames)

Barnsdall House (F. Lloyd Wright)

Wayfarers' Chapel (Lloyd Wright)

Schindler House (Schindler)

Malibu/Canyons

The Santa Monica and San Gabriel mountains form a crescent barrier to the north and east of LA, creating what **Carey McWilliams** called "an island on the land." The mountains define the boundaries of the flatlands, trap the smog, and offer a welcome escape from the growing pressures of urban life.

Mountains and ocean meet at **Malibu**—a place where reality and image sometimes conflict. Everything you have heard about its laid-back hedonism is true, but the celebrated beach with its sun-tanned beauties and avid surfers is largely walled off from public view along **Pacific Coast Highway** by a 6-mile stretch of what look more like hillbilly shacks than million-dollar homes. And

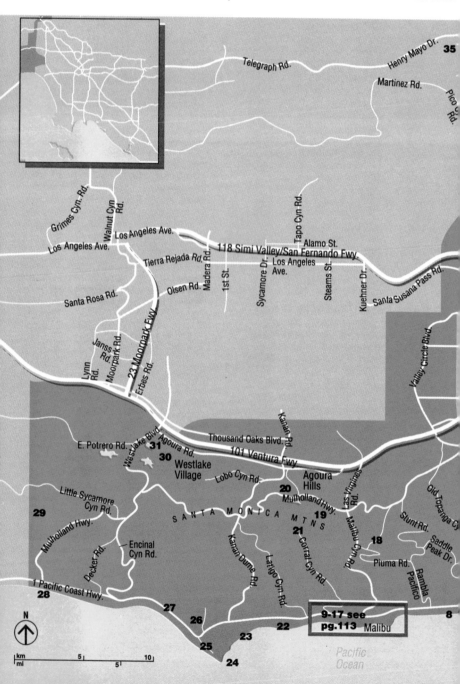

the commercial strip development is as undistinguished here as anywhere else. The Malibu of legend has to be stalked.

The first perfect bodies here were the deer, for whom the **Chumash Indians** named the area. In 1805, the **Topanga-Malibu-Sequit** rancho, an expanse that included over 22 miles of pristine Pacific oceanfront, was granted to **José Tapia**. In 1887, **Frederic H. Rindge**, a wealthy easterner, bought the entire rancho and began lifetime efforts (which his widow continued) to keep outsiders away. They built a private railroad, planted alfalfa, resorted to dynamite, and carried their protest to the State Supreme Court. Eventually, the government won. In 1929, the Pacific Coast Highway (then called the **Roosevelt Highway**) was officially opened and development came to the ocean. Sixty years later, the voters of Malibu, administered by LA County, are seeking incorporation as an independent city.

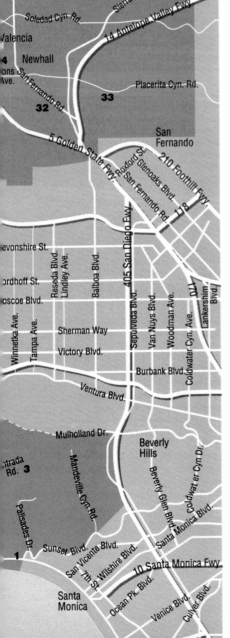

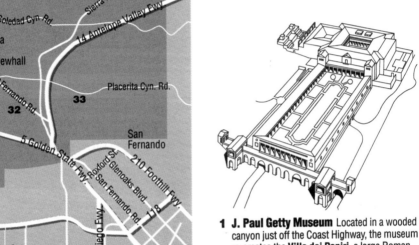

1 J. Paul Getty Museum Located in a wooded canyon just off the Coast Highway, the museum re-creates the **Villa dei Papiri**, a large Roman seaside villa at Herculaneum that was buried in AD 79 by the eruption of **Mount Vesuvius** and has yet to be fully excavated. When it opened in 1974 some critics compared this brightly colored facsimile to Disneyland; since then, architectural fashions have changed, and the building and its immaculate formal gardens seem almost mainstream. It was J. Paul Getty who conceived this new home for his extensive collections of Roman and Greek antiquities, European paintings, and French decorative arts. He endowed the museum with a trust that is now worth $3 billion—of which 4.2 percent must be spent each year on the trust's 7 operating programs, including the museum—making the Getty the richest institution of its kind in the world.

Among the antiquities are a superbly restored 6th-century Greek *kouros* (standing youth) and an outstanding collection of classical Greek vases. Paintings range from a magical **Vittore Carpaccio** panel of a hunt on the Venetian Lagoon, through the Renaissance masters (splendid works by **Pontormo** and **Mantegna** have recently been added), to **Monet, Renoir**, and **van Gogh**. French furniture, porcelain, and silver of dazzling quality are shown in period rooms.

Since Getty's death, the museum has made important acquisitions, including 3 new collections. There is a small but exquisite selection of Old Master drawings with works by **Raphael**,

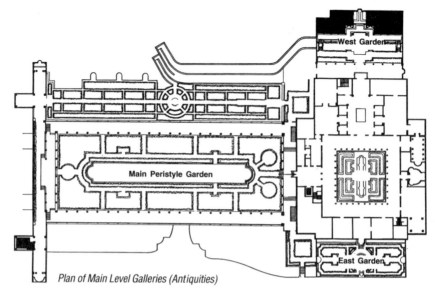

Plan of Main Level Galleries (Antiquities)

Veronese, Dürer, and the elder **Cranach**. Also on display are changing groups of extraordinary

Malibu/Canyons

illuminated manuscripts, and classic photographs from collections that feature work by **Nadar, August Sander, Lazlo Moholy-Nagy,** and **Man Ray**. When the **J. Paul Getty Center**, currently being designed by **Richard Meier** for a 110-acre hilltop site in Brentwood, opens in the 1995, the antiquities will inherit the entire villa, and a larger selection of the other collections will be exhibited in the new galleries. The study center and other Getty programs and offices will also be housed here amid terraced gardens in a complex of buildings designed to preserve the natural beauty of the site and to enhance its sweeping vistas of mountains, ocean, and city.

A well-stocked bookstore sells cards and reproductions. The **Garden Tea Room** serves lunches and afternoon snacks; no picnicking on the grounds. Orientation talks and gallery lectures are given daily. You can also teach yourself about the Greek vases and medieval manuscripts by using the interactive video discs developed for these exhibitions. For information on Friday afternoon and evening concerts, lectures, and other educational programs, call 459.7611. Parking is limited, so advance reservations are required for all visitors arriving by car, van, or charter bus. Visitors may also come by bicycle, taxi, RTD bus No. 434 (request a museum pass from the bus driver), or may be dropped off at the gatehouse by private car without advance reservations. Walk-in traffic is restricted to RTD bus passengers with passes. The museum is accessible to the handicapped. ◆ Free. Tu-Su 10AM-5PM. 17985 Pacific Coast Hwy. 458.2003

Museum Bests

John Walsh
Director, J. Paul Getty Museum

The first view of the **Getty Museum villa** as you climb the Roman road from the Pacific Coast Highway.

The Drawing Lesson by Jan Steen at the Getty.

The Getty's Aphrodite—an over life-size Greek cult figure, worth a trip to Los Angeles all by itself.

East Garden and **Pompeian mosaic fountain.**

View from the **second floor balcony** across the gardens toward the ocean.

Collection of **drawings by the great masters**, including Dürer, Raphael, Rubens, Rembrandt, and Watteau.

Cabinet by AC Boullee made about 1670, probably for Louis XV.

Andrea Mantegna's *Adoration of the Magi.*

Young Hercules Killing a Dragon by Gianlorenzo Bernini.

Changing display of **illuminated manuscripts** of the Middle Ages and Renaissance.

Rotating selection of **photographs** from one of America's best collections.

2 Sassafras Nursery Miniature vegetables and grand gardens with an emphasis on the English country look. ◆ Daily 9AM-5PM. 275 N. Topanga Canyon Blvd. 455.1933

3 Topanga State Park Nine thousand untouched acres to explore and enjoy. The high peaks offer superb views of the ocean and San Fernando Valley. A self-guided trail explains the ecology. Grassy meadows and woodlands are perfect for picnics. Water and sanitary facilities are available. No overnight camping. ◆ Free. Daily 8AM-7PM. 20825 Entrada Rd (Entrada Rd leads off Topanga Canyon Blvd. There are no park signs on Topanga Canyon Blvd, so watch carefully.) 455.2465

4 Topanga Canyon Before anyone ever hand-painted a VW bus, before anyone other than a Mexican wore *huaraches*, Topanga was an alternate community. Its bucolic homes are sheltered on the hillsides under large groves of sycamores, or scattered along the creek running through the base of the canyon. Indian settlements in the area have been dated to at least 5000 years ago. The name Topanga means *mountains that run into the sea.*

5 Will Geer's Theatricum Botanicum Outdoor theater established by the late Will Geer that presents **Shakespeare** and new and classic modern plays, June-September. ♦ 1419 N. Topanga Canyon Blvd. 455.3723

6 Inn of The Seventh Ray ★$$ Four miles from the Coast Highway is this bucolic New Wave restaurant, with tables set up beside a stream where you can absorb the benign vibrations and recorded harpist while enjoying a salad, grilled fish, and a glass of Chardonnay. ♦ Health food ♦ M-F 11:30AM-3PM, 6-10PM; Sa-Su 10:30AM-3PM, 6-10PM. 128 Old Topanga Canyon Rd. 455.1311

Santa Monica Mountains

In 1978, the Santa Monicas were designated a National Recreation Area, administered by the National Park Service. They offer numerous breathtaking views of the Los Angeles Basin and the San Fernando Valley from their summits, while retaining a wild environment within their ridges and valleys. The mountains are part of a chain that rises from the floor of the Pacific, forming the Channel Islands, the beach plateau, and the series of peaks that extend into the city center at heights averaging 1000 to 2000 feet. Slopes are covered with a collection of evergreen shrubs and scrubby trees known as chaparral. This plant life includes chamise and sage on the lower, drier hills, and a denser cover of scrub oak, sumac, wild lilac, and manzanita along stream beds. The wild plants seen everywhere, oats and mustard, were introduced only 200 years ago by the Franciscan *padres*. Fire is a major hazard in this region. Plant life is bone-dry in the summer and the smallest spark or flame can ignite a raging brush fire that will quickly spread over thousands of acres.

For a fast look at the wilderness and the housing that imperils it, you can drive the length of Mulholland Drive, a narrow country road that snakes 50 miles along the crest of the Santa Monicas, from the Hollywood Freeway to Leo Carillo State Beach. It was named for the self-taught Irish engineer who developed the first major aqueduct in the city, thus spurring its rapid growth.

7 Las Tunas Beach The name does not refer to canned fish, but is Spanish for the fruit of the prickly pear cactus.

8 Moonshadows $$$ Bountiful salads, steaks, and piped-in sounds of surf, plus the view of the breakers. ♦ American ♦ M-Th 5-11PM; F-Sa 5PM-midnight; Su 4-11PM. 20356 Pacific Coast Hwy. 456.3010

9 Tidepool Gallery One of the area's finest seashell stores also sells art inspired by the ocean. ♦ Tu-Su 10AM-5:30PM. 22762 Pacific Coast Hwy. 456.2551

9 La Salsa ★$ A huge rooftop figure marks the site of this popular takeout overlooking the ocean. The fresh vegetables, grilled chicken, fish, and meat tacos have won acclaim. ♦ Mexican ♦ Daily 8AM-10PM. 22800 Pacific Coast Hwy. 456.6299

10 Malibu Beach Inn $$$ Spanish-style hotel on the beach. Every room in the low pink stucco range has a balcony looking onto the sand; the prices match this privileged location. ♦ 22878 Pacific Coast Hwy. 465.6444, 800/462.5428

10 Saint Honoré French Bakery Loaves and brioches, fresh juices, and sandwiches attract a

steady stream of enthusiasts. ♦ M-F 6:30AM-7PM; Sa 7:30AM-7PM; Su 7:30AM-5PM. 22943 Pacific Coast Hwy. 456.2651

11 Malibu Surfrider State Beach Affectionately known as *the Bu* by surfers, it has a world-famous right reef point break. The surfing here is best in August and September when south swells are in evidence. A good location to watch surfers in action is from the adjacent Malibu pier.

11 Malibu Pier (1903, **Frederick Rindge**) Built as a landing point for ranch supplies and for Rindge's private railroad, the pier was reconstructed in 1946 and is now owned by the state. Fishing is permitted. ♦ 23000 Pacific Coast Hwy

On Malibu Pier:

Alice's ★$$ Long noted for its view of surf and sunsets, it now has a good chef, **André Guerrero**, and is worth more than a drink at the bar. Unlike most other beachfront restaurants, the menu is light and healthy, with an emphasis on salads and mesquite-grilled chicken and fish, though some of the more elaborate dishes are worth a try. ♦ California ♦ M-Sa 11:30AM-9:30PM; Su 10AM-9:30PM. 456.6646

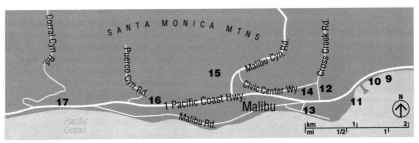

Malibu Sport Fishing Landing Located on the pier, with boats that make regular day and half-day surface fishing cruises. The bait and tackle shop rents equipment for pier or boat use. Fishing licenses are sold for boat fishing; no license is necessary for pier fishing. ◆ Daily 6AM-6PM. 456.8030

11 Adamson House (1929, **Stiles O. Clements**) Romantic Spanish Colonial house that is preserved the way its owner, **Rhoda Rindge Adamson**, left it at her death in 1962. It is a showcase of colorful Malibu tiles and a reminder of the imperious family that once owned 17,000 acres in and around Malibu. The house and adjoining **Malibu Lagoon Museum** are open for frequent 45-minute tours. ◆ Admission. Tours W-Sa 10AM-1:15PM. 23200 Pacific Coast Hwy. 456.8432

12 Malibu Art and Design A contemporary general store of domestic and personal items coupled with an art gallery that shows leading local artists. ◆ M-Sa 10AM-6PM; Su noon-5PM. 3900 Cross Creek Rd. 456.1776

12 La Scala Malibu ★$$$$ The flower-filled patio overlooking Malibu Creek is a lovely place

Malibu/Canyons

for lunch, and for dinner there's a cozy interior. Smoked salmon and pasta with eggplant, risotto, calamari salad, and herbed roast chicken have all been praised. In the Malibu Country Mart. ◆ Italian ◆ M-Th 11:30AM-2:30PM, 5:30-10:30PM; F 11:30AM-2:30PM, 5:30-11PM; Sa 5:30-11PM; Su 5:30-10PM. 3874 Cross Creek Rd. 456.1979

12 Malibu Deli Authentic deli treats, from lox to corned beef to egg creams. ◆ M-Th, Su 7AM-8PM; F-Sa 7AM-9PM. 3894 Cross Creek Rd. 456.2444

13 Malibu Beach Colony At last, a listing about where the movie stars *do* live. An exclusive and very private beach for the famous and wealthy since 1926, when silent movie queen **Anna Q. Nillson** moved here. Many of the beach cottages have bedrooms sufficient to sleep the staff of the *Tonight Show* and hot tubs big enough to soak the Olympic swim team. The drives and beach here are private, but the dramatic **Stevens House** by **John Lautner** can be seen from Pacific Coast Highway as a double-height concrete quarter-circle rising into the sky. Private residences. ◆ Webb Wy off Pacific Coast Hwy

13 Granita Wolfgang Puck promises a casual Mediterranean-style beach restaurant, which may have as great an impact on the area as **Spago** has had on the Westside. January 1991. In the Colony Plaza Shopping Center. ◆ Pacific Coast Hwy at Webb Wy

14 Godmother of Malibu ★★$$ There are a few tables, but this is primarily a catering service and takeout—for which it is praised above all the restaurants in Malibu. A young, enthusiastic staff prepares such specialties as vegetable lasagna, truffled chicken breast, and

stuffed veal. ◆ Italian ◆ Tu-F 9:30AM-7:30PM; Sa 9:30AM-6PM; Su 9:30AM-4PM. 23410 Civic Center Wy. 456.5203

14 Malibu Books Food for the mind, and an invaluable resource for resident writers (and compulsive readers). The stock is rich and varied. ◆ M-Sa 10AM-6:30PM. 23410 Civic Center Wy. 456.1375

14 Malibu Adobe ★$$ Celebrity hangout designed by **Ali McGraw** in southwestern style. In the past, the kitchen has done little to distract from star-gazing, but the cooking seems to have improved. Salads, grills, and pasta with smoked chicken are favorites. ◆ Southwestern ◆ 23410 Civic Center Wy. 456.2021

14 Tops Malibu Southwestern furniture, jewelry, and accessories. ◆ M-Sa 11AM-6PM; Su noon-5PM. 23410 Civic Center Wy. 456.6002

15 Pepperdine University Popularly known as *Surfers U* for its oceanfront site, this is actually a respected 4-year college that offers bachelor's and master's degrees in 50 major subject areas. It has a law school, 3 satellite centers in Southern California, and a year-in-Europe program at Heidelberg University. ◆ 24255 W. Pacific Coast Hwy. 456.4000

16 24955 Pacific Coast Highway (1989, **Goldman Firth Architects**) Crisp low-rise commercial development that lifts the spirits of motorists speeding by.

17 Beau Rivage ★$$$ A warm and cozy roadhouse with a piano indoors and a patio in back. The rich, steeply-priced menu has drawn mixed reviews, but locals throng in. ◆ French ◆ Daily 5-11PM. 26025 Pacific Coast Hwy. 456.5733

18 Saddle Peak Lodge ★★★$$$$ Wonderful hearty food served in a romantic mountain lodge (once a bordello) with a roaring fire and stags' heads on the walls. Seasonal game is the specialty—the roast venison is especially good, but so are the vodka-cured salmon and the carpetbagger steak. Well worth a long drive, but don't go without a reservation. ◆ American ◆ W-Sa 6-11PM; Su 5-11PM. 419 Cold Canyon Rd, Calabasas. 818/340.6029

19 Malibu Creek State Park Four thousand acres including **Malibu Creek**, 2-acre **Century Lake**, ageless oaks, chapparal, and volcanic rock. There is excellent day hiking on almost 15 miles of trails. Movie companies sometimes film on location in this secluded park. No camping. May be entered from Malibu Canyon. ◆ Free. 28754 Mulholland Hwy, Agoura. Parking charge. 818/706.1310

20 Paramount Ranch From the early 1920s on, Westerns have been shot on the standing set and what was formerly a 4000-acre expanse of hills. Ranger-guided hikes over the ranch and movie set are offered on weekends; 330 acres of wooded countryside are open daily for riding, walking, and picnicking. Silent films shown under the stars on summer Sundays. Information: 874.2276, 818/597.9191. ◆ Daily dawn to dusk. 2813 Cornell Rd, Agoura (Cornell Rd exit south off the Ventura Fwy) 818/880.4508

21 Sunset viewing A 360-degree panorama of ocean, mountains, and the San Fernando Valley. Drive to the end of Corral Canyon Rd, beyond Malibu Canyon, and climb to the boulders on the crest of the hill.

22 Geoffrey's ★$$$$ Go for the fabulous cliff-edge terrace with its sweeping ocean view, or the handsome **Richard Neutra** interior, ribbed like the interior of a boat hull. The health-conscious menu includes grilled fresh fish, pastas, salads, and some hearty dishes such as steak in peppercorn sauce and rack of lamb. ◆ California ◆ M-Th noon-4PM, 5-10PM; F noon-4PM, 5-11PM; Sa noon-4PM, 6-11PM; Su 10AM-4PM, 6-10PM. 27400 Pacific Coast Hwy. 457.1519

23 Paradise Cove A private beach full of nooks and crannies for walking and exploring. The **Sandcastle**, a staid, inexplicably popular restaurant, overlooks the ocean. ◆ Admission. Paradise Cove Rd off 28100 block of Coast Hwy

24 Point Dume Named in 1782 by **George Vancouver**, the English explorer, for **Father Dumetz**, a Jesuit at the Ventura Mission. A residential area with a hard-to-get-to beach. Until the 20th century, the point was high and peaked, but the top has been shaved off for a housing development.

25 Splash California ★$$$ Intimate, elegant rooms facing the ocean and a rich, innovative menu. ◆ French ◆ Daily 4-10PM. 6800 Westward Beach Rd. 457.5521

26 Zuma Canyon Orchids Prize-winning plants bred here are sent all over the world. ◆ Daily 10AM-4PM. 5949 Bonsall Dr. 457.9771

27 Trancas $$ Long-established nightclub offering dancing and entertainment nightly; also comedy, dance, and stage productions. The restaurant is open all day and there's even an outdoor patio. ◆ Restaurant: daily 7AM-9PM. Nightclub: 9PM-2AM. 30765 Pacific Coast Hwy. 457.5516

28 Leo Carrillo State Beach A broad and clean sandy beach named for the Los Angeles-born actor **Leo Carrillo** (1880-1961). Descendant of one of California's oldest families and son of the first mayor of Santa Monica, Carrillo became famous as *Pancho*, the sidekick to TV's *Cisco Kid*. There is surfing at the northern end of the beach.

29 Point Mugu State Park A secluded and idyllic park with 70 miles of trails, a tall-grass prairie preserve, beautiful sycamores, and lovely canyons. Excellent for day hikes and picnics. Camping hook-ups are provided. Advance camping reservations required. ◆ No. of Pacific Coast Hwy, across from Leo Carrillo State Beach. 818/706.1310

30 Boccaccio's $$$ Dependable standby that—despite its location in the midst of a housing development—offers some degree of sophisticated service and a truly marvelous oak tree and lakeside view. ◆ International ◆ M-F 11:30AM-2:30PM, 6-10PM; Sa 6-10PM; Su 5:30-9PM. 32123 W. Lindero Canyon Rd, Westlake Village. 889.8300

31 Tuscany ★★$$ Serious eating in a remote location. Herb-flavored veal chops, cheese-stuffed chicken breast, and inventive antipasti. **Tommaso Barletta** runs a tight ship. ◆ Italian ◆ M-F 11:30AM-2PM, 6-10PM; Sa-Su 6-10PM. 968-4 Westlake Blvd, Westlake Village. 818/880.5642

32 William S. Hart Park *While I was making pictures, the people gave me their nickels, dimes, and quarters. When I am gone, I want them to have my home.* With this testament, silent film cowboy star **William S. Hart** bequeathed his 253-acre ranch for use as a public park. One hundred and ten acres have been preserved as a wilderness area. The developed portion of the property includes an animal compound stocked with domestic beasts and a herd of buffalo, picnic sites, and Hart's ranch-style home, **La Loma de los Vientos**, which contains paintings and sculptures by **Charles M. Russell**. ◆ Park: daily 10AM-dusk. Museum: W-Su 11AM-4PM, mid June-mid Oct; W-F 10AM-1PM, Sa-Su 11AM-4PM, mid Oct-mid June. 24151 Newhall Ave at San Fernando Rd, Newhall. 805/254.4584

Malibu/Canyons

33 Placerita Canyon Park and Nature Trail A 314-acre native chaparral park located in a picturesque canyon amid stands of California live oak. There is a nature center and self-guided tour designed to illustrate the relationships of the plants and animals in the area. ◆ Free. Nature Center daily 9AM-5PM. 19152 Placerita Canyon Rd, Newhall. 805/259.7721

34 California Institute of the Arts Founded with an endowment from **Walt Disney** in 1970, Cal-Arts is an elite cutting-edge college with schools of film, dance, theater, art, and music. Graduates (including **David Salle** and **Eric Fischl**) have invigorated the art world on both coasts. ◆ 24700 McBean Pkwy, Valencia. 805/255.1050

35 Six Flags Magic Mountain If the kids want thrills and fun, but you want a day in the country, the 100 rides and attractions of Magic Mountain are the answer. The amusement park is set into 260 beautifully landscaped acres atop the rolling hills of **Valencia**, with grassy knolls, trees, and shrubbery, creating a spacious and sylvan feeling quite different from the crowded hurly-burly of the conventional entertainment park.

Rides at Magic Mountain are guaranteed to be fast and scary. There are 5 roller coasters to test your mettle. The **Colossus** is billed as the largest, fastest, highest, and steepest wooden roller coaster ever built. After 9200 feet at speeds up to 65 miles per hour, who could argue? The **Revolution** offers a 360-degree vertical loop at 60 miles per hour; the **Shock Wave** gives thrill seekers the opportunity to loop the loop while standing up. The **Gold Rusher** is a theme roller coaster on which you become a passenger aboard a runaway mine train. The

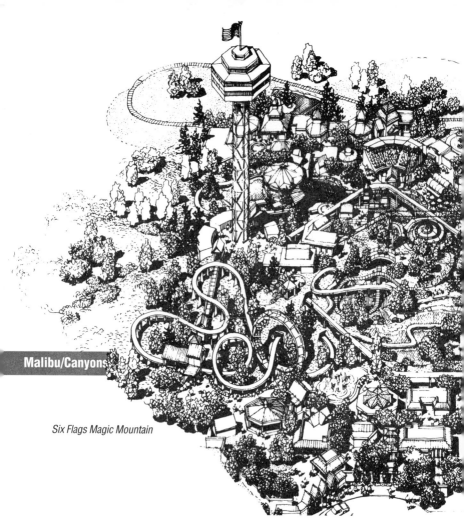

Six Flags Magic Mountain

latest addition is **Viper**, a roller coaster with several loops and an 18-story drop!

Magic Mountain has some memorable rides for those who like to get soaking wet as part of the fun. Similar in concept and course, the rides differ in modes of conveyance: the **Tidal Wave** takes you by boat over a 50-foot waterfall, the **Log Jammer** features hollowed-out logs; the **Jet Stream**, speed boats; the **Roaring Rapids**, white-water rafts.

For panoramic views of the surrounding territory, try the **Eagle's Flight Tramway**, a 40-degree inclined funicular railroad to the top of Magic Mountain, or the **Sky Tower**, a ride to the observation deck of a 384-foot *space needle* structure.

Fast fun on the level is featured at **Sand Blasters**, where dunebuggies are powered by electric motors, or **Grand Prix**, where visitors can play at being **Mario Andretti**.

The past is not forgotten at Magic Mountain. The **Grand Carousel** is an exquisitely restored 1912 merry-go-round. At **Spillikin Handcrafters Junction** such traditional American crafts as glassblowing and

blacksmithing are demonstrated and goods are sold in quaint shops.

Nighttime attractions for teenagers include **Back Street**, a high-energy city block, and **After Hours**, a high-tech dance club. The 1200-seat **Magic Moments Theater** presents *California Dreamin'*; and there's plenty of rocking at the **Contempo Pavilion**. Divers and dolphins are the stars at the **Aqua Theater**, exotic animals take center stage at the **Greenwillow Theater**. A fireworks extravaganza explodes over **Mystic Lake** nightly through the summer.

Bugs Bunny, Daffy Duck, Wile E. Coyde, and other Warner Brothers' cartoon characters welcome youngsters to the 6-acre **Bugs Bunny World** with its 15 pint-size rides, and they can enjoy a magic show through the summer in the **Valencia Falls Pavilion**. And don't miss the petting zoo.

Food is plentiful in the park, although a half-hour wait after meals before hitting the larger rides is recommended. The **Four Winds**, at the summit of Magic Mountain, offers a delicious salad buffet at lunchtime and hot meals in the evening. The **Timbermill** serves hearty American-style food. **Food Etc.** is a fast-food

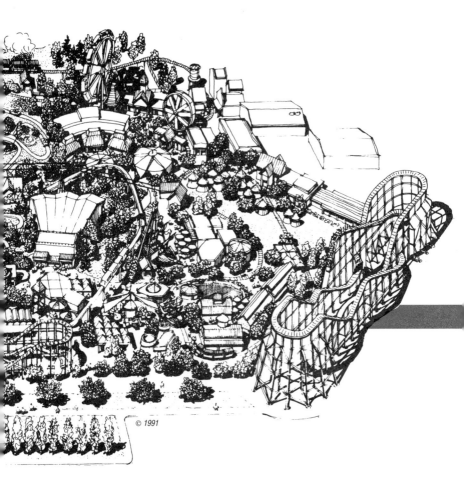

© 1991

restaurant with a surprisingly sophisticated Mondrian-influenced decor by **Shari Canepa**. Other spots include **Valencia Terrace, La Cantina**, and **Suzette's Bakery**. Naturally, hot dogs, soda pop, etc., are abundant everywhere.

One admission fee at Magic Mountain conveniently covers all rides and attractions. Height and weight restrictions on some rides.

♦ M-Th, Su 10AM-10PM; F-Sa 10AM-midnight, Memorial Day-Labor Day. Rest of year weekends and school holidays only, from 10AM; call for closing times. Magic Mountain Pkwy off Interstate 5, Valencia. 818/367.5965, 818/992.0884, 805/255.4100

Michael McCarty
Michael's Restaurant

Mr. Chow's in Beverly Hills: lobster and ginger, Peking duck, Tattinger Rosé.

Spago in West Hollywood: prosciutto pizza, goat-cheese-and-basil calzone, Joseph Phelps Insignia.

Valentino in Santa Monica for Friday lunch. Whatever Piero wants, plus *Angelo Gaja Barbaresco, Maurizio Zanella Ca del Basco Reserve.*

West Beach Cafe in Venice. Only after midnight: old Cabernets and lots of Champagne.

My house in **Malibu**. Lunch after tennis: Krug 71, 71 *Romanee-Conti*, 78 *Musigny, Comte de Vogue*, BBQ pork tenderloin with Maui onions, cilantro, jalepeño, olive oil, salsa, red and yellow peppers, basil, and balsamic vinegar.

Easter, 4th of July, Labor Day, and Thanksgiving: 12-hour eating fest for 50 wild partygoers.

Paul Gurian's. BBQ shrimp.

Don Henley's. Ribs. The Woody Creek smoked hearty meat-fest every New Year's.

72 Market Street in Venice. Florida stone crabs, Stoli's.

Michael's in Santa Monica. Phil Reich's computerized wine list and my food, such as shad roe, roach crabs, white-truffle pasta, Killian's red Olympic onion rings, foie gras sauté, all the sauces! The dreaded Health Bar.

Angeli. Magnums of everything, whatever John and Evan suggest.

John's Garden Grocers. Best fruit and sandwiches in town.

San Fernando Valley

You drive out of the LA Basin and look down from the crest of the hills. As far as the eye can see is a vast sprawling city, surpassing in scale anything you might have imagined. At night it's spectacular: colorful and glittering with millions of lights in every direction, its mountain-ringed boundaries disappearing into the sky. It is a Doppelgänger metropolis added to the urban original on the flip side of the Santa Monicas. It is the **San Fernando Valley**. Even though it is separated from the city proper by a full-blown mountain range, most of the San Fernando Valley (known to residents as *The Valley*) is part and parcel of the city of Los Angeles. Some things distinguish it, however, and they are: *space* —a lot of it, predominantly flat; *heat*—more of it, since the valley is usually 10-20

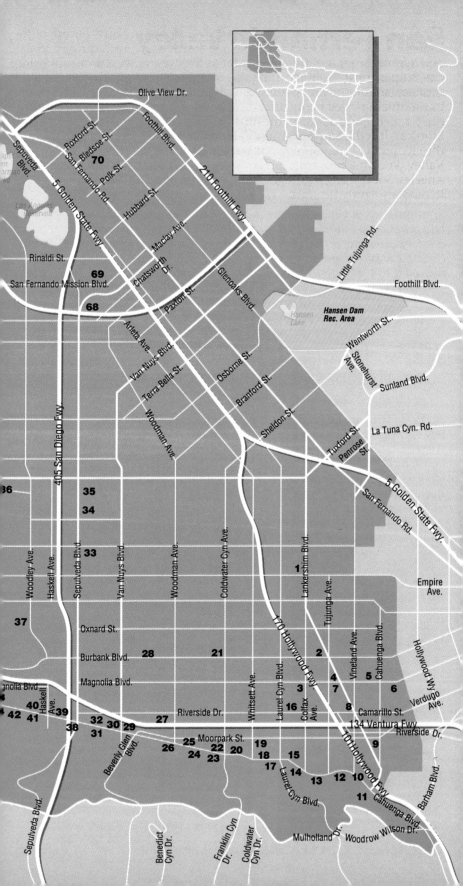

degrees warmer than the LA Basin; *people*—over one million, a third of the population of the city of Los Angeles and nearly as many as the city of Dallas; *streets* and *cars*—an extended grid of seemingly endless boulevards and streets crosses the length and breadth of the valley, reinforcing its dominant car culture. Hopelessly inadequate public transit makes an automobile a necessity here. For anyone accustomed to eastern American or European cities, the valley is unimaginable. When on 22 May 1915, the City of Los Angeles originally annexed the San Fernando Valley, it effected a land grab that added 177 square miles to its existing 108 square miles.

For a long time land use in the valley was limited to ranching and non-irrigated agriculture; the land boom of the 1880s quickly fizzled out. Speculators anticipated the arrival of the **Owens River Aqueduct** in 1913, buying up thousands of acres of valley property. To share in the water this brought, ranchers voted to join the municipality of Los Angeles. Property values boomed, and one group of investors profited on their investment at a ratio of about 8 to one. Boom succeeded boom, and hundreds of thousands moved into the valley, encouraged by jobs in nearby aviation, electronics, and entertainment industries. Several decades of accelerated development made the area famous for rapid-start tracthouse neighborhoods and instant shopping centers. The vast spaces were quickly filled up due to a low-density development pattern: only 7.2 people per acre here compared to the Wilshire District's 38.9 persons per acre. The valley is predominantly residential and almost 80 percent white, remarkably homogeneous for such a large population group. The west and south sides are more affluent than the

San Fernando Valley

east, and heavy industry is almost exclusively concentrated in the northern area around **San Fernando**, **Sylmar**, and **Pacoima**. With these few exceptions, it is basically all of one fabric, very middle class, and extremely mobile. Until recently, single-family ranch-style homes outnumbered multiple dwellings two-to-one, leaving it a place where it is still possible to maintain a semblance of the American dream: to own one's own home with a spacious yard and a 2-car garage.

Area code 818 unless otherwise noted.

1 The Palomino $$ The primo country-western club in the city, also featuring R&B and blues; a favorite of **Jerry Lee Lewis**. The long tables and rustic decor add atmosphere. Arrive early for a good seat and a generous helping of barbecue. ♦ American ♦ Cover. M-Sa 7:30PM-2AM. 6907 Lankershim Blvd, N. Hollywood. 764.4010

2 Norah's Place ★$ Quinoa, the sacred grain of the Incas, is a key ingredient in the distinctive cuisine of Bolivia. So are a few of that country's hundred-plus kinds of potato. Other dishes are more familiar —empanadas, *lomo saltado* (sirloin tips). Live folk music and dancing on weekends. ♦ Bolivian ♦ Tu-Th 5-11PM; F-Su noon-3PM, 5-11PM. 5667 Lankershim Blvd, N. Hollywood. 980.6900

3 Erawan ★$$ Good cooking in a nondescript setting. Recommended: the beef curry and the special seafood dish, which includes shrimp, squid, and clams in a delicious spicy sauce. ♦ Thai ♦ Tu-F 11AM-2:30PM, 5-10PM; Sa noon-10PM; Su noon-9PM. 5145 Colfax Ave, N. Hollywood. 760.1283

4 Salomi ★$$ Exceedingly hot curries of high quality. ♦ Indian ♦ M-Th noon-2:30PM, 5-10PM; F noon-2:30PM, 5-11PM; Sa 5-11PM; Su 5-10PM. 5225 Lankershim Blvd, N. Hollywood. 506.0130

5 Arte de Mexico Create your own hacienda from the 7 warehouses crammed with crafts from Mexico and the southwest. ♦ M-Sa 9:30AM-5:30PM; Su 10AM-5:30PM. 5356 Riverton Ave, N. Hollywood. 769.5090

6 Beograd ★$ Hearty Serbo-Croatian food, wine, and songs enliven this friendly home-away-from-home for expatriates. The music and celebration can be infectious on weekends. ♦ Yugoslavian ♦ W-Th, Su 5-10PM; F-Sa 5PM-2AM. 10580 Magnolia Blvd, N. Hollywood. 766.8689

7 China Chef Wang ★$$ The lighting isn't romantic and the flowers may be plastic, but it's got some of the best Chinese food in the valley. Mostly Szechuan and Mandarin. There may be a wait on weekends. ♦ M-Th, Su 11AM-10PM; F-Sa 11AM-11PM. 5049 Lankershim Blvd, N. Hollywood. 509.9999

8 La Maida House $$$ A 1920s Mediterranean villa surrounded by lush gardens offers bed, breakfast, and if you order in advance, de-

Restaurants/Clubs: Red   Hotels: Blue
Shops/Parks: Green   **Sights/Culture**: Black

licious dinners. Pretty rooms and suites offer a civilized alternative to the chain hotels. ♦ 11159 La Maida St (Lankershim Blvd) N. Hollywood. 769.3857

9 Barsac Brasserie ★★$$ Delicious bistro food in a cool setting. Duck-and-mushroom salad, penne with olives and tomatoes, and choucroute with veal sausage have been praised. ♦ French ♦ M-F 11:30AM-2:30PM, 5:30-10:30PM; Sa 5:30-11PM; Su 5:30-10:30PM. 4212 Lankershim Blvd. 760.7081

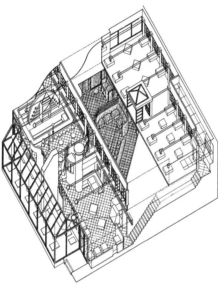

Drawing Courtesy Johannes Van Tilburg

9 L'Express $$ (1986, **Johannes Van Tilburg**) A stunning interior helps sustain the popularity of this café/restaurant with different age groups and at different times of day—for a business lunch, a quiet dinner in the enclosed room upstairs, or action at the stand-up bar. It is located in the base of a large brick-and-glass wedge designed to catch the attention of motorists speeding by Universal City on the freeway. ♦ California ♦ Daily 7AM-1:30AM. 3575 Cahuenga Blvd, Universal City. 763.5518

9 Thai Barbecue $$ A slick, reliable Thai eatery. The usual Thai egg rolls and *mee krob* (sweet fried noodles), plus deep-fried squid and sautéed baby clams. ♦ Thai ♦ M-F 11:30AM-3PM, 5-10:30PM; Sa-Su 5-10:30PM. 3737 Cahuenga Blvd, N. Hollywood. 760.9691

9 The Baked Potato $$ One of LA's best established clubs for contemporary jazz, where **Lee Ritenour** and **Larry Carlton** got their start. Loud and intimate. Shrimp-and-cheese stuffed potatoes are a specialty. ♦ Cover. Daily 7AM-2AM. 3787 Cahuenga Blvd, N. Hollywood. 980.1615

10 The Racquet Center For a small annual fee you can reserve any one of the 20 lighted tennis courts and 10 racquetball courts, and use the well-appointed locker room. ♦ M-F 6AM-midnight; Sa-Su 7AM-midnight. 10933 Ventura Blvd, Studio City. 760.2303

11 Mary's Lamb ★$ Cozy restaurant and take-out where everything is homemade, from the meat loaf and fried chicken to the pies and baked goods. ♦ American ♦ Tu-F 7AM-3PM, 5:30-10PM; Sa-Su 9AM-3PM, 5:30-10PM. 10820 Ventura Blvd, Studio City. 505.6120

12 Hortobagy ★$$ Named for the plains region of Hungary, home of the fabled Hungarian horsemen, so it's no surprise that the food here is solid, spicy, unpretentious stuff. There are stews, rich soups, grilled and breaded meats, as well as amazing homemade sausages. There's a small deli case and a selection of Hungarian wines. ♦ Hungarian ♦ Tu-Su 11AM-9:30PM. 11138 Ventura Blvd, Studio City. 980.2273

12 Sushi Nozawa ★★$$ Victorian table manners are observed at this splendidly old-fashioned restaurant, but the stern warnings on what not to do or eat are worth it: chef Nozawa serves some of the best and freshest sushi in town. ♦ Japanese ♦ M-F noon-2PM, 5-10PM; Sa 5-10PM. 11288 Ventura Blvd, Unit C, Studio City. 508.7017

13 Jitlada ★★$$ One of the best Thai restaurants in LA, specializing in shellfish. Among the stars: crunchy fried squid, barbecued chicken, Thai sausage salad, and Bangkok duck. ♦ Thai ♦ M-Th, Su 11:30AM-3PM, 5-10PM; F-Sa

San Fernando Valley

11:30AM-3PM, 5-11PM. 11622 Ventura Blvd, Studio City. 506.9355

13 St. Moritz ★$$ Long-time area favorite that draws an older crowd with its reliable central European cuisine—notably the *wienerschnitzel*—served in generous portions. There is a lovely patio. ♦ Swiss ♦ Daily 5-9PM. 11720 Ventura Blvd, Studio City. 980.1122

14 La Loggia ★★$$ Movie moguls and power brokers keep this modern trattoria jumping. Its popularity hasn't waned since the day it opened—locals describe it as the valley's answer to Spago. Pasta and risotto are standouts. ♦ Northern Italian ♦ M-Th 11:30AM-2:15PM, 5:30-10:30PM; F 11:30AM-2:15PM, 5:30-11PM; Sa 5:30-11PM; Su 5-10PM. 11814 Ventura Blvd, Studio City. 985.9222

14 Teru Sushi ★$$ Hugely popular sushi bar that launched what is now LA's favorite grazing fare. Theatrical presentation: the chefs are from Central Casting. Also serves other Japanese specialties. ♦ Japanese ♦ M-Th noon-2:30PM, 5:30-11PM; F-Sa noon-2:30PM, 5:30-11:30PM; Su 5-10PM. 11940 Ventura Blvd, Studio City. 763.6201

15 Wine Bistro ★$$ Wine and pretty good bistro fare in a warm and woodsy setting. ♦ French ♦ M-F 11:30AM-10:30PM; Sa 5:30-10:30PM. 11915 Ventura Blvd, Studio City. 766.6233

16 Dutton's Bookstore Well-stocked branch of the store in Brentwood. ♦ M-F 9:30AM-9PM; Sa 9:30AM-6PM; Su 11AM-6PM. 5146 Laurel Canyon Blvd, Studio City. 769.3866

17 San Pietro Bar & Grill ★★$$ Prawns with rice-wine sauce, pasta with salmon and cucumber, and grilled meats and vegetables are good bets at this improved version of the Bel Air pizza place. Valley girls, too. ♦ Italian ♦ Daily 11:30AM-midnight. 12001 Ventura Blvd, Studio City. 508.1177

17 Le Pavillon ★$$ Café food with an organic bent. Crêpes, omelets, and more than generous salads. ♦ French ♦ M-Th 11AM-10PM; F-Sa 11AM-11PM. 12161 Ventura Blvd, Studio City. 980.0225

17 Paris Express Cafe $ Pâtisserie and elegant light meals; fresh croissants even on Sundays. No longer connected to the original in Beverly Hills. ♦ French ♦ M-Sa 10AM-10PM; Su 10AM-8PM. 12321 Ventura Blvd, Studio City. 508.9977

18 Art's Deli $$ A full-service deli that is a favorite among valley tennis players. Pastrami is a

San Fernando Valley

house specialty. ♦ Deli ♦ Daily 7:30AM-8:30PM. 12224 Ventura Blvd, Studio City. 769.9808

19 Oyster House Saloon and Restaurant $$ The oyster bar and the pasta with seafood are the main attractions in this popular watering hole. ♦ Seafood ♦ M-Sa 11AM-2AM; Su 4PM-midnight. 12446 Moorpark St, Studio City. 761.8686

20 Sportsmen's Lodge and Sportsmen's Lodge Restaurant ★$$$ A moderately priced hotel ($$) in a verdant setting. Inside, the glass-walled dining room looks out onto ponds, a stream, and a waterfall. All this beauty and the food is good, too. ♦ American ♦ Tu-Sa 5:30-10PM; Su 4:30-10PM. Hotel: 12825 Ventura Blvd, Studio City. 769.4700. Restaurant: 12833 Ventura Blvd. 984.0202

21 Tujunga Wash Mural The world's longest mural (a half-mile and still unfinished) occupies the west wall of a concrete flood control channel, and tells the history of California from the age of the dinosaurs to the present. Anger brings history to life, as in the revolutionary murals of Mexico City, and though this collaborative effort is no artistic masterpiece, it's a provocative learning experience for participants and visitors. **Judy Baca** has directed the project over the past 10 years for **SPARC**, a nonprofit Venice arts group. ♦ Coldwater Canyon Blvd (Burbank Blvd-Oxnard St) N. Hollywood

22 Iroha Sushi ★★$$ Excellent sushi in a quiet, caring bar that's well hidden from the street. ♦ Japanese ♦ M-Th noon-2:30PM, 6-10:30PM; F noon-2:30PM, 5:30-11PM; Sa 5:30-11PM. 12955 Ventura Blvd, Sherman Oaks. 990.9559

22 La Serre ★$$$$ Considered by some to be the best restaurant in the valley—but others doubt it's worth the Beverly Hills tab. Rich food served in a pretty flower-filled room. ♦ French ♦ M-Th noon-2:30PM, 6-10:30PM; F noon-2:30PM, 6-11PM; Sa 6-11PM. 12969 Ventura Blvd, Sherman Oaks. 990.0500

23 Bistro Garden ★$$$ Indoor version of the Beverly Hills favorite for the ladies who lunch. Light, airy room with traditional decor, good service, and long menu; stick to the simplest dishes. ♦ Eclectic ♦ M-F 11AM-11PM; Sa 6-11PM; Su 11AM-3PM. 12950 Ventura Blvd, Sherman Oaks. 501.0202

23 Marrakesh ★★$$ Couscous with lamb, chicken with olives, and *b'stilla* (chicken with spices, nuts, and fruit beneath a flaky pastry crust) amid authentic decor. ♦ Moroccan ♦ M-Th, Su 5-10PM; F-Sa 5-11PM. 13003 Ventura Blvd, Sherman Oaks. 788.6354

24 The Great Greek $$$ Greek food in an exuberant atmosphere. The appetizers are a better bet than the entrees. Music and dancing nightly. The 14-course banquet, intended to serve one, is enough for any 3 people we know. ♦ Greek ♦ Daily 11:30AM-midnight. 13362 Ventura Blvd, Sherman Oaks. 905.5250

24 Mistral ★$$ Generally good French bistro, with warm atmosphere and a touch of Provence in the generous use of herbs to enliven the baked mussels and grilled steak. ♦ French ♦ M-Th 11:30AM-3PM, 5:30-10:30PM; F-Sa 5:30-11PM; Su 5:30-10:30PM. 13422 Ventura Blvd, Sherman Oaks. 981.6650

25 Camille's ★★$$$ Reasonably priced yet innovative cuisine served in a romantic setting of white trellised booths and colors that grandma will love. Viennese chef **Peter Schawalder** has a deft hand for the classics—including a fine *Sachertorte*. ♦ French ♦ Tu-F 11:45AM-2PM, 6-10PM; Sa 6-10PM. 13573 Ventura Blvd, Sherman Oaks. 995.1660

25 Prezzo ★$$$ Favorite meeting place for the valley's *jeunesse dorée*, yet the food is surprisingly good. Scallops in red pepper sauce, pasta with smoked chicken, and grilled swordfish are recommended. ♦ Italian ♦ M-F 11:30AM-2:30PM, 5:30PM-midnight; Sa-Su 5PM-1:30AM. 13625 Ventura Blvd, Sherman Oaks. 905.8400

26 Moonlight Tango Cafe ★$$ A band in white suits plays rhumbas on white instruments in a '40s setting; all it needs is **Carmen Miranda** to sashay on stage and lead a conga line. The food can be good—seafood gumbo, juicy lamb, fettucine with wild mushrooms, and spicy homemade sausages. ♦ Eclectic ♦ M-Th, Su 5PM-midnight; F-Sa 5PM-2AM. 13730 Ventura Blvd, Sherman Oaks. 788.2000

27 Sherman Oaks Fashion Square One of the first large shopping plazas in the area. Anchored by **Bullock's** and **The Broadway**, the brick-paved outdoor promenades are lined with quality shops. ♦ M-F 10AM-9PM; Sa 10AM-6PM; Su noon-5PM. 14006 Riverside Dr (Hazeltine Ave), Sherman Oaks. 783.0550

27 Sunkist Headquarters Building (1969, **A.C. Martin & Associates**) Striking concrete crate built for the industry that is synonymous with Southern California. Sunkist is the trademark of a citrus-growing collective of ranches all over the Southland. ♦ 14130 Riverside Dr, Sherman Oaks

28 Cevicheria El Silencio ★$ South American seafood of rare authenticity. Standouts include *ceviche* of scallops, deep-fried stuffed potatoes, and fried rice with seafood. ♦ Peruvian ♦ M, W-Su noon-10PM. 14111 Burbank Blvd, Van Nuys. 997.9412

29 Gen Mai-Sushi $$ Peace, love, and sushi. This spot, run by disciples of **Masahisa Goi**, serves vegetarian and macrobiotic dishes as well as sushi with brown rice. ♦ Organic ♦ Tu-F 5:30-midnight; Sa 5:30-11PM. 4454 Van Nuys Blvd. Suite M, Sherman Oaks. 986.7060

30 Lannathai ★$$ An elegant setting—diners sit around what was once a swimming pool, now full of koi. The menu boasts 86 specialties. ♦ Thai ♦ M-F 11:30AM-2:30PM, 5:30-10:30PM; Sa 5-11PM; Su 5-10PM. 4457 Van Nuys Blvd, Sherman Oaks. 995.0808

30 Outer Limits Contemporary pop culture—American and European adult comics, fantasy, and science fiction—art works, and collectibles. ♦ M-Th 11AM-9PM; F-Su 11AM-11PM. 14513 Ventura Blvd, Sherman Oaks. 995.0151

30 Le Cafe $$$ Simple dishes served in a strikingly modern setting. The **Room Upstairs** features top-flight jazz talent nightly. ♦ American ♦ Daily 8AM-2AM. 14633 Ventura Blvd, Sherman Oaks. 986.2662

31 L'Express $$$ Unfortunately, the view from the sidewalk café is of Ventura Blvd, but nevertheless, L'Express tries to be a lively French bistro. Steak and *pommes frites* and pâté with cornichons in the valley. ♦ French ♦ Daily 7AM-1AM. 14910 Ventura Blvd, Sherman Oaks. 990.8683

32 La Frite $$ Crêpes, omelets, quiche, all nicely prepared and served until late. ♦ French ♦ M-Th 11AM-11PM; F 11AM-midnight; Sa 10AM-12:30AM; Su 10AM-11PM. 15013 Ventura Blvd, Sherman Oaks. 990.1791. Also at: 22616 Ventura Blvd, Woodland Hills. 347.6711

33 Kenny's Kitchen ★$ A friendly couple from Bombay offers good home-cooking in a mini-mall. The vegetable dishes are outstanding, as are the chicken in garlic sauce and lamb *korma*. ♦ Indian ♦ Tu-Su 11:30AM-9:30PM. 14126 Sherman Wy, Van Nuys. 786.4868

34 Western Bagel Jalapeño and blueberry are among the 18 varieties, freshly baked and sold 24 hours a day. ♦ 24 hours. 7814 Sepulveda Blvd, Van Nuys. 786.5847

35 Dr. Hogly-Wogly's Tyler Texas BBQ ★★$ The Real Thing, good enough to bring tears to the eyes of a Lone Star exile. People line up to eat down-home ribs, links, chicken, and beans, despite the lack of amenities. ♦ Barbecue ♦ Daily noon-10PM. 8136 Sepulveda Blvd, Van Nuys. 780.6701

36 94th Aero Squadron Headquarters Restaurant $$ A 1973 version of a French farmhouse complete with bales of hay in the front yard. A fun place to take the kids. Located near the Van Nuys Airport. ♦ American ♦ M 11AM-3PM, 5-10PM; T-F 11AM-3PM, 5-11PM; Su 9:30AM-2:30PM, 5-11PM. 16320 Raymer St, Van Nuys. 994.7437

37 Arts Park An ambitious attempt to bring serious culture to the valley. Leading California architects—**Morphosis**, **Mark Mack**, Hodgetts-Fung—have designed the elements of a 50-million-dollar arts center on 60 acres of the **Sepulveda Dam Recreation Area**. The **San Fernando Valley Cultural Foundation** is now trying to secure funding and win over the **Sierra Club** and the **Army Corps of Engineers**, who would rather keep the space green. Meanwhile, in **Woodley Park**, to the north, there's another kind of high flying. Every weekend, the **San Fernando Valley Fliers** meet here to show off their model planes. This is serious stuff—a 9-foot-long replica of the **Concorde** has been spotted. ♦ 6335 Woodley Ave, Van Nuys. 341.7194

38 India Palace ★$$ Chicken *tikka* and lamb *vindaloo* are standouts at this serious restaurant. ♦ Indian ♦ M-Sa 11:45AM-2PM, 5:30-10PM; Su 5:30-10PM. 4523 Sepulveda Blvd, Sherman Oaks. 986.8555

San Fernando Valley

39 Shihoya ★★$$ Another strict sushi bar, where (as at **Nozawa's** in Studio City) you obey the rules and enjoy outstandingly fresh and beautiful sashimi and sushi. ♦ Japanese ♦ M, W-Sa 5:30-10:30PM; Su 5:30-9:30PM. 15489 Ventura Blvd, Sherman Oaks. 986.4461

40 Angkor ★$ Steamed sole in yellow-bean sauce, charbroiled pork, and poached salmon in lemon-grass sauce are standouts in this simple but satisfying storefront. ♦ Cambodian ♦ M-Sa 11AM-3PM, 5-10PM; Su 5-10PM. 16161 Ventura Blvd. Suite B, Encino. 990.8491

41 Benihana of Tokyo ★$$$ The teppan-grill tradition of Japan, raised to the level of theater by a chef trained to handle a knife like a samurai. ♦ Japanese ♦ M-F 11:30AM-2:30PM, 5:30-10:30PM; F 11:30AM-2:30PM, 5:30-11PM; Sa 5-11PM; Su 5-10PM. 16226 Ventura Blvd, Encino. 788.7121

42 Tempo $ A taste of the Middle East, welcome for its unfamiliarity. Try the falafel, hummus, and shish kebab. ♦ Israeli ♦ Daily 11AM-12:30AM. 16610 Ventura Blvd, Encino. 905.5855

43 Rancho de los Encinos State Historical Park Leave the traffic behind and recall the stagecoach era, when dusty travelers stopped off here to refresh themselves. Among the 5 acres of expansive lawns, duck ponds, and tall eucalyptus are a 9-room adobe built in 1849 by **Don Vicente de la Osa** and a 2-story limestone French-style home designed in 1870 by **Eugene Garnier**. ♦ Admission. Grounds: W-Su 10AM-5PM. Home tours: W-Su 1-4PM. 16756 Moorpark St, Encino. 784.4849

44 Stratton's ★$$$ A branch of the cozy restaurant in Westwood Village that has drawn praise for its veal chops, braised ribs, and steaks. ♦ American ♦ M-Th 11:30AM-3PM, 5-10:30PM; F-Sa 11:30AM-3PM, 5-11:30PM; Su 5-10:30PM. 16925 Ventura Blvd, Encino. 986.2400

44 Akbar ★★$$ Superb Mogul cooking, with excellent tandoori dishes. A branch of the original in Marina del Rey. ♦ Indian ♦ M-F, Su 11:30AM-2:30PM, 5:30-10:30PM; Sa 5:30-10:30PM. 17049 Ventura Blvd, Encino. 905.5129

45 Town and Country Shopping Center and Plaza de Oro Unusual for the absence of large department stores. Both plazas are open, rambling complexes, with different levels and handsome landscaping. Shopping here has a relaxed, almost villagelike quality. ♦ M-F 10AM-9PM; Sa 10AM-6PM; Su noon-5PM. 17200 Ventura Blvd, Encino. 788.6100

Within the Town and Country Shopping Center and Plaza de Oro:

Oak Tree An astonishing oak tree, estimated to be over 1000 years old. The branches spread 150 feet and the trunk is over 8 feet in diameter. ♦ Louise Ave, just south of Ventura Blvd

Bao Wow ★$ Dim sum, salads, and noodle dishes served in a high-tech dining room or on

San Fernando Valley

the patio. ♦ Chinese ♦ M-Th 11:30AM-10PM; F-Sa 11:30AM-11PM; Su noon-9PM. 17209 Ventura Blvd. 789.9010

Lalo & Brothers ★★$$$ Ambitious blend of nouvelle California and *nuevo* Mexican presented in a romantic dining room and elegant patio. Specialties have included cabbage stuffed with lobster, grilled shrimp in tequila, lamb with wild mushrooms and the trufflelike fungus *Huitlacoche*. Monday is Mexican night, with regional specialties, live marimba music, and handshaken margaritas. ♦ California/Mexican ♦ M-F noon-2:15PM, 6-10PM; Sa 6-10PM. 17237 Ventura Blvd. 784.8281

Silver Grille ★$$ In the same shopping mall is a health-conscious restaurant serving such dishes as tortilla soup laden with fresh herbs, grilled tuna with an orange-ginger sauce, chicken quesadillas, and a great *tarte tatin*. ♦ California ♦ M-F noon-3:30PM, 5-10PM; Sa-Su noon-3:30PM, 5:30-10:30PM. 17239 Ventura Blvd. 784.4745

The LA Cabaret Comedy Club $$ Lively talent draws enthusiastic regulars. Restaurant and separate bar. Call for showtimes. ♦ Cover. Restaurant: M-Th 6-10:30PM; F-Sa 6PM-midnight; Su 6-10:30PM. 17271 Ventura Blvd. 501.3737

46 Juel Park Lingerie for perfectionists from Sue Drake, a designer who joined the firm (long in Beverly Hills) a year after its founding in 1929. She created form-fitting bias-cut silk gowns for Jean Harlow, Carole Lombard, and Norma Shearer, so you are buying not only a work of art but a piece of a legend. Custom-made negligees and teddies in satin, lace, and organdy.

Poules de luxe and the men who want to flatter them are equally welcome. By appt. only. ♦ 17940 Rancho St, Encino. 213/276.3292

47 Adam's $$$ Ribs broiled over oak and mesquite, a 55-foot salad bar, an authentic soda fountain, an extensive historical photo collection of the San Fernando Valley, and 350 potted plants. One of the most popular and lively places in the valley. ♦ American ♦ M-Th 11:30AM-3PM, 4:30-10PM; F-Sa 11:30AM-3PM, 4:30-11PM; Su 10AM-2PM, 4:30-10PM. 17500 Ventura Blvd, Encino. 990.7427

47 Domingo's Well-stocked family-run Italian grocery and deli. ♦ Tu-Sa 9AM-6PM; Su 10AM-4PM. 17548 Ventura Blvd, Encino. 981.4466

48 Mon Grenier ★★$$$ If your attic had French cooking like this, your house would be jammed, too. Reliable standbys include salmon en croûte and pheasant with wild mushrooms. Service can be surly. ♦ French ♦ M-Th 6-9PM; F-Sa 6-9:30PM. 18040 Ventura Blvd, Encino. 344.8060

49 The Country Club $$ Top country-western, rock, New Wave, R&B, etc., in a concert setting. Live music most nights. Full restaurant; soft drinks only. Free parking. Days and shows vary. ♦ Cover. 18415 Sherman Wy, Reseda. 881.5601

50 Silver Chopsticks ★$ Bold Szechuan dishes, including noodles with chicken and sesame paste, wonderful *siu mai* (pork-filled noodle dumplings), and wontons in peanut chili sauce. ♦ Chinese ♦ M-Sa 11:30AM-9:30PM; Su 4-9PM. 19538 Ventura Blvd, Tarzana. 344.6112

51 Los Angeles Pierce College A branch of the Los Angeles Community College system specializing in agriculture, horticulture, landscape architecture, and animal husbandry. ♦ 6201 Winnetka Ave, Woodland Hills. 347.0551

Drawing Courtesy Annie Kook

51 Farm Tour The Animal Husbandry Department at Pierce College offers a free guided tour of one of the last working farms in the city. It's all here: cows milking, hens laying, goats bleating, pigs wallowing. Children will love the close look at farm life, while adults appreciate the picturesque bucolic setting. Reservations must be made one week in advance for the tours, held only during the school year. ♦ School tours Tu, Th 10AM; other groups Sa 10AM. 6201 Winnetka Ave, Canoga Park. 719.6425

Restaurants/Clubs: Red   Hotels: Blue
Shops/Parks: Green   **Sights/Culture:** Black

52 La Paz ★$ Pork baked with annato seeds in banana leaves, barbecued goat, and garlicky octopus, plus whole baked fish and paella make **Oscar Iturralde**'s Yucatan eatery a culinary adventure. ◆ Mexican ◆ M-Th, Su 11AM-9PM; F-Sa 11AM-10:30PM. 21040 Victory Blvd, Woodland Hills. 883.4761

52 Gaetano's Bistro ★★$$ Delicious shrimp with green beans, fusilli with smoked duck, and grilled whole bass with a sauce of wild mushrooms are among the standouts at this *simpatica* trattoria. In the Trillium Building. ◆ Italian ◆ M-F 11:30AM-2:30PM, 5:30-10:30PM; Sa 5:30-10:30PM. 6336 Canoga Ave, Woodland Hills. 596.5900

53 Woodland Hills Promenade One of the poshest of the indoor malls. Clustered around **Saks Fifth Avenue** and **Bullocks Wilshire**, the tiled corridors are lined with luxury mercantiles. Lighting, fountains, and indoor landscaping add to the cool elegance of the place. ◆ M-F 10AM-9PM; Sa 10AM-7PM; Su 11AM-5PM. Topanga Canyon Blvd (Oxnard-Erwin Sts) Woodland Hills. 884.7090

54 Brother's Sushi ★★$$ Wonderful sushi, but don't miss the ultrafresh oysters, deep-fried soft-shell crabs in season, or the crackly salmon skin. ◆ Japanese ◆ M-F 11:30AM-2PM, 5:30-10:30PM; Sa 5:30-10:30PM. 21418 Ventura Blvd, Canoga Park. 992.1284

55 Lautrec $$ Lamb and seafood are the specialties of this stylish restaurant. ◆ Eclectic ◆ M-Th 11AM-3PM, 5-10PM; F-Sa 11AM-3PM, 5-11PM; Su 5-9PM. 22160 Ventura Blvd, Woodland Hills. 704.1185

56 Adagio ★★$$ Pastas, fish, and meat dishes all excel, and the *penne all'amatriciana* and fried calamari have won applause. ◆ Italian ◆ Tu-F 11:30AM-2:30PM, 5:30-10PM; Sa-Su 5:30-10PM. 22841 Ventura Blvd, Woodland Hills. 346.5279

57 Calabasas Inn $$$ An expansive garden setting, popular for dinner and drinks at sundown. ◆ American ◆ Tu-F 11:30AM-3PM, 5-10PM; Sa 5-11PM; Su 10AM-3PM, 4:30-10PM. 23500 Park Sorrento, Calabasas. 888.8870

57 Sagebrush Cantina $ Movie-set Old West saloon and patio housing a lively singles bar and a popular restaurant serving mostly Mexican standards. ◆ Mexican ◆ M-Th 11AM-10PM; F 11AM-11PM; Sa-Su 10AM-11PM. 23527 Calabasas Rd, Calabasas. 888.6062

57 Leonis Adobe The home-improvement tendencies of the San Fernando Valley may be traced back to 1879, when **Miguel Leonis** decided to upgrade a one-story 1844 adobe that he owned. A second level and balcony in the modish style of Monterey, then the capital, were added to the simple rectangular structure, thus making it the first chic home in the area. ◆ Free. W-Su 1-4PM. 23537 Calabasas Rd, Calabasas. 712.0734

Ordinance is passed prohibiting the serenading of women without a license. **1838**

58 Canoga Mission Gallery (1936, Francis Lederer) Early film star Francis Lederer designed and built this as a mission-style stable. Later, Mrs. Lederer remodeled it for use as a gallery and gift shop of Californian and Mexican arts. ◆ W-Su 11AM-5PM. 23130 Sherman Wy, West Hills. 883.1085

59 Shadow Ranch A restored 1870 ranch house built by LA pioneer **Albert Workman** and located on 9 acres that were at one time part of a 60,000-acre wheat ranch. The stands of eucalyptus on the property, planted in the late 19th century, are purported to be the parent stand of the trees that are now one of the most prominent features of Southern California botany. The ranch is presently used as a community center. ◆ Free. Tu-Th 9AM-9PM; W 9AM-10PM; Sa 8AM-5PM. 22633 Vanowen St, Canoga Park. 883.3637

60 Antique Row Over 28 shops specializing in Americana. The range is memorabilia to publications, with an emphasis on golden-oak Victorian furniture, bric-a-brac, and collectibles. A good place to start is the **Antique Company**. ◆ Daily 11AM-5PM. 21513 Sherman Wy, Canoga Park. 347.8778

61 Orcutt Ranch Horticultural Center (1920, C.G. Knipe) Originally part of a 200-acre estate belonging to **William** and **Mary Orcutt**. The ex-

tensive gardens, lush landscaping, and venerable trees accented by statuary are relaxing and lovely. There are spots for picnics, hiking trails, and horticultural demonstrations. House tours given the last Sunday of each month from 2-5PM, September-June. ◆ Free. Ranch daily 7AM-5PM. 23600 Roscoe Blvd, West Hills. 883.6641

62 Les Sisters Southern Kitchen ★$ Authentic down-home fare—shrimp jambalaya, potent gumbo, the best fried chicken and hush puppies. BYOB. ◆ Southern ◆ Tu-F 11AM-2:30PM, 5-9PM; Sa 5-9PM; Su 5-9PM. 21818 Devonshire St, Chatsworth. 998.0755

63 Alexis $ An exceptional deli/market—sandwiches, salads, Greek specialties, and imported groceries. ◆ Greek ◆ M-Th 11:30AM-3PM, 5-9PM; F-Sa 11:30AM-3PM, 5-10PM. 9034 Tampa Ave, Northridge. 349.9689

64 Thai Gourmet ★$ Great northern Thai/Laotian food, absolutely the spiciest in town. Don't be a tough guy and ask them to make it hot. Cartoon smoke will pour out of your ears and you won't be able to taste the rest of your dinner. Not for everyone, but certainly interesting, is a jackfruit ice cream with garbanzo beans in it. ◆ Thai ◆ M-F 11:30AM-3PM, 5-10PM; Sa-Su 5-10PM. 8650 Reseda Blvd, Reseda. 701.5712

65 California State University at Northridge A branch of the California State University system offering both undergraduate and graduate courses in a number of liberal arts and science disciplines. **Richard Neutra** was made architect of the campus in 1960 but designed only the 1961 **Fine Arts Building**. ◆ 18100 Nordhoff St, Northridge. 885.1200

66 Paru's ★$ Delicious vegetarian dishes—curries, pilafs, *samosas*, and crunchy pancakes—served in a tiny white storefront. No alcohol. ◆ Indian ◆ M, W-Su 11:30AM-9PM. 9545 Reseda Blvd, Northridge. 349.3546. Also at: 5140 W. Sunset Blvd, Hollywood. 213/661.7600; 9340 Pico Blvd, Beverly Hills. 213/273.8088

67 Luneburg Deli-Cafe $ Black Forest ham on pumpernickel, or a paprika-flavored sausage with potato salad and red cabbage are among the inexpensive lunches served in this old-world café. And there's an even larger choice of provisions at the deli counter. ◆ German ◆ M-F 7:30AM-8PM; Sa 7:30AM-6PM. 18041 Chatsworth St, Granada Hills. 368.9005

68 Andres Pico Adobe (c. 1834) This is the second oldest home in Los Angeles, built by Mission San Fernando Indians. **Andreas Pico**, brother of the one-time governor, bought it in 1853, and with his son **Romulo** added a second story in 1873. By the early 1900s it had fallen into disuse, but in 1930 the curator of the **Southwest Museum** purchased and restored it. It was bought by the City of Los Angeles in 1967. The **San Fernando Historical Society** has its headquarters here. ◆ W-Su 1-4PM; weekdays by appointment. 10940 Sepulveda Blvd, Mission Hills. 365.7810

San Fernando Valley

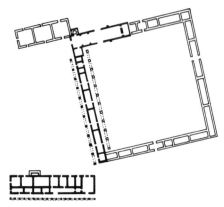

69 Mission San Fernando Rey de España Founded in 1797 by **Friar Fermin Lasuen**. Until the dissolution of the missions in the mid-1830s, San Fernando was an essential part of the economic life of Los Angeles, supplying a great portion of the foodstuffs for the fledgling community. The original buildings were completed in 1806, but were subsequently destroyed by earthquake and replaced in 1818. History repeated itself in the 1971 Sylmar/San Fernando earthquake, when the church again sustained damage so grave that it had to be reconstructed in 1974. The adobe construction of the early period had a simple yet monumental quality that achieved richness through the repetition of structural elements. This quality is best observed in the 243-foot-long convento, where 19 semicircular arches supported by

massive square pillars form a loggia over time-hollowed tiles. Tours of the mission include working, sleeping, and reception areas, giving visitors a sense of day-to-day life during the early days of the complex. ◆ Admission. Daily 9AM-5PM. 15151 San Fernando Mission Blvd, Mission Hills. 361.0186

70 Merle Norman Museum Vast assortment of classic cars, nickelodeons, and 19th-century musical instruments, including the **Emperor Franz Joseph**'s piano, which are played on the 2 daily tours, Tuesday-Saturday 10AM and 1:30PM. Reservations must be made 6 weeks in advance. ◆ 15180 Bledsoe St, Sylmar. 367.1085, tour information 367.2251

Bests

Merry Norris
Former President, Board of Cultural Affairs Commissioners; Art Consultant

Beverly Hills Civic Center Expansion (**Charles Moore** and **Urban Innovations Group**) Sensitively attuned to the City Hall and other existing structures. Integrates quietly and charmingly with surrounding city/civic activity.

Museum of Contemporary Art (MOCA) (**Arata Isozaki**) A true jewel box, perfectly sited, and a beautiful counterpoint to the rash of new glass/granite highrise buildings that are beginning to dominate the downtown arena.

Figueroa at Wilshire, Mitsui Fudosan (**Albert C. Martin and Associates/Gerald Hines**) This may prove to be the most impressive office building in downtown Los Angeles. The wide plazalike sidewalk provides a major amenity for those who will never have occasion to use the building.

First Interstate World Center (**I.M. Pei and Partners/Maguire Thomas Partners**) A real *beacon* that has already reshaped the Los Angeles skyline. One of the most interesting aspects of this astonishing building is how the perspective changes according to one's approach.

72 Market Street (**Morphosis Architects**) Inspired use of materials for the facade as well as an enormous sash window that allows the dining experience to interact with street activity.

Pacific Design Center (**Cesar Pelli and Associates**) The dialogue between the Blue Whale and the Green UFO is particularly dynamic and best understood from the West Hollywood Recreation Park on San Vicente Boulevard.

Hollyhock House (**Frank Lloyd Wright**) I want to live there and be *Queen of the Hill* or *Empress of Barnsdall Art Park!* Beautiful location, buildings sadly in need of repair, overall landscaping a disaster—everything calls for loving attention on an ongoing basis.

Watts Towers (**Sam Rodia**) Staggering in concept, amazing in execution. One of the all-time treasures of Los Angeles.

Restaurants/Clubs: Red		**Hotels:** Blue
Shops/Parks: Green		**Sights/Culture:** Black

Griffith Park/ North Central

Northeast of Hollywood in the foothills of the Santa Monica Mountains are 2 of LA's most attractive neighborhoods and its grandest park. **Griffith Park** covers over 4000 acres, making it one of the largest urban green spaces in America. It is named for **Colonel Griffith J. Griffith**. Immensely rich, he bought the land in 1882 and donated it to the city in 1896.

South of the park are the residential communities of **Los Feliz** and **Silver Lake**. Begun in the '20s before the advent of pad construction, in which bulldozers take huge bites out of hillsides to create level tracts, the homes here conform to the picturesque undulations of the land. The winding roads and tiled roofs massed on the slopes around the 1907 **Silver Lake Reservoir** resemble a Mediterranean hill town; there are stunning views of the city and a road around the lake for biking and jogging. This area also has LA's highest concentration of modern masterpieces, notably by **Richard Neutra**, **Rudolph Schindler**, **Gregory Ain**, and **John Lautner**.

Surrounded by freeways, **North Central** LA is an island of cultural and geographic diversity. The dialects of nearly every Latin American country can be heard on the streets. The area includes the communities of **Echo Park, Elysian Park, Highland Park**, and **Eagle Rock**.

1 Griffith Park The park is divided into 2 main areas: the flatlands, with their golf courses, picnic areas, pony and train rides, tennis courts, **Merry-Go-Round**, the **Zoo**, **Travel Town**, the **Observatory**, and the **Greek Theatre**; and the mountainous central and western areas, which have been left undeveloped except for numerous hiking and horse trails. There are 4 main entrances to the park: Western Canyon Road, off Western Avenue north of Los Feliz Boulevard, leading to Ferndell; Vermont Avenue and Hillhurst Avenue, north of Los Feliz Boulevard, leading to the Greek Theatre and the **Bird Sanctuary**; Crystal Springs Drive, off Riverside Drive, leading to the Ranger Station, Merry-Go-Round, and golf courses; and the junction of the Golden State (Interstate 5) and Ventura (California 134) freeways, leading to the Zoo and **Travel Town**. Rangers lead a hike on the first Saturday of the month at 9AM from the Merry-Go-Round parking lot. **Sierra Club** tours include evening outings during full moon. Call 665.5188 for schedule. There are no specific bike paths, but regular paved roads are open to cyclists. Bikes are not permitted on the fire roads or horse trails. Eighteen picnic areas are located in the park. Some have benches and tables; those in Ferndell and Vermont Canyon have barbecues and water. **Park Center** and **Mineral Wells** have some areas with cooking facilities. Visitors may also picnic on the grass. ♦ Daily 5:30AM-10:30PM, mountain roads close at sunset. Visitors Center: 4730 Crystal Springs Dr. 665.5188

1 Ranger Station Information, free road and hiking trail maps. ♦ Daily 6AM-10PM. 4730 Crystal Springs Dr. 665.5188

2 Merry-Go-Round A well-preserved merry-go-round on the green, constructed in 1926 and moved to the park in 1936. ♦ Admission. Daily mid June-mid Sep; Sa-Su and LA public school holidays 10AM-4:30PM, mid Sep-mid June. Park Center Picnic Area, off Griffith Park Dr. 665.3051

3 Baseball A baseball diamond in the **Crystal Springs Picnic Area** is open by permit. It is used by city college teams for their league games.

4 Golf There are 3 golf courses; 2 are full-size 18-hole courses. City-registered golfers may make reservations; others will be allowed on the green as space becomes available. ♦ 485.5566

5 Zoo The zoo opened in 1966 and has over 2000 animals, grouped according to continent of origin, on 75 landscaped acres. Many of the animals are in environments that simulate their natural habitat with surrounding moats,

thus allowing visitors to see them without bars. The zoo preserves 78 endangered species. Explore the **Koala House** and the **Aviary**; go for a camel or elephant ride; take in a bird show. Children may mingle with gentle beasts and explore the American Southwest on **Adventure Island**. The **Animal Nursery** proudly displays the newest arrivals. Baby stroller and wheelchair rentals, picnic tables, snack bar, and tram tour are available. ♦ Admission. Daily 10AM-6PM. 5333 Zoo Dr, near the junction of the Golden State and Ventura Fwys. 666.4090, recorded information 666.4650

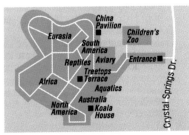

6 Gene Autry Western Heritage Museum

The singing cowboy of movies, radio, and television opened this wonderful tribute to the spirit of the West in 1988. **Walt Disney Imagineering** has brought the memorabilia, art works, and movie clips to life, so that you can get a visceral sense of what it was like to be a settler, a cowboy, or a sheriff. Scholarship and show biz are fruitfully combined, and the museum presents regular exhibitions as well as the permanent collection. ♦ Admission. Tu-Su 10AM-5PM. 4700 Zoo Dr. 667.2000

7 Travel Town

The romance of the rails lives at this open-air museum of transportation, displaying many antique railroad and trolley cars, locomotives, planes, and automobiles. An enclosed structure houses several fire trucks and a circus animal wagon. Many of the exhibitions are open for children to climb on board. Members of a model train club work on an enormous train layout on Saturday. ♦ Free. M-F 10AM-4:30PM; Sa-Su 10AM-5:30PM. Zoo Dr, near Forest Lawn exit from Ventura Fwy. 662.9678

7 Live Steamers The Los Angeles Live Steamers **Club** brings its tiny steam locomotives to an area just northeast of **Travel Town** each Sunday. The trains run on tracks only 7 inches apart, but they're authentic in every detail and powerful enough to pull several fully loaded cars. Children are given free rides and a chance to examine the miniatures. ◆ Su 10AM-2:30PM. 1 mile W of the zoo in Griffith Park, E of Travel Town. 669.9729

8 Equestrian Center and Cricket Fields Two fields are located in the center of the equestrian track near Riverside Drive. The equestrian track near Riverside Drive functions as a practice area that leads to all trails. There are 43 miles of horse trails within the park. While the Department of Parks and Recreation does not maintain stables, several commercial stables on the outskirts of the park rent horses by the hour. All accept cash only and require a security deposit. ◆ Daily 8AM-4PM. 840.8401

Restaurants/Clubs: Red   **Hotels:** Blue
Shops/Parks: Green   **Sights/Culture:** Black

8 Riding and Polo Club Schools for riding and polo, livery stables, and an indoor polo arena, lounges, and a restaurant are located in this facility that is a part of the park's **Equestrian Center**. Professional polo matches are held in the spring and fall on Saturday at 8:15PM. The restaurant serves regional American dishes. ♦ Club: M-Sa 11AM-3PM, 5-10PM; Su 11AM-3:30PM. Café Polo: M-W 11AM-3PM; Th-Su 11AM-3PM, 5-10PM. 480 Riverside Dr, Burbank. 818/841.5981

9 Circle 'K' Stables ♦ M-F 8AM-5PM; Sa-Su 7:30AM-5PM. 910 S. Mariposa St, Burbank. 818/843.9890

10 Bar 'S' Stables ♦ Daily 8AM-4PM. 1850 Riverside Dr, Glendale. 818/242.8443; riding lessons 818/547.0203

11 Sunset Ranch The Old West in the heart of the city, with photogenic stables and moonlit rides to the top of the mountains with stupendous views over LA. Night rides every Friday at 5PM, "first come first served"; groups by appointment on other nights. ♦ Daily 9AM-5PM. 3400 N. Beachwood Dr. 469.5450

12 The Ferndell A natural glade along a spring-fed stream, planted with native and exotic ferns. Paths and picnic tables make this an outstanding place to retreat from the world for an al fresco meal. ♦ Daily 6AM-5PM. Fern Dell Dr bounded by Black Oak Dr, Red Oak Dr (off Los Feliz Blvd near Western Ave)

Griffith Park/North Central

13 Observatory and Planetarium (1935, **John C. Austin** and **F.M. Ashley**) The restored copper-domed moderne structure dominates the Hollywood Hills and commands a view over the city and (on rare clear days) to Catalina. Get a closeup of the heavens through the observatory's twin refracting telescope; clear nights only, 7-10PM. Displays in the **Hall of Science** explain astronomy and physical sciences in participatory exhibitions. The pendulum in the center of the rotunda hypnotizes visitors with its constant gentle swing. A fascinating show in the **Planetarium Theatre** re-creates eclipses, northern lights, and cycles of the stars through the use of a huge Zeiss projector. For sci-fi lovers, a show in the **Laserium** surrounds the audience with laser light, laser rock, and starship-sound. For more information on this popular show, call 997.3624.
♦ Admission. Hall of Science: Free. M-F, Su 12:30-10PM,

Sa 11:30AM-10PM, June-Sep; Tu-F 2-10PM, Sa-Su 12:30-10PM, Oct-May. Planetarium: Admission. Shows afternoons and evenings. Closed Monday in winter. Northern end of Vermont Ave. 664.1191

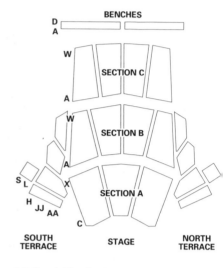

14 Greek Theatre An amphitheater presenting mostly popular music, June through the first week in October. It is ringed by picnic tables; box suppers may be purchased from concessionaires inside. Bring a sweater. Beer and wine available. ♦ Seats 6000. Admission. 2700 N. Vermont Ave. Tickets and schedules 410.1062, subscription information 468.1767

15 Bird Sanctuary A wooded canyon with ponds and a stream where birds are encouraged to nest. There are picnic tables. ♦ Daily dawn-dusk. Vermont Canyon Rd, just north of the Greek Theatre

16 Tennis Twelve day-use courts. City-registered players may make reservations; others will be allowed to play as courts become available. Refreshments sold. ♦ Fee. Courts daily 7AM-9PM. Vermont Ave at Vista del Valle Dr. Reservations 661.5318.

Vermont Canyon Peppertree Lane Four day-use courts. No reservations taken. ♦ Fee. Courts daily 7AM-7PM. Griffith Park Dr at Los Feliz Blvd

17 Train Ride Another tiny train, this one runs daily. Adults as well as children may ride. ♦ Fee. M-F 10AM-4:30PM; Sa-Su 10AM-5PM. Crystal Springs Dr. 664.6788

Observatory and Planetarium

17 Pony Rides A safe, small track with ponies for children. ♦ Daily 10AM-5PM. Crystal Springs Dr. 664.3266

18 Swimming Pool An Olympic-size pool is open during the summer at the **Griffith Recreation Center**. ♦ M-F 11AM-3PM, 4-7PM; Sa-Su noon-3PM, 4-7PM mid June-mid Sep. 485.5559

19 Tam O'Shanter Inn $$ **Lawry's** runs this haven for expatriate Scots; prime rib is the best choice from a straightforward menu. For true believers, *haggis* is served on **Robert Burn**'s birthday. If you don't know what haggis is, don't ask. ♦ Scottish ♦ M-Th 11AM-3PM, 5-10PM; F 11AM-3PM, 5-11PM; Sa 5-11PM; Su 10:30AM-2:30PM, 4-10PM. 2980 Los Feliz Blvd. 664.0228

19 La Strada $$ The attraction here is opera, sung tableside by professionals. The atmosphere sometimes gets zany, with singers singing, waiters serving, and patrons coming and going. ♦ Italian ♦ Tu-Su 6-11PM. Show: Sa 8:30PM. 3000 Los Feliz Blvd. 664.2955

19 Woody's Bicycle World Griffith Park is full of bike trails, and this is the place to rent your wheels. ♦ M, W, F 9AM-6PM; T, Th 9AM-7PM; Sa 9AM-4:50PM. 3157 Los Feliz Blvd. 661.6665

22 Mise en Place Kitchen gadgets, pots, pans, tableware, and linens in profusion. ♦ M-Sa 10AM-6PM. 2120 Hillhurst Ave. 662.1334

22 Pierre's Los Feliz Inn ★$$$ For those who want to eat in a formal atmosphere as respectable Angelenos did 50 years ago, with no surprises, good or bad, this fills the bill. It was once a **Brown Derby**, and it still serves the signature Cobb salad. ♦ Continental ♦ M-Th 11:30AM-11PM; F 11:30AM-midnight; Sa-Su 5PM-midnight. 2138 Hillhurst Ave. 663.8001

23 SanSui ★$ *Healthy food in a peaceful room* is the goal of owner-chef **Shinichi Kishi**, and he delivers on both promises. The Shojin dinner includes 10 small vegetarian courses; the music that wafts through sounds like wind on a mountaintop. ♦ Japanese ♦ Tu-F noon-2PM, 5:30-9:30PM; Sa-Su 5:30-9:30PM. 2040 Hillhurst Ave. 660.3868

23 Los Feliz Wine Shop An unusually good selection of wines and a very pleasant gourmet market. ♦ M-F 11AM-8PM; Sa 10AM-8PM; Su 10AM-4PM. 2044 Hillhurst Ave. 665.7687

23 Yuca's Hut ★$ People come from miles to eat the *carnitas, carne asada tacos*, and burritos made by **Dora** and her family at this little stand. Grab a beer and join the gang. ♦ Mexican ♦ M-Sa 10:30AM-6PM. 2056 N. Hillhurst Ave. 662.1214

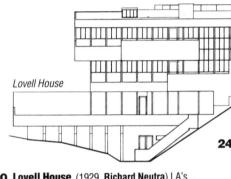

Lovell House

20 Lovell House (1929, **Richard Neutra**) LA's finest example of International Style architecture: a steel-framed, stucco-clad composition of stacked planes flowing out from a hillside. It launched Neutra's 40-year career as the most productive and prestigious of LA's modern architects. The best view is from below on Aberdeen Avenue. Private residence. ♦ 4616 Dundee Dr

21 Ennis-Brown House (1924, **Frank Lloyd Wright**) A Mayan temple on a hill overlooking the city. This is the most impressive and best-sited of Wright's concrete block houses. It is a private residence; however tours of the interior, which has been sensitively restored to its original appearance, are given on the second Saturday of each odd-numbered month from noon on. ♦ Admission. 2607 Glendower Ave. Tour reservations 660.0607

22 La Conversation One of the 2 or 3 best French bakeries in LA with tables for those who cannot wait to carry the goodies home. Croissants with lox and cream cheese are a specialty. ♦ M-Th 7:30AM-7PM; F-Sa 7:30AM-10PM; Su 7:30AM-2:30PM. 2118 Hillhurst Ave. 666.9000

24 Duplex ★★$$ Comfortable, quirky restaurant run by a hip neighborhood couple. The menu is small but interesting (spinach and oyster soup, noodle pancakes, and tea-smoked chicken), and the desserts really shine. ♦ American ♦ Tu-F 11:30AM-2:30PM, 6-10:30PM; Sa 6-10:30PM; Su 5-10:30PM. 1930 Hillhurst Ave. 663.2430

24 The Pasta Shoppe Pasta in every shape and flavor—from squid to spinach. ♦ M-F 10:30AM-6:30PM; Sa 9:30AM-5:30PM. 1964 Hillhurst Ave. 668.0458

24 Katsu ★★★★$$$ One of the city's most popular Japanese restaurants, and perhaps one of the best restaurants in the USA. If we were giving 5 stars Katsu would deserve the extra one. The stunning black-and-white interior features a collection of **Mineo Mizuno** ceramics on the walls and on the tables, and dramatic paintings by contemporary California artists. Chef **Katsu Michite** is a magician with the knife, using the freshest seafood to create exquisite dishes that display an unerring sense of culinary and esthetic harmony. ♦ Japanese ♦ M-F noon-2PM, 6-10PM; Sa 6-10PM. 1972 Hillhurst Ave. 665.1891. Also: **Cafe Katsu**, 2117 Sawtelle Blvd. 477.3359; **Katsu III**, 8636 W 3rd St. 273.3650

24 Trattoria Farfalla ★$ A hole in the wall where the delicious pizzas, pastas, and desserts are worth the wait—or you can carry them home. Bring your own wine. ♦ Italian ♦ M-F 11:30AM-3PM, 5-10PM; Sa-Su 5-10:30PM. 1978 Hillhurst Ave. 661.7365

25 Chatterton's Book Store A high-ceilinged airy white barrel brimming with books. One of the best selections of American and foreign literature, contemporary poetry, and literary periodicals in the city. Music plays, and there are seats for reading. ♦ M-Sa 10AM-10PM; Su noon-9PM. 1818 N. Vermont Ave. 664.3882

25 Palermo $ Popular pizza place. ♦ Pizza ♦ Tu 5-10:30PM; W-Th 11AM-10:30PM; F-Sa 11AM-11:30PM. 1858 N. Vermont Ave. 663.1430

26 Tepparod Thai Restaurant ★$$ For a quieter experience. Spicy Thai food, a blend of Chinese, Indian, and French influences, served in serene rooms. The mint chicken is amazing; the refreshing coconut ice cream improbably contains nuggets of corn. ♦ Thai ♦ Tu-Th 11AM-3PM, 5:30-10PM; F 11AM-3PM, 5:30PM-11PM; Sa 5PM-11PM; Su 5-10PM. 4645 Melbourne Ave. 669.9117

26 Sarno's Cafe Del Opera $$ The piano in the front room is the center for opera and popular tunes by professionals and amateurs, some of whom have stage bravado that makes up for lack of vocal equipment. The action starts after

Griffith Park/North Central

8PM. Bring your own music and tell the pianist if you want to join the fun. ♦ Italian ♦ Daily 11AM-1AM. 1714 N. Vermont Ave. 662.3403

27 Mercedes Designer Resale Slightly worn designer labels at a discount. ♦ M, F-Su 11AM-6PM; Tu-Th 11AM-8PM. 1775 Hillhurst Ave. 665.8737

28 Maps to Anywhere A stock of maps and guides plus language tapes to match the area's ethnic diversity. Polynesian, anyone? ♦ M-F 9AM-6PM; Sa-Su 10AM-5PM. 1514 Hillhurst Ave, 2nd fl. 660.2101

29 El Chavo $$ The menu features *rinones fritos* (sautéed kidneys with chopped vegetables), tongue in Spanish sauce and mole, and a wonderful, tender poached chicken. Also excellent grilled steaks. Pleasant, softly lit atmosphere and music that is thankfully unobtrusive. ♦ Mexican ♦ M-Th 11AM-10:30PM; F-Sa 11AM-11:30PM. 4441 Sunset Blvd. 664.0871

30 Uncle Jer's Peace and love live on in this selection of floral, gauze, and tie-died clothing. A share of the profits go to environmental groups. ♦ Tu-F 11AM-7PM; Sa 10AM-5PM; Su noon-5PM. 4447 Sunset Blvd. 662.6710

31 L.A. Nicola Restaurant ★★$$ A local hot spot, thanks to personable owner/chef **Larry Nicola**, the architectural whimsy of **Morphosis**, and a menu that includes good grills, salads, and fried calamari. Adjoining the restaurant is

an upscale bar with art on the walls, cool jazz on the stereo, and a lively buzz from local residents and neighboring KCET staffers. ♦ California ♦ M-F 11:30AM-2PM, 6PM-10PM; Sa 6-10PM. 4326 Sunset Blvd. 660.7217

31 El Cid $$ The food in this Spanish Colonial cabaret is only run-of-the-mill, but the flamenco guitar and flamenco dancing are remarkable. Located on the site of **D. W. Griffith**'s studio, where the 150-foot-high set of *Babylon* rose in 1916. ♦ Mexican/Spanish ♦ W 6:30-10PM; Th 6:30-11:30PM; F-Sa 6:30PM-1:45AM; Su 11AM-3PM, 6:30-11:30PM. 4212 Sunset Blvd. 668.0318

32 Say Cheese Great neighborhood resource for fresh cheeses, teas, coffees, and imported delicacies. ♦ T-Su 10AM-6:30PM. 2800 Hyperion Ave. 665.0545

33 Red Lion Tavern ★$$ Not a place for nibbling, this unpretentious, inexpensive neighborhood place is the real home-cooked German article. Delicious food and lots of it: schnitzel, bratwurst, smoked pork loin, veal loaf, sauerkraut, potato salad, etc. Also *weiss beer* and *dortmunder ritter* on tap and a fine selection of after dinner liqueurs such as kirschwasser, *slivovitz*, and apple schnapps. ♦ German ♦ M-Sa 11AM-2AM; Su 11AM-midnight. 2366 Glendale Blvd, Silver Lake. 662.5337

34 Neutra House (1933/64, Richard Neutra) The architect built a daringly experimental house for himself in his first decade of work, and when it was destroyed by fire in 1963, he created a more romantic version. Private residence. On the **2200** block of Silver Lake is a concentration of Neutra houses, dating from 1948-61. They are at Nos. 2250, 2242, 2240, 2238, 2226, 2218, 2210, and 2200. Private residences. ♦ 2300 E. Silver Lake Blvd

35 Olive House (1933, Rudolph Schindler) A wonderfully complex house by **Neutra**'s compatriot and rival, who was more innovative and less successful in his LA career. This street has a uniquely rich concentration of classic modern houses. Private residence. ♦ 2236 Micheltorena St

36 Casita Del Campo $$ Pleasant eating at an outdoor patio. ♦ Mexican ♦ Daily 11AM-midnight. 1920 Hyperion Ave. 662.4255

37 Seafood Bay $$ Some of the cheapest fresh seafood dinners in town. There's little atmosphere here but the enthusiasm of the customers makes up for it. Doubles as a fish market. ♦ Seafood ♦ M-Sa 11:30AM-10PM; Su 4-10PM. 3916 Sunset Blvd. 664.3902

The word smog was coined to describe the combination of smoke and fog, first noticed in Los Angeles in 1943. Ironically, LA's severe smog problem is exacerbated by 2 of its greatest assets: the mountains, which hold the pollutants in place instead of allowing them to be dispersed, and the sunshine, which cooks the pollutants into a visable hazy layer. An atmospheric phenomenon known as an *inversion layer* holds automobile and industrial pollutants trapped by warm air currants from above in a low, poorly ventilated layer.

38 Millie's $ Authentic Depression-era decor (with a portrait of **FDR** on the wall) and traditionally hearty breakfasts. ♦ American ♦ Tu-F 8AM-4PM, 5-10PM; Sa-Su 8AM-4PM. 3524 Sunset Blvd. 661.5292

39 Amok Bookstore Eclectic range of literature from the macabre to the philosophical. ♦ Tu-Su noon-8PM. 1067 Hyperion Ave. 665.0956

40 Longest staircase The earliest moviemakers built studios in Silver Lake and filmed on its streets. **Laurel and Hardy** tried to carry a grand piano up these steps in *The Music Box* (1932). ♦ 927 Vendome St, Silver Lake

40 Tropical Bakery Guava cream cheese pie and good coffee are specialties. ♦ M-Su 6AM-10PM. 2900 Sunset Blvd. 661.8391

41 Netty's $ Soups, pasta, grilled chicken, and dishes of the day, to go or to eat at a few small tables. ♦ American ♦ Tu-Sa noon-9PM. 1700 Silver Lake Blvd. 662.8655

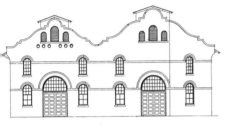

42 Olive Substation (1907) Restored by the **Jerde Partnership**. This was originally one of several Mission-style stations in the city taken over by the Pacific Electric Railway Company in 1911. Private office. ♦ 2798 Sunset Blvd

43 Los Arrieros ★$ You'd be delighted to find a place like this in Bogota. The good news is you don't have to risk your life in this friendly neighborhood restaurant to enjoy boudin, chicken, and black beans. ♦ Colombian ♦ Daily noon-10PM. 2619 Sunset Blvd. 483.0074

44 Minnette's Antiques Etcetera Americana, vintage silver and jewelry, and much more are crammed into this tiny store. ♦ M-Sa noon-6PM. 2209 Sunset Blvd. 413.5595

44 Managua $ Tasty dishes include the *nacatamal* (sweet pork-filled tamale made with corn meal and raisins) and *picadillo* (spicy ground meat with chopped onion, peppers, tomatoes, olives, raisins, and garlic). Try the nonalcoholic *cacao* or *tamarindo*, and save room for the flan. ♦ Nicaraguan ♦ Daily 10AM-10PM. 1007 Alvarado St. 413.9622

44 Burrito King $ A takeout stand offering wonderful burritos at low prices. ♦ Mexican ♦ Daily 6AM-3AM. Sunset Blvd at Alvarado St. 413.9444

The community of **Tarzana** in the west San Fernando Valley can trace its name back to Tarzan, the character created by **Edgar Rice Burroughs**, who lived in the area.

After World War II, tourists flocked to sunny California, where the sight of acres of orange trees was a popular attraction.

North Central

Tucked into 2 pockets of steep hills and bordered by freeways at the northern end of downtown, this is predominately a blue-collar Hispanic-American district. The small frame houses perched high on the tightly woven streets give the appearance of a rural setting, and huge stands of eucalyptus trees run across the hillsides and into the canyons. Trails form a network through the overgrown wild areas across slopes and ravines leading up to **Mount Washington**. A mix of romance and economy makes this residential area attractive to creative young people.

The first residents of the neighborhood were the Yang-Na Indians, who camped in the Elysian Park Hills and hunted for small game with bows and arrows. Several hillside springs fed by the Los Angeles River supplied the Indians with water. When the pueblo's first settlers arrived, they continued to use these water sites and added a waterwheel and rope system to bring the water down to the settlement from the hills. Around 1910, moviemakers came to the neighborhood, among them Mack Sennett, who built his first studio near Glendale Boulevard.

45 Les Freres Taix $$ Largest and oldest of LA's French restaurants. Wholesome budget-priced dishes and reasonably priced wines are served family-style at long tables. ♦ French ♦ M-Sa 11:30AM-10PM; Su 11:30AM-9PM. 1911 Sunset Blvd. 484.1265

Griffith Park/North Central

46 Angelus Temple In the '20s and '30s, **Aimee Semple McPherson** preached her Foursquare Gospel within this circular structure. The large domed classical building was based on the design of the Mormon Tabernacle in Salt Lake City. ♦ M-F 9AM-5PM. 1100 Glendale Blvd. 484.1100

47 Echo Park During the 1870s, **Echo Park Lake** provided water for nearby farms. In 1891, the land was donated to the city for use as a public park. **Joseph Henry Tomlinson** designed the layout utilizing the plan of a garden in Derbyshire, England. The 26-acre park is attractively landscaped with semitropical plants and a handsome lotus pond. The lake has paddle boats available for hourly rental. Special events include an annual celebration by the local Samoan community. ♦ Daily 5AM-10:30PM. Glendale Blvd at Park Ave

48 Barragan Cafe $$ A neighborhood favorite for Mexican food, with usual dishes and old favorites honestly prepared. Nightly entertainment in the bar. One of the best in town. ♦ Mexican ♦ M-Th, Su 6AM-10:30PM; F-Sa 6AM-11:30PM. 1538 Sunset Blvd. 250.4256

Restaurants/Clubs: Red	Hotels: Blue
Shops/Parks: Green	Sights/Culture: Black

Kentuckian fur trapper **William Wolfskill** came to LA in the early 1830s and planted the area's first orange grove.

49 Angelino Heights LA's first commuter suburb, begun in the land boom of 1886-87 when it was linked by cable car along Temple Street to the stores and offices downtown, just over a mile away. The hilltop site offered impressive views and a cool refuge (with 3 tennis courts) from the noise and dust of Spring Street. Professionals moved into handsome Queen Anne and Eastlake houses, but the boom soon fizzled. The 1300 block of **Carroll Avenue** is a time capsule of the period, and has been lovingly restored by its residents, who organize an annual house tour to raise money for improvements, including the installation of period street lamps and the burying of overhead wires. It's a favorite location for film and television crews, but it has kept an authentic neighborhood atmosphere, especially on the adjoining streets, where Craftsman

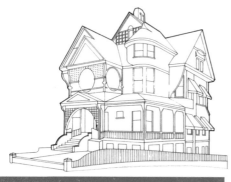

Griffith Park/North Central

bungalows are interspersed with the Victorians. Highlights on Carroll Ave include **No. 1316**, a treasury of virtuoso Eastlake carpenter work with a restored carriage barn in back; **No. 1330**, a Moorish design with fine spindle work designed by **Joseph Cather Newsom**; and **No. 1334**, a delicate Gay Nineties house with a witch's hat corner turret. Eleven other houses have been designated LA cultural historical monuments. For a detailed flier, information on the May house tour and other events, call the **Carroll Avenue Restoration Foundation**, 250.5976. Private residences.

50 Dodger Stadium (1962, **Emil Prager**) At the heart of Chavez Ravine, surrounded by one of the world's largest parking lots, is the the home of the **LA Dodgers** baseball team. The unique cantilevered construction eliminates view-blocking pillars within. Boxes are usually in short supply because they are generally sold to season ticket holders. All levels of the stadium are well supplied with food stands selling the famous *Dodger Dogs*; you might ask for the unadvertised spicy dog, a Polish sausage on an onion roll. And this is one of the only fields in America that sells sushi. Numerous kiosks sell such Dodger-imprinted merchandise as T-shirts, baseball equipment, stuffed animals, and team pennants. A giant color screen in the outfield flashes instant replay, baseball quizzes, batting averages, and the scores of other games around the country. The screen also acts as an electronic cheerleader, signaling when it is time to

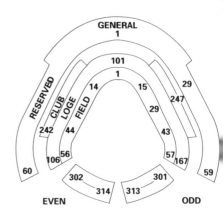

bellow the Dodger cheer, *Charge!* The screen cannot be seen from the bleachers. Ticket office in the parking lot. ♦ Seats 56,000. Ticket office M-Sa 8:30AM-5:30PM. 1000 Elysian Park Ave. 224.1400

51 Elysian Park The second largest park in the Los Angeles area (over 600 acres), occupying several hills and valleys. The parkland was set aside for public use at the founding of the city in 1781. The main part of the park has been left in its natural state, the slopes covered with the shrubs and low trees known as chaparral. These areas are crisscrossed with hiking trails. **Chavez Ravine Arboretum**, the area in Stadium Way from Scott Avenue to Academy Road, was planted with rare trees at the end of the 19th century; many mature and beautiful specimen remain. The center of the park along Stadium Way has picnic areas, some with cooking facilities. A scenic plaza with a small manmade lake is located a quarter-mile north of the end of Stadium Way. There is also a small children's play area. A small café at the **Police Academy** is open to the public weekdays from 6AM-3PM and serves hearty reasonably-priced meals. ♦ 1880 Academy Dr. 222.9136

52 Lawry's California Center ★$$$ Help yourself to hearty food in flower-filled pavilions and patios. The evening steak Fiesta Dinner offers barbecued New York steak, fresh swordfish or salmon, and hickory-smoked chicken. Mariachi music. Culinary takeout offered in the excellent wine and gift shop. Fiesta Dinners 15 April-15 November. ♦ Mexican/American ♦ Tu-Th 11AM-3PM, 5-10PM; F-Sa 11AM-3PM, 5-10:30PM; Su 11AM-3PM, 4-9PM. Mariachi music: M-F 5:30-9:30PM. Jazz: Tu 6-9PM; Sa 2-5PM. Tours: 11:30AM, 12:30, 1:30, 2:30PM. 568 San Fernando Rd. 224.6850, advance reservations for 10 or more 224.5783

53 Lummis House (1898-1910) A unique owner-built residence conceived and executed by **Charles Fletcher Lummis**, founder of the Southwest Museum and the first city librarian. Constructed of granite boulders from the nearby arroyo, hand-hewn timbers, and telephone poles, the structure is a romantic combination of styles. Most of the original furniture is gone, but the home and gardens remain as a monument to a most extraordinary man. ♦ W-Su 1-4PM. 200 East Ave 43. 222.0546

54 Heritage Square Museum The President of the National Trust described this as an *architectural petting zoo*, and certainly these vintage houses had a greater impact on the city when they occupied their original sites. But just as zoos preserve endangered species, so the **LA Cultural Heritage Board** has rescued these 8 historic buildings (1865-1920) from the insatiate greed of developers. They include the **Hale House**, the **Palms Railroad Depot**, and the **Lincoln Avenue Methodist Church**. Tours, special events, and gift store. ♦ Admission. Sa-Su noon-4PM, June 10-mid Sept; Su 11AM-4PM, mid Sep-May. 3800 N. Homer St (Ave 43 exit off Pasadena Fwy)

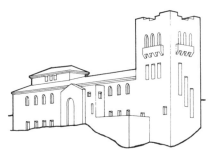

55 Southwest Museum One of the city's sleepers. A magnificent collection of Native American arts, from Alaska to South America, housed in a Mission-style building on a hill overlooking the Pasadena Freeway. The permanent displays of art and artifacts from the Southwest, the Great Plains, the Northwest Coast, and California have been dramatically improved. Notable among the holdings are the **Poole Collections** of American Indian basketry, Navajo blankets, pottery, and a full-size Blackfoot tepee. Loan exhibitions, lectures, and workshops for the entire family are held throughout the year. A *Festival of Native American Arts*, with food, music, and dance, is held every October. There is also a well-stocked gift and book store, and the important **Braun Research Library** for scholarly reference. Immediately below the museum and open the same hours is the **Casa de Adobe**, a replica of an 1850s Mexican California hacienda, constructed in 1918 by the **Hispanic Society of California**. Its rooms are built around a central patio and display decorative arts of the period. ♦ Admission. Tu-Su 11AM-5PM. 234 Museum Dr (Ave 43 exit from Pasadena Fwy). Recorded information 221.2163, offices 221.2164

56 Judson Studios This studio has been well known for its stained-glass work since 1897. The Moorish and Craftsman-style building is owned by a 4th-generation Judson descendant. ♦ Lobby M-F 8AM-4:30PM. 200 S. Ave 66. 255.0131

57 San Encino Abbey (1909-25, **Clyde Brown**) A hybrid of California Mission and European Gothic styles. Brown imported parts of old European castles and monasteries to create his own medieval environment. Private residence. ♦ 6211 Arroyo Glen

58 Sparklett Drinking Water Corporation (1929) LA is full of Islamic pastiches; this mosque is one of the finest. The minarets were shaken down in the 1971 earthquake. ♦ 4500 Lincoln Ave

Griffith Park/North Central

59 Occidental College A small liberal arts college founded in 1887, formerly affiliated with the Presbyterian Church. It is currently broadening its enrollment and undertaking a major building program. The campus core was designed by **Myron Hunt** after the college's move to the Eagle Rock area in 1914. Occidental figures as Tarzana College in **Aldous Huxley**'s *After Many a Summer Dies the Swan*. The inventively designed 400-seat **Keck Theatre** presents a wide range of plays and visiting dance companies throughout the year. ♦ 1600 Campus Rd. 259.2500, box office 259.2737

60 Eagle Rock A massive sandstone rock, 150 feet high and imprinted with a natural formation resembling an eagle in flight on its southwest side. It was described by **Dr. Carl Dentzel**, the late director of the Southwest Museum, as the most distinctive natural landmark in the city. Visible from the 134 Freeway traveling east from Glendale to Pasadena. ♦ Northern end of Figueroa St

61 Eagle Rock Playground Clubhouse (1953, **Richard Neutra**) A significant building with a magnificent view. ♦ 1100 Eagle Vista Dr

Restaurants/Clubs: Red	Hotels: Blue
Shops/Parks: Green	Sights/Culture: Black

Los Angeles' population is exceeded by only 4 other **states**(not including California).

Burbank/Glendale

They seem like the Siamese twins of the eastern San Fernando Valley, but the 2 stubbornly independent cities of **Glendale** and **Burbank** are as unlike each other as border mates can be. Although they share a common boundary at the base of the **Verdugo Mountains**, Glendale is a conservative bedroom community, while Burbank is a land of papier-mâché bricks, styrofoam trees, rubber boulders, and breakaway walls.

Both cities were originally part of Mission San Fernando and were deeded in 1794 to **José Maria Verdugo**, the captain of the guards at the San Gabriel Mission. The 433-square-mile *Rancho San Rafael* remained in the Verdugo family until a financial crisis forced foreclosure in 1869. By 1883, 13 Americans had arrived and were working farm plots in a townsite the Americans chose to call Glendale, the name coming from the title of a painting one of the group had seen. In 1887, 5 speculators filed plans for the town of Glendale.

Within the year, a small town was founded nearby by real-estate promoters on the site of the *Rancho La Providencia*, which had been owned by a physician/ sheep rancher, **Dr. David Burbank**. The 2 cities grew slowly until the 1904 extension of the **Pacific Electric Railway** brought hundreds of new citizens. In 1906, Glendale incorporated, followed by Burbank in 1911. **Tropico**, a competing city, sprang up south of Glendale in 1911. The site of photographer **Edward Weston**'s first studio, the town's main economic activity was strawberry farming. Glendale annexed Tropico in 1918. Many of Glendale's homes date from the 1920s, when it flourished as a suburban haven for transplanted Midwesterners. Glendale still retains a *Main Street USA* image on some of the older downtown streets. Its southern portion is predominantly commercial while the northern has the original residential array of small, pastel-colored stucco homes. A series of newer, more affluent subdivisions has recently been constructed on the steep hillsides of the Verdugo Mountains. The intersection of Adams and Palmer streets was the site of the first Baskin-Robbins ice-cream store in 1948.

Much of Burbank's growth is attributable to the opening in 1928 of a small airplane manufacturing site near the Burbank airfield. **Alan Loughead**'s (he later changed the spelling to **Lockheed**) prototype industrial plant spawned a huge aerospace and electronics industry employing thousands, centering on the **Burbank-Glendale-Pasadena** airport. To the visitors, Burbank's fame and fortune is not in fuselages, but in its 4 major television and film studios (**NBC**, **Universal**, **Burbank**, and **Disney**). With the exception of the closed Disney lot, guided tours are available to show you what the stars do when they go to work. **Johnny Carson**'s jokes about "beautiful downtown Burbank" are enjoying a new lease on life as an odd assortment of colorful Postmodern towers enlivens the skyline. **Warner Bros.** has spread off the lot into what looks like an inhabited junglegym and a block whose curved mirror-glass facade reflects passing traffic as though in a fun-house mirror. This provides the best free entertainment in Burbank.

Area code 818 unless otherwise indicated.

1 Burbank-Glendale-Pasadena Airport
Nine airlines serve a variety of domestic destinations, making this a convenient alternative to LAX for those living on the north side of LA. The airport is located between 3 freeways, No. 170 (Hollywood), No. 134 (Ventura), and No. 5 (Golden State). Adjoining the terminal are expensive short and long-term parking lots (enter from Empire Ave). A free shuttle runs to a remote lot on Winona Ave, west of Hollywood Way, which is open daily 6AM-11PM. Ground transportation to and from the airport by **Super Shuttle**, 244.2700. ♦ 2627 Hollywood Wy, Burbank. 840.8847

2 Barron's Cafe $ Hearty food served by friendly waitresses in a traditional coffeeshop. ♦ American ♦ M-F 7AM-7:30PM; Sa 8AM-1PM. 4130 W. Burbank Blvd. 846.0043

3 Cafe Mediterranean ★$ Middle Eastern standards in an informal, all-pink setting. ♦ Lebanese ♦ Daily 11AM-11PM. 10151 ½ Riverside Dr, Tuluca Lake. 769.0865

4 Universal Studios Tour Movie mogul **Carl Laemmle** moved his studio from Hollywood to the undeveloped hills of Universal City in 1915, anticipating the need for a huge backlot. This visionary augmented revenue with the first studio tour: for a quarter, visitors could watch films being shot and buy eggs from "Uncle" Carl's hatchery as they left. The tour was discontinued when it proved too distracting to moviemakers, but in 1963 a tram ride was inaugurated, and the tour has now drawn over 50 million visitors, making it the most popular manmade attraction in the US after the 2 Disney parks.

Compulsively humorous guides escort visitors on a 2-hour tram ride around the lot, which brings you face to face with a 30-foot-high **King Kong** (smell the bananas on his breath!) and the giant mechanical shark from *Jaws*. You will barely survive an avalanche, a collapsing bridge, and the parting of the Red Sea. The latest attraction is *Earthquake—the Big One*, a simulation of what most Angelenos expect to experience without paying for the privilege. Visitors are invited to participate in demonstrations on the **Special Effects Stage** that reveal the astounding developments in movie magic, from the early years to the fantasies of **Steven Spielberg**.

From the tram you can glimpse over 500 outdoor sets, ranging from the Bates mansion for *Psycho* to the facades for *Back to the Future* and *Kojak*. Artificially-aged streets are redressed for every new movie and television series: here are the New England village, the frontier town, and the Mexican square you've seen a hundred times in different guises on the screen. The tour pauses at **Prop Plaza** (summer only) for a close-up look at over-size props from television's *Land of the Giants* and *The Incredible Shrinking Woman*. Visitors can pose in front of a giant telephone and test their *bionic* strength by lifting a fullsize van.

After the tour, visitors can wander at will in the **Entertainment Centre**. The star attraction is *The Adventures of Conan*, a 4.4-million-dollar sword and sorcery extravaganza, featuring lasers, flashing sword fights, and a fire-breathing dragon. When you've got your breath back, you can have a shot at stardom in the **Screen Test Comedy Theatre** (and watch the results on video), thrill to the *Western Stunt Show*, enjoy the antics on the *Animal Actors Show* and talk back to K.I.T.T., the speaking car from *Knight Rider*. Star lookalikes from **Charlie Chaplin** to the *Phantom of the Opera* will pose with you for photos, and special celebrations are held in the Centre throughout the year. Food stands and gift stores abound. Fifty acres of free parking. At press time: a fire in Fall 1990 destroyed portions of Universal Studios, so call in advance for hours and tours. ♦ Admission. 100 Universal City Plaza, Universal City. 508.9600, 508.5444

Burbank/Glendale

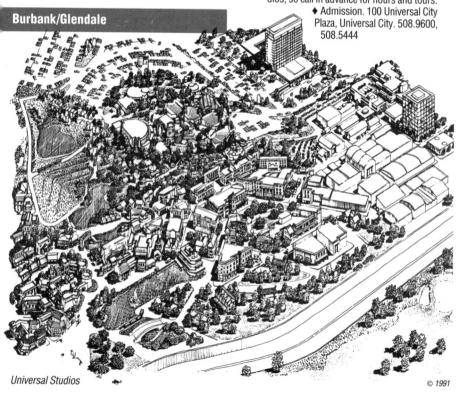

Universal Studios

© 1991

Within Universal Studios:

Universal Amphitheatre The theater presents a full range of pop entertainment year-round. ♦ Seats 6251. 980.9421, ticket charge line 213/480.3232

Cineplex Odeon Universal City Cinemas The latest motion picture spectacle is not a movie but a multiplex: the world's largest, comprising 18 theaters with 5600 seats and a 1400-car garage all under one roof. This is the latest venture from the Canadian company that has become the fastest-expanding exhibitor in the US. ♦ 508.0588

4 Victoria Station $$ One of many re-creations of London's famous train station. This family-oriented steak house has a funicular railroad from the parking lot to the restaurant. ♦ American ♦ M-Th 11:30AM-10PM; F-Sa 11:30AM-11PM; Su 10:30AM-10PM. 3850 Lankershim Blvd, Universal City. 760.0714

5 Campo de Cahuenga The treaty ending the war between Mexico and America was signed here on 13 January 1847 by **Lt. Col. John C. Fremont** and **Gen. Andreas Pico**. The historic meeting opened the way for California's entry into the Union. The declaration was known as the *Treaty of Cahuenga*, after this building constructed by **Thomas Feliz** in 1845. The existing structure is a 1923 replica of the original, which was demolished in 1900. ♦ Free. M-F 8AM-4PM by reservation, or ask the caretaker. 3919 Lankershim Blvd. 763.7651

6 Sheraton Universal $$$ A 25-year-old tower block that offers solid comfort and attractive weekend packages with free tickets to the Universal Studios Tour. ♦ 333 Universal Terrace Pkwy, Universal City. 980.1212, 800/325.3535; fax 985.4980

6 The New Registry Hotel $$$$ The former **Sheraton Premiere**, a handsome 24-story steel-and-glass tower with elegant, spacious rooms, has a new owner. It remains the best place to stay for miles around. ♦ Deluxe ♦ 555 Universal Terrace Pkwy, Universal City. 506.2500, 800/247.9810; fax 519.2058

Within the New Registry Hotel:

Oscar's ★★$$$ The decor is a bit overdone in that fancy hotel restaurant kind of way, but the service and American regional cooking is first-rate. **Philipe Astruc**, formerly at **La Serre**, is the chef. ♦ American ♦ Tu-Sa 6-9PM. 506.2500

7 Smoke House $$ A good, long-established steak house that takes care with the thing that really matters—meat. They age their own and grill it over hickory. ♦ American ♦ M-Th 11AM-10PM; F 11AM-11:30PM; Sa 11:30AM-11:30PM; Su 10:30AM-10:30PM. 4420 Lakeside Dr, Burbank. 845.3731

8 Warner Bros. Studios Begun in 1925 for **First National** and long occupied by **Warner Bros.**, the lot is now shared with independent companies, which produce television shows and feature films in comfortable cohabitation. A **VIP Tour** is available by advance reservation. Tours are limited to 12 adults per group and involve a lot of walking—wear comfortable, casual clothes. Unlike the Universal Studios Tour, the Burbank tours are designed as an introduction to the actual, behind-the-scenes technical workings of the motion picture crafts. At the end of the tour, guests may dine, at extra charge and subject to space availability, in the **Blue Room**, the studio commissary, where a number of actors and technicians take their meals. By reservation only. No cameras allowed. Additional reservations must be made for the Blue Room. ♦ Admission. Tours M-F 10AM, 2PM. Reservations only. 4000 Warner Blvd. 954.1744

9 La Scala Presto $$ Another branch of **La Scala** in Beverly Hills, serving antipastos, pizzas, and pastas. ♦ Italian ♦ M-Th 11:30AM-10PM; F-Sa 11:30AM-11PM. 3821 Riverside Dr, Burbank. 846.6800

10 NBC Television Studios Famous as the home of *The Tonight Show*, NBC Television Studios are the largest color facilities in the United States. A 75-minute tour of the complex is offered for visitors. During the progress through a number of sound stages, guides explain the videotape process and use of communication satellites for transcontinental transmission. A huge prop warehouse stores everything from breakaway chairs to silicone cobwebs. You can see yourself on camera and participate in new sound and special effects shows. **Studio 1**, home of *The Tonight Show*, is open for inspection, as is the wardrobe department. Tickets to attend taping of NBC shows are available. A number of seats are on a stand-by basis. Out of state visi-

tors should write to: Tickets, NBC Television, 3000 W. Alameda, Burbank, California 91523. No tickets will be sent out of state, but a letter of priority will be returned, which gives the holder first chance at the Burbank ticket line. Because of frequent changes in availability, it is recommended that would-be taping attendees call the studio for current information. ♦ Admission fee for tour; show tickets free. M-F 9AM-4PM; Sa 10AM-4PM; Su 10AM-2PM, closed holidays. 3000 W. Alameda Ave, Burbank. 840.3537

10 Chadney's $$ A friendly, hospitable steakhouse that is a favorite hangout for people from across the street at NBC. ♦ American ♦ M-F 11:30AM-10PM; Sa-Su 5-10PM. 3000 W. Olive Ave, Burbank. 843.5333

11 Safari Inn $$ A '50s period piece, conveniently close to the Burbank studios, with restaurant and pool. ♦ 1911 W. Olive Ave, Burbank. 845.8586, 800/845.5544 (CA), 800/782.4373 (US)

12 Genio's $$ An upbeat Italian menu that changes constantly but achieves consistent quality. ♦ Italian ♦ M-Th 11AM-10PM; F 11AM-11PM; Sa 4-11PM. 1420 W. Olive Ave, Burbank. 848.0079

Restaurants/Clubs: Red   Hotels: Blue
Shops/Parks: Green   **Sights/Culture: Black**

139

13 Burbank City Hall (1941) A PWA moderne classic with its tall fretted screen, fountain, and jazzy lobby. ◆ Olive Ave at 3rd St

14 Boulder Bungalows (c. 1920) Boulders were once a favorite building material in the foothills; these are fine examples of the style. Private residences. ◆ Olive Ave at 9th St, Burbank

15 Castaways $$ Go for drinks and a truly spectacular night view of the LA Basin. ◆ Polynesian ◆ M-Th 11:30AM-2:30PM, 5-11PM; F-Sa 11:30AM-2:30PM, 5PM-midnight; Su 10AM-3PM, 5-10PM. 1250 Harvard Rd, Burbank. 848.6691

16 Theodore Payne Foundation An organization devoted to the preservation and propagation of native California flora, named for the pioneer California botanist. The foundation maintains a nature trail up the hillside and a nursery where seeds and plants are sold at very reasonable prices. ◆ Free. Tu-Sa 8:30AM-4:30PM. 10459 Tuxford St, Sun Valley. 768.1802

17 McGroarty Cultural Arts Center A historic house, the former home of **John Steven McGroarty**, congressperson, poet, and historian, now maintained by the City of Los Angeles as a

Burbank/Glendale

showcase of mementos and as a community arts center. ◆ M-F 9AM-5PM; Sa 8:30AM-5PM. 7570 McGroarty Terrace, Tujunga. 352.5285

18 Brand Library (1904) The exotic *El Miradero* was inspired by the East Indian Pavilion at the 1893 Chicago World's Fair. The white-domed Saracenic-style home with minarets was built for **Leslie C. Brand**, who donated it to the city of Glendale with the stipulation that the property be used as a public library and park. In 1956, it was opened as an art gallery that exhibits contemporary Southern California art, a lecture and concert auditorium, and arts and crafts studios. The extensive, beautifully landscaped grounds are lovely for picnicking. The Queen Anne-style **Doctor's House** has been moved into the grounds and restored. ◆ Free. Tu, Th 12:30-9PM; W, F-Sa 12:30-6PM. Tours Su 2-4PM. 1601 W. Mountain St at Grandview Ave, Glendale. 956.2051

19 Casa Adobe de San Rafael Thomas A. **Sanchez**, one-time sheriff of Los Angeles County, also lived on Rancho San Rafael. His one-story hacienda is surrounded by huge eucalyptus trees planted by **Phineas Banning**, founder of the Los Angeles Harbor. The historic house was restored in 1932 by the city of Glendale. ◆ W, Su 1-4PM. 1330 Dorothy Dr, Glendale

20 First Church of Christ, Scientist (1989, **Moore Ruble Yudell**) A new church in the arts and crafts tradition, beautifully lit. ◆ 1320 N. Brand Blvd, Glendale

21 Gennaro's ★$$$ Discreet decor and honest food, including clam soup, Caesar salad, and osso buco; also a good wine list. ◆ Italian ◆ M-F 11:30AM-2:30PM, 5:30-10:30PM; Sa 5:30-10:30PM. 1109 N. Brand Blvd, Glendale. 243.6231

22 Phoenicia ★$$$ A local institution that has drawn some very mixed reviews. There is a prix-fixe dinner of mammoth proportions and a good wine list with some older Californian vintages at reasonable prices. Chicken baked in clay is the signature dish. ◆ French ◆ M 11:30AM-2:30PM; Tu-F 11:30AM-2:30PM, 5:30-10PM; Sa-Su 5:30-10PM. 343 N. Central Ave, Glendale. 956.7800

23 Aoba $$ Excellent food served in a simple setting. ◆ Japanese ◆ Tu-Th 11:30AM-2PM, 5:30-9PM; F 11:30AM-2PM, 5:30-10PM; Sa 5:30-10PM; Su 5-10PM. 201 W. Harvard St, Glendale. 242.7676

24 Red Lobster $$ The decor is slightly fast-food, but the fish is fresh, quickly cooked over charcoal. A good value. ◆ American ◆ M-Th, Su 11AM-10PM; F-Sa 11AM-11PM. 919 S. Central Ave, Glendale. 243.1195

25 Osteria Nonni ★★$$ High-tech setting and a sharply focused menu, inspired by the **Trattoria Angeli** in West LA. Tiny clams in a white wine and prosciutto sauce, designer pizza, lightly-fried baby salmon, and breaded calamari are all good choices. ◆ Italian ◆ M-F 11:30AM-3PM, 5:30-10:30PM; Sa 5:30-10:30PM. 3219 Glendale Blvd, Atwater. 213/666.7133

Court of Honor in the Great Mausoleum contains a stained-glass interpretation of da Vinci's *The Last Supper*, as well as reproductions of famous Italian statuary. The world's largest religious painting, entitled *The Crucifixion*, by Jan Stykam, measuring 195 feet by 45 feet, is displayed every hour on the hour in the Hall of Crucifixion-Resurrection. A companion behemoth, *The Resurrection*, by Robert Clark, is revealed every hour on the half-hour in the same hall. The Court of Freedom displays objects from American history, as well as a 20- by 30-foot mosaic copy of Turnbull's *The Signing of the Declaration of Independence*. Additional attractions are the collection of originals of every coin mentioned in the Bible; the Court of David, containing a reproduction of Michelangelo's famous work; and the chance to pay your respects to the earthly remains of a number of Hollywood luminaries, such as Clark Gable, W.C. Fields, Nat King Cole, and Jean Harlow. The exact whereabouts of graves is never disclosed by the Forest Lawn staff. ◆ Free. Daily 8AM-5PM. 1712 S. Glendale Ave, Glendale. 241.4151

27 Gourmet 88 ★$$ Fresh seafood delicately prepared with spicy sauces to add punch. Rock cod comes steamed with ginger and scallions, scallops are served with garlic or lemon sauce. ◆ Chinese ◆ M-Th, Su 11:30AM-10PM; F-Sa 11:30AM-10:30PM. 315 S. Brand Blvd, Glendale. 547.9488

27 Fresco ★★★$$$ Chef **Antonio Orlando** and maître d' **Lino Autiero**, alumni of **Valentino's**, have maintained its reputation as the best in Glendale. A skylit Roman villa is the setting for complex and original dishes that subtly combine different textures and flavors: lobster salad with grapefruit, corn crêpes stuffed with duck, and a heavenly tiramisù, in addition to terrific risottos, seafood, and veal. Reservations are essential; this treasure does not want for admirers. ◆ Italian ◆ M-F 11:30AM-2:30PM, 5:30-11PM; Sa 5:30-11PM. 514 S. Brand Blvd, Glendale. 243.6908

28 Mann's Alex Theatre A dramatic streamline moderne movie house whose 1939 facade is dominated by a fluted pylon. The columned lobby has flowerlike chandeliers. ◆ 216 N. Brand Blvd, Glendale. 241.4194

28 Far Niente ★$$ The rich menu draws crowds, though the results are uneven. Pasta with peas, prosciutto and cream, veal chop with a meaty sauce, and the chocolate soufflé are good bets —and should take care of your calorie intake for the week. ◆ Italian ◆ M-F 11:30AM-2:30PM, 6-9:30PM; Sa 6-10PM. 204 1/2 Brand Blvd. 242.3835

28 Panda Inn ★$$ Dependable contemporary Chinese. ◆ Chinese ◆ Daily 11:30AM-10:30PM. 111 E. Wilson Ave (Brand Blvd) Glendale. 502.1234

29 Churchill's $$ High-quality English prime rib haven. ◆ English ◆ M-Th 11AM-3PM, 4:30-10PM; F-Sa 11AM-3PM, 4:30-11PM; Su 10AM-3PM, 4-10PM. 209 N. Glendale Ave, Glendale. 247.3130

30 Scarantino $ Home-cooked minestrone, chicken *roletine*, baked zucchini, and spaghetti Napoletana. ◆ Italian ◆ Tu-Sa 4:30PM-10PM; Su 3-9PM. 1524 E. Colorado St, Glendale. 247.9777

31 Derby House (1926, Lloyd Wright) A superb example of the architect's precast concrete block houses patterned after pre-Columbian designs. Also in the neighborhood are Lloyd Wright's **Calori House**, 3021 E. Chevy Chase Dr, and his **Lewis House**, 2948 Graceland Way. Private residences. ◆ 2535 Chevy Chase Dr, Glendale

32 Catalina Verdugo Adobe (1875) The Catalina Verdugo Adobe was built for **José Maria Verdugo**'s blind daughter, **Dona Catalina**, on part of the original Rancho San Rafael. The single-story adobe is now a private residence in excellent condition. ◆ 2211 Bonita Dr, Glendale

33 Descanso Gardens The 165-acre gardens are famous for their collection of camellias, with over 100,000 plants representing 600 varieties. The landscaping also includes extensive displays of azaleas, roses, deciduous trees and shrubs, and bulb flowers, all located in a mature California live-oak grove. The variety of plants ensures that something is almost always blooming. The camellias perform from late December through early March. The serene teahouse is nestled in a Japanese-style garden that features a flowing stream forming waterfalls and pools. Tea and cookies are served daily from 11AM-4PM. **Hospitality House** sells books and gifts and offers exhibitions of flower

arrangements and art. Concerts and plays are presented outdoors in summer. ◆ Nominal admission. Daily 9AM-5PM. Tram tours on the hour Tu-F 1-3PM; Sa-Su 11AM-3PM. 1418 Descanso Dr, La Canada-Flintridge. 790.5571

34 The Epicurean ★★$$ Havana-born **Xiomara Ardolina** runs this tiny, exquisite restaurant, whose ingredients are worthy of the finest kitchens. Chicken sautéed with rosemary, lamb chops with gorgonzola, salads (especially the fresh mozzarella with tomatoes), and the tiramisù are outstanding. ◆ Eclectic ◆ M-F 11:30AM-2PM, 5:30-10PM; Sa-Su 5:30-10PM. 913 Foothill Blvd, La Canada-Flintridge. 790.5565

35 Jet Propulsion Laboratory (JPL) Fifty years ago, a group of Cal Tech graduates performed what one described as rather odd experiments in rocketry. Today, the JPL covers 175 acres of the Verdugo foothills, has 200 buildings, and employs 5000. From the 1958 *Explorer 1*, America's first satellite, to the *Voyager* missions that blazed a trail to the edge of the solar system, it has brought the sights and sounds of space to scientists and into our living rooms. Occasional tours, call for schedule. ◆ 4800 Oak Grove Dr, La Canada-Flintridge. 354.8594

Pasadena

Pasadena's international fame rests on a single day's activity: the annual New Year's Day **Tournament of Roses Parade** and the post-parade **Rose Bowl** football game. Parade festivities have been held yearly since 1890, when a *Battle of the Flowers* was first fought. Citizens draped garlands of fresh flowers over horse-and-buggy teams and carts in a celebration of the Southland's mild winter climate and climaxed the event with a gala Roman chariot race. The races were thought to be too dangerous and so a substitute event, the national football college championship game known as the Rose Bowl, has been held since 1916.

Those who feel overwhelmed by the epic scale and relentlessly wholesome quality of the Rose Parade may enjoy a rival venture, the November **Doo Dah Parade**, which is fast becoming an institution. The Doo Dah has no floats, no queens (except, perhaps, in drag), and best of all, no television celebrities. Its stars are the precision briefcase drill team and assorted zanies with lawnmowers, supermarket carts, and odd musical instruments.

Pasadena had a false start in 1873, when midwestern pioneers established a farming community here, giving it a name that means Crown of the Valley in the Chippewa Indian language. The tiny settlement exploded during the real-estate boom of 1886. In that year, Pasadena had 53 active real-estate agencies for a population of less than 4500. Promoters arranged 5 daily trains to Los Angeles and a special theater express for downtown 3 nights a week. Salespeople advertised the region's sunny, healthful climate, hotels were quickly erected, and get-rich-quick schemes proliferated. The city incorporated, but the boom

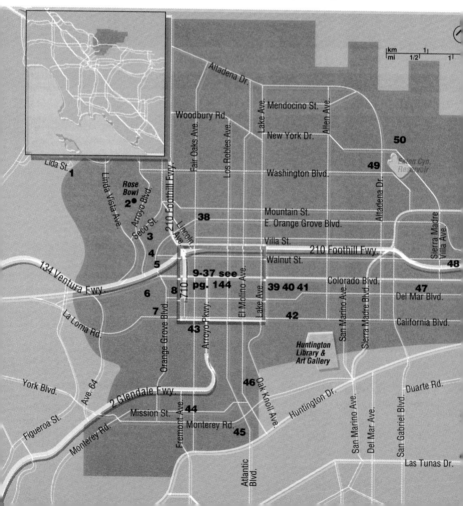

collapsed, the population dwindled, and town lots, once clamored for, grew weeds. But the clear air, citrus blooms, and mountain views (now but a memory) drew a steady stream of affluent Easterners. The **Huntington-Sheraton** and the **Hotel Green** (now converted to apartments) are reminders of an era when this was a fashionable winter resort. And the Craftsman bungalows of the **Greene** brothers recall how some travelers stayed on.

Pasadena's population increased through several small booms in the '20s, and it soon became the most important suburb of Los Angeles. LA's first freeway—the 1942 **Arroyo Seco Parkway**—stimulated commuter traffic. Today Pasadena has 100,000 residents, a mixture of old money to the north and low income in the south, opulent homes and lush gardens, and outstanding scientific and cultural resources.

Area code 818 unless otherwise indicated.

1 Art Center College of Design (1977, **Craig Ellwood**) The college is housed in a Miesian steel-framed bridge that spans a ravine. The center, established in 1930, has an international reputation as a school of industrial design, photography, graphics, illustration, and fine arts. The hilly 175-acre campus is an idyllic setting for artworks. Changing exhibitions of work by students and established artists and designers are held in the center's gallery.
♦ Campus and gallery M-Th 9AM-10PM; F-Sa 9AM-5PM. 1700 Lida St. 584.5000

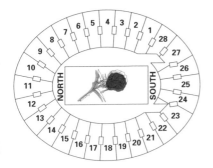

2 The Rose Bowl Since 1902, the Midwest has met the West here in the most famous college football match of all, and UCLA plays its home games here. Special events throughout the year. ♦ Seats 104,700. Bowl M-F 9AM-4PM. 991 Rosemont Blvd. 557.3106

Los Angeles Wins in the Rose Bowl

1923	USC over Penn State	14-3
1932	USC over Tulane	21-12
1933	USC over Pittsburgh	35-0
1939	USC over Duke	7-3
1940	USC over Tennessee	14-0
1944	USC over Washington	29-0
1945	USC over Tennessee	25-0
1953	USC over Wisconsin	7-0
1963	USC over Wisconsin	42-37
1966	UCLA over Michigan	14-12
1968	USC over Indiana	14-3
1970	USC over Michigan	10-3
1973	USC over Ohio State	42-17
1975	USC over Ohio State	18-17
1976	UCLA over Ohio State	23-10
1977	USC over Michigan	14-6
1979	USC over Michigan	17-10
1980	USC over Ohio State	17-16
1983	UCLA over Michigan	24-14
1984	UCLA over Illinois	45-9
1985	USC over Ohio State	20-17
1986	UCLA over Iowa	45-28
1990	USC over Michigan	17-10

At the Rose Bowl:

Rose Bowl Flea Market Held on the second Sunday of each month. This bargain-pickers' paradise offers everything from junk to antiques. ♦ Admission. 2nd Su of every month 9AM-3PM. 588.4411

3 Prospect Boulevard and Prospect Crescent The stone entrance gates at Orange Grove and Prospect boulevards were designed by **Charles** and **Henry Greene** in the 1910s. Along this boulevard lined with camphor trees is the Greenes' 1906 **Bentz House** at 657 Prospect Blvd. At No. 781 is **Alfred** and **Arthur Heineman's Hindry House**, half hidden behind shrubbery. A narrow street entered from the southwest side of the boulevard is Prospect Crescent. This leads to **Frank Lloyd Wright**'s 1923 **Millard House** at No. 645, which resembles a small pre-Columbian tower, giving it the name of **La Miniatura**. (The studio house near the pond was designed by Wright's son, **Lloyd Wright**, in 1926.) The house is set in a ravine, and there's a better view from below on Rosemont Street. All are private residences.
♦ Prospect Blvd (Orange Grove Blvd-Seco St)

Gamble House

4 Gamble House (1908, **Charles & Henry Greene**) A masterpiece of craftsmanship and planning, from the silkily polished teak and original furnishings to the cross ventilation that provides natural air conditioning. The best-known of the Craftsman-style bungalows was commissioned by the **Gamble** family (of **Proctor & Gamble**) in Cincinnati who, like other affluent sun-starved Easterners, wintered here at the turn of the century. It is now maintained by the **USC School of Architecture** as a study center and retreat for visiting scholars. Docents lead public tours, explaining the Japanese influences on the home's deep overhanging roofs and crafted woodwork. The house is furnished with tables, chairs, and Tiffany glass works designed by the architects. (Next door is the **Cole House** at 2 Westmoreland Place. This 1906 Greene and Greene house is now part of the **Neighborhood Church**.) ♦ Admission. Tours Th-Su noon-3PM. 4 Westmoreland Pl. 793.3334

4 Arroyo Terrace Behind Westmoreland Place is the loop of Arroyo Terrace, with its colony of **Greene and Greene** bungalows. All are worth

Pasadena

noting, although some are in better condition than others. They are **Charles Sumner Greene House** (1906) at No. 368; **White Sisters House** (1913) at No. 370, home of Charles Greene's sisters-in-law; **Van Rossen-Neill House** (1903, 1906), at No. 400, has a wall of burnt clinker brick and Arroyo boulders; **Hawkes House** (1906), at No. 408, resembles a Swiss chalet; **Willet House** (1905), at No. 424, is a remodeled bungalow; and at No. 440 is the **Ranney House** (1907). Also notable is the Greenes' **Duncan-Irwin House** (1900, 1906) close by at 240 N. Grand Ave. Private residences.

5 Pasadena Historical Museum (Fenyes Mansion) (1905, **Robert Farquhar**) The Neo-classical residence, formerly the home of the **Finnish Consul**, is now occupied by the **Pasadena Historical Society Museum**. The main floor retains its original furnishings, including antiques and paintings. The basement houses a display of Pasadena history, including memorabilia, paintings, and photographs. The adjacent library is open to researchers only. The 4-acre grounds are beautifully landscaped and contain a wandering stream with several pools as well

as **Sauna House**, a replica of a 16th-century Finnish farmhouse with a display of Finnish fo[lk] art. ♦ Free. Tu, Th, Su 1-4PM. 470 W. Walnut (Orange Grove Blvd) 577.1660

6 Colorado Boulevard Bridge Pasadena's *Pont du Gard*: splendid high concrete arches spanning Arroyo. ♦ Colorado Blvd at Arroyo Se[co]

7 Wrigley Mansion The broad Mission-style home is surrounded by a rolling lawn and well-kept gardens. It is an example of the grand ma[n]-sions found on the boulevard in the first deca[de] of the century. This is now the headquarters o[f] the **Tournament of Roses Association**. ♦ Garden: daily sunrise-sunset. Tours: W 2, 3, 4PM, Feb-Aug. 391 S. Orange Grove Blvd. 449.7673

8 Ambassador College A 4-year liberal arts i[n]-stitution emphasizing theology. The campus also houses the headquarters of the **Worldwid[e] Church of God**. Formerly part of *millionaires row*, the college contains 4 fully-restored mansions, as well as several newer buildings. Campus tours weekdays and Sunday at 10AM, noon, and 2PM, weather permitting, from the Hall of Administration. ♦ 300 Green St. Inform[a]-tion and group reservations 304.6123

8 Ambassador Auditorium Herbert von Karajan chose to conduct the **Berlin Philharmonic** here; other top artists have included **Vladimir Horowitz, Leontyne Price**, and the **Juilliard Quartet**. Extraordinary acoustics, exce[l]-lent sightlines, and sumptuous decor make thi[s] LA's top hall for serious concerts. ♦ Seats 120[0]. 300 W. Green St. Schedule and tickets 304.61[00]

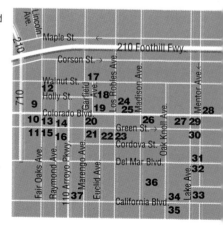

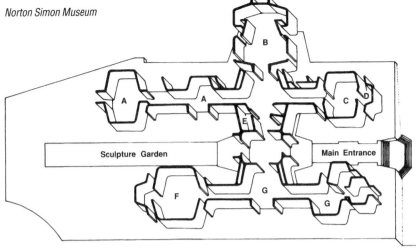

A European Painting	**C** Renaissance	**E** Special Exhibitions	**G** 19th & 20th Century
B 20th Century	**D** Early Italian	**F** India & Southeast Asia	

9 Norton Simon Museum One of America's greatest collections of European and Southeast Asian art housed in a dog of a building. Norton Simon installed his holdings here after the failure of the Pasadena Museum of Modern Art (a good idea later reborn as MOCA). The spacious galleries are hung with works according to school or century, spanning over 2000 years. Among the notable holdings are Indian and Southeast Asian sculpture; Old Master paintings and drawings, including works by **Rembrandt, Reubens, Tiepolo, Raphael, Breughel**, and **Hals; Goya** etchings; tapestries; 17th-century botanical watercolors; Impressionist paintings and sculpture, including works by **Cézanne, Toulouse-Lautrec, Renoir**, and **Van Gogh**; a large selecton of work by **Degas**, including an exquisite series of small bronze dancers; **Picasso; Maillol**; and work by the German Expressionists. So rich is the permanent collection that outstanding exhibitions can be generated in house, without recourse to outside loans. The museum shop has one of the finest selections of art books in the city and also offers prints and cards. ♦ Admission. Th-Su noon-6PM. 411 W. Colorado Blvd (Colorado-Orange Blvds) 449.6840

Museum Bests

Sarah Campbell
Chief Curator, Norton Simon Museum

Jacopo da Ponte's *Flight into Egypt.*

Paul Cézanne's *Tulips in a Vase.*

Edgar Degas' *Dancer in the Wings.*

Vincent van Gogh's *Portrait of a Peasant.*

Pablo Picasso's *Woman with Book.*

Pierre-August Renoir's *Pont des Arts.*

Francisco de Zurbaran's *Lemons, Oranges and a Rose.*

Restaurants/Clubs: Red   Hotels: Blue
Shops/Parks: Green   Sights/Culture: Black

10 Old Town Bakery Jog that extra mile and reward yourself with one (or more) of these sinfully rich pastries. ♦ M-Th, Su 9AM-11PM; F-Sa 9AM-midnight. 166 W. Colorado Blvd. 792.7943

11 Pasadena Heritage An energetic preservation society that offers walking tours and seminars, rescues historic buildings, and raises public awareness. ♦ 80 W. Dayton St. 793.0617

11 The Folk Tree Folk art, fine art, and textiles, mostly from Latin America; don't miss the seasonal theme exhibitions. Down the street is the **Folk Tree Collection**, specializing in antique

Pasadena

and contemporary crafts and furniture (217 S. Fair Oaks Ave, 795.8733). ♦ M-W, F-Sa 11AM-6PM; Th 11AM-8PM; Su noon-5PM. 199 S. Fair Oaks Ave

12 Armory Center for the Arts Contemporary art shows and an operating base for the **Pasadena Art Workshops**, which give kids a hands-on experience of the arts. ♦ Free. Tu-Sa noon-5PM. 145 N. Raymond Ave. 792.5101

13 Old Town Vintage small-scale buildings, recycled. There are a number of interesting gift and antique shops. Both sides of Colorado Boulevard are lined with small shops. Along Holly are a number of shops selling antiques and memorabilia. Within the Old Town is another attractive group of restored buildings, the **Pasadena Marketplace**. ♦ Bounded by Delacey Ave, Arroyo Pkwy, Holly and Green Sts

13 Merida $ The distinctive cooking of Yucatan is featured in an intimate dining room and a pretty outdoor patio. Specialties include *cochinita pibil* (pork steamed with spices in banana leaves), good seafood, and tortillas with chicken and black beans. ♦ Mexican ♦ M-Su 9AM-10PM. 20 E. Colorado Blvd. 792.7371

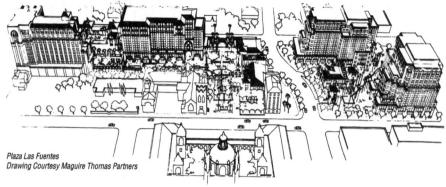

Plaza Las Fuentes
Drawing Courtesy Maguire Thomas Partners

13 Birdie's Cafe $ Delicious salads and hot muffins, with avian decor. ♦ American ♦ M-Th, Su 7:30AM-9PM; F-Sa 7:30AM-10PM. 17 S. Raymond Ave. 449.5884

14 Espresso Bar $ Funky, crowded coffeehouse serving fine desserts until late. Live music and performance. ♦ Café ♦ M-Th noon-1AM; F-Sa noon-2AM; Su noon-midnight. 34 S. Raymond Ave. 356.9095

14 Distant Lands A traveler's bookstore, run by **Adrian Kalvinskas**, offering maps, videos, and over 4500 book titles. ♦ Tu-Th 1:30AM-7PM; F-Sa 1:30AM-9PM; Su 11AM-5PM. 62 S. Raymond Ave. 449.3220

15 Hotel Green Apartments One of the 2 remaining examples of Pasadena's grand hotel era. Architect **Frederick Roehrig**'s grand Moorish and Spanish Colonial design is an immense extension to the older Hotel Green structure, originally known as the **Webster Hotel**, and built in 1890 for promoter **E.C. Webster** and patent medicine manufacturer **Colonel G.G.**

Pasadena

Green. In the 1920s Roehrig more than tripled the hotel's size with elaborate bridged and arched additions that include the domed and turreted **Castle Green Apartments** built in 1897 across the street at 99 S. Raymond Ave, and the **Green Hotel Apartments** (1903) at 50 E. Green St, newly renovated and modernized as a senior citizen's home.

16 Santa Fe (AMTRAK) Railroad Station (1935) Colorful Spanish Colonial depot with **Batchelder** tiles in the waiting room. Here, in the '30s before the completion of Union Station in downtown LA, movie stars made splashy departures on the *Super Chief* to Chicago, and on to New York aboard the *Twentieth Century Limited*. Now there's one train a day —the *South West Chief*—and a connecting bus to Bakersfield. ♦ 222 S. Raymond Ave. Amtrak information 800/872.7245

17 Pasadena Public Library (1927, **Hunt and Chambers**) A Renaissance-style building at the north end of the Civic Center axis. ♦ M-Th 9AM-9PM; Sa 9AM-6PM; Su 1-5PM. 285 E. Walnut St. 405.4066

18 Plaza Las Fuentes (1989, **Moore Ruble Yudell**; landscape design, **Lawrence Halprin**) A 200-million-dollar 6-acre development by **Maguire Thomas Partners**, comprising a hotel, offices, retail, and restaurants, to the east of City Hall. In a break with the concrete boxes that have proliferated in recent years, the architects have sought to integrate buildings and gardens, drawing on the Beaux-Arts spirit of the Civic Center and the Hispanic tradition. They have created a sequence of pedestrian spaces enlivened by fountains, with low buildings and plantings to soften the impact of major blocks. ♦ Bounded by Colorado and Los Robles Blvds, Walnut and Euclid Aves

18 Doubletree Hotel $$$ Luxury hotel with 360 rooms and suites. Low weekend rates. Within the hotel is the **Oaks Restaurant**, which offers an adventurous though uneven menu in a grand space. The bar offers tapas, 4-7PM, and light dining until midnight. ♦ 191 N. Los Robles Ave. 792.2727, 800/528.0444; fax 795.7669

19 Pasadena City Hall (1925, **John Bakewell, Jr.,** & **Arthur Brown, Jr.**) A handsome domed Baroque structure located at the junction of 2 broad avenues designed by the firm responsible for San Francisco's City Hall. As notable as the architecture are the formal courtyard garden and fountain. ♦ 100 N. Garfield Ave

20 Plaza Pasadena **Terry Schoonhoven**'s trompe l'oeil mural enlivens the 60-foot vault of this otherwise conventional shopping mall. ♦ M-F 10AM-9PM; Sa 10AM-7PM; Su 11AM-6PM. Colorado Blvd (Marengo-Los Robles Aves) 795.8891

21 Civic Auditorium (1932) Handsome home to the **Pasadena Symphony Orchestra** and varied music, dance, and theater events. Don't miss a concert that showcases the mighty Wurlitzer. The auditorium is the centerpiece of a convention center built of concrete in a disagreeably brutal style. ♦ Seats 3000. 300 E. Green St. 449.7360

22 Miyako ★$$ The house specialty is sukiyaki, a mixture of meat and vegetables cooked in a seasoned sauce, prepared at your table by a kimono-clad waitress. Traditional Japanese decor enhances the meal. ♦ Japanese ♦ M-F 11:30AM-2PM, 5:30-10PM; Sa 5:30-10PM; Su 4:30-9PM. 139 S. Los Robles Ave. 795.7005

23 Pasadena Hilton $$$ Conveniently located hostelry. ♦ 150 S. Los Robles Ave. 577.1000, 800/445.8667; fax 584.3148

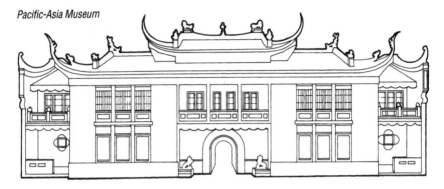

Pacific-Asia Museum

24 Pacific-Asia Museum (1924) **Grace Nicholson** commissioned the firm of **Mayberry, Marston and Van Pelt** to design a traditional Northern Chinese building to house her extensive collection of Far Eastern art. The building is an imaginative amalgam of rare beauty and serenity, and features changing exhibitions on the arts of the Far East and Pacific Basin. ♦ Donation requested. W-Su noon-5PM. 46 N. Los Robles Ave. 449.2742

25 Warner Building (1927) Sensational Art Deco frieze of seashells. ♦ 481 Colorado Blvd

26 Pasadena Playhouse Founded in 1917, it flourished for 50 years, nurturing the careers of **Gene Hackman, Kim Stanley, William Holden**, and other leading actors. The 1925 building closed in the mid '60s and stayed dark for the next 20 years. It was elaborately restored and reopened in 1986 with **Shaw**'s *Arms and the Man* in the 700-seat proscenium-arch auditorium. There is also a 99-seat Equity waiver performance space. Both are flourishing under Artistic Director **Susan Dietz**. Behind-the-scenes tours on the second Saturday of the month led by theater alumni, 11AM-1PM. ♦ 37 S. El Molino Ave. Tickets 356.7529, information 763.4597

26 Stottlemeyer's $ One-hundred-and-fifty sandwiches, each named for a famous personality. Great desserts. ♦ American ♦ M-Sa 10AM-6:30PM. 712 E. Colorado Blvd. 792.5351

27 Lake Avenue One of the main shopping streets with numerous specialty shops clustered around **Bullock's** and **I. Magnin**. Three arcades are notable: **The Commons** (quality food stores); **The Colonnade and Burlington Arcade** (elegant imports); **Haskett Court** (flowers, toys, and curios from *Merrie Englande*). ♦ California-Colorado Blvds

27 Beadle's Cafeteria $ Plain American food, freshly prepared. The prime rib and leg of lamb are favorites with the regulars who line up daily. ♦ American ♦ Daily 11AM-7:45PM. 850 E. Colorado Blvd. 796.3618

28 The Ice House Lily Tomlin, Robin Williams, and **Steve Martin** got their start here and you may catch tomorrow's top talent at this friendly night spot. Three-act comedy show Tuesday-Saturday at 8:30PM (late show Friday-Saturday, 10:30PM); also in **Footsies**, a smaller room, shows Friday 9PM, Saturday 8:30PM. Dinners and dancing are also offered at an adjoining restaurant. ♦ 24 N. Mentor Ave. 577.1894

29 Marianne's ★$$$ Gourmet French cooking in a proper dining room. A row of private booths with adjustable lighting and lace curtains for romantic trysts are available by request. Mousse and quenelles of remarkable lightness. ♦ French ♦ Tu-Th 11:30AM-2PM, 6-9:30PM; F 11:30AM-2PM, 5:30-9:30PM; Sa 5:30-9:30PM; Su 5-9:30PM. 45 S. Mentor Ave. 792.2535

30 Crocodile Cafe $ A junior version of the Parkway Grill, serving eclectic cuisine—pizza, papaya chicken, and Cuban pork with black beans—in a noisy, popular room. ♦ California ♦ M-Th 11AM-11PM; F-Sa 11AM-midnight; Su 11AM-10PM. 140 S. Lake Ave. 449.9900

31 Konditori $ Open-face Danish sandwiches are the specialty of the house. Breakfast offers smoked salmon and eggs or Swedish meatballs. The umbrella-shaded patio is a lovely spot to relax with pastry and coffee. ♦ Scandinavian ♦ M-Sa 7:30AM-5PM; Su 8AM-4PM. 230 S. Lake Ave. 792.8044

Pasadena

32 Saw Mill $$ Good steaks, chicken, and seafood; a self-serve salad bar. The cocktail lounge has a comfortable living room feeling with a fireplace. Entertainment nightly from 9PM. ♦ American ♦ M-Th 11AM-10:30PM; F-Sa 11AM-11:30PM; Su 4-10:30PM. 340 S. Lake Ave. 796.8388

33 The Chronicle ★★$$$$ A lovingly restored Victorian house reminiscent of San Francisco that serves competent classic cuisine—including oysters Rockefeller, poached salmon, and broiled swordfish. The front room is lace-curtained; the back is draped in elegance. The wine list emphasizes California vintages and is one of the best in the city. ♦ Continental ♦ M-Th 11:30AM-2:30PM, 5-10PM; F-Sa 11:30AM-2:30PM, 5-11PM; Su 5-10PM. 897 Granite Dr (S. Lake Ave) 792.1179

34 Burger Continental $ A self-serve counter that offers hamburgers in native or exotic dress. Middle Eastern specialties are a surprise on the menu. The rear patio is tree-shaded by day, lit with Christmas bulbs in the evening. ♦ American/Middle Eastern ♦ M-Th, Su 6:30AM-10:30PM; F-Sa 6:30AM-11:30PM. 535 S. Lake Ave. 792.6634

35 Rose Tree Cottage ★$ Book early for an authentic English tea complete with fresh scones, Devonshire cream, and strawberry jam. Light fare is available throughout the day. A pretty place. ♦ English ♦ Daily 10AM-5:30PM. 824 E. California Blvd. 793.3337

36 Kidspace Interactive exhibitions for children from 2 to 12 include *Splashsports* (how to swim without getting wet), *Human Habitrail* (popular science), a TV studio, grownup tools, and a live ant colony. Special events throughout the year; large groups and birthday parties by arrangement. ♦ Admission. W 2-5PM, Sa-Su 12:30-5PM, Oct-May; M-F 1-5PM, Sa-Su 12:30-5PM, June-Sep. 390 S. El Molino Ave. 449.9144

37 Parkway Grill ★★$$$ Outstanding Contemporary Californian cuisine by chef **Hugo Molina** in the aggressively creative tradition of Spago. Eating here is a delicious lesson in topsy-turvy geography: gumbo, applewood-smoked chicken with chutney, hot oysters with corncakes, sausage and a *tomatillo* sauce, pasta, and of course the ubiquitous pizza straight from the wood-burning oven. The obligatory bustling open kitchen is the centerpiece of the warm and attractive high-beamed brick room. ♦ California ♦ M-F 11:30AM-2:30PM, 5:30-10PM; Sa-Su 5-10PM. 510 S. Arroyo Pkwy. 795.1001

38 James/Randell Authentic hand-crafted reproductions of Greene and Greene furniture. ♦ M-F 8AM-6PM; Su varies. 768 N. Fair Oaks Ave. 792.5025

39 Roxxi ★$$ Popular newcomer that calls itself Fresh Western, serving shallot-and-garlic pizza, pasta with spinach and scallops in broth, and crisp roasted duck with Zinfandel and plum

Pasadena

sauce. ♦ California ♦ M-F 11:30AM-2:30PM, 5:30-10:30PM; Sa-Su 5:30-10:30PM. 1065 E. Green St. 449.4519

39 Pasadena Post Office (1913, **Oscar Wenderoth**) An Italian Renaissance building. ♦ 1022 E. Colorado Blvd

40 Maldonado's ★$$$ Well-prepared and handsomely presented food accompanied by song and opera. One of the most successful combinations of food and entertainment in the city. Chicken Marengo is recommended. ♦ Continental ♦ Tu-F 11:30AM-2:30PM, 6PM-midnight; Sa 6PM-midnight; Su 5:30PM-midnight. 1202 E. Green St. 796.1126

41 Pasadena City College A 2-year college, part of the Pasadena Area Community District. ♦ 1570 E. Colorado Blvd. 578.7123

42 California Institute of Technology World-famous for physics, engineering, and astronomy, its faculty and alumni have won 21 Nobel prizes and it has spawned a plethora of high-technology firms in the area. **Albert Einstein** once taught here. It is a far cry from **Throop University**, its forerunner, founded in

1891 to *foster higher appreciation of the value and dignity of intelligent manual labor.* Architect **Bertram Goodhue** laid out the plan of the institute in 1930, inspired by a medieval scholastic cloister. Other buildings of that era were designed by **Gordon Kauffman**, notably the **Spanish Renaissance Atheneum Faculty Club** on nearby Santa Bonita Street. ♦ Campus tours M, Th, F 3PM; Tu-W 11AM; architectural tours 4th Th of every month 11AM (reservations required). No tours December, July, August. 1201 E. California Blvd. 356.6228

At the California Institute of Technology:

Beckman Auditorium This auditorium hosts lectures, concerts, film, plays, and dance. ♦ Seats 1165. S. Michigan Ave at Constance St. Schedule and tickets 356.4652

43 Bristol Farms A 4-star market with the freshest produce and fish, a dazzling array of wines and groceries, and exemplary service. ♦ M-Sa 9AM-9PM; Su 10AM-7PM. 606 S. Fair Oaks Ave. 441.5450. Also at: 837 Silver Spur Rd, Rolling Hills Estates. 213/541.9157

44 Restaurant Shiro ★★★$$ Chef **Hideo Yamashiro** left the **Cafe Jacoulet** to open this delectable storefront restaurant and bring joy to the neighborhood. The freshness of the fish and the delicacy of the sauces have won acclaim. Standouts have included seafood salad, ravioli stuffed with shrimp and salmon mousse, and whole sizzling catfish. ♦ French/Japanese ♦ Tu-Su 6-10PM. 1505 Mission St, South Pasadena 799.4774

45 Miltimore House (1911, **Irving Gill**) A purified Mission revival house by a master. Private residence. ♦ 1301 Chelten Wy, South Pasadena

46 The Huntington Hotel & Cottage $$$ The last functioning resort hotel from Pasadena's golden age. The cottages and other buildings are open while the original block is being restored to its former glory. This work should be completed by early 1991. ♦ 1401 S. Oak Knoll Ave. 792.0266; fax 792.9572

47 Acapulco $ A casual family restaurant that offers imaginative interpretations of Mexican favorites. The crab enchilada is famous. ♦ Mexican ♦ M-Th 11AM-10PM; F-Sa 11AM-midnight; Su 10AM-10PM. 2936 E. Colorado Blvd. 795.4248

48 Panda Inn $$ One of a dependable group of Pandas serving spicy food in a cool Postmodern room. ♦ Chinese ♦ Daily 11:30AM-10:30PM. 3488 E. Foothill Blvd. 793.7300

49 Domenico's $$ A family-run pizzeria for more than 20 years. Good pizza and delicious toppings. ♦ Pizza ♦ Tu-F 3PM-11PM; Sa noon-midnight; Su 12:30-10PM. 2411 E. Washington Blvd. 797.6459

50 Eaton Canyon Nature Center Just east of central Pasadena. One-hundred-and-eighty-four acres of native California plants. The small museum contains displays on the ecology of the area and gives leaflets for self-guided tours through the canyon. **The Naturalists Room** houses live animals and natural history objects.

50 San Gabriel Mountains True wilderness is found in the San Gabriel Mountains, which were inaccessible to anyone but a seasoned outdoorsman until 1935, when the Angeles Crest Highway (State 2) was opened. It was the first of an interlacing network of mountain highways that brings travelers to secluded destinations. Route 2 begins in La Canada and leads to the 691,000 acre Angeles National Forest, of which the San Gabriels are only a part.

Some of the more remote sections of the region have colorful histories. The discovery of placer gold deposits triggered a small gold rush as early as 1843 near the east and west forks of the San Gabriel River. At the end of the decade a town named Eldoradoville sprang up and soon rivaled northern Gold Rush towns as a den of iniquity. The town was later destroyed by heavy floods. Gold fever revived during the Depression, when jobless Southern Californians improvised a camp and panned for hardscrabble gold with kitchen utensils.

During the boom of the 1880s, Angelenos made the horse trail up Mt. Wilson a favorite vacation spot. Professor T.S.C. Lowe opened up the Mt. Lowe Railroad in 1893 to bring delighted tourists 3000 feet up the steep incline to the mock-alpine hamlet near Echo Mountain's peak. The railway was destroyed by fire, but another famous landmark, the Mt. Wilson Observatory, still stands near the peak of 5710-foot Mt. Wilson. The observatory grounds and an astronomical photo exhibition are open daily 10AM-4PM, information 440.1136.

The San Gabriels are popular for hiking, bicycling, fishing, birdwatching, and in winter, a variety of snow sports. The quiet trails are seldom crowded—the only groups you might see are Boy Scout troops. There are great contrasts in vegetation and terrain; water makes all the difference (Crystal Lake is one of the most spectacular sights). One moment you may be walking in a fern dell, the next taking in an arid chaparral landscape. Wildflowers abound, including poppies, Indian paintbrush, lupines, and wild tiger lilies. Skunk cabbage grows near springs, and at altitudes over 5000 feet, pine trees flourish.

Three levels of ranges add variety to hiking pleasure. The front slopes near Altadena are good for day hikes, with well-maintained trails leading through waterfalls and pools and near cliffs and ravines. Vegetation here is primarily alders, oaks, and cedars. In places such as Bear Canyon, the middle ranges take you to the last reserves of mountain lions and bighorn sheep in Southern California. At the top of the range, many of the slopes are stark and are a rugged rock climber's paradise. One of the most challenging of the higher areas is Mt. San Antonio, or Old Baldy, at 10,080 feet the county's highest peak. Sightseeing drives will provide only a

sample of the wealth that the San Gabriels contain. Getting out and walking around is the best way to understand this area. Much is virgin territory, and the thrill of trailblazing is still available. It is recommended that visitors stop at the Red Box Ranger Station for trail and road information, brochures, and books. ♦ Route 2 at Mt. Wilson junction. To phone ahead, call the O operator and ask for Red Box No. 2 Station

Bests

Jane Pisano
President of The 2000 Partnership

Mark Pisano
Executive Director, Southern California Association of Governments

For a foretaste of 21st century LA:

Tour the **Port of Los Angeles**. International trade will be an important engine of economic growth.

Attend a ballgame at **Dodger Stadium**. Today, this is the only place in town where people from all ethnic groups and income levels come together, foreshadowing 21st-century multiethnic Los Angeles.

Hike from the **Griffith Park Observatory** to the top of Mt. Hollywood. Take a long view of Los Angeles. It will look the same in the 21st century.

Visit **Union Station**. This 50-year-old structure is the future site of an intermodal transportation center linking metrorail and light rail lines now under construction.

Stroll along Grand Avenue from the **Music Center** to the **Museum of Contemporary Art**. With the completion of **Disney Hall**, designed by Frank Gehry, this area will be an internationally recognized arts center and

Pasadena

the esthetic heart of downtown Los Angeles in the 21st century.

Sip coffee at the restaurant atop the **Holiday Inn** in Brentwood and observe the rush-hour traffic on the 405 Freeway. Most Angelenos will still travel by car in the 21st century. It will probably take them longer than it does today.

Christine and Joachim Splichal
Patina Restaurant

Play tennis at the **Los Angeles Tennis Club**.

Walk our dog Coco around **Hollywood Lake**.

Eat sushi at **Katsu**.

Drink great Burgundies with dinner.

Stay at the **Jerome Hotel** when we go skiing in Aspen.

Go to the fish market early in the morning.

Go to old car auctions and rare wine auctions.

Play the stock market (Joachim only).

Stay at the **Highlands Inn** in Carmel for a romantic weekend.

Visit art galleries.

San Gabriel Valley

In the 1920s and '30s, the **San Gabriel Valley** was a near paradise of dense orange, lemon, and walnut groves, with such exotic attractions as lion, ostrich, and reptile farms in between. Over the past 15 years the Anglo population has sharply declined as Hispanics and, most recently, Asians have flocked in. The small communities of the valley, nearly all independent cities, have sprawled one into another, creating a large suburban region of small stucco homes extending some 30 miles.

The first settlement of the Los Angeles region was made here in 1771, when 2 priests, 14 soldiers, and 4 mule drivers chose a spot near the banks of the San Gabriel and Rio Hondo rivers to found the **Mission San Gabriel Archangel**.

While life at San Gabriel was relatively peaceful, revolution was brewing in Mexico. Colonials in California and Mexico resented Spain's civil and economic restrictions, and the revolt of 1821 successfully created a new government. Church and state were split asunder when Mexican authorities declared a secularization of the mission regime. The Indians who were to have

shared in ownership of mission properties lost out to counter claims by settlers of European descent. By the time California became part of the Union, the San Gabriel Valley area was a well-known stopping place on the traveler's route into Los Angeles. Several small towns popped up in the San Gabriel region as the *ranchos* began to be broken up into small farm tracts. One of the first was **El Monte**, started as a trading post for Americans arriving overland from the East. For many years thereafter, El Monte was the region's hog-ranching center. The site of **Alhambra** is part of the former Rancho San Pascual and was later acquired by **J.D. Short** and **Benjamin D. Wilson**. Short and Wilson laid out a subdivision in 1874 and named it Alhambra because one of their relatives saw a resemblance between **Washington Irving**'s *stern melancholy country* and the landscape around the tract.

The next big spurt of development in this eastern valley came in 1903, when **Arcadia** and **San Marino** were founded by 2 of the wealthiest men of the times. **E.J. "Lucky" Baldwin** named his subdivision Arcadia after the district in Greece whose poetic name meant a place of rural simplicity, while **Henry E. Huntington** named his palatial estate after the Republic of San Marino and created a small independent city of luxurious homes.

Area code 818 unless otherwise indicated.

1 Wonder Seafood ★★$ How do you like cobra—served in a soup with abalone and mushrooms? It's delicious, and those with adventurous tastes won't be disappointed by this authentic Cantonese restaurant. But there's plenty more familiar fare, including steamed oysters with black-bean sauce, asparagus with scallops, wonderful crab and shrimp, and sliced chicken with geoduck clam. ♦ Chinese ♦ Daily 11:30AM-10PM. 2505 W. Valley Blvd, Alhambra. 308.0259

2 Pine Garden ★$$ Excellent sushi, fine tempura, clams steamed in sake, and *bentos* (lunch boxes) to go. Dancing to live bands. ♦ Japanese ♦ Daily 5:30PM-midnight. 323 W. Valley Blvd, San Gabriel. 289.1000

3 El Emperador Maya ★$ Specialties of this local treasure include Yucatan seafood dishes, turkey tostadas, and mild mole sauces. ♦ Mexican ♦ Tu-Sa 11AM-9PM. 1823 S. San Gabriel Blvd, San Gabriel. 288.7265

4 Edward's Steak House $$ Nicely grilled steaks and chops, a surprise or 2 (like lamb shanks), and at least one fresh fish each day. The sawdust-on-the-floor informality makes this a good place for kids. ♦ American ♦ M-F 11:15AM-10:15PM; Sa 3-11PM; Su 3-10:15PM. 9600 E. Flair Dr, El Monte. 442.2400

5 Middle East ★$ Bargain eating in a tiny shack. Two Druze from Lebanon prepare aromatic stews and couscous, stuffed chicken and lamb with yogurt, plus all the traditional starters and desserts. A treasure. No alcohol. ♦ Lebanese ♦ M-Sa 11AM-10PM. 645 E. Main St, Alhambra. 576.1048

Restaurants/Clubs: Red	Hotels: Blue
Shops/Parks: Green	**Sights/Culture:** Black

6 Panchito's ★$$ Everything from the salsa to the building itself has been made by the owner, and the personal involvement shows. The 18-ingredient secret family recipe marinade soaks flavor into steaks and seafood. The grapevine that shelters the patio comes from rootstock at the San Gabriel Mission. ♦ Mexican ♦ Tu-F 11:30AM-10PM; Sa 5-11PM; Su 4-11PM. 261 S. Mission Dr, San Gabriel. 289.9201

7 San Gabriel Civic Auditorium This immense auditorium was designed especially for **John Steven Groarty**'s *Mission Play*, a favorite tourist attraction during the 1920s. The authentic Mission-style building was created by **Arthur Benton** who modeled the playhouse after the Mission San Antonio de Padua in Monterey County. Heraldic shields of the Spanish provinces, donated by Spanish **King Alfonso** on the playhouse's opening in 1927, adorn the interior. Fine theater organ, used for concerts and to accompany silent movies. ♦ Seats 1500. 320 S. Mission Dr, San Gabriel. 308.2865

8 Mission San Gabriel Archangel Founded in September 1771 by fathers **Pedro Cambon** and **Angel Somera**. The present Mission Church consists of the remains and renovation of the one built by Indian workers from 1791 to 1805. Constructed of stone, mortar, and brick, it has an unusual design because the north side is the major facade. Its capped buttresses and narrow windows were influenced by the style of the Cathedral of Cordova, Spain. The church originally had a vaulted roof but it was damaged in the earthquake of 1803. In 1812 the church tower on the facade was toppled by another earthquake. When the church was completely restored in 1828, a new bell tower was constructed on the north wall of the altar end. The bell-tower wall with its 3 rows of arched openings creates the characteristic image of the mission. Interior closed for

San Gabriel Valley

repairs from earthquake damage. ♦ Gardens, cemetery, gift shop daily 9:30AM-4:15PM. 537 W. Mission Dr, San Gabriel. 282.5191

9 Ortega-Vigare Adobe (Blessed Hope Church of San Gabriel) Begun approximately in 1795, this is one of the oldest adobes in Southern California. Built by **Don Juan Ortega** and purchased by **Don Juan Vigare** in 1859, only half of the original structure remains; a former hallway is now the front porch. ♦ 616 S. Ramona St, San Gabriel

10 Tokyo Lobby $$ Decorated with folk art; a Japanese restaurant that appeals to Americans. ♦ Japanese ♦ M-F 9PM. 927 Las Tunas Dr, San Gabriel. 287.9972

11 Alex's $$ Good pizza, good lasagna, good value. ♦ Italian ♦ Tu-Su 4-11PM. 140 Las Tunas Dr, Arcadia. 445.0544

12 Julienne ★$ Charming café serving great homemade bread, delicious salads, roast chicken, and daily specials. ♦ French ♦ M, F 8AM-6PM; Tu-Th 8AM-9PM; Sa 8AM-5PM. 2649 Mission St, San Marino. 441.2299

13 El Molino Viejo (1816) The first water-powered gristmill in Southern California is maintained by the **California Historical Society**. ♦ Admission. Tu-Su 1-4PM. 1120 Old Mill Rd, San Marino. 449.5450

14 Huntington Library, Art Collections, and Botanical Gardens A 207-acre estate, formerly the home of **Henry E. Huntington** (1850-1927), pioneer railroad tycoon and philanthropist, and one of the greatest attractions in Southern California. The Huntington residence, designed by **Myron Hunt** and **Elmer Grey** in 1910, now houses the art gallery. The collection emphasizes English and French painting of the 18th century. Among the famous works displayed are **Gainsborough**'s *Blue Boy*, **Lawrence**'s *Pinkie*, **Reynold**'s *Sarah Siddons as the Tragic Muse*, and **Romney**'s *Lady Hamilton*. The gallery also exhibits an impressive collection of English and French porcelains, tapestries, graphics, drawings, and furniture. Acquisitions include a full-length **Van Dyck** portrait, *Mrs. Kirke*, and a late **Turner** canvas with the rather literary title, *Neapolitan Fishergirls Surprised Bathing by Moonlight*.

The library, designed by Myron Hunt and **H.C. Chambers** in 1920, houses extensive holdings of English and American first editions,

Mission San Gabriel Archangel

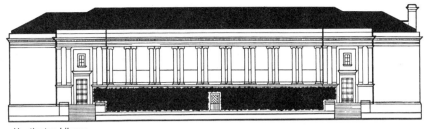
Huntington Library

manuscripts, maps, letters, and incunabula. Displayed are a number of the most famous objects in the collection, including a **Gutenberg Bible**, the **Ellesmere** manuscript of Chaucer's *Canterbury Tales*, the double elephant folio edition of **Audubon**'s *Birds of America*, and an unsurpassed collection of the early editions of **Shakespeare**'s works. In the west wing of the library is the **Arabella Huntington Memorial Collection** of French porcelain, furniture, sculpture, and Renaissance paintings.

With the 1984 opening of the **Virginia Steele Scott Gallery of American Art**, designed by **Warner and Gray**, the Huntington added another dimension to its collections. Works range in date from the 1730s to the 1930s, and in-

clude paintings by **Mary Cassatt** (*Breakfast in Bed*), **Gilbert Stuart, Winslow Homer, John Singleton Copley, Edward Hopper**, and **Robert Henri**. American artifacts and furniture, including pieces by **Gustav Stickley**, are distributed throughout the gallery and matched with paintings from the appropriate period. There is also temporary exhibition space for photographs and works on paper.

 The gardens were designed and developed by **William Hertrich** beginning in 1904. In addition to expansive lawns and formal planting arrangements that incorporate 17th-century Italian sculpture, they contain extensive rose and camellia gardens, a Shakespearean garden of plants mentioned by *the Bard*, and a number of

Huntington Library Botanical Garden

annual beds. The Japanese garden is entered through a moongate over an arched bridge spanning a koi pond. It features an authentically furnished 16th-century teahouse, specimens of bonsai, and a Zen rock garden. The astonishing 12-acre desert garden has the largest and most unique variety of cacti and succulents in the world. Sunday visitors must make advance reservations. ◆ Admission. Galleries and gardens: Tu-Su 1-4:30PM. Huntington Patio Restaurant: Tu-Su 1-4:30PM. 1151 Oxford Rd, San Marino. Information 405.2100, directions 405.2274, reservations 405.2273

15 Peony ★★$$ **Michael Chang**, formerly of **Joss** in West Hollywood, has created a sophisticated decor and menu. Standouts include *Pin pei* chicken (crispy-skinned and served like Peking duck), fish broth with ginger and cilantro, diced fish with pine nuts, and clams with satay sauce. ◆ Chinese ◆ Daily 11AM-10PM. 7232 N. Rosemead Blvd, San Gabriel. 286.3374

16 Talk of the Town $$ A clublike steakhouse serving large, well-prepared portions. The bar is decorated with horse-racing memorabilia (the owner is a former jockey) and, during the season at Santa Anita, is quite a hangout for the racing crowd. ◆ American ◆ M-Th 11:30AM-2PM, 5-10:30PM; F 11:30AM-2PM, 5-11PM; Sa 5-11PM. 3730 E. Foothill Blvd, Pasadena. 793.6926

When it is 12 noon (Standard Time) in Los Angeles, the corresponding times around the world are:

Hawaii	10AM
Chicago	2PM
New York	3PM
London	8PM
Moscow	midnight
Bombay	1:30 AM (next day)
Tokyo	5AM (next day)

17 Restaurant Lozano ★$$ Folksy setting for healthy, flavorful food. Black-bean soup, stuffed peppers, and AHA-approved burgers are specialties. ◆ Southwestern ◆ M-Th, Su 11AM-9PM; F-Sa 11AM-10PM. 44 N. Baldwin Ave, Sierra Madre. 355.5945

18 LA Arboretum No need to go to Africa or Brazil to visit a jungle—a visit to the arboretum and the lake where **Humphrey Bogart** once pulled the *African Queen* through the slimy muck, leeches and all, is certainly more economical. Located on a 127-acre portion of the former **Rancho Santa Anita**, the arboretum houses plant specimens from all over the world, arranged by continent of origin. The lake in the middle of the property is spring fed, a result of natural waters seeping up along the Raymond fault, which runs across the property. The **Gabrieleno Indians** used this as a water source for hundreds of years before **E.J. "Lucky" Baldwin** bought the rancho in 1875. The **Baldwin Ranch** was not only a working ranch but one of the earliest botanical collections in the Southland. Witness several exceedingly tall *Washingtonia robusta* palm trees; at 121 feet they might set a world record. Peacocks and guinea fowl roam among the lush plantings, delighting with their vivid promenades and startling with their raucous cries. Demonstration gardens show California domestic horticulture at its best. A snack bar offers refreshment; a gift shop sells books and gifts. ◆ Admission. Daily 9AM-4:30PM. 301 N. Baldwin Ave, Arcadia. 446.8251

Within the LA Arboretum:

Lucky Baldwin Queen Anne Guest Cottage (1881) Baldwin, a high-living and often outrageous silver-mining magnate, owned the rancho between 1875 and 1909. The exuberant red-and-white gingerbread Queen Anne-style building was created as a lavish guesthouse for

San Gabriel Valley

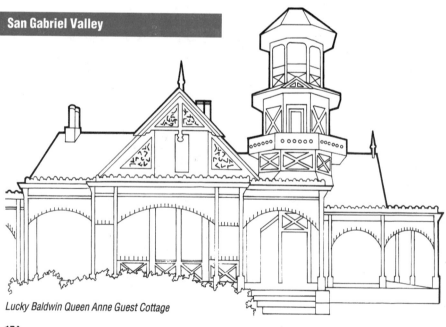

Lucky Baldwin Queen Anne Guest Cottage

visitors to the estate. The cottage with its delicately scrolled woodwork is a favorite location for film and television crews. Close by, and in the same style, are stables, a dog house, and an 1890 railroad station.

Hugh Reid Adobe A reconstruction of Reid's original 1839 structure, and built of more than 15,000 handmade adobe blocks. Reid owned the 13,319-acre Rancho Santa Anita between 1841 and 1847.

19 Chez Sateau ★★★$$$ An oasis in the culinary desert, conveniently close to Santa Anita and the LA Arboretum. Japanese chef **Ryo Sato** combines his own traditions with inventive French cooking, delighting diners with such unusual dishes as grapefruit consommé and oyster-veal mousse. Nice service makes up for the plain decor. Sumptuous picnics to go, here and at **Chez Sateau Pâtisserie** next door (574.0702). ◆ French ◆ Tu-F 11:30AM-2:30PM, 5:30-9:30PM; Sa 5:30-9:30PM; Su 9AM-2:30PM, 5:30-9:30PM. 850 S. Baldwin Ave, Arcadia. 446.8806

20 Santa Anita Race Track Thoroughbred horses race against the backdrop of the San Gabriel mountains on one of the most beautiful race tracks in the country. The park features a lushly landscaped infield, children's playground, and numerous eating places that run the gamut from hot dogs to haute cuisine. Weekdays, the public is invited to watch morning workouts (a Continental breakfast is served at **Clocker's Corner**); on Saturday and Sunday, a free tram tour of the grounds is offered. The action in the saddling enclosure and walking ring may be viewed immediately prior to post time. In addition to the regular season, the **Oak Tree Racing Association** sponsors thoroughbred racing in October through mid November. ◆ Admission. Season: 26 Dec-late April. Post time: 1PM. Morning workouts: 5-9:30AM. Tram tours: Sa-Su 8:30AM. 285 W. Huntington Dr, Arcadia. 574.7223

21 Aztec Hotel (1925, Robert Stacy-Judd) A wonderfully eccentric, freshly-restored stucco facade designed by an enthusiastic advocate of the pre-Columbian revival style. ◆ Foothill Blvd (Magnolia Ave) Monrovia. 358.3231

22 La Parisienne ★★$$$ A venerable, unpretentious restaurant with highly professional service and traditional French cooking. The portions are generous and the pastries win raves. ◆ French ◆ M-F 11:30AM-2PM, 5:30-9PM; Sa 5:30-9PM. 1101 E. Huntington Dr, Monrovia. 357.3359

23 Raging Waters A 44-acre family water park extravaganza, waves and a sandy beach offer welcome relief from scorching days. A popular summer attraction is **Dive-in Movies**, where you can watch everything from *Splash* to *Creature from the Black Lagoon* while floating in an inner tube. ◆ Admission. Daily 10AM-6PM, April through May; daily 10AM-7PM, late May through mid-June; M-F 10AM-6PM, Sa-Su 9AM-10PM, mid-June through mid-Sep; Sa-Su 10AM-6PM, mid-Sep through mid-Oct. 111 Via Verde, San Dimas (Via Verde exit from Foothill Fwy, I 210) 714/592.6453

24 Fluke's for Fine Food ★$$ Mini-mall oasis of interesting food, including crabcakes and chicken with coriander. ◆ American ◆ Tu-F 11AM-2:30PM; Sa 5-10PM. 2350 E. Amar Rd (Nogales St), West Covina. 965.3996

Bests

Gil Friesen
Music Industry Executive

A view of the **Los Angeles basin** on a clear night from the air.

Tower Records late at night.

Irvine Ranch Market for bountiful fresh fruit and vegetables and unobstructed aisles.

Early morning walks on the beach, particularly in April/May for dolphin sightings.

Browsing at **Book Soup** on Sunset.

Shopping for bonzai at **Yamaguchi.**

Will Rogers Park and, of course, his home.

Greene and Greene's **Gamble House** in Pasadena.

The **Apple Pan** on West Pico for almost anything.

A day's sailing out of the **Marina.**

Adolfo V. Nodal
General Manager, Cultural Affairs Department

The **Wilshire Boulevard Historic Neon Corridor**—from Alvarado Street to La Brea Avenue between 4th and 8th Streets. Over 40 vintage neon signs cram the rooftops of this historic part of mid Wilshire. They were turned off during the air-raid scare of World War II. Today some are languishing, some have been restored—a few were never turned off.

Jay's Jayburger, Meaty Meat Burger, Tommy's, Oki Dog, and other early Los Angeles food stands throughout the city.

San Gabriel Valley

Bunker Hill Steps, the **Toluca Yard Tunnel**, the **Union Pacific Pedestrian Overpass** (now closed), the **Superset Light Church Courtyard, St. Elmo's Village**, and other high-quality human-scale open spaces in Los Angeles.

The **Watts Towers** and the conceptual plan for the "Cultural Crescent" expansion of the Tower grounds, which will include an expansion of the **Watts Towers Arts Center** and additional park area linking with the Watts Train Station and the new light-rail transit system.

Louisiana/LA, the **African Marketplace, St. Elmo's Village Festival, Watts Towers Drum Festival**, the **Pacific Island Festival**, and other citywide outdoor cultural festivals that are rapidly making this a festival town. (For information call 213/485.2433.)

The **Sequel**, the **Pick-Me-Up, Café Java, Cafe Largo** and other of the new breed of coffeehouses and cabarets that are catering to Los Angeles' new bohemians and turning this city into the Paris of the '90s.

South and East Central

This is the true Los Angeles Basin, edged by mountains and water, scored by railroad tracks, freeways, and rivers. Industry provides the economic base of the area; the flat expanse offers no obstacles to construction of factories and roads. The development of this region was largely dependent on the **Southern Pacific Railroad** and the **Pacific Electric Interurban Railroad**. Buying up huge tracts of land as they built their lines, the transportation giants later subdivided their holdings into a series of communities for workers and their families.

The flat expanses, right-angled streets, and unimpeded vistas seemed familiar to newcomers from the Midwest and South who had responded to the

boosterism and land fever of the 1880s and 1920s. Many of these communities have remained unincorporated; like the jigsaw patterns of the other parts of Los Angeles County, the boundaries between city and county hop and skip around each other.

East LA is overwhelmingly Hispanic; it has the largest concentration of Latinos in the country—from the view homesites of **Boyle Heights** through the flatlands to the ranch homes of the **Whittier Hills**. South-Central—from **Baldwin Hills** to the plains area that includes **Watts, Willowbrook,** and **Compton**—is home to the county's largest concentration of black residents. **Monterey Park** is the preferred destination for Chinese immigrants.

Culver City

Formerly home to 3 major motion picture studios: **Metro-Goldwyn-Mayer, Selznick International Studios**, and **Hal Roach Studios**. At one time this small town outstripped Hollywood to become the producer of half of the films made in the United States.

1 Artemide The best in contemporary lighting from European and American designers. ◆ M-F 9AM-5PM. 4200 Sepulveda Blvd. 837.0179

1 Allied Model Trains One of America's largest stores for model train buffs of all ages has relocated to these larger premises designed as a miniature of Union Station. ◆ M-Sa 10AM-6PM. 4411 Sepulveda Blvd. 313.9353

2 Columbia Pictures Studios How are the mighty fallen! **Metro-Goldwyn-Mayer**, once an empire, with 5 lots, theaters, and studios around the world, and *more stars than there are in heaven*, surrendered its last piece of turf to the producer of TV's *Dallas* and *Falcon Crest* and is now located in a bland Beverly Hills office building. The sequel is even more ironic. Columbia Pictures, born on Gower Street's **Poverty Row** in the same year as MGM, has relocated here from Burbank—a poor-boy-makes-good story worthy of the movies. Meanwhile, you can see the exteriors of the 2 major buildings on the lot: the 1916 **Triangle Company** office, with its classical colonnades, which MGM took over in 1924, and the monumental moderne **Thalberg Building** of 1939, named for MGM's legendary head of production. And, of course, there are the echoes—of **Lillian Gish** and **Greta Garbo, Clark Gable** and **Joan Crawford, Judy Garland** and **Gene Kelly**. Not open to the public. ◆ 10202 W. Washington Blvd. 818/954.6000

3 Versailles ★$ Roast pork with black beans, chicken with garlic, and paella are delicious in this modest, budget-priced restaurant. ◆ Cuban ◆ Daily 11AM-10PM. 10319 Venice Blvd. 558.3168

4 The Beaded Bird Depression-era glass, bakelite jewelry, porcelain, and other pre-1940

South and East Central

collectibles. ◆ M-F 10AM-5PM; Sa 11AM-5PM; open 2nd Sunday of each month 9AM-4PM. 9416 Venice Blvd. 204.3594

4 Sacks Fashion Outlet Popular unisex sportswear, deeply discounted. ◆ M-Tu 10AM-6PM; W-F 10AM-8PM; Sa 10AM-7PM; Su 11AM-6PM. 9608 Venice Blvd. 559.5448

5 Culver City Studios **King Kong** roared, Atlanta burned, and boy wonder **Orson Welles** directed *Citizen Kane* on this lot. Its southern plantation offices were built by pioneer producer **Thomas Ince**, later housed **RKO**, and were the trademark of **David O. Selznick**'s company long before he built *Tara* on the land cleared by torching the surviving sets of **Cecil B. De Mille**'s *King of Kings*. All of this history has gone with the wind, leaving only the facade and a cluster of vintage rental stages. Not open to the public. ◆ 9336 W. Washington Blvd

5 Warehouse conversions (1988, Eric Moss) Expressive remodelings of the old **Paramount Laundry**, across from the **Culver City Studios** and another '20s industrial facility. ◆ 3958-60 Ince Blvd, 8522 National Blvd

6 The Antique Guild (1930) A block-long moderne building, formerly the home of **Helms Bakeries**. It now houses a collection of stores specializing in antiques and period reproductions. A small tearoom is located among the departments devoted to furniture, jewelry, books, plants, and gifts. ◆ M-F 10AM-7PM; Sa 10AM-6PM; Su 11AM-6PM. 8800 Venice Blvd. 838.3131

7 Design Express (1989, Michele Saee & Ma Massie) A huge contemporary design showroom that is itself a design statement, in the striking way a drab warehouse has been recycled. ◆ M-F 10AM-7PM; Sa 10AM-6PM; Su noon-5PM. 3410 S. La Cienega Blvd, LA. 935.9451. Also at: 8806 Beverly Blvd, W. Hollywood. 859.7177; 6459 De Soto Ave, Woodland Hills. 818/346.4709

7 Baldwin Hills Village (1940-41) A rare model of planned housing that forms a tight-knit community, well-integrated with its landscaping. Private residences. ◆ 5300 Rodeo Rd

8 Oil Wells Driving north on La Cienega (a good shortcut into town from LAX if the San Diego Freeway is doubling as a parking lot), you pass this surviving patch of unimproved oil wells nodding away like mechanical storks. Much of LA looked like this in the early years of the century

9 Fox Hills Mall Large, popular shopping mall, with a **May Co** and **J. C. Penney**, plus 131 other stores on 3 floors selling everything from fresh-roasted nuts to bolts of cloth as well as clothing for all ages. The electronic game center is a popular spot with youngsters. ◆ M-F 10AM-9PM; Sa 10AM-7PM; Su 11AM-6PM. Sepulveda Blvd at Slauson Blvd, Fox Hills. 390.7833

10 Dinah's $ Good and cheap basic food—from fried chicken to apple pancakes—in a setting so time-hallowed it should be in the Smithsonian. Eat in or takeout. ◆ American ◆ Daily 6AM-11PM. 6521 S. Sepulveda Blvd. 568.1964

11 Centinela Ranch House Built in the 1840s for **Ignacio Machado**, this well-preserved house is made of adobe with a wood-shingle roof, and is furnished with 19th-century antiques. Some of the original planting is maintained. ◆ Free. W, Su 2-4PM. 7634 Midfield Ave. 649.6272

12 Harriet's Cheesecakes Unlimited $ Over 36 flavors of cheesecake to go or by the slice. Try the chocolate amaretto, apple'n'spice, or coffee flavors if the exquisite French vanilla is too tame for you. ◆ Takeout ◆ Tu-Sa noon-8PM. 1515 Centinela Ave, Inglewood. 419.2259

13 JB's Little Bali ★$$ Multidish rijstaffel is the only meal but you may think you've eaten your way through an entire menu. ◆ Indonesian ◆ Th-Su 6-10PM. 217 E. Nutwood St, Inglewood. 674.9835

14 Hollywood Park Thoroughbred racing April through July on a track landscaped with lagoons and tropical trees. A computer-operated screen offers patrons a view of the back stretch, as well as stop-action replays of photo finishes and racing statistics. Refreshments at the elegant **Turf Club Terrace**, **International Food Fair**, **Wine and Cheese Cellar**, and **Carnation Ice Cream Parlor**. Children's play area. ♦ Admission. Post times M-F 2PM; Sa-Su 1:30. 1050 S. Prairie Ave, Inglewood. 419.1500

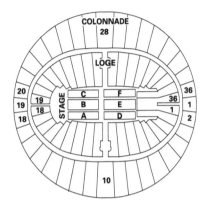

15 The Forum Concerts, ice hockey, basketball, tennis, boxing, and other sports and public events. From October through April, it is home to the **Los Angeles Lakers** basketball team and the **Los Angeles Kings** hockey team. ♦ Seats 17,000. Admission varies with event. Box office daily 10AM-6PM. Manchester Ave at Prairie Ave, Inglewood. 673.1300

16 Academy Theatre (1939, **S. Charles Lee**) A streamline moderne landmark, notable for its spiral-finned tower, now used as a church. ♦ 3100 Manchester Blvd at Crenshaw Blvd, Inglewood

17 Museum in Black Part museum, part store. Features traditional African art and African-American memorabilia. ♦ Free. Tu-Sa noon-6PM. 4327 Degnan Blvd. 292.9528

18 Harold & Belle's ★★$$ Generous helpings of fabulous gumbo, jambalaya, hot sausage, shrimp creole, and barbecued ribs in pleasant surroundings draw enthusiastic crowds. ♦ Cajun/Creole ♦ M-Th 11AM-10PM; F 11AM-midnight; Sa 1PM-midnight; Su 1-10PM. 2920 W. Jefferson Blvd. 735.9023

19 William Grant Still Community Arts Center A community arts center named for the famous late black composer and long-time resident of LA. Offers exhibitions, festivals, and workshops. ♦ Free. Tu-Su noon-5PM. 2520 West View St, LA. 734.1164

20 Clark Memorial Library English literature and music of the 17th and 18th centuries are well-represented in this research library, bequeathed to UCLA in 1934 by **William Andrews Clark, Jr.**, in memory of his father, **Senator William A. Clark**. The Italian Renaissance building is decorated with murals and ceiling paintings by **Allyn Cox**, and is furnished with period antiques. The underground vaults are covered with formal gardens. Tours by appointment only. Open to researchers weekdays 9AM-4:45PM. ♦ 2520 Cimarron St (West Adams Blvd) 731.8529

20 Amateur Athletic Foundation of LA The **Paul Ziffren Sports Resource Center** was built with proceeds from the 1984 Olympics, and named for the chairman of the LAOOC. It houses a state-of-the-art sports library and archive, which is open to the public by appointment. ♦ 2141 W. Adams Blvd. 730.9696

21 Janet's Original Jerk Chicken $ Pork, ribs, chicken, and Jamaican roast beef are the tasty treats in this storefront restaurant. ♦ Jamaican ♦ M-Sa noon-9PM; Su 1-8PM. 1541 Martin Luther King, Jr. Blvd. 296.4621

22 Jamie's ★$ One of several bare-bones restaurants/takeouts in the area that offer the tasty Creole/Caribbean dishes of Belize, where *The Mosquito Coast* was filmed. Sunday specialties include *relleno* (baked chicken stuffed with ground pork served with a sauce of roasted chiles) and *escabeche* (sautéed chicken with onion and vinegar). Weekday treats include conch and cowfoot soups. ♦ Belizian ♦ M-Tu, Th-Su 8AM-10PM. 4307 S. Vermont Ave. 231.1207

23 El Sol ★$ Don Julio, the Chinese/Peruvian owner/chef serves delicious ceviche and tripe, lamb with cilantro sauce, and fried red snapper at very reasonable prices—as he did at the previous location in Hollywood. Live music on weekends. ♦ Peruvian ♦ Tu-Sa 11AM-10:30PM; F-Sa 11AM-midnight; Su 11AM-9PM. 15651 Hawthorne Blvd, Lawndale. 973.2486

24 El Pollo Inka ★$ Marinated spit-roasted chickens are the signature dish, but just as delicious are the braised lamb in cilantro sauce and potato slices with a walnut-chile sauce. ♦ Peruvian ♦ Daily 11:30AM-9PM. 15400-D Hawthorne Blvd, Lawndale. 676.6665

25 Kanpachi $$ An exceptional sushi bar. ♦ Japanese ♦ M-Sa 5:30PM-midnight; Su 5-9PM. 14813 S. Western Ave, Gardena. 515.1391

South and East Central

26 New Meiji Market Foods of the Pacific Rim in mind-numbing variety. Begin browsing and you may decide to change your diet. ♦ M-Sa 8AM-9PM; Su 8AM-8PM. 1620 W. Redondo Beach Blvd, Gardena. 323.7696

27 Ascot Speedway Escape the frustrations of speed limits and pollution consciousness with a visit to the Valhalla of heavy horsepower. See sprint cars do the half-mile in less than 20 seconds and motorcycles leave the ground in daredevil leaps. Dirt-track racing is presented Wednesday through Sunday night. ♦ Admission. 18300 S. Vermont Ave, Gardena. 323.1142, speedway information 515.5115

Restaurants/Clubs: Red   **Hotels:** Blue
Shops/Parks: Green   **Sights/Culture:** Black

28 Goodyear Blimp The best-known, best-loved corporate symbol in the United States—192 feet long, 59 feet high, 50 feet in diameter, with a volume of 202,700 cubic feet. Deflated, she weighs 12,000 pounds; filled with helium, an inert lighter-than-air gas, her weight drops to 150 pounds. Cruising speed is 35 miles per hour; top speed is 53 miles per hour. The normal cruising altitude of 1000-1500 feet gives the blimp and its logo maximum recognition from the ground. The blimp is used for a number of purposes besides advertising. It acts as a camera platform for TV coverage of sports and public events; it assists the American Cetacean Society with the annual count of the California gray whales during their winter migration; and it has carried instruments aloft for a number of scientific experiments. The *Columbia* travels 6 months out of the year, but you are most likely to see her on the ground in the early morning or at twilight from the intersection of the Harbor and San Diego freeways. ♦ 770.0456

29 Dominguez Ranch Adobe A relic of the Spanish settlement of California. **Juan José Dominguez** traveled as a soldier with Father Serra's original expedition from Mexico to found the California missions. In 1782 he was rewarded for his service with a land grant covering the harbor area south of the Pueblo de Los Angeles, over 75,000 acres. His nephew built an adobe in 1826, and its interior has been restored as a historical museum, displaying many of the original furnishings. The adobe is now part of the **Dominguez Memorial Seminary**, operated by the Claretian Order. Groups over 10 must make advance reservations.
♦ Free. Tu-W 1-4PM; 2nd and 3rd Su of every month 1-4PM. 18127 S. Alameda St, Compton 631.5981, 636.6030

30 Watts Towers (1921-54, **Sam Rodia**) A dream made real, one of the world's greatest works of folk art, now shrouded in scaffolding. An unlettered plasterer created these masterpieces, framing them from salvaged steel rods, dismantled pipe structures, bed frames, and cement. He worked alone. *How could I have help?* asked Rodia, *I couldn't tell anyone what to do...most of the time I didn't know what to do myself.* Building without conscious plan—though he may have been inspired by childhood memories of similar structures used in an annual fiesta near Naples—scaling the

Watts Towers Drawing by Rik Olsen

heights of his work using a window washer's belt and bucket, Rodia's glistening fretwork grew slowly over the years until the central tower topped out at 107 feet. Glass bottle fragments, ceramic tiles, china plates, and over 70,000 seashells embellish his creation, encrusting the surface so thickly that they seem to be the primary building material, forming a skin that has the calcified delicacy of coral. When the towers were completed, Rodia deeded his property to a neighbor and left LA forever. He died in 1965 in Martinez, CA, unwilling to the end to talk about his life work. Vandals disfigured the spires, and they were threatened with demolition. Citizens rallied and saved them. Extensive renovation work commenced in 1978 and is ongoing under the direction of the **LA Cultural Affairs Department**. Public access to interior limited to the July music festival and the Days of the Drum in October. Be aware of high crime rate in the area. ♦ 1765 E 107th St, Watts. 271.9711

30 The Watts Towers Art Center A community art center that hosts exhibitions, art classes, and special programs of music, dance, and poetry reading. ♦ T-Sa 9AM-4PM. 1727 E 107th St, Watts. 569.8181

30 Watts Train Station (1904) Recently restored as a railroad museum and office for the **Department of Water and Power**. It is meant as a symbol of the CRA's efforts to revitalize Watts, and the new light rail line from Long Beach to downtown LA will stop close by—much as the Big Red Cars used to. ♦ 103rd St (Grandee Ave) Watts

31 Winnie and Sutch Company Building (1939) One of the best streamline moderne buildings in LA, especially since the Pan Pacific Auditorium was torched. ♦ 5610 S. Soto St, Huntington Park

32 Farmer John's Pig Mural Little pigs romp and play in a painted, life-size farm landscape that becomes a part of the real building. Real trees become inseparable from painted ones and pigs peer into windows, real and painted. The murals, begun in 1957, were done by **Les Grimes**, a scenic artist who usually worked for movie studios. When he fell to his death from a scaffold in 1968 the **Arco Sign Company** assumed responsibility for maintaining and extending the murals. ♦ 3049 E. Vernon Ave, Vernon

33 Dunbar Hotel (1928) The first hotel in America built specifically for blacks—when white hotels refused to take them. During its heyday in the 1930s, almost every prominent black who visited Los Angeles stayed here. It is now being restored and converted to seniors housing. ♦ 4225 S. Central Ave

34 Street Clock A vintage free-standing clock is the centerpiece of a delightful row of Art Deco storefronts in a section that has retained its original flavor. ♦ 2423 Broadway, Lincoln Heights

35 Hollenbeck Park A 21-acre park donated to the city in 1892. There are a number of old trees, including a lovely stand of jacaranda. The clubhouse sponsors recreation programs. ♦ Daily 8AM-10PM. 415 S. St. Louis St. 261.0113

36 El Mercado For Mexican flavor without leaving LA County, try El Mercado, a bustling combination of food market, shops, and restaurants moving to the music of mariachis on the mezzanine and Latin records in the basement. The main floor is a market full of stalls selling the ingredients for Mexican cooking; along the walls on this level are a *tortillaria*, a bakery, snack bars with food to go, and delicatessens. The mezzanine has a series of cafeteria-style restaurants where a large variety of dishes are available. Mariachis play from around noon until midnight on this level; they'll take special requests for a small donation. In the basement are shops selling everything from furniture to Mexican crafts to utilitarian domestic goods. ♦ Shops: 9AM-9PM. Restaurants: daily noon-midnight. 3425 E 1st St. 268.3451

37 La Parilla ★★$ Authentic Mexican cuisine at the heart of the barrio where little English is spoken, but the welcome is as friendly as it is south of the border. Handmade tortillas, fresh and feisty salsa, deep-fried snapper, and well-garlicked shrimp. ♦ Mexican ♦ M-Th, Su 8AM-midnight; F-Sa 8AM-1AM. 2126 Brooklyn Ave. 262.3434

38 Los Angeles County USC Medical Center The highly visible 20-story moderne structure, completed in 1934, covers 89 acres and is the largest general acute-care hospital in the country. ♦ 1200 N. State St, Lincoln Heights. 226.2622

39 Lincoln Park One of the oldest parks in the city, the 46 acres were purchased in 1874. Over 300 varieties of trees grace the grounds; a number of them are rare and enormous, dating back to the beginning of the park. ♦ M-F 9AM-10PM; Sa 9AM-5:30PM; Su 10AM-6PM. N.

Mission Rd at Valley Blvd, Lincoln Heights. 237.1726

Within Lincoln Park:

Plaza de la Raza Fronting on the park's small lake, it is a complex of theater, classroom, and office space serving as a cultural and educational center. It is the main forum for activities of interest to LA's Spanish-speaking community. Activities include musical performances, dance, drama, and seasonal festivals based on themes related to Mexican holidays and family life. ♦ Nominal admission. 3540 N. Mission Rd. 223.2475

Restaurants/Clubs: Red   **Hotels:** Blue
Shops/Parks: Green   **Sights/Culture:** Black

Greater Los Angeles encompasses over 40,000 square miles.

40 California State University, Los Angeles A branch of the California State University system. ♦ 5151 State University Dr (Eastern Ave) 343.3000

41 Ocean Star Seafood ★★$$ No-frills, authentic Cantonese seafood—including steamed live shrimp and scallops, baked lobster, and fish prepared in several distinctive ways. Duck soup with citrus peel and beef hotpot are also recommended. ♦ Chinese ♦ M-Th, Su 5PM-3AM; F-Sa 5PM-4AM. 112 N. Chandler Ave (Garvey Ave) Monterey Park. 818/300.8446

44 East Los Angeles College Free, public 2-year community college with undergraduate courses and occupational programs. One of the first colleges to offer free, noncredit courses to anyone in the community. ♦ 1301 Brooklyn Ave, Monterey Park. 265.8650

45 Tamayo $$ An ambitious restaurant named for Mexican muralist **Rufino Tamayo**, whose artworks adorn this handsome, restored 1927 building with its painted wood ceilings. It's a delightful oasis, except for the food, which has drawn mixed reviews at best. ♦ Mexican ♦ M-Th, Su 11AM-10PM; F-Sa 11AM-11PM. 5300 E. Olympic Blvd. 260.4700

The Citadel Drawing Courtesy Sussman-Prejza & Company, Inc.

41 Dragon Regency ★★$$ Extraordinary preparations of shrimp, crab, and sole put most Western seafood restaurants to shame. ♦ Chinese ♦ Daily 9AM-10PM. 120 S. Atlantic Blvd, Monterey Park. 282.1089

42 Fragrant Vegetable ★★$$ One of the best vegetarian restaurants in LA. Forbidden meats are convincingly simulated with tofu; elsewhere on the menu, real vegetables play starring roles. In the Garfield Lincoln Center. ♦ Chinese ♦ M-Th, Su 11AM-9:30PM; F-Sa 11AM-10PM. 108-110 N. Garfield Ave, Monterey Park. 818/280.4215

42 Cocary ★$ Frantic and fun. A Mongolian barbecue where you select (from refrigerated

South and East Central

cases down one wall) such delicacies as tiger prawns, baby clams, and fish dumplings to grill or simmer in a pot at your table. Bring a crowd of friends and a good appetite. ♦ Chinese ♦ Daily 11AM-1AM. 112 N. Garfield Ave, Monterey Park. 818/573.0691

43 NBC Seafood ★★$$ Sister of **ABC** in Chinatown; can CBS be long in coming? Like its sibling, it specializes in Cantonese seafood, fresh from the tank. Perch steamed with ginger, catfish with garlic, and live crab prepared to order are highly recommended. Dim sum are served for breakfast and lunch. ♦ Chinese ♦ Daily 8AM-10PM. 404 S. Atlantic Blvd, Monterey Park. 818/282.2323

The Squaw Man, directed and produced by **Cecil B. DeMille**, was the first Hollywood movie; it was made in 1913 in a horse barn at Selma and Vine.

46 The Citadel (1929, **Morgan, Walls & Clements**) Sound the trumpets! The Assyrian fortress, designed as an impressive facade for the **Samson Tire and Rubber Factory**, is being restored and redeveloped. Long a forlorn landmark glimpsed from the freeway by tourists who wondered if they had misread the map and arrived early at Disneyland, it will soon be pulling them into a 130,000 square foot factory outlet retail center whose stores will face onto **The Grand Plaza**. A stylish food court will be roofed with existing trusses and skylights, and the facade building will be remodeled as corporate offices. This ambitious project, due for completion in late 1991, has been designed by **Sussman-Prejza & Co**. ♦ 5675 Telegraph Rd (Santa Ana Fwy) City of Commerce

47 All American Home Center Family-owned store, comprising 21 departments on 4 acres and another 6 acres of parking. It claims to be the best-stocked in the US and—more important—to motivate its staff through profit sharing. So, if you want to build your dream house.... ♦ M-Sa 8AM-9PM; Su 8AM-7PM. 7201 E. Firestone Blvd, Downey. 927.8666

48 Magdalena ★★★$$$ Sophisticated cooking in an improbable location. Chef **Stephen White** prepares such dishes as salmon quenelles in a 3-mustard sauce, breast of pheasant, and lamb stuffed with a julienne of vegetables. ♦ French ♦ Tu-Th 11AM-3PM, 5-9:30PM; F 11AM-3PM, 5-10PM; Sa 5-10PM. 17818 Bellflower Blvd, Bellflower. 925.6551

49 Heritage Park Restored 1880s ranch and history museum in 6 acres of gardens. Close by is the **Clarke Estate** (1919, **Irving Gill**), one of the best-preserved works by this landmark architect. ♦ 12100 Mora Dr, Santa Fe Springs. 946.6476

50 Pio Pico State Historic Park/Casa de Pio Pico Don Pio Pico, former governor of California, built this hacienda on his 9000-acre El Ranchito in 1850. The U-shaped house is a 13-room 2-story adobe mansion with 2- to 3-foot-thick walls. Covered porches link the side wings to the central portion of the house; a well is located in the courtyard. The house is closed for restoration through 1994. ◆ Park W-Su 9AM-5PM. 6003 Pioneer Blvd, Whittier. 695.1217

51 Whittier Narrows Nature Center A 127-acre sanctuary for an enormous variety of birds, plants, and animals located along the San Gabriel River. The small museum has exhibitions that describe the aquatic environment. ◆ Free. Daily 9AM-5PM. 1000 N. Durfee Ave, El Monte. 444.1872

52 El Monte Historical Museum Located in a 1936 WPA building, the museum contains 3 main sections: archives of pioneer diaries, books, maps, photographs, and other printed material; a reproduction of the interior of an El Monte home, c. 1870-1890; and a depiction of the town (known as **Lexington** until 1868), c. 1855, including a general store, barber shop, police department, and school. ◆ Free. Tu-F 10AM-5PM; Sa 10AM-3PM. 3150 N. Tyler Ave, El Monte. 818/444.3813

53 Do-Nut Hole (1958) One of the city's great pop monuments. You can drive through the 2 giant donuts and pick up one, or a bag to go, at any hour of the day or night. ◆ 24 hours. Elliott Ave at Amar Rd (Hacienda Blvd) La Puente

54 Workman & Temple Homestead Relive the colorful history of Los Angeles, from the first American settlers of the 1840s (when California was still under Mexican rule) through the booms of the 1870s and 1920s. Each of these formative decades is dramatically evoked by historic buildings on a 6-acre site, restored by the **City of Industry** as an educational showpiece. The major attraction is a 26-room Spanish-revival house built in the '20s with the profits from an oil strike and furnished in period style, complete with wind-up Victrola and a bearskin in the hall. The original mid 19th-century adobe, an English-style manor house, a lacy gazebo, and a private cemetery are also featured. The Homestead has become an important cultural resource, scheduling art fairs, concerts, lectures, and seasonal activities. ◆ Guided tours on the hour Tu-F 1-4PM; Sa-Su 10AM-4PM; closed the 4th weekend of every month. 15415 E. Don Julian Rd, City of Industry. 968.8492

55 China Pavilion ★★$$ Lemon scallops, hot spicy garlic chicken, and double-pleasure sole are standouts from the 200-item menu. There's a virtuoso noodle maker and elegant decor. ◆ Chinese ◆ Daily 11:30AM-10PM. 2140 S. Hacienda Blvd, Hacienda Heights. 818/330.5388

Restaurants/Clubs: Red   Hotels: Blue
Shops/Parks: Green   **Sights/Culture: Black**

Drawing by Willie Heron

LA Murals
Murals are the most democratic of art forms, as the great Mexican muralists demonstrated after their revolution. In LA, the movement began as part of the counterculture in the late 1960s, and they are scattered around the city, notably in East LA, downtown, and Venice. Twelve freeway murals were commissioned for the 1984 Olympics. Two of the finest are on the north side of the Hollywood Fwy (US 101): **Frank Romero**'s *Going to the Olympics* (at Alameda Blvd) and **John Wehrle**'s *Galileo/Jupiter/Apollo* (at Broadway). Veteran **Terry Schoonhoven** did a mirror view

---

South and East Central

of downtown on the west side of the Harbor Freeway, north of Wilshire Blvd. **Kent Twitchell**'s portrait of fellow artists **Lita Albuquerque** and **Jim Morphesis** lurks beneath the 7th St overpass on the Harbor Fwy. Other Twitchell murals are located off surface streets at Broadway and 2nd St (*Bride and Groom*), at Hill and 10th streets (*Ed Ruscha*), at Fountain Ave and Kingsley Dr (*Strother Martin*), and on the side of the Otis Art Institute on Carondelet St at Wilshire Blvd (*Trinity*). His most celebrated, *Old Lady of the Freeway*, on Hollywood near the Harbor interchange, was painted over. Another classic, created in El Pueblo de Los Angeles in 1932 by **David Siqueiros**, the outspoken Marxist artist, was immediately painted over for political reasons. It is now being restored. The **LA Mural Conservancy** (PO Box 860244, LA, CA 90086-0244) has published a guide to the latest and best works.

LAX/South Bay/Long Beach

From **Venice** to **Naples** extends a succession of beach towns, each with its own distinct character and specialty—bathing, surfing, sailing, fishing. The sandy expanses are interrupted by manmade **Marina del Rey**, the rocky outcrop of the **Palos Verdes** peninsula, and by the industrial enclave around the **Los Angeles Harbor, San Pedro,** and **Long Beach**. Inland is LA's real harbor: **LAX** the fourth busiest airport in the world.

1 Los Angeles International Airport The hub of the LA regional airport system, which also includes **Ontario** to the east, **Burbank** and **Van Nuys** to the north, **Long Beach** and **John Wayne** to the south. In 1988 it handled 622,427 landings and takeoffs and 44,398,611

passengers (up from 7 million when jet service began in 1962). There are 4 east-west runways on a 3500-acre site, and the buildings are constantly being improved.

The central complex comprises 7 separate terminals around the perimeter of a 2-level loop, with parking, a restaurant, heliport, and control tower within the loop. The 5-level million-square-foot **Tom Bradley International Terminal** at the end of the loop includes **Skytel**, in which weary travelers can take a shower or rent sleeping space by the hour—a facility European airports have offered for years.

Terminal No. 2 has been expanded to provide improved service to overseas destinations. Airlines frequently merge and move terminals; for up-to-date information call 646.5252.

Departures are made from the upper level, where ticket counters and check-in, restaurants, newsstands, and gift stores are located. The lower arrival level includes baggage claim areas, car rental agencies, information on hotels, and ground transportation.

Free blue, green, and white **Airline Connections** buses link each terminal at both levels. Other free buses will take you to satellite parking lots and the **West Imperial Terminal**. **Handicapped Connections** is a free minibus with extra-wide doors and a ramp lift for wheelchairs.

Getting to the airport by car There is short-term parking (8800 spaces) in 9 central lots at reasonable rates; lots are often full at holidays or peak periods. Long-term parking at 2 major satellite lots (16,400 spaces): **Lot C** (corner of Sepulveda Blvd and 96th St) and **Lot B** (corner of La Cienega Blvd and 111th St). Both of these satellite lots have 24-hour bus service running every 10-20 minutes to each of the 8 terminals. (**Lot D** is used as a spill-over from the adjoining Lot C at peak times.) There are also privately owned lots scattered around the airport offering greater convenience at higher cost. ◆ Information 670.8164

Ground transportation A bewildering array of buses and vans circle the loop, stopping at the center island outside each baggage claim. Be sure to stand at the correct pick-up sites. Major services include:

Super Shuttle Bright blue vans offering door-to-door service from LAX to most destinations in Los Angeles and Orange Counties, including the major airports. Fares are somewhat below taxi rates. For pick-up at the airport, call 417.8988 after you have collected your baggage; 24 hours in advance from your home or hotel.

Van Service covers the following routes; other stops by arrangement with the driver.

Downtown Area Stops Hotels: Bonaventure, Hilton, Figueroa, Hyatt Regency, Biltmore, New Otani. Greyhound-RTD Terminal.

Wilshire District Stops Hotels: Hyatt-Wilshire, Sheraton Town House.

Beverly Hills-Century City Stops Hotels: Century Plaza, Beverly Hilton, Regent Beverly Wilshire.

Hollywood-Universal City Stops Hotels: Hollywood Roosevelt, Holiday Inn, Sheraton-Universal.

Pasadena Stops Hotels: Pasadena Hilton, Holiday Inn.

Orange County Buses go to hotels and sites in Anaheim, Disneyland, Santa Ana, Long Beach Airport, and John Wayne Airport.

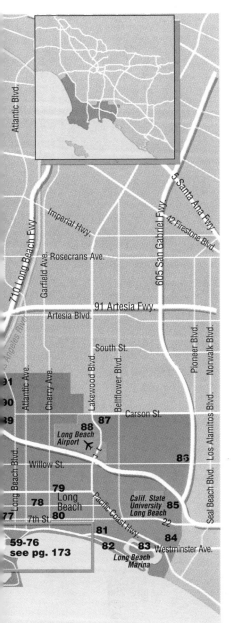

Los Angeles produces nearly half of the California economy.

Santa Monica Area Santa Monica Flight Line's white vans service the Miramar Sheraton, Huntley House, Holiday Inn, Pacific Shore, and Ocean Village hotels; call 2 hours in advance. ♦ Daily 6AM-9PM. 971.8265

Eastern San Fernando Valley FlyAway bus service to the Van Nuys Airport Terminal at 7610 Woodley, corner of Saticoy. At the airport, board buses in the center island outside of the baggage claim area. ♦ 818/994.5554

Western San Fernando Valley and Ventura Area The Great American Stage Lines brown-and-gold big buses go regularly to and from Woodland Hills, Thousand Oaks, Oxnard, and Ventura. ♦ 805/499.1995

For other ground transportation services, check the ticket/information booths on the sidewalk outside each baggage claim.

RTD Airport Services Regular bus services link many parts of town with the bus terminal at Lot C. Free 24-hour connector bus stops at each of the airline terminals and runs every 10-20 minutes. ♦ 626.4455

Theme Building Rising 135 feet above the terminal area, the Theme Building houses the **California Place Restaurant**, an 80-foot observation deck, and a branch of the Bank of America. ♦ Observation Deck: daily 9AM-5PM. Restaurant: M-Sa 11AM-4:30PM, 5-9:30PM; Su 10AM-2:30PM. 646.5471

West Imperial Terminal A separate terminal just south of the main airport handles charter flights and supplemental carriers. A free blue-and-green bus marked *West Imperial Terminal* (WIT) connects you with the main terminal every half-hour 7AM-12:30AM. Take the bus from the center island in front of each baggage claim area. ♦ 6661 W. Imperial Hwy. 646.2011

Information Inside the airport, yellow telephones are available to reach the Airport Information Aides. ♦ Multilingual information and assistance daily 7AM-11:30PM. 656.5252

2 Quality Inn $$ A moderately priced hotel. Outdoor pool, exercise room, 2 restaurants. Complimentary 24-hour airport shuttle. Room service. Ballroom and conference rooms. ♦ 5249 W. Century Blvd 645.2200, 800/228.5151; fax 641.8214

3 Hilton Hotel $$$ Huge conference center and 1280 rooms. ♦ 5711 W. Century Blvd. 410.4000, 800/445.8667; fax 410.6241

3 Marriott Hotel $$$ Another caravanseray for families and business travelers. Health club with Jacuzzi and sauna, children's game room, beauty salon, 3 restaurants, 24-hour airport shuttle, 24-hour room service, concierge. ♦ 5855 W. Century Blvd. 641.5700, 800/228.9290; fax 337.5358

4 Sheraton Plaza La Reina Hotel $$$ Conveniently located near the airport and beaches. Bonuses include transportation to **Disneyland**, **Universal Studios**, and **Knotts Berry Farm**. In-house restaurants and disco. Handicapped accommodations. ♦ 6101 W. Century Blvd. 642.1111, 800/325.3535

4 Hyatt Hotel $$$ A cut above the other airport hotels. Health spa, pool, and Jacuzzi, 24-hour airport shuttle. Four Gold Passport floors, Regency Club, and lounge. ♦ 6225 W. Century Blvd. 670.9000, 800/228.9000; fax 641.6924

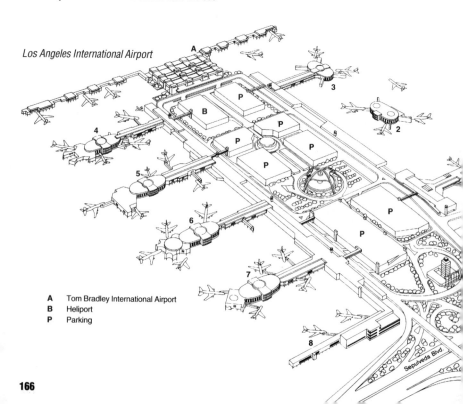

Los Angeles International Airport

A Tom Bradley International Airport
B Heliport
P Parking

5 Loyola Theater (1946) Once a luxurious pre-view theater for **20th Century-Fox**, now gutted. The swan's-neck facade survives. ◆ Sepulveda Blvd at Manchester Ave

6 AMFAC Hotel $$$ A luxury hotel. Complimentary shuttle to Fox Hills Mall and Marina del Rey. Amenities include complimentary parking, an exercise room, jogging track, tennis courts, and an adjacent bowling alley. ◆ 8601 Lincoln Blvd. 670.8111, 800/227.4700; fax 337.1883

7 Loyola Marymount University The successor to **St. Vincent's**, the first college in Los Angeles, founded in 1865. Now a coeducational private Catholic university. ◆ Loyola Blvd at W 80th St. 642.2700

8 Lannan Foundation Changing art exhibitions are presented in the garden and galleries of this adventurous philanthropic venture. Amid the new Puritanism, Lannan's support for controversial art and literature is of key importance. ◆ Tu-Sa 11AM-5PM. 5401 McConnell Ave. 306.1004

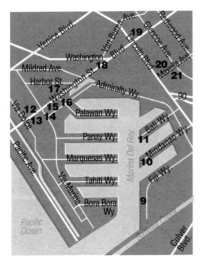

Marina del Rey

Home to the world's highest concentration of finely honed blond singles: a waterfront community laid out in the '60s on marshy land between Venice and the airport. It is also the world's largest manmade small-boat harbor, with moorings for 10,000 private pleasure craft. The adjoining open space of Playa Vista, bought by Howard Hughes for aircraft testing in the '40s, is being redeveloped as a planned community by a talented group of designers working for Maguire Thomas Partners.

9 Fisherman's Village Quaint restaurants and shops with a good view of the Marina Channel. Harbor cruises offered. ◆ 13755 Fiji Wy. 823.5411

9 Marina del Rey Sportfishing Charter fishing boats go offshore for 1/4 and 1/2 day cruises. Dock fishing, boat, and tackle also available. ◆ Daily 6AM-5PM. 13759 Fiji Wy. 822.3625

10 Burton Chace Park Perfect for yacht watching, fishing, kite flying, or moon-gazing from the watchtower. Picnic facilities and restrooms make this a good place for a family outing. ◆ End of Mindanao Wy past Admiralty Wy

11 Marina del Rey Hotel $$$ A luxury hotel surrounded by water on 3 sides, making it an ideal base for sailors. The **Crystal Seahorse** restaurant overlooks the marina's main channel. ◆ 13534 Bali Wy. 301.1000, 800/862.7462 (CA), 800/882.4000 (US); fax 301.8167

12 Siamese Garden ★★$$ Friendly little place with a delightful courtyard. Specialties include barbecued chicken, grilled shrimp, steamed crab claws, and fine *pad thai* noodles. ◆ Thai ◆ M-Th 11:30AM-3PM, 5-10PM; F 11:30AM-3PM, 5-11PM; Sa 11:30AM-11PM; Su 11:30AM-10PM. 301 Washington St. 821.0098

13 Bird Sanctuary Perhaps the only natural retreat remaining of the miles of duck marshes once covering the area. It is a sylvan haven, hemmed in by concrete roads on both sides. ◆ Washington St-Admiralty Wy

14 Cheesecake Factory $$ Specialty drinks include the *Flying Gorilla* and the *Strawberry Creamsicle.* Combine one of these with the house's varied cheesecakes and kiss your diet goodbye. Or you can choose something less calorific from a vast menu. Popular patio. ◆ American ◆ M-Th, Su 11:30AM-11:30PM; F-Sa 11:30AM-12:30AM. 4142 Via Marina. 306.3344

15 Marina City Towers (1971, **Anthony Lumsden for DMJM**) Rounded shapes that resemble enormous horseshoe magnets tugging at each other. ◆ 4333 Admiralty Wy

LAX/South Bay/Long Beach

16 Jamaica Bay Inn $$ A pleasant place with its own beach. Forty-two units with kitchenettes in 12. Bayside and cityside room rates. Café. Shuttle to airport available. ◆ 4175 Admiralty Wy. 823.5333; fax 823.1325

16 Marina International and Marina Beach Hotels $$$$ Neighboring luxury hotels operated by **Doubletree** and both commanding views of the marina. The International has 25 popular theme villas in which you can pretend you're an astronaut, a great white whale, or a movie star. Marina Beach has **Stones**, a stylish restaurant with a sophistiscated menu. ◆ 4200 Admiralty Wy. 301.2000, 800/862.78462 (CA), 800/882.4000 (US); fax 301.6687

17 Akbar ★★$$ Mughal cooking of unusual quality, with excellent tandoori and vegetarian dishes. ♦ Indian ♦ M-Th 11:30AM-2:30PM, 6-10PM; F-Sa 11:30AM-2:30PM, 6-10:30PM; Su 6-10:30PM. 590 Washington St. 822.4116

18 Roger's Marina Cafe ★$$ A local version of a Parisian bistro; crabcakes and pastas are good choices. ♦ Eclectic ♦ Daily 11:30AM-10PM. 822 Washington Blvd. 822.7221

19 Miami Spice ★$ A Day-Glo coffee shop that changes its personality through the day. Breakfast on sweet toast and café *con leche*; lunch on *media noche* (a composite sandwich) washed down with a tropical fruit shake, and save room for a dinner of roast chicken with rice, beans, and fried plantains. Then dance to a salsa reggae band with an eclectic crowd. ♦ Cuban ♦ Daily 6AM-11:30PM. 13515 Washington Blvd. 306.7978

20 Marina Marketplace Serious shopping comes to the land of throwaways with branches of **Gelson's** supermarket, **Polo/Ralph Lauren**, **Kent & Curwen**, **State of the Art** (furniture and lighting), and **Ecru** (American and European women's clothes). ♦ 13455 Maxella Ave. 822.2000

Within Marina Marketplace:

Angeli Mare ★★★$$$ (1989, **Michele Saee**/Building) Ribbed, wavelike space that is sharp-edged and sensual, woodsy and watery. Pizza and roast chicken are carried over from the other Angeli restaurants, but it's the seafood that wins this place its extra star. Tuna carpaccio, fish soup, and pastas, plus the daily specials are outstanding. ♦ Seafood ♦ M-F 11:30AM-11:30PM; Sa-Su 11AM-11:30PM. 822.1984

21 Aunt Kizzy's Back Porch ★★$ Catfish and fried chicken, short ribs and smothered pork chops, just like down-home in the old South. ♦ Southern ♦ M-Th, Su 11AM-10PM; F-Sa 11AM-midnight. 4325 Glencoe Ave. 578.1005

Beach Cities of El Segundo, Manhattan, Hermosa, and Redondo
A jumble of pastel cottages squeezed along a stretch of beachfront marks a series of former summer resorts, now prospering as permanent communities. El Segundo has the least developed waterfront, being hemmed in by the airport and

LAX/South Bay/Long Beach

a huge oil refinery. Manhattan Beach is part family neighborhood, part singles capital of the beach party circuit. Next is Hermosa Beach, the prototype beach town with its concentration of T-shirted surfers, T-shirted families, and T-shirted elderly retirees. At the south end is Redondo Beach, a mixture of affluent new and slightly seedy old, with an interesting and well-kept pier and marina complex.

22 Radisson Plaza Hotel $$$ Luxury hotel with its own golf course, complimentary airport shuttle, shuttle service to the beach, and concierge. Continental breakfast, full health club, and pool. ♦ 1400 Parkview Ave, Manhattan Beach. 546.7511, 800/228.9822; fax 546.7520

Within the Radisson Plaza Hotel:

Califia ★★$$$ Inventive cuisine with a French twist in a pretty gray-and-pink dining room. ♦ California ♦ M-F 11:30AM-2PM; Tu-Sa 6-10PM. 546.1668

22 Sausalito South $$$ A San Francisco look, with Tiffany lamps and hanging plants, a young crowd, pretty good fresh seafood, and a friendly oyster bar. ♦ Seafood ♦ M 11AM-10PM; Tu-Sa 11AM-11PM; Su 10AM-10PM. 3280 Sepulveda Blvd, Manhattan Beach. 546.4507

22 Saint Estephe ★★★$$$$ New Mexico goes to art school: chef **Steve Garcia** continues the tradition established by **John Sedlar**. Poached salmon with 3 chili-based sauces appears suspended in a delicate cloudscape; pastas and desserts are patterned after Native American petrographs. This may sound too precious to be good, but the proof is in the tasting; this is much more than decorative frou-frou. Visiting Japanese, with their own refined *kaiseki* tradition, adore it; but so will anyone looking for something distinctively different. Don't be fazed by the fact that this exclusive restaurant stands next to a Ralph's in the Manhattan Village shopping center; the interior is cool, all-white, and tasteful. ♦ Southwestern ♦ Tu-F 11AM-2PM, 6-10PM; Sa 6-10PM. 2640 Sepulveda Blvd, Manhattan Beach. 545.1334

23 Barnaby's $$$ A Victorian fantasy hotel—Charles Dickens by Disney—but somehow the leaded glass, deep carpets, marble statuary, and thousands of dollars worth of antiques come together in a charming, elegant whole. Rooms have old books and fourposter beds, plus well-disguised modern conveniences. There's a pool, and a garden that's so pretty you may have to share it with a string of wedding receptions. High-quality service. Call for special weekend rates. Intimate Victorian restaurant (**Barnaby's**) serves traditional cuisine daily. **Rosie's Pub** is popular with locals and guests; it offers nightly entertainment and dancing on weekends. ♦ 3501 Sepulveda Blvd, Manhattan Beach. 545.8466, 800/562.5285; fax 545.8621

24 Sloopy's Beach Cafe $ A favorite for lunch. Sandwiches, burgers, and salads are served before the hearth in winter, or at sidewalk tables when the weather cooperates. ♦ American ♦ Tu-Su 11AM-4PM. 3416 Highland Ave, Manhattan Beach. 545.1373

25 Café Pierre $$ Rustic and comfortable. ♦ French ♦ M-F 11:30AM-2:30PM, 5:30-10PM; Sa 5:30-11PM; Su 5:30-10:30PM. 317 Manhattan Beach Blvd, Manhattan Beach. 545.5252

26 Manhattan Beach State Pier A 900-foot municipal facility, without tackle or snack shops. ♦ 24 hours

27 Hermosa Beach Fishing Pier A 1320-foot municipal pier. Shop rents equipment and sells bait. Snack bar available. ♦ Pier: 24 hours. Bait shop: daily 7AM-midnight. 372.2124. End of Pier Ave, Hermosa Beach

The only culture in LA can be found in the yogurt.
Johnny Carson

27 The Lighthouse In the block next to the pier is one of the best and oldest jazz clubs in Los Angeles. Fine music and top-flight performers rather than fancy decor have kept its doors open since the '50s. ♦ Cover. M-F 4PM-1:30AM; Sa-Su 10AM-1:30AM. 30 Pier Ave, Hermosa Beach. 372.6911, 376.9833

28 The Either/Or Bookstore Writer **Thomas Pynchon** used to come in here to pick up the latest in fiction when he lived nearby. ♦ Daily 10AM-11PM. 124 Pier Ave, Hermosa Beach. 374.2060

28 Ajeti $ Owner **Din Ajeti** gives you a warm welcome and heaping platters of roast lamb and other native specialties. ♦ Albanian ♦ Tu-Sa 5-10PM; Su 4-8:30PM. 425 Pier Ave, Hermosa Beach. 379.9012

28 Comedy & Magic Club Good food, Art Deco decor, and eclectic humor in this friendly club. ♦ Cover. Call for showtimes. 1018 Hermosa Ave, Hermosa Beach. Reservations required. 372.1193

28 Pedone's $ A very good thin-crusted pizza. ♦ Pizza ♦ Daily 11AM-10PM. 1501 Hermosa Ave, Hermosa Beach. 376.0949

29 Habash Cafe ★$ Homemade Arab specialties by the owner include barbecued lamb, hummus, baba ghanouj, and tabouleh. ♦ Middle Eastern ♦ M-Sa 10AM-9:30PM. 233 Pacific Coast Hwy, Hermosa Beach. 376.6620

30 Monstad Pier Two hundred-foot privately-owned pier. Tackle shop rents and sells equipment and bait. ♦ Pier: admission. 24 hours. Tackle Shop (Tony's Fish Market): daily 5:30AM-9PM. 376.6223. Restaurant (Redondo Coffee Shop Bait and Tackle): 318.1044. Coral Wy, Redondo Beach

30 Fisherman's Wharf Many unusual shops line the narrow path leading to the end of the pier, as well as places to buy and eat fresh fish and the ubiquitous souvenir shops. A popular place on summer nights when many restaurants are open late. ♦ Redondo Beach

30 Portofino Inn $$$ Every room has a view overlooking picturesque King's Harbor in this middling-size oceanfront hotel. Complimentary shuttle to and from airport. Health club. Hospitality bar in every room. All rooms have a balcony and view. ♦ 260 Portofino Wy, Redondo Beach. 379.8481, 800/468.4292 (CA), 800/338.2993 (US); fax 372.7329

30 Redondo Sport Fishing Choose from a short 45-minute harbor cruise, local offshore fishing, or deep-sea cruises to Catalina and Santa Barbara islands. An exciting seasonal whale watch allows you to observe the migration of the California gray whale from breathtakingly close range. ♦ 233 N. Harbor Dr. 24-hour reservations 372.3566, 772.2064

30 Redondo Sportfishing Pier Two-hundred-fifty-foot privately owned pier. Tackle shop rents and sells equipment and bait. Snack bar available. ♦ Pier: 24 hours. Tackle shop: daily 4:30AM-9PM. End of Harbor Dr and Portofino Wy, Redondo Beach. 372.2111

31 Abbruzzese Elegant French lingerie for women who indulge themselves and for men looking for a sophisticated present. Semi-annual sales bring the stiff prices down a tad. ♦ M-Sa 10AM-6PM. 1706 S. Catalina Ave, Redondo Beach. 540.9406

31 Palos Verdes Inn $$$ Medium-size hotel 2 blocks from the beach. ♦ 1700 S. Pacific Coast Hwy, Redondo Beach. 316.4211, 800/352.0385 (CA), 800/421.9241 (US); fax 316.4863

31 Chez Mélange ★★$$ There's a sushi bar, a wine counter, and a dining room serving contemporary international cuisine in chef **Robert Bell**'s exciting restaurant. Warm lamb salad with mixed greens, seafood specials, and fresh fruit tarts are among the standouts. The wine-tasting dinners are celebrated citywide. Located in the **Plush Horse Inn**. ♦ Eclectic ♦ M-Th 7-11AM, 11:30AM-4PM, 5-11PM; F-Sa 7-11AM, 11:30AM-4PM, 5-11:30PM; Su 8AM-2:30PM, 5-10:30PM. 1716 S. Pacific Coast Hwy, Redondo Beach. 540.1222

Palos Verdes Peninsula
In 1913, New York banker Frank Vanderlip bought most of this hilly peninsula and planned to turn it into a millionaires' colony. Slightly less ambitious developments began in the 1920s, creating a series of exclusive, often gated residential enclaves and modest commercial centers—in very conservative taste. Ranch houses alternate with Spanish haciendas, horse trails, and countless lovely hiking paths leading through the forests of eucalyptus. The hills are a succession of 13 marine uplift terraces created by Palos Verdes' slow rise from the ocean floor.

32 Malaga Cove Plaza (1924, **Webber, Staunton & Spaulding**) In their 1922 plan for Palos Verdes, **Charles H. Cheney** and the **Olmsted brothers** envisioned 4 area community centers. This was the only one built. It is a Spanish revival design of 2-story shops in an arcade. The plaza has a picturesque brick bridge over Via Chico and a fountain inspired by the *Fountain of Neptune* in Bologna, Italy. ♦ 200 Palos Verdes Dr (Via Corta) Palos Verdes

LAX/South Bay/Long Beach

32 La Rive Gauche ★$$$ Well-prepared food in a rustic and chic room. The roasted quail with raspberries is a standout. ♦ French ♦ Tu-Sa 11:30AM-3PM, 5:30-10PM; Su 10AM-3PM, 5:30-10PM. 320 Via Tejon, Palos Verdes. 378.0267

Six thousand in-the-water privately owned yachts are docked and another 3000 boats are in dry storage at **Marina del Rey** the world's largest small-craft harbor, also known as LA's Riviera.

Restaurants/Clubs: Red   Hotels: Blue
Shops/Parks: Green   **Sights/Culture:** Black

33 Wayfarer's Chapel (1946, **Lloyd Wright**) Occupying a prominent hillside location overlooking the ocean, this chapel is the national monument to **Emmanuel Swedenborg**, Swedish theologian and mystic. The glass structure, supported by a redwood frame, is transparent and blends with the surrounding redwood grove. ♦ Daily 9AM-5PM. Services Su 11AM. 5755 Palos Verdes Dr. S, Rancho Palos Verdes. 377.1650

34 Borelli's $$ Lovely Mediterranean decor. The service is particularly solicitous. ♦ Italian ♦ M-F 11:30AM-2:30PM, 5-10PM; Sa-Su 11:30AM-2:30PM, 5-11PM. 672 Silver Spur Rd, Rolling Hills Estates. 541.2632

35 South Coast Botanic Gardens A model experiment in land reclamation. Until 1956 the site was a diatomaceous earth mine. When mining activity ceased, the trash dumping began—3,500,000 tons were poured in. Starting in 1960, the **Los Angeles Department of Arboreta and Botanic Gardens** initiated a planting program. Beautifully landscaped, the 87-acre gardens now contain mature specimens from all continents except Antarctica. Plants are grouped according to botanical family. The gardens also offer horticultural and botanical displays, a gift shop, gardening demonstrations every Sunday at 2PM, and a picnic area. ♦ Admission. Daily 9AM-5PM.

LAX/South Bay/Long Beach

26300 S. Crenshaw Blvd, Rolling Hills Estates. 377.0468

36 Fino ★★$$ Rustic bistro serving hearty aromatic Mediterranean cuisine. From the imported olives and cured meats to the rabbit braised in a wine sauce with pine nuts to the marscapone cheesecake, this is a place to set you dreaming of scenic, faraway places. ♦ Mediterranean ♦ M-Sa 5-10:30PM. 24530 Hawthorne Blvd, Torrance. 373.1952

37 Big Wok ★$ The Golden Horde never had it so good. They had to eat as they galloped over the steppes; you can serve yourself from a buffet in an opulent room and add sauces to taste at your table. ♦ Mongolian ♦ Tu-F 11:30AM-

9:30PM; Sa-Su 4-9:30PM. 24012 Vista Montana (Anza Ave-Pacific Coast Hwy), Torrance. 375.1513

38 Symphonie ★★★$$ **Susumu Fukui**, chef of the late, great **La Petite Chaya** in Silverlake has moved to this new post. His *cuisine inventive* is an unfailing delight. ♦ French/Japanese ♦ M-F 11:30AM-2PM, 5:30-10PM; Sa 5:30-10PM; Su 5-9PM. 23863 Hawthorne Blvd, Torrance. 373.8187

39 Del Amo Fashion Center Over 350 stores in 2.4-million-square-feet of space—the largest center of its kind. Department stores include **The Broadway, Sears, J.C. Penney, Robinson's, Bullock's, I. Magnin** and **Wards**. Also independent fashion stores, 30 restaurants, and dramatic interior spaces. ♦ M-F 10AM-9PM; Sa 10AM-7PM; Su 11AM-6PM. Bounded by Hawthorne, Sepulveda, Torrance Blvds, Madrona Ave, Torrance. 542.8525

40 Lomita Railroad Museum Housed in a replica of the 19th-century Greenwood Station in Wakefield MA, the museum displays memorabilia from the steam era of railroading. The station is flanked by an impeccably restored 1902 steam locomotive and a 1910 wooden caboose, both of which may be boarded. The annex across the street has picnic benches, a fountain, and a 1913 boxcar. Gift shop. ♦ Admission. W-Su 10AM-5PM. 250th St at Woodward Ave, Lomita. 326.6255

41 Alpine Village Inn $$ You can quaff a stein and down huge portions of German-Swiss food while listening to the band in the beer garden. Children may pet domestic animals in the farm or take a ride in the amusement park. Twenty-four shops offer an array of goods in a replica of an Alpine Village. ♦ Farm: daily 11AM-7PM. Restaurant: daily 11AM-9PM, dancing until midnight. 833 Torrance Blvd (W of Harbor Fwy), Torrance. 327.4384

42 Paradise ★$$ **Scott Johnson** designed the contemporary Polynesian interior for this welcome oasis at the junction of the Harbor and San Diego freeways. The menu features a potpourri of exotic drinks and contemporary favorites like goat-cheese salad, Santa Fe pizza, and tuna niçoise. ♦ Eclectic ♦ M-Th 11AM-2:30PM, 5-10PM; F 11AM-2:30PM, 4:30-11PM; Sa 4:30-11PM; Su 5-10PM. 889 W 190th St, Gardena. 324.4800

Los Angeles Harbor

In 1876, the first railroad arrived in Los Angeles, but the city still lacked access to the sea. Despite its shallow, unprotected harbor, San Pedro outmaneuvered Santa Monica for federal funding and became the main port-of-entry for the emerging metropolis. Work began in 1899 on a new breakwater and a major port expansion. In 1909, LA annexed San Pedro and Wilmington, creating the famous shoestring strip, a stretch of city land, at places only a half-mile wide, from downtown to the harbor, which provided for a seaport and transportation route entirely within city limits. Today's harbor is the largest canning and fishing port in the nation, a hub of industry (notably oil refineries and aircraft plants), and the foremost port-of-call in Southern California for passenger vessels.

At the center of the harbor is Terminal Island, linked to San Pedro by the Vincent Thomas Bridge and to Long Beach by the Gerald Desmond Bridge. The streets of downtown San Pedro (pronounced by natives as *San Peedro*) retain much of the flavor of their colorful past as a seaman's port town. The region's commercial fishing fleet is a major part of the area economy, employing many mariners of Portuguese, Greek, and Yugoslav descent. Strong ethnic traditions make shopping in the multitude of small food stores a delightful experience.

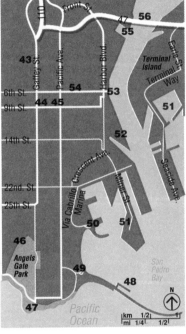

43 San Pedro Grand Hotel $$$ A misnamed hostelry; this is a small European-style hotel with Victorian decor, though the prices are quite grand. ♦ 111 S. Gaffey St, San Pedro. 514.1414, 800/248.3188; fax 831.8262

44 Babouch Moroccan Restaurant ★$$ Authentic food (couscous, lamb, and chicken *tajine*) served in an Arabian Nights setting. ♦ Moroccan ♦ Tu-Su 5-10PM. 810 S. Gaffey St, San Pedro. 831.0246

45 The Grand House ★$$ A gift store specializing in artist-designed jewelry that doubles as an adventurous restaurant. Dishes have included sweetbread pâté with prunes and pistachio nuts, salmon chowder, and beef tongue with lentils. ♦ Eclectic ♦ Store: 9AM-5PM and during restaurant hours. Restaurant: Tu-F 11:30AM-2PM, 6-9PM; Sa 6-9:30PM; Su 11AM-2PM, 6-10PM. 809 S. Grand Ave, San Pedro. 548.1240

| Restaurants/Clubs: Red | Hotels: Blue |
| Shops/Parks: Green | Sights/Culture: Black |

46 Fort McArthur Military Reservation and Angel's Gate Park Currently headquarters for the Army's **47th Artillery Brigade**, the fort has been under government jurisdiction since 1888. The lower reservation was used during World War II as a training center and was one of the primary West Coast defense fortifications. The 20-acre park offers a spectacular view of the Pacific and Point Fermin. ♦ Free. Park daily 5:30AM-10:30PM. Ft McArthur, San Pedro. 832.9611

47 Point Fermin Park Thirty-seven landscaped acres on the palisades overlooking the Pacific and Los Angeles Harbor. The lookout point has coin-operated telescopes; the whale-watching station offers information on the California gray whale regarding its annual winter migration to the Gulf of California. The Victorian Eastlake-style lighthouse, constructed in 1874 from bricks and lumber brought around Cape Horn by sailing ship, is not open to the public. The lighthouse originally used oil lamps approximating 2100 candlepower until 1925, when electric power was installed. This park is a popular place to watch hang gliders. ♦ Gaffey St at Paseo del Mar, San Pedro. 548.7756

48 Cabrillo Beach Fishing Pier A 1500-foot publicly owned fishing pier. Shop sells equipment and live bait; no rentals. No license or fee required. ♦ Daily during daylight hours. End of Stephen White Dr, San Pedro. Life guard 832.1179

49 Cabrillo Beach Marine Museum (1981, **Frank Gehry**) Children will love the imaginative displays of marine life and the behind-the-scenes glimpses of how they are maintained. To emphasize the spirit of fun, Gehry has designed a villagelike cluster of small buildings housing acquaria, classrooms, offices, and a theater,

LAX/South Bay/Long Beach

dramatically enclosed with chain-link fencing, which suggests a playground to the kids, who are the prime audience. Museum volunteers are always on hand for tours and workshops. The museum's former quarters, in the renovated 1928 **Cabrillo Beach Boathouse**, house more exhibitions, including dioramas, fossils, and over 15,000 seashells. For information on whale-watching tours, late December-early April, call 832.4444. ♦ Free. Tu-Su 10AM-5PM. 3720 Stephen White Dr, San Pedro. 548.7562

49 The Point Fermin Marine Life Refuge A tidepool community next to the museum. Brochures for a self-guided exploration of tidepool biology are available at the museum.

50 Madeo Ristorante ★★$$$ Larger, more glamorous version of the Westside original, serving great pastas, veal, and Florentine steak. ◆ Italian ◆ M-Th, Su 11:30AM-2:30PM, 5:30-10:30PM; F-Sa 11:30AM-2:30PM, 5:30-11:30PM. 295 Whaler's Walk (take 22nd St to Via Cabrillo Marina) San Pedro. 831.1199

51 Fisherman's Dock and Fish Harbor Centers for the commercial fishing industry—on the western side of the main channel and on the southern side of Terminal Island, respectively.

52 Ports O'Call Village and Whaler's Wharf At the harbor's edge is a replica of other times and other places. Nineteenth-century New England, a Mediterranean fishing village, and early California live again in this shopping and eating complex. The **Village Boat House**, located in Ports O'Call Village, offers daily cruises of the harbor area where visitors can see the inner harbor, yacht harbor, freighter operations, scrapping yards, and the Coast Guard base. Tour hours vary with the season; for information call 831.0287. ◆ Ports O'Call. Berth 77, San Pedro

53 Maritime Museum A nautical history collection located in an old ferry building, refurbished by **Pulliam & Matthews**. Much of the old ferry gear remains, giving visitors a sense of imminent departure. There is a fine view of harbor operations from the promenade deck. Next to the museum, the bow section of the US Navy cruiser *Los Angeles* offers a chance to explore. Museum collections include a number of ship models, including a 16-foot scale model of the *Titanic*, built from cardboard and match sticks by a 14-year-old boy. The **Naval Deck** is replete with Navy memorabilia, including the bridge deck of the *Los Angeles*. A timeline history of the harbor beginning in 1840 gives a graphic summary of the dredging and construction. ◆ Free. Tu-F 10AM-5PM; Sa-Su 10AM-5PM. Berth 84, San Pedro. 548.7618

54 Papadakis Tavern ★$$ A lively restaurant where, if the mood is right, the waiters dance and the customers break plates. Very popular. ◆ Greek ◆ M-Th, Sa-Su 5-10PM; F noon-2PM. 301 W 6th St, San Pedro. 548.1186

LAX/South Bay/Long Beach

55 Terminals On the western side of the main channel are the container terminals, piled high with steel freight containers, and the passenger liner terminals. The terminal for the *Catalina Steamer* and the Catalina helicopter is located just north of this point.

56 Vincent Thomas Bridge Spanning the main channel between San Pedro and Terminal Island. Clearing the water by 185 feet so that military planes can fly under it, the 6500-foot-long turquoise suspension bridge is the most visible landmark in the harbor. Freighters are berthed on the northern side of Terminal Island. Drydocks are located across the back channel in the Long Beach side of the harbor and in the Naval Shipyard on the southeastern end of Terminal Island.

57 Gen. Phineas Banning Residence Museum In 1864 Phineas Banning, father of the Los Angeles harbor, built this Greek Revival clapboard home of lumber from the Mendocino coast, Belgian marble, and European colored glass. The house is now decorated with period furnishings. Tours through the building include the restored kitchen, where food is cooked using **Katherine Banning**'s recipes, as well as family and public rooms of the mansion. The museum is located in 20-acre **Banning Park**, which offers picnic facilities and playground equipment. Access to the house by tour only. ◆ Donation requested. Tours Tu-Th, Sa-Su 12:30, 1:30, 2:30, 3:30PM. 401 E. M St, Wilmington. 548.7777

57 Drum Barracks The last remaining building of **Camp Drum**, a 7000-soldier Union Army outpost. Although California sympathized with the Confederacy during the Civil War, this large Union military presence kept the state in the blue ranks. The barracks have been refurbished as a museum of Civil War memorabilia. ◆ Admission. Tu-F 9AM-1PM. Tours Sa-Su 12:30, 1:30, 2:30PM. 1053 Cary Ave, Wilmington. 548.7509

Long Beach

East of the harbor is the City of Long Beach, which was founded in 1880 and flourished with the oil boom of the 1920s and the improvements to the port. A few wells survive in Signal Hill to the northeast; for a short time this was the world's most productive field. From the sandy strand south of Long Beach, you can see the tropical camouflage created to conceal the almost 600 still-producing offshore oil wells; each palm-clad fake island covers 10 acres of sound-proofed oil wells. The Long Beach harbor is new, constructed since 1940. It is a major port for automobile imports and

Alaskan crude oil, and a major West Coast port-of-entry. Long Beach was devastated by the 1933 earthquake; many of the pleasing Art Deco buildings erected in its wake have since been destroyed by massive urban redevelopment. The city center is currently raw and unappealing, but elsewhere historic landmarks and districts can still be found. The *Blue Line* light rail (similar to San Diego's *Tijuana trolley*) runs along the route once used by the *Red Car*, from Long Beach Boulevard and Willow, 21 miles north to downtown LA. ♦ Daily 5:30AM-8PM

58 Naval Shipyard You may tour a Navy ship by advance reservation, Saturday at 9AM and 1PM. Call weekdays 8 days in advance and a free pass will be mailed. ♦ 547.7219

59 Port of Long Beach Cargo handling can be watched from the observation deck atop the **Port Administration Building**. If you want to see the harbor in style (with up to 300 of your closest friends), you can charter the *Wild Goose*, the late **John Wayne**'s private yacht, 828.3813 ♦ M-F 8AM-5PM. 925 Harbor Plaza, port end of Queens Bay Bridge. 590.4123

60 Viscount Hotel $$$ Formerly the **Queensway Bay Hilton**, now extensively renovated. Waterfront site, a short walk from the *Queen Mary*. ♦ 700 Queensway Dr. 435.7676, 800/255.3050; fax 437.0866

Drawing by Rik Osen

61 Queen Mary This majestic 50,000-ton passenger liner, the largest ever built, is now permanently berthed in Long Beach Harbor. Launched in 1934, the vessel epitomized Art Deco luxury when she and her crew of 1200 cruised the North Atlantic. In 1964, she was retired from service, purchased by the City of Long Beach, and converted into a tourist attraction and luxury hotel. Her upper decks have been refurbished and one of her 4 propellers and the main turbine put on display. Special exhibitions include a sound and light show in the engine room and wheelhouse, model ships, and lifeboat demonstrations. Restaurants include **Sir Winston's** (American cuisine), the **Chelsea** (seafood and lunch buffet), and the **Promenade Cafe** (light meals). Sunday brunch is served in the **Grand Salon**, formerly the first-class dining room. ♦ Pier J at the end of the Long Beach Fwy. 435.3511

Aboard the Queen Mary:

Queen Mary Hotel $$$ First-class state-rooms have been refurbished to create this hotel, with its pool and health club, concierge service and free shuttle to LAX and Long Beach airports. A wonderful way to recapture the luxury of travel in the '30s. ♦ 435.3511, 800/642.5391 (CA), 800/421.3732 (US); fax 437.4531

Drawing by Rik Osen

61 The Spruce Goose The world's largest clear-span aluminum dome houses the largest wooden airplane ever built, with its 320-foot wingspan, 219-foot length, and 80-foot-high tail. Conceived by **Howard Hughes** in 1942 as the prototype for a fleet of troop transports, its construction was delayed and it flew only once, on 2 November 1947. A raised platform allows visitors a close-up view of the cockpit, cargo areas, and flight deck. Audiovisual displays dramatize Hughes' career as an aviation pioneer; *Time Voyager* is a special-effects adventure through time and space. The Spruce Goose and the *Queen Mary* are under the same management; one ticket admits to both. ♦ Daily 10AM-6PM. Pier J, next to the *Queen Mary*. 435.3511

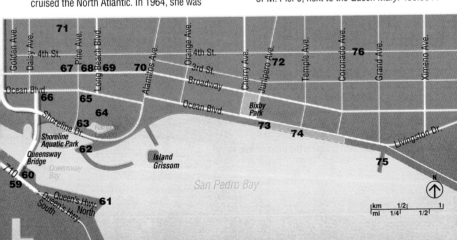

62 Shoreline Village Another cutely historical waterfront shopping center with quaint stores and popular restaurants. One genuine item amid the fakery is the 1906 **Charles Loof** carousel. ♦ Daily 10AM-10PM. 407 Shoreline Dr. 590.8427

63 Hyatt Regency $$$ Luxurious atrium hotel adjacent to the Convention Center. Outdoor pool and Jacuzzi, 2 restaurants, and 2 Regency Club floors. ♦ 200 S. Pine Ave. 491.1234, 800/228.9000; fax 435.0027

64 Long Beach Convention and Entertainment Center From rodeos to rock concerts, symphony to ballet. The center is home to the acclaimed **Long Beach Ballet, Civic Light Opera,** and **Symphony Orchestra and Opera.** The latter is one of America's most adventurous companies, noted for its innovative staging of rare and classic works, and the quality of its guest artists. ♦ Terrace Theater seats 3141. Center Theater seats 862. 1300 E. Ocean Blvd. Ticket information: 436.3661. 24-hour recorded event information: 436.3660. Ballet: 427.5206. Civic Light Opera: 432.7926. Opera: 596.5556. Symphony: 436.3203

65 Visitor Center Information for tourists and conventions. Next door is the transit information office ♦ M-F 8:30AM-4:30PM; Sa-Su 9AM-5PM. 180 E. Ocean Blvd. Suite 150. 436.3645, 436.9982

66 Giorgio's Place ★★$$ High-ceilinged pink dining room in the **Arco Center,** serving innovative food of rare quality. Salmon in a celery puree, chicken breast with a puree of asparagus, excellent risotto, and *tagliolini al pesto* have been acclaimed. ♦ Italian ♦ M-F 11:30AM-2:30PM, 5:30-10PM; Sa 5:30-10PM. 300 Oceangate. 432.6175

67 Amis Stephen White, owner of **Magdalena's** in Bellflower, plans a rustic bistro offering such hearty dishes as cassoulet. ♦ French ♦ M-Th 11AM-3PM; F 11AM-3PM, 5-10:30 PM; Sa 5-10:30PM. 217 Pine Ave. 495.8935

68 Long Beach Mural A '30s Federal Arts Project mosaic by **Henry Nord** taken from the now-demolished **Municipal Auditorium** and installed on a parking structure. ♦ Long Beach Plaza at W 3rd St

69 Acres of Books Ray Bradbury acclaims this vast used-book emporium as a treasure; ex-

plore its riches before the local planning board closes it down in the name of progress. ♦ Tu-Sa 9:15AM-5PM. 240 Long Beach Blvd. 437.6980

70 Acapulco y Los Arcos $ A chain operation that consistently serves innovative and delicious food. ♦ Mexican ♦ M-Th, Su 11AM-10PM; F-Sa 11AM-11PM. 733 E. Broadway. 435.2487

71 Collage ★$$ Confusing mix of traditional and trendy; best bets include the homemade lamb sausage, the Santa Fe bean cakes with sour cream and salsa, the fine ice creams, and the crème brûlée. ♦ Eclectic ♦ M 11:30AM-2:30PM; Tu-F 11:30AM-2:30PM, 5:30-10PM; Sa-Su 5:30-11PM. 762 Pacific Ave. 437.3324

72 Carroll Park Historic district of large houses built in 1910s, and '20s bungalows. ♦ 3rd-4th Sts (Junipero-Wisconsin Aves)

73 Long Beach Museum of Art Located in a 1912 Craftsman-style home, the museum sponsors changing exhibitions that emphasize contemporary Southern California art. The archives of artists' videotapes are the largest on the West Coast. The permanent collection includes work by the *Laguna Canyon School* of the '20s and '30s and regional WPA-sponsored pieces. The carriage house has a bookstore and exhibition gallery. Sculpture by prominent contemporary artists is displayed around the beautifully landscaped site. ♦ Free. W-Su noon-5PM. 2300 E. Ocean Blvd. 439.2119

74 Bluff Park Historic district containing diversified houses fronting Ocean Blvd. On fine days, model plane enthusiasts meet in the park. ♦ Temple Ave (Ocean Blvd)

75 Belmont Pier Thirteen hundred-foot municipal pier. The bait shop also rents equipment. Snack bar. ♦ Bait shop: daily 6AM-8PM. 434.6781. Snack Bar: Tu-Th 11AM-6PM; F-Su 8AM-8PM. End of 39th Pl

76 Fourth Street At the less expensive end of the shopping spectrum, Fourth Street has a number of little shops ranging from chic to modest that carry antiques, Art Deco accessories, crafts, and clothes. ♦ Redondo Ave-Lucille Ave

77 Drake Park Third of Long Beach's historic districts comprising almost every architectural style known to man. ♦ Daisy Ave at Loma Vista (7th-11th Sts)

78 Long Beach Firefighters Museum Five motorized engines, 2 horse-drawn steamers, handcarts, and memorabilia dating back a hundred years. ♦ Free. 2nd Sa of every month 10AM-3PM. 1445 Peterson Ave. 597.0351

79 The Foothill Club Honky-tonk dance hall offering live hillbilly, fried chicken, and pizza. ♦ Daily 5PM-2AM. 1922 Cherry Ave, Signal Hill. 494.5196

80 Battambang ★$$ A smattering of Khmer will help you order the authentic dishes; the standard menu is much less interesting. Try ordering the "A" or "C" dinners—and such dishes as lobster soup with banana blossoms, and minced pork in coconut milk (*praw hok ktee*). ♦ Cambodian ♦ Daily 7AM-9PM. 2501 E. Anaheim St. 439.9301

81 Shenandoah Café $$ Southern cooking in an atmospheric setting. ♦ Southern ♦ M-Th, Su 4:30-10PM; F-Sa 4:30-11PM. 4722 E 2nd St. 434.3469

81 Legends Popular sports bar with 4 projection screens and 2 news tickers in a wood-and-brick room filled with memorabilia. ♦ M-Th 11AM-midnight; F-Su 11AM-2AM. 5236 E 2nd St. 433.5743

81 Cafe Gazelle ★$$ Pretty, friendly restaurant famous for its hefty portions at reasonable prices. The soups, salads, desserts, and cappuccinos shine; do try the creamy pine-nut soup. ♦ Italian ♦ M-F 11AM-11PM; Sa-Su 10AM-11PM. 5325 E 2nd St. 438.2881

Naples

At the same time Kinney was creating his version of Venice, another American romantic, Arthur Parson, was dredging Alamitos Bay to create his picture-perfect pastiche of Italy. He built cottages on curving streets and along canals that were spanned by quaint footbridges. By the end of the '20s, the community was complete. Today, Naples seems more midwestern than Italian, with well-maintained shingled homes and carefully tended gardens. The perimeter of the island is bordered by walkways that overlook the bay and a small beach. In the center, Colonnade Park is encircled by the Rivo Alto Canal. Although the island is accessible by car, its true charm is seen only by the pedestrian. This is a wonderful place for an afternoon of strolling, picnicking, and boat-watching. ♦ 2nd St (Marina Dr)

82 Gondola Getaway One-hour cruises by gondola through the canals of Naples, with costumed opera-singing gondoliers. A basket of bread, salami, and cheese is provided. BYOB. Reserve 2 weeks in advance. ♦ 5437 E. Ocean Blvd. 433.9595

83 Endo's Waterski Werks Waterskis for rent and sale, lessons for those with their own boats. ♦ Tu-W noon-6PM; Th-F 10AM-6PM; Sa 10AM-4PM. 5612 E 2nd St. 434.1816

83 Justina's ★$$ *A Celebration of Food* proclaims the awning, and this pretty little restaurant lives up to its motto with well-prepared shrimp in sherry sauce, chicken breast with ratatouille, and beef stew. ♦ French ♦ Tu-Th 8AM-9PM; F-Sa 8AM-10PM; Su 8AM-3PM. 5620 E 2nd St. 434.5191

83 Morry's of Naples Long-established wine and liquor store. ♦ M-Th, Su 7AM-10PM; F-Sa 7AM-midnight. Wine tastings W-F 6-9PM. 5764 E 2nd St. 433.0405

84 Bogart's $$ If you liked *Casablanca*, try Bogart's. Wicker, ceiling fans, potted palms, plus dancing and live entertainment. ♦ American ♦ Daily 8PM-2AM. 6288 E. Pacific Coast Hwy (No of Westminster in Marina Pacifica Mall) 594.8976

85 Rancho Los Alamitos Another part of the original 1784 Nieto land grant. The adobe house has been enlarged 4 times since it was built in 1806. The interior is very much as it was when the **Bixby** family occupied it during the 1930s and '40s. The grounds contain a dairy and horse barns, a blacksmith's shop, and a 5-acre native California garden planted with cacti and succulents, kitchen vegetables and herbs, and exquisite Chinese and Japanese wisteria. Visitors must be accompanied by docents. ♦ Free. W-Su 1-5PM. 6400 Bixby Hill Rd. 431.3541

86 El Dorado Park An 800-acre recreational facility. **El Dorado East Regional Park** is an unstructured activity area containing meadows and several lakes where fishing is permitted. The largest lake rents paddleboats. There are over 4 miles of bicycle and rollerskate paths and an archery range. **El Dorado West City Park** offers an 18-hole golf course, night-lit tennis courts, a tennis shop, rollerskate rental, 6 baseball diamonds, a duck pond, a children's playground, a bandshell, a branch of the Long Beach Public Library, and a number of game courts. The **El Dorado Nature Center**, located in the east section, is an 80-acre bird sanctuary and native chaparral community. The small museum in the center of one of the 2 lakes exhibits material about the natural history of Southern California. Maps available at museum. Vehicle admission fee. ♦ East Park: daily 7AM-6PM. West Park: daily 7AM-7PM. 429.6310. Nature Center: Tu-Su 10AM-4PM. 421.9431. 7550 E. Spring St

87 Outdoor Antique and Collectible Market Over 700 dealers offer every kind of collectible, from the serious to the silly. ♦ Admission. 3rd Su of every month, 1st Su of Nov 8AM-3PM. Long Beach Veterans Memorial Stadium, Lakewood Blvd at Conant St, Long Beach. 655.5703

88 Long Beach Airport Served by 6 airlines. Fourteen coaches a day to LAX. Several public and private bus companies provide transportation between Long Beach Airport and Long Beach, Los Angeles and Orange Counties, including **Long Beach Transit System** (714/636.RIDE), and **Airport Service, Inc.** (596.1662). ♦ Lakewood Blvd exit north from San Diego Fwy. 421.8293

89 Bixby House (1895, **Ernest Coxhead**) One of the few remaining examples of English architect Coxhead's residential work, this is a shingle-style house built for a member of the Bixby family. The wood-shingle Victorian house has Craftsman design elements. Private residence. ♦ 11 La Linda Dr, Bixby Knolls

90 Rancho Los Cerritos The romance of the old rancho days is recalled at this restored 1844 Monterey-style adobe. The 2-story residence was built by **Don Juan Temple** on part of the 1784 Nieto land grant. Subsequently enlarged, the house is furnished as it was between 1866 and 1881, when the **Bixby** family used it as headquarters for their ranching empire. Exhibitions include the children's room, complete with dolls and toys; the weaving room; and the foreman's bedroom. The exhibi-

tion wing features material relating to social and economic aspects of rancho life and a research library of California materials. Some of the original walks and trees planted in the mid-19th century remain in the restored 5-acre garden. ♦ Free. W-Su 1-5PM. 4600 Virginia Rd, Long Beach. 424.9423

91 Johnny Reb's Southern Smokehouse $ Peanut shells on the floor, seafood gumbo, barbecued ribs, and pecan pie. ♦ Southern ♦ M-Th, Su 7AM-9PM; F-Sa 7AM-10PM. 4663 Long Beach Blvd. 423.7327

Restaurants/Clubs: Red   Hotels: Blue
Shops/Parks: Green   **Sights/Culture: Black**

Catalina

An island paradise 26 miles offshore that lives up to its reputation as a romantic getaway. Arriving by boat you see first the misty green peaks of a mountain range that rises from the ocean floor to form this and the other Channel Islands. Next, gleaming white buildings climbing the hillside above the Mediterranean-style port of **Avalon**, and its round casino on a spur of land. And finally, you enter the harbor, thronged with pleasure boats and backed by picturesque, winding streets lined with red-tiled houses and shops. Hotel rooms are in short supply and pricey during the summer; most visitors come for the day on ferries that take as little as an hour for the crossing.

Avalon's resident population of 2500 is far outnumbered by the influx of up to 15,000 visitors a day, and the town, established 75 years ago, is straining at the seams. There is a plan to ease the pressure by adding houses, small hotels, and civic amenities over the next 15 years, without sacrificing the small-town charm. Happily, most of the island has been preserved in its unspoiled natural state, and traffic is generally limited to golf carts and the buses that ferry visitors along the back roads. You can see still more if you hike. Herds of wild bison (left by a movie crew several decades ago), boars, and goats roam free over the back region of the island. A buffalo joyously rolling over on its back like a big puppy is a sight not quickly forgotten. Catalina is 28 miles long and up to 8 miles wide; the perfect spot for a lazy or strenuous vacation.

Most of the island has been privately owned since the native Indians were re-settled on the mainland in 1811. Avalon was named in 1888 by the sister of an early developer, **George Shatto**, after the island of Avalon in **Tennyson**'s *Idylls of the King*, the refuge of blessed souls in Celtic mythology. In 1919, **William Wrigley, Jr.**, the chewing-gum scion, purchased the Santa Catalina Island Company, built the casino in Avalon and a mansion for himself, promoted

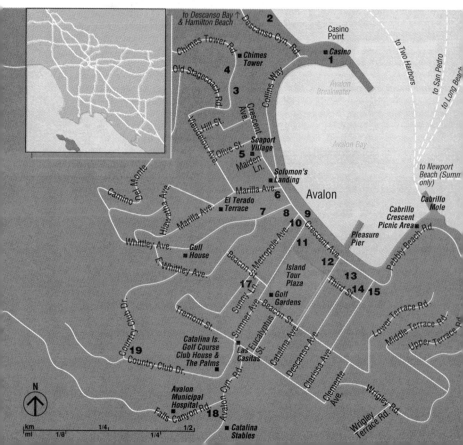

deepsea fishing, and established a spring training camp for his baseball team, the **Chicago Cubs**. Avalon became a popular tourist spot during the 1930s, but most of the interior of the island and much of the coastline remained undeveloped. A nonprofit conservancy acquired title to about 86 percent of the island in 1975 and now administers this unique open space in conjunction with the County of Los Angeles. Visitor information: 510.1520; fax 510.2762.

1 Casino (1928, **Webber & Spaulding**) The island's signature building, a circular Spanish-Moderne structure on a rocky promontory at the northwest end of Crescent Bay. It houses one of America's most beautiful movie palaces, a 1000-seater with fanciful underwater murals and a working organ. There's a splendid Art Deco box office, restored tiles, and murals around the entrance. Above is a grand ballroom where thousands can dance to big bands as they did 50 years ago. You can reserve the space for a terrific private party. There is also a small museum and art gallery. Daytime tours of the casino and

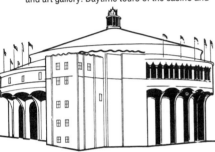

evening showings of new movies are presented daily in summer, weekends off-season. ♦ Movie schedule 510.0179; private parties 510.0550

2 Descanso Beach Family cookouts daily—you barbecue your own steak or hamburgers and the beach provides the salad and trimmings. A short walk from the Casino. ♦ Reservations 510.2780

3 Wolfe House (1928, **Rudolph Schindler**) An icon of modernism, comprising a stack of balconied floors that exploit the steep site and extraordinary views. Private residence. ♦ 124 Chimes Tower Rd

4 The Zane Grey Hotel $$$ Tahitian teak beams in an open-beam ceiling, a hewn-plank door, a log mantle, and walls of mortar mixed with goat's milk combine with blessed isolation and an extraordinary view of the ocean and the hills in this, the former Avalon home of the foremost writer of the American West. Now a hotel and reachable by bus, the pueblo was originally built for Zane Grey in 1929 as a haven for his literary labors and fishing desires. Amenities include complimentary taxi pick-up, outdoor pool, and complimentary tea or coffee throughout the day. Lower rates in winter. ♦ 199 Chimes Tower Rd. 510.0966

5 Seaport Village Inn $$ New hotel, close to the beach, with spa, suites, and off-season packages. Amenities include color TV with cable, private baths, studio suites with view, fully furnished kitchens, and wet bars. ♦ Maiden Lane. 510.0344

6 Hotel Villa Portofino $$$ A 34-room waterfront hotel with the ambitious Italian **Ristorante Villa Portofino** restaurant. Two-bedroom family units available. Amenities include a large sundeck and honeymoon accommodations. ♦ 111 Crescent Ave. Hotel 510.0555, restaurant 510.0508, 800/34OCEAN

7 Hotel Catalina $$ The charm of yesterday in a renovated Victorian hotel only a half-block from the beach. Movies for guests every afternoon, and Jacuzzi are provided. ♦ 129 Whittley Ave. 510.0027

8 Channel House $ A lunch of a salad or sandwich on the terrace overlooking the harbor is a treat; dinners are forgettable. ♦ American ♦ Daily 11AM-2PM, 5:30-10PM. 205 Crescent Ave. 510.1617

9 Armstrong's Seafood Restaurant ★$$ Specialties include mesquite-grilled swordfish, fresh lobster, and abalone. ♦ Seafood ♦ M-Th, Su 11AM-9PM; F-Sa 11AM-9:30PM. 300 Crescent Ave. 510.0113

9 Busy Bee $ Chinese chicken salad with ginger dressing, hamburgers, and sandwiches are offered in this pleasant café. ♦ American ♦ Daily 8AM-10PM. 306 Crescent Ave. 510.1983

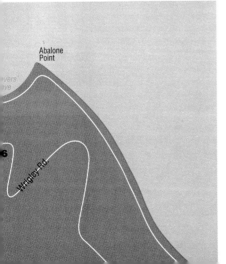

177

10 Chi-Chi Club Live jazz and bluegrass. Call for hours and programs. ♦ Cover weekends during summer. 107 Sumner Ave. 510.2828

11 Glenmore Plaza Hotel $$$ Charming re-decorated Victorian hotel, with Jacuzzis and a tree-filled courtyard. **Clark Gable** slept here and you can rent his suite. Amenities include whirl-pool tubs in all rooms, Continental breakfast, wine and cheese in afternoon, and free shuttle to boat area. ♦ 120 Sumner Ave. 510.0017, 800/422.8254

12 Hotel Vista del Mar $$$ New beachfront hotel, with fireplaces and Jacuzzis, located in the center of town. ♦ 417 Crescent Ave. 510.1452

13 Pavilion Lodge $$ On the beach in the heart of town. Large central courtyard. Free cable TV. Group rates. ♦ 513 Crescent Ave. 510.1788, 800/428.2566; fax 510.2300

14 Garden House Inn $$$ Eight-room bed-and-breakfast, just off the beach. ♦ 125 Clarissa Ave. 510.0356

15 Cafe Prego $$ Old-world warmth and charm. Try linguine with clams, sautéed calamari, and piccata of veal. ♦ Italian ♦ Daily 5:30-10PM. 603 Crescent Ave. 510.1218

16 Inn on Mt. Ada $$$$ The **Wrigley Mansion** has been converted into a luxurious bed-and-breakfast with just 6 guest rooms, all with ocean or harbor views. Guests enjoy full break-fast, gas-powered golf cart, wine and hors d'oeuvres. ♦ Wrigley Terrace Dr. 510.2030

17 Hotel St. Lauren $$$ (1987) Victorian decor and harbor views, a block from the water. Amenities include 42 guest rooms, Continental breakfast, kingsize beds, whirlpool tubs, and ocean views. ♦ 232 Metropole Ave. 510.2299

18 The Sand Trap $ A local favorite serving soup, burgers, and omelets. ♦ American ♦ Daily 7:30AM-3PM. Avalon Canyon Rd, en route to Wrigley Botanical Garden. 510.1349

19 Catalina Canyon Resort Hotel $$$ Sauna and pool and adjoining tennis and golf in a se-cluded setting. Courtesy van. Meeting facilities. ♦ 888 Country Club Dr. 510.0325, 800/253.9361; fax 510.0900

20 Cove of Catalina Resort Luxury villas in a new private community with golf, tennis, a se-cluded beach, and boat moorings. ♦ Hamilton Cove, No of Avalon. 510.1220

Catalina

21 Two Harbors Idyllic destination for a day trip, by boat or **Safari Bus** (510.2800) from Avalon. Be sure to pack a picnic. ♦ Center of island

21 Banning House Lodge $$ Eleven rooms in a converted classic. A peaceful retreat with no television. Dining room, solarium, and hill-top view of both sides of island. Be sure to book well ahead. ♦ Two Harbors. 510.0303, 800/888.4228; fax 510.0303 ext 243

Restaurants/Clubs: Red   **Hotels:** Blue
Shops/Parks: Green   **Sights/Culture:** Black

How To Get To Catalina

Boat Year-round service from the ports of Long Beach and San Pedro. Fast (less than 2 hours) big boats; refreshments. Mid-June through mid-September: 5 trips daily from both ports. Mid-September through mid-June: 3 trips daily. During peak months, service direct to Two Harbors/Isthmus area is available. Reservations for all sailings advisable. Call 800/888.5939 (from LA and Orange County), 514.3838 (from South Bay). Group information: 547.0802. Catalina Channel Express offers 55-minute trips daily, year-round, from a dock beside the *Queen Mary* in Long Beach to Avalon, and 90-minute trips from San Pedro and Redondo Beach to Avalon and Two Harbors aboard stabilized vessels with airline-style seating (519.1212), group information (519.7957, 800/257.2227). Catalina Passenger Service operates luxury catamarans from Balboa Pavilion in Newport Beach (714/673.5245).

Helicopter Charter flights and hydrofoil service from Long Beach are available, but the most convenient ac-cess to Catalina is by helicopter. Helitrans offer a mini-mum of 5 flights daily (weather permitting) from San Pedro's Catalina Terminal to Pebbly Beach, 5 minutes by van from Avalon (548.1314, 800/262.1472). The flight takes about 18 minutes. Island Express flies from San Pedro and from the Queensway Bay Hilton in Long Beach (491.5550, 510.2525).

Getting to the Terminals Long Beach terminal: take RTD bus 456 from downtown LA to Long Beach Blvd at 1st St. Walk from bus stop 'A' to stop 'D' and take Long Beach bus 12 or 186. San Pedro terminal: take RTD bus 446 from downtown LA to Anaheim St, and change to RTD bus 146.

Getting Around

Driving Rental cars are not allowed in the interior. If you have a friend with a car on the island, you may ob-tain a temporary card key to drive outside of Avalon from Santa Catalina Island Conservancy.

Hiking Permits are required to hike into the interior and may be obtained free of charge at the Visitor's In-formation Center in Avalon or at the Catalina Cove and Camp Agency at the Isthmus.

Camping Arrangements for camping at Black Jack or Little Harbor must be made through the County De-partment of Parks and Recreation (PO Box 1133, Avalon CA 90704, 510.0688). A brochure describing the trails may also be obtained from the department. Arrangements for camping at Little Fisherman's Cove (Two Harbors) must be made through Catalina Cove and Camp Agency (PO Box 5044, Two Harbors CA 90704, 510.0303). All camping by permit only and ad-vance reservations are required.

Recreation

Visit Wrigley's Memorial Botanical Garden, or try fish-ing, swimming, golf, or tennis. There are all sorts of sightseeing tours, such as the glass-bottom boat trip, flying-fish boat trip, and scenic terrace drive. Tours range from 40 minutes to 4 hours. A 3-hour *Around the Island Tour* departs Avalon daily at noon. It in-cludes El Rancho Escondido, which is home to some of America's finest Arabian horses. ♦ Catalina Sightseeing Tours: 510.2000, 800/428.2566. Catalina Adventure Tours: 510.2888. Catalina Safari Bus (back-packing tours): 510.2800. Island Navigation (water taxis to all points): 510.0409

Bikes, horses, baby strollers, fishing tackle, etc., can easily be rented. If you want to bring your bike along, contact your cross-channel carrier for details. Argo Diving Service (510.2208), and Catalina Sportfishing Charter (510.1078) offer rental equipment.

Accommodations

Beach Realty (PO Box 812, Avalon CA 90704, 510.0039) can arrange cottage rentals. Note that most hotels require a 2-day or even a one-week minimum stay during the summer. A Chamber of Commerce information office on the green pleasure pier in Avalon is open daily.

Native wildlife in Catalina's underdeveloped interior is extraordinary; more than 100 species of birds make Catalina their permanent or part-time home. There are 400 species of native plant life, including 8 types found only on Catalina. They include Catalina ironweed, the wild tomato, and the dudleya hassel, whose generic name means live forever.

Bests

Ira E. Yellin

Attorney, Developer, The Yellin Company

Grand Central Market. A traditional Central Market in downtown Los Angeles, open since 1917; a must see—represents the melding of the Hispanic and Anglo cultures. Some of the best Mexican tastes in the city.

Langer's Delicatessen. Best pastrami in all of Los Angeles.

Diamonds Bakery on Fairfax. Arguably, the best raisin, pumpernickel, and rye bread in the West.

La Brea Bakery on La Brea. The best currant rolls and ficelles.

Polo Lounge at the Beverly Hills Hotel. Neil McCarthy salad.

Brentwood Country Mart. Reddi Chick, chicken-and-fries basket. Saturday just would not be the same without sitting in the courtyard of this West LA haunt.

Le Dome. Vertical chicken and duck ravioli. Great food, great for lunch, great for star-gazing.

Patrick's Roadhouse. Pacific Coast Highway at Entrada—adequate food, crowded counters, often a wait, but with the mix of music, people, and the ocean view, it's one of the better breakfast "experiences" in town.

John O'Groats. Best breakfast in town. I love the corned-beef hash, but everything, including the coffee, is great. Be prepared to wait for a table.

Book Soup on Sunset. For book browsing and buying; have a cappuccino or bowl of Book-Soup at **Chaya Diner** next door.

Dutton's Books in Brentwood. Great books but terrific CD section. Ask Jim for advice and you can't go wrong.

Huntington Library. The cactus garden is a unique and special treat; also the camellias and azaleas when in bloom in winter and the Chinese magnolias in the spring.

The **Million Dollar, Orpheum**, and **Los Angeles Theaters** on Broadway in downtown Los Angeles, where you can still experience, albeit in tattered condition, the best of the movie palaces of the '20s and '30s.

House Tours given by **MOCA, LACMA**, and the **LA Conservancy.** LA is a city of houses so try to make one of these tours.

Da Camera Society. Great (usually classical) music superbly performed in historic places.

Jim Morris. Weight trainer and former Mr. America. He can teach you everything you, or anyone else, want to know about your body.

World's Gym, Venice. Where Joe Gold yells at you for dropping his weights; where you can pump iron with Arnold, have Jim Morris train you, and work off all the food from the above eateries.

A stroll through the flatlands of Hollywood to experience the Hollywood bungalow era of the '20s and '30s, and a drive through the Hollywood Hills (take any street) to see our version of the hills of Italy or France.

The **Andalusia** on Havenhurst Avenue in West Hollywood. The purest and most satisfying of Los Angeles' famous courtyard apartment buildings.

Neil Lane in the **Antiquarium** on Beverly Boulevard in West Hollywood. The best antique jewelry.

Some favorite LA foods

Tortilla—an unleavened bread in the form of a pancake, made of wheat flour or cornmeal.

Chile—a podlike fruit that is an essential ingredient of Mexican cooking, ranging in spiciness from the mild chile *poblana* to the incendiary chile jalapeño.

Quesadilla—a folded tortilla enclosing melted cheese and green chiles.

Taco—a tortilla fried then folded in half and filled with shredded meat, beans, tomato, shredded lettuce, and cheese.

Burrito—beans, meat, cheese, and chiles wrapped in a large flour tortilla.

Salsa—a spicy mixture of chiles, tomato, onion, and cilantro, used to enhance food.

Tamale—cornmeal dough filled with a meat and chile mixture, then wrapped in a corn husk and steamed.

Tequila—a liquor distilled from the juice of the Agave cactus.

Margarita—a cocktail of tequila, triple sec, and lemon juice blended to a froth with ice and served in a salt-rimmed glass.

Avocado—a thick-skinned fruit with a buttery yellow flesh, used in salads, omelets, and innumerable other dishes.

Catalina

Guacamole—a thick sauce made of mashed avocado, tomato, and chiles, often used as a dip for small fried triangles of tortilla.

Abalone—a single-shelled gastropod native to the Pacific; it is pounded until tender, dipped in egg batter, and sautéed.

Teriyaki—chicken, fish, or meat grilled in a soy-based sauce that has a touch of sweetness.

Sake—a rice wine, usually served warm in thimble-size cups.

Orange County North

Like the San Fernando Valley, **Orange County** has become a separate metropolis of over 2 million and still growing. This boom has occurred in the last 3 decades—since **Walt Disney** opened his **Anaheim** entertainment park in 1955 and the Irvine Ranch was finally developed in the 1970s. Orange County shares many of the same problems as LA—traffic congestion and deteriorating air quality high among them—but it is set apart by its newness. It is an embryo city, half finished, only now acquiring the institutions and resources to match its wealth and ambitions. It is a maze of separate communities that can be divided, like Hollywood, into 2 areas: the less prosperous north, with its ethnic and blue-collar enclaves and huge entertainment parks, centered on Anaheim; and the affluent south, with its luxurious homes, hotels, and restaurants, and its burgeoning cultural scene.

The ranchos of the Spanish and Mexican periods became the farms and orchards of the Yankees in the middle of the 19th century. In 1857, a coopera-

tive agriculture colony was established by 50 Germans, who named their community Anaheim, combining the name of the local river, the Santa Ana, and the German word for home, *heim*. Originally part of Los Angeles County, the area's autonomy was mandated by the California legislature in 1889. For the first 50 years of the 20th century, Orange County seemed a land of milk and honey. Well-tended groves of Valencia orange trees stretched as far as the eye could see, perfuming the air with the fragrance of their blossoms. In the 1950s, land values began to skyrocket, fueled by a postwar generation eager for a suburban lifestyle. As land became more valuable for homes and developments, the groves began to disappear. By the next century, the trees will be just a memory, immortalized in the names of streets and condominium tracts.

Area code 714 unless otherwise indicated.

Public transportation Erratic, at best. An unusual way to reach **Disneyland** is the brief (about 35 minutes) and delightful **Amtrak** local to Fullerton from Union Station (800/USARail). (From the Fullerton train station, walk about 1¹/₂ blocks to Commonwealth and Harbor. From there you can board **Orange County Transit District (OCTD)** bus No. 41/43 to get to the Disneyland Hotel.) The OCTD has extensive service throughout the county and, within limited areas, **Dial-a-Ride** curb-to-curb service (636.7433).

The **Southern California Rapid Transit District** has service from its main terminal at 6th and Los Angeles streets in LA to major locations in Orange County. **Greyhound** (620.1200) and **Trailways** (742.1200) serve Anaheim and Santa Ana from LA; Greyhound also covers Newport Beach and Laguna Beach en route to San Diego. From the Westside of LA, a convenient way to get to Orange County is the regularly scheduled **Airport Coach Service** from Los Angeles International Airport. The coaches take you directly to the major hotels, to Disneyland, and to the Orange County Airport.

A reliable and convenient shuttle service runs between the major amusement parks and hotels in the Anaheim-Buena Park area, South Coast Plaza, and Newport Beach. Called the **Funbus**, it circulates about every 35 minutes, its hours approximating the hours the parks are open.

For local transportation there is **Anaheim Yellow Cab** (535.2211), but for extensive travel to specific places away from the major tourist sites a car is the only practical option. For more information about transportation, special events, sightseeing services, or accommodations, the **Anaheim Area Visitors and Convention Bureau** has an office at the **Anaheim Convention Center** (800 W. Katella Ave, 999.8999).

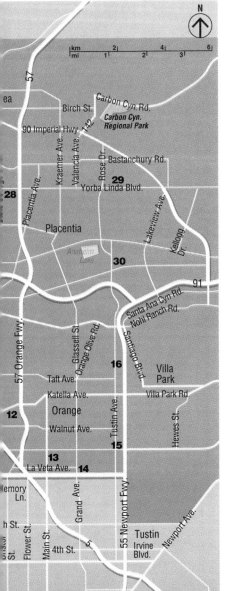

1 Los Alamitos One of LA's top tracks features quarter horse racing from mid-November through January, and May through mid-August. Harness racing is held from late February through April. ♦ Admission. Post time 7:30PM. 4961 Katella Ave, Los Alamitos. 995.1234

2 Hobby City Doll and Toy Museum Puppet shows and a display of 2500 antique dolls from around the world. ♦ Daily 10AM-6PM. 1238 S. Beach Blvd, Anaheim. 527.2323

3 Anaheim Country Inn $ A 1910 Queen Anne mansion has been converted to a small, moderately priced bed-and-breakfast with a front porch and a large garden. ♦ 856 S. Walnut St. Anaheim. 778.0150

260 acres a day become housing tracts. Farming ceases to be a major industry.
1965

4 Disneyland The kingdom where fantasy and magic are around the next turnstile and dreams are as advertised. The complex covers 76 acres and has cost over $200 million to build. New attractions are added almost every year. You can expect to spend at least 8 hours. A good way to get an overview of the Park is from the **Monorail** or the perimeter **Railroad**.

The Magic Kingdom is divided into 7 areas: **Main Street, Adventureland, New Orleans Square, Critter Country, Frontierland, Fantasyland**, and **Tomorrowland**.

Main Street Close to the entrance to the Park is Main Street, USA, an idealized turn-of-the-century small town. Small shops with wooden floors that resound under your feet and glass display cases at precisely the right height for children's noses sell a variety of nostalgic merchandise. In the nearby **Opera House**, *Great Moments with Mr. Lincoln* brings our 16th president to life through the magic of audio-animatronics.

The Plaza, hub of the Park, is located at the end of Main Street. From this point, the other Park areas spread out and you may enter the land of your choice via its unique theme gate.

The cannons in **Town Square** on Main Street are authentic, and were used by the French army in the 19th century.

Facial designs for the figures in the **Pirates of the Caribbean** were modeled after Walt Disney Company staff members.

In the early years of the Park, the **Rivers of America** in Frontierland was stocked with catfish and fishing was allowed off the docks of **Tom Sawyer Island**.

Original plans for the **Jungle Cruise** in Adventureland called for real wild animals, but zoologists warned Walt Disney that the animals would be asleep during operating hours.

Orange County North

Dust and cobwebs are brought into the **Haunted Mansion** to compensate for air conditioning suction.

22k gold leafing covers the spires of **Sleeping Beauty Castle**.

Real mermaids used to sit atop the coral reef of the lagoon in Tomorrowland's **Submarine Voyage**.

Adventureland The *Jungle Cruise* takes you down the Nile, Congo, and Amazon in a flat-bottomed boat: elephants bathe, crocodiles guard a ruined temple. More audioanimatronic magic is at work in the **Enchanted Tiki Room**, where exotic birds come to life in an amusing show.

Frontierland Next to Adventureland. There are battles, a blazing fort, and the **Golden Horseshoe Jamboree**, which you can enter through the swinging doors of a Western saloon and see cancan dancers. The Rivers of America run along the shore and are plied by an amazing assortment of vessels. **Big Thunder Mountain Railroad** is an exciting ride through a deserted mine during

©1991

Theme Park Drawings © The Walt Disney Company

which riders confront floods, swarms of bats, and fierce animals—and live to tell the tale.

New Orleans Square On the Rivers of America. Filigreed balconies overlook winding streets ablaze with flowers and lined with quaint shops. Every day is Mardi Gras with Dixieland music heralding the parades. Take a ride with the **Pirates of the Caribbean** on flat-bottomed boats that explore a haunted grotto hung with Spanish moss and glide into a seaport for pillage and plunder. Ghosts inhabit the **Haunted Mansion**, which uses holography to bring many of the 999 residents to wonderfully disembodied life.

Critter Country An audioanimatronic jamboree of mechanical bears will set your toes tapping. **Davy Crockett's Explorer Canoes** let you paddle along

the Rivers of America. A new attraction is **Splash Mountain**, a spectacular log flume adventure.

Fantasyland Enter this magical land through **Sleeping Beauty Castle**. Over the drawbridge and through the stone halls is the world of storybook characters familiar since childhood. The *Casey Jr. Circus Train* chugs past **Cinderella's** castle, **Pinocchio's** village, and the home of the **Three Little Pigs.** The whirling teacups of **Mad Tea Party** will leave your head spinning. Boats glide through **It's a Small World** with scenes of children of many lands all singing the same tune in their own native tongue.

The most popular ride in Fantasyland is the **Matterhorn**, a 14-story replica of the Swiss mountain built for white-knuckle fun. You are hoisted aloft in tandem bobsleds for a plunge through ice

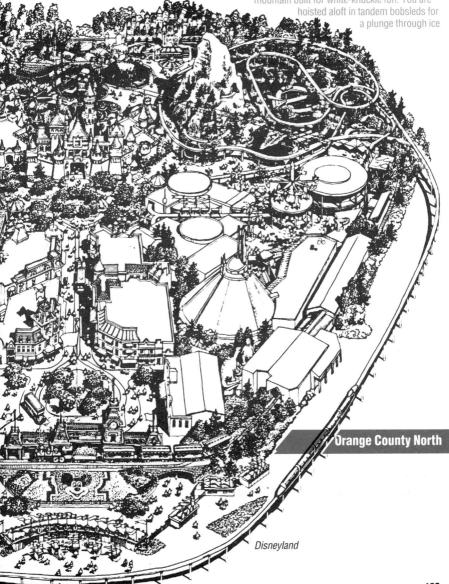

Orange County North

Disneyland

caverns and hairpin curves that ends with a splashy finale. **Videopolis** is a popular nightspot, with dancing to music videos on 70 monitors.

Tomorrowland Science fantasy—and a vision of how the real world may be (with monorails and people-movers now being introduced 25 years after their Disneyland de-

but). The **Mission to Mars** and **Rocket Jets** may prove equally prophetic. The Magic Eye Theater presents *Captain EO*, George Lucas' 3D extravaganza, directed by Francis Coppola and starring Michael Jackson. Another Lucas production is *Star Tours*, a simulated space flight with an awesome sense of realism. The aquatic world is equally accessible via the **Submarine Voyage**. The perils of outer space will thrill you on **Space Mountain**, a 20-million-dollar high-speed journey to the stars. Visitors enter through a simulated NASA control center and board rockets that travel aloft through a series of optical effects. The downward plummet is equally spectacular, with showers of meteors illuminating the ride home.

Summer nights in Disneyland offer a series of special events. The Main Street **Electrical Parade** is held every evening at 8:45 and 11PM; fabulous floats and Disney characters are illuminated by 100,000 sparkling lights. The parade is capped by a spectacular fireworks display. Music fills the air in almost every corner of the Park. The **Plaza Garden** features big band music and dancing. **Tomorrowland Terrace** has rock concerts and dancing. Continuous Dixieland jazz on the **French Market Stage** enlivens the atmosphere in New Orleans Square.

In addition to formally scheduled concerts, Disneyland is full of roving minstrels, troubadours, and musicians. Food, ranging from non-alcoholic drinks and light snacks to multicourse dinners, is widely available in the more than 25 restaurants and snack centers. The menu in each place is keyed to complement the neighboring attractions. **Harbor Gallery** is a recent addition offering good chowder and grilled fish. Admission to Disneyland admits you to all rides and shows without further charge. The Park offers numerous services, such as pet kennels, package lockers, baby stroller rentals, a baby-changing station, and a first-aid dispensary. Some rides have height and age minimums. Guided tours are available for first-time visitors.

Orange County North

♦ Admission. Daily 8AM-1AM, Memorial Day-Labor Day; M-F 10AM-6PM, Sa 9AM-midnight, Su 9AM-9PM, rest of year; extended hours on holidays. Harbor Blvd, exit off Santa Ana Fwy, follow signs to Disneyland. 999.4000, 213/626.8605, ext 4565

Restaurants/Clubs: Red   **Hotels:** Blue
Shops/Parks: Green   **Sights/Culture:** Black

5 Disneyland Hotel $$$ Three towers surround a water garden, **Seaports of the Pacific**, that evokes the spirit of the Magic Kingdom, to which it is linked by monorail. There are 10 tennis courts, 3 pools, a tropical beach, a shopping mall, and 16 restaurants and cafés. ♦. 1150 W. Cerritos Ave, Anaheim. 778.6600, 800/642.5391; fax 956.6582

6 Anaheim Convention Center Just down the street from Disneyland, it has a 9100-seat arena, two 100,000-square-foot exhibition halls, and 27 meeting rooms set in attractively landscaped grounds. The center is used for events ranging from concerts to conventions. ♦ 800 W. Katella Ave, Anaheim. 999.8999

6 JW's ★★★$$$ Romantic, librarylike dining room and imaginative, sometimes great cooking by **John McLaughlin**, who has traveled the world in search of fresh inspiration. Specialties have included rack of lamb with garlic sauce, veal medallions with mushrooms, and Grand Marnier soufflé. Within the **Anaheim Marriot**. ♦ Eclectic ♦ M-Th 6-10PM; F-Sa 6-10:30PM. 700 W. Convention Wy. 750.8000

6 Inn at the Park $$ Adjacent to the Convention Center. ♦ 1855 S. Harbor Blvd, Anaheim. 750.1811, 800/421.6662; fax 971.3626

7 Hansa House $$ A Scandinavian all-you-can-eat smorgasbord. The groaning boards feature some unusual dishes, like corn fritters and a herring plate, as well as a wide range of entrees and unusually good salads. Recommended for families. ♦ Scandinavian/American ♦ Daily 7:30-10:30AM, 11:30AM-3PM, 4:30-9PM. 1840 S. Harbor Blvd, Anaheim. 750.2411

8 Hyatt Regency $$$ The live flamingos, pools, and 60-foot palms in the glass atrium suggest a tropical island—an appropriate image for a hotel created by **Princess Cruises** (of *Love Boat* fame). There's also tennis, a spa, and stylish decor. ♦ 100 Plaza Alicante (Harbor Blvd-Chapman Ave) 971.3000, 800/228.9000; fax 740.0465

9 Belisle $ Fresh sandwiches, meatloaf, and pies served in heaping portions. ♦ American ♦ 24 hours. 12001 Harbor Blvd, Garden Grove. 750.6560

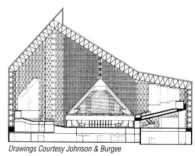

Drawings Courtesy Johnson & Burgee

10 Crystal Cathedral (1980, **Johnson & Burgee**) Only a few blocks away from Disneyland is the all-glass Crystal Cathedral of the **Garden Grove Community Church**. Made of white steel trusses and tempered silver glass, it is a shimmering extravaganza 415 feet long, 207 feet wide, and 128 feet high that seats 2862. The

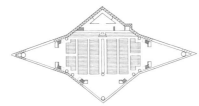

church's previous center was designed by architect **Richard Neutra** in 1961. It is an International-Style steel-and-glass church where services were made visible to passengers inside 1400 automobiles assembled for drive-in services. Neutra's son **Dion** designed the adjacent 15-story **Tower of Hope** for the expanding church administration in 1967. ♦ Tours M-Sa 9AM-3:30PM every ¹/₂ hour. Services Sunday 9, 11AM, 6:30PM. 12141 Lewis St, Garden Grove. 971.4000

11 Dover's ★★$$$ Soaring light-filled room serving such highly praised dishes as conch chowder, duck breast with honey and horseradish, and pork noisettes with yellow peppers. Within the **Doubletree Hotel**. ♦ Eclectic ♦ M-F 11:30AM-2PM, 6-10PM; Sa-Su 10:30AM-3PM, 6-10PM. 100 City Dr, Orange. 634.4500

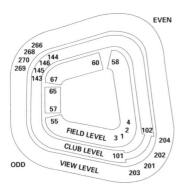

12 Anaheim Stadium Home of the **California Angels** baseball team and the **Rams** football team. The stadium features comfortable seats and good visibility. ♦ Seats 70,000. 2000 S. State College Blvd, Anaheim. 634.2000

13 La Brasserie Restaurant ★$$$ An intimate and relaxed bistro specializing in home-style soups, well-prepared fish, and veal. The library dining room is appealing. ♦ French ♦ M-F 11:30AM-2PM, 5-10PM; Sa 5-10PM. 202 S. Main St, Orange. 978.6161

14 Yen Ching ★★$$ Wonderful food is served in a cool, modern setting, and the unusually friendly service makes this a consistent favorite. Specialties include crispy duck, pot stickers, and whole fish with garlic sauce. ♦ Chinese ♦ M-Th 11:30AM-2:30PM, 4:40-9:30PM; F 11:30AM-2:30PM, 4:40-10:30PM; Sa noon-10:30PM. 574 S. Glassell St, Orange. 997.3300

15 Caffe Piemonte ★$$ Sparkling trattoria in a lackluster shopping center. Polenta, salmon-filled agnolotti, and the rack of lamb have been praised. ♦ Italian ♦ Tu-Su 5-10PM. 1835 E. Chapman Ave, Orange. 532.3296

16 Doll City USA Claims to be the world's largest store for dolls, buggies, and related books. ♦ M-Sa 10AM-5PM. 2040 N. Tustin Ave, Orange. 998.9384

17 Angelo's $ A classic drive-in with pert carhops on roller skates, a great neon sign, and occasional rallies of vintage wheels. ♦ American ♦ M-Th, Su 10AM-midnight; F-Sa 10AM-2AM. 511 S. State College Blvd, Anaheim. 533.1401

18 Werner's $ Honest home cooking in the plastic desert. **Helen Werner** offers chicken with dumplings, braised short ribs, and old-fashioned pies, all at old-fashioned prices. ♦ American ♦ Tu-Sa 4:30-8:30PM; Su 11:30AM-8PM. 1001 W. Lincoln Ave, Anaheim. 535.5505

18 Hansen House (Mother Colony House) Built in 1857, this white clapboard house with a narrow front porch is in the Greek Revival style. This was the first house in Anaheim, built by **George Hansen**, founder of the **Mother Colony**, a group of Germans who left San Francisco to grow grapes in Southern California. Inside the restored home is an exhibition on Anaheim's history. ♦ Free. W 3-5PM; Su 1:30-4PM. 414 N. West St, Anaheim. Library 999.1880

19 Museum of World Wars and Military History Hundreds of firearms, uniforms, posters, and military vehicles dating from 1776 through World War II. ♦ Admission. M-F, Su 11AM-7PM; Sa noon-7PM. 7884 E. La Palma, Buena Park. 952.1776

20 Knott's Berry Farm The oldest theme amusement park in the world had its start in 1934 when **Mrs. Cordelia Knott** began selling homemade chicken dinners to supplement income from the family's berry farm. Mrs. Knott's chicken kitchen not only survived the Depression, it spawned a 150-acre entertainment facility that emphasizes the wholesome aspects of an idealized and simpler America. There are 5 theme areas, comprising 165 rides, attractions, live shows, restaurants, and stores.

Ghost Town A replica of an 1880s Old West boom town, complete with cowboys, cancan dancers, and gold panning. Old-time melodramas are presented in the **Birdcage Theatre**. The **Butterfield Stagecoach** tours the countryside, making riders bless the day that shock absorbers were invented. Plan on getting wet if you choose to take a **Log Ride**, where your log boat floats through old sawmill and logging camps before splashing 42 feet in its final descent.

Roaring '20s A nostalgic glimpse of a vintage amusement park enhanced by the latest technology and featuring **Kingdom of the Dinosaurs**, a 7-minute ride through prehistoric times. The 20-story **Sky Jump** allows riders to parachute to the ground at free-fall speeds.

Camp Snoopy High in the Sierra Mountains, **Snoopy** and his **Peanuts** friends welcome youngsters to rides, shows, an 1896 merry-go-round, and performing animals.

Fiesta Village A tribute to California's Latino heritage. Parades, piñatas, parrots, mariachis, and *mercados* are found within a lushly landscaped and tiled plaza. A dance area features Latin and rock music. The **Marionette Theatre** is particularly artful and appealing to children. One of the most popular rides is **Montezooma's Revenge**, a roller coaster with cars that spin through a 360-degree loop at 55 miles per hour and then shoot backward. Also located in this area is **Dragon Swing**, a Viking ship dangling from a huge A-frame, thrilling riders by swinging back and forth until it achieves a 70-degree arc.

Wild Water Wilderness Turn-of-the-century California, featuring **Bigfoot Rapids**. Other thrill rides include **XK1**, in which riders can control their planes 70 feet above ground; **Whirlpool**, which gives riders the feeling of being beneath the ocean; and an extravaganza on **Reflection Lake**, *The Incredible Waterworks Show*. The **Good Time Theatre** presents roller-skating shows daily.

Knott's Market Place Just outside the park is a separate dining and shopping village. Here you can sample the chicken dinners and boysenberry pies that launched Knott's, enjoy the **Family Steakhouse** or **Cable Car Kitchen**, a salad, burger, or barbecue. Gifts, baked goods, and clothes are also on sale.

Height and age restrictions on some rides. Admission ticket provides access to everything except **Pan for Gold** and the

arcades. ◆ Admission. M-F 10AM-midnight, Sa 10AM-1AM, June-Aug; M-F 10AM-6PM, Sa 10AM-10PM, Su 10AM-7PM, Sep-May. 8039 Beach Blvd, Buena Park. 827.1776, recorded information 220.5200

21 Movieland Wax Museum Over 230 lifelike replicas of Hollywood stars are displayed in 130 sets of classic movies. **Arnold Schwarzenegger, Mel Gibson, Captain Kirk**, and **Spock** have joined the **Marx Bros, John Wayne**, the **Keystone Kops**, and **Shirley Temple**. Bring your camera for a close-up of your favorites, quake in the **Chamber of Horrors**, and pick yourself up in the pizza restaurant. ◆ Admission. Daily 10AM-8PM. 7711 Beach Blvd, Buena Park. 522.1154

22 Medieval Times If you haven't overdosed on good cheer at one of the theme parks, you might end your day here in a mock castle that offers a tournament with knights on horseback as you are being served dinner by costumed serfs and wenches. ◆ Admission. M-Th 10AM-9PM; Sa 10AM-3AM; Su shows at 1, 4:45, 7:30PM. 7662 Beach Blvd, Buena Park. 521.4740, 800/438.9911 (CA), 800/826.5358 (US)

Knott's Berry Farm

22 Ming's Family Restaurant $$ Where the Orange County Chinese hold their banquets. Hong Kong noodles and seafood specialties such as crispy shrimp in baked salt. ◆ Chinese ◆ M-Th, Su 11:30AM-9:30PM; F 11:30AM-10:30PM; Sa 10:30AM-10:30PM. 7880 Beach Blvd, Buena Park. 522.8355

23 International Museum of Graphic Communication Working antique printing machines, a printer's office c. 1900, and a myriad of other exhibitions going back to **Gutenberg**. ◆ Admission. Tu-Sa 11AM-7PM; Su noon-5PM. 8469 Kass Dr, Buena Park. 523.2080

24 La Mirada Civic Theater Broadway shows, concerts of every kind, and film lecture series are presented here. ◆ Seats 1300. 14900 La Mirada Blvd (No of Buena Park) Box office 994.6310, 213/944.9801

25 Muckenthaler Cultural Center Located in a lovely Spanish Baroque house that overlooks the valley. The 1923 house was given to the city of Fullerton by the Muckenthaler family in 1963 and is used for art exhibitions, classes, receptions, and cabaret theater. ◆ Free. Tu-Sa 10AM-4PM; Su noon-5PM. 1201 W. Malvern Ave, Fullerton (E of Buena Park) 738.6595

26 La Habra Children's Museum Railroad cars, hands-on displays, and a hands-off beehive are housed in a restored 1923 depot. ◆ Admission. Tu-Sa 10AM-4PM. 301 S. Euclid St, La Habra. 526.2227

27 Ruby Begonia's A comfortable spot to ease the cares of the day. The intimate dance club is a favorite with locals. ◆ American ◆ No cover. M-Th 11:30AM-2:30PM, 5:30-9PM; F 11:30AM-2:30PM, 5:30PM-1AM; Sa 5:30PM-1AM; Su 10AM-2PM, 5:30-9PM. 1500 S. Raymond, Fullerton. 635.9000

28 California State University at Fullerton A branch of the California State University system. ◆ 800 N. State College Blvd, Fullerton. 773.2011

29 Richard M. Nixon Library and Birthplace (1990, **Langdon & Wilson**) Admirers and haters of the deposed president should be equally rewarded by a visit to the Spanish-style museum and the transplanted boyhood home. Those with a serious need to know can make an appointment to visit the research library with its Shaker-inspired interior designed by **Gere Kavanaugh**. ◆ Admission. Daily 8:30AM-5PM. 18001 Yorba Linda Blvd, Yorba Linda. 993.3393

30 Bessie Wall's Fine Food and Spirits $$$ A hideaway restaurant in a revamped Spanish-style home. Warm hospitality and attention to detail make the extra drive worthwhile. ◆ Mexican ◆ M-F 11AM-2:30PM, 5-10PM; Sa 5-10PM; Su 10AM-2:30PM. 1074 N. Tustin Ave, Anaheim. 630.2812

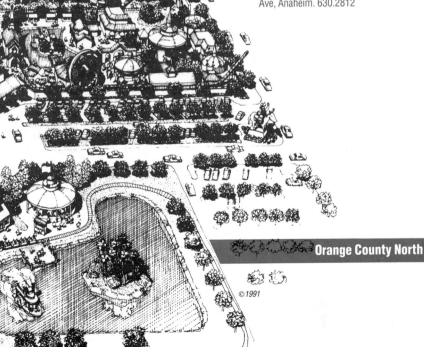

Orange County North

© 1991

Restaurants/Clubs: Red   Hotels: Blue
Shops/Parks: Green   Sights/Culture: Black

Orange County South

The **California Gold Coast** is an earthly paradise: temperate climate, sandy beaches and rocky promontories, green canyons and rolling hills, with something of the French and Italian Rivieras. Along the coast, boating, golf, tennis, and other recreation are the major businesses, while the interior hills are devoted to education and high-tech industry.

The beaches have distinct identities: **Huntington Beach** is a surfer's paradise; **Newport Beach** and **Balboa** are havens for the yachting crowd; **Corona del Mar** is a quiet beachside community; **Laguna Beach** is an artists' colony;

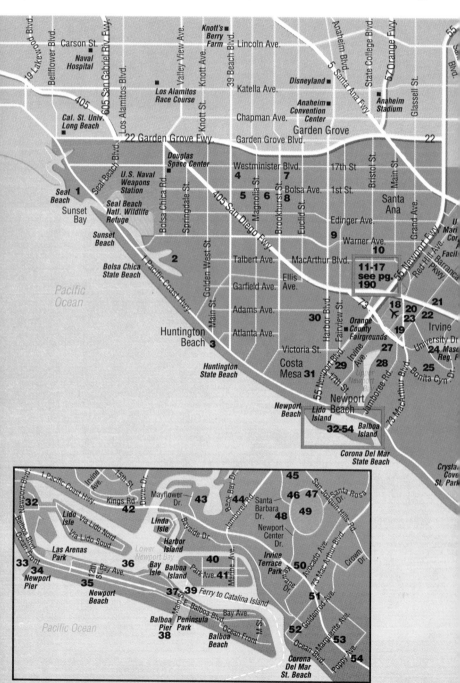

Dana Point is newly developed with a large marina; and **San Juan Capistrano** and **San Clemente** are gracious residential areas.

Developed as planned communities in the '60s, thousands of tract homes cover the hilly acreage formerly devoted to farming and orange groves on the Irvine Ranch. The new town of **Irvine** surrounds the newest campus of the **University of California**. Businesses in **Orange County South** are usually housed in one-story tilt-up slab concrete buildings, the best examples of which are seen in the **Irvine Industrial Park**. The area is a mecca for high-technology—electronics and computers forming the most important sector of the economy.

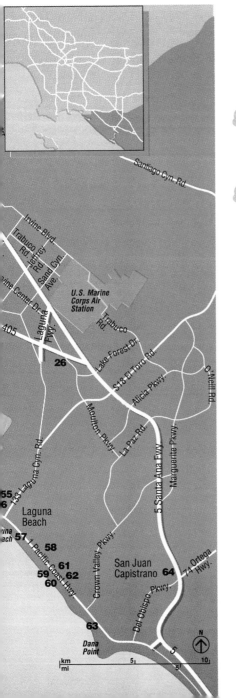

Area code 714 unless otherwise indicated.

1 Seal Beach Inn $$$ Ask for a room facing the flower-filled courtyard in this bed-and-breakfast gem. Nearly all the 24 rooms and suites have period furnishings, a fully-equipped kitchen, and books. The beach and fishing pier are just 2 blocks away. ♦ 212 5th St, Seal Beach. 493.2416

2 Bolsa Chica Ecological Reserve A 530-acre wildlife sanctuary. Guided 90-minute tours at 9AM on the first Saturday of the month, October-March. ♦ Entrance and parking inland from Pacific Coast Hwy (Warner Ave-Golden West St) Huntington Beach. 897.7003

3 Huntington Pier The first surfing contests were held at Huntington Beach and it remains a worldwide haven for surfers, who congregate at the Huntington Pier to enjoy unusual wave conditions created by the agglomeration of pilings; this is the best place to watch the year-round action. ♦ End of Main St, Huntington Beach

4 Seafood Paradise II ★★$$ Dim sum for connoisseurs in 3 dozen varieties are served daily for lunch; the regular Cantonese menu includes such treats as drunken chicken, salty duck, shredded jellyfish, and 5-flavor beef. ♦ Chinese ♦ M-Th, Su 10AM-9:30PM; F-Sa 10AM-10PM. 8602 Westminster Blvd, Westminster. 893.6066

5 Grand Garden ★$ Catfish hot pot, eel braised in coconut milk, and spicy shrimp braised in a clay pot are offered at this modest seafood restaurant. ♦ Vietnamese ♦ M, W-Th, Su 10AM-9:30PM; F-Sa 10AM-10PM. 8894 Bolsa Ave, Westminster. 893.1200

6 Bahn Cuon Tay Ho ★$ Sautéed ground meat and shrimp ears, dried shrimp, cold sausage, and barbecued pork are among the fillings for this café's sheer, steamed rice sheets. ♦ Vietnamese ♦ Tu-Su 8AM-8PM. 9242 Bolsa Ave, #C, Westminster. 895.4796

7 Pagolac ★$ A standout in Little Saigon for its 7-course meal of beef—delicate morsels that are chopped, simmered, charbroiled, or rolled in rice paper and served with lettuce, mint, and cilantro. ♦ Vietnamese ♦ Tu-F noon-10PM; Sa-Su 11AM-10PM. 14564 Brookhurst St, Westminster. 531.4740

8 Nui Ngu ★$ Tiny storefront serving such Hue specialties as *bahn bot loc* (transparent rice tortellini enclosing unshelled shrimp) and *bo Hue* (a spicy beef-and-rice vermicelli soup). ♦ Vietnamese ♦ Tu-Th 9AM-6PM; F-Sa 9AM-8PM. 10528 McFadden Ave, Garden Grove. 775.1108

189

9 Gen Kai Country Pub ★★$$ Simple wood tables, a long sushi bar, and a lone tatami platform make up the decor, but don't be deterred—this is a favorite eating place for local Japanese chefs and the rustic dishes taste wonderful. Highlights include marinated squid, asparagus and sausage, stewed fish with vegetables, and hot-pepper eggplant with onion. ◆ Japanese ◆ M-Th 11:30AM-2PM, 5:30-11PM; F-Sa 11:30AM-2PM, 5:30PM-2AM; Su 11:30AM-2PM, 5:30-10PM. 16650 Harbor Blvd, Fountain Valley. 775.3818

10 Gemmell's ★★★$$$ One of Orange County's finest classic French restaurants, with a young but thoroughly professional staff. Don't miss the home-smoked salmon, the foie gras, and the lobster in Sauternes cream sauce. ◆ French ◆ M-F 11:30AM-2PM, 6-11PM; Sa 6-11PM. 3000 Bristol St, Costa Mesa. 751.1074

11 Horikawa ★★$$ Versatile branch of the distinguished restaurant in LA's Little Tokyo, offering *teppan-yaki*, sushi, and classic dishes in a setting of elegant simplicity. ◆ Japanese ◆ Tu-Th 11:30AM-2PM, 6-10PM; F 11:30AM-2PM, 6-11PM; Sa 5:30-11PM; Su 5:30-9:30PM. 3800 S. Plaza Dr (No side of South Coast Plaza Village) 557.2531

11 Antonello ★★$$ Excellent Northern Italian food, including cioppino and scampi in mussel sauce, is served with flair in a village street setting. Owner **Antonio Cagnolo** is a caring host and maintains an excellent wine list. ◆ Italian ◆ M-Th 11:30AM-2PM, 6-10PM; F 11:30AM-2PM, 6-11PM; Sa 6-11PM. 3800 S. Plaza Dr (No side of South Coast Plaza Village) 751.7153

11 Gustaf Anders ★★★$$$$ Spacious elegance and wonderful food. As in its former La Jolla location, the standouts are the sugar- and salt-cured salmon, smoked sandwich, black caviar sandwich, marinated beef, and crusty home-baked breads. ◆ Scandinavian ◆ Daily 11:30AM-2:15PM, 6-10:30PM. 3810 S. Plaza Dr (No side of South Coast Plaza Village) 668.1737

11 Gandhi ★★$$ Outstanding in looks and cuisine, Gandhi offers terrific *naan* (bread), exemplary tandoori, *masalas*, and regional dishes. ◆ Indian ◆ M-Th 11:30AM-2PM, 5:30-10PM; F-Sa 11:30AM-2PM, 5:30-11PM. 3820 S. Plaza Dr (No side of South Coast Plaza Village) 556.7273

12 South Coast Plaza Buyer's heaven: over 270 stores on the main landscaped plaza and

busiest mall in Southern California, with over 20 million visitors a year, as worthy a visit as any theme park. ◆ M-F 10AM-9PM; Sa 10AM-7PM; Su 11AM-6PM. 3333 Bristol St (off I 405, San Diego Fwy) 241.1700

At South Coast Plaza:

Rizzoli's International Bookstore The most elegant, literate, and beautiful bookstore chain now has a nearby LA address. ◆ M-F 10AM-9PM; Sa 10AM-6PM; Su noon-5PM. Between Jewel and Crystal Cts. 957.3331

Gianni ★$$ Excellent fried mozarella, unusual pizzas and pastas. ◆ Italian ◆ M-Sa 11AM-10PM; Su 11AM-7PM. Crystal Ct. 540.3365

13 Westin South Coast Plaza Hotel $$$ The Weekend Specials are a good value. ◆ 666 Anton Blvd. 540.2500, 800/228.3000; fax 754.7996

14 California Scenario Artworks are scattered throughout South Coast Plaza, but the treasure (worth the drive from LA) is **Isamu Noguchi**'s 1.6-acre sculpture garden. Framed by reflective glass towers and the blank white walls of parking structures, this oasis is often overlooked by visitors. Noguchi created a contemporary version of a traditional Japanese garden in which natural rocks, sandstone structures and paving, trees, cacti, and running water symbolize different aspects of the state of California. ◆ Free. Daily 8AM-midnight. Free parking off Ave of the Arts

15 Security Pacific Gallery (1989, **Frederick Fisher**) A 9000-square-foot showcase for contemporary artworks from the bank's huge collection. ◆ Free. Tu-Su 11AM-5PM. 555 Anton Blvd, South Coast Metro Center. 433.6000

16 South Coast Repertory Theatre The **Mainstage** and **Second Stage** present a diversified program of live drama September through June. ◆ Seats 507, 161. 655 Town Center Dr. Box office 957.4033

17 Orange County Performing Arts Center From the **Kirov Ballet** to *Cats*, from *Fiddler on the Roof* to the **American Ballet Theatre**, the center has become a rival to LA's Music Center since its opening in 1986. The auditorium is named for **Henry T. Segerstrom**, who developed

Orange County South

the adjoining **Crystal, Carousel,** and **Jewel Courts,** including 8 department stores (**Bullock's, I. Magnin, May Co, Nordstrom, Saks Fifth Avenue, Sear's, Broadway** and **Robinson's**). In between is a selection to rival Beverly Hills: **Gucci, Cartier, Saint Laurent, Polo/Ralph Lauren, Charles Jourdan, Barneys New York, Jaeger, Louis Vuitton, Scribner's Books,** and **Godiva Chocolatier.** It is also the

South Coast Plaza and spearheaded the effort to make it a center for the arts. Concerts and opera are also regularly featured. ♦ Seats 3000. 600 Town Center Dr. Box office 556.2787, ticket charge 634.1300

18 John Wayne Airport Thirteen American airlines serve this busy alternative to LAX. As the population of Orange County exploded (from 200,000 in 1950 to well over 2 million today), the airport's terminal and parking capacity became sorely strained. Fortunately, major expansion was completed in September 1990. Terminal parking is expensive and inadequate; travelers are advised to park in the north lot and take the free shuttle bus to the terminal, daily 5:30AM-11PM at 15-minute intervals. For transportation to LAX, hotels, and tourist attractions, call 973.1100. ♦ 18741 Airport Wy (So of I 405, San Diego Fwy, and I 55, Newport Fwy) Santa Ana. 755.6500

19 Pascal ★★$$$ Superb seafood, with a hint of Provence in the bold colors and seasonings. Mussels steamed with saffron, bass with thyme, and chicken with olives are among the signature dishes. ♦ French ♦ M-Th 11:30AM-2:30PM, 6-9:30PM; F 11:30AM-2:30PM, 6-10:30PM; Sa 6-10:30PM; 1000 N. Bristol St, Newport Beach. 752.0107

20 Chanteclair $$$ French farmhouse decor offers a romantic setting for such dishes as filet Wellington, veal Oscar, and grilled swordfish. ♦ Continental ♦ M-F 11:30AM-2:30PM, 6-10PM; Sa 11:30AM-2:30PM, 6-11PM. 18912 MacArthur Blvd (across from John Wayne Airport) Irvine. 752.8001

21 Morell's ★★★$$$ Specials include the seafood grill, tarragon-flavored lobster sausage, and duck with pomegranate sauce (a Persian recipe). Excellent service, complimentary appetizers, and a string quartet on weekends. Within the **Irvine Hilton**. ♦ Eclectic ♦ M-Th 11:30AM-1:30PM, 6-10PM; F 11:30AM-1:30PM, 6-11PM; Sa 6-11PM. 17900 Jamboree Rd, Irvine. 863.3111

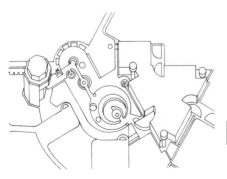

22 Fluor Corporation Building (1976, **Welton Becket & Associates**) Futuristic glass-clad structures with rooftop pods for air-conditioning equipment. It is best viewed from the San Diego Freeway (I 405). ♦ 3333 Michelson Dr, Irvine

22 Prego ★★$$ A happy, crowded place, modeled on a Tuscan villa, that serves inventive pizzas, rabbit, duck, and free-range chicken from the rotisserie, and such special treats as tortellini filled with ricotta, chard, and sage. ♦ Italian ♦ M-Th 11:30AM-11PM; F 11:30AM-midnight; Sa 5PM-midnight; Su 5-10PM. 18420 Von Karman Ave, Irvine. 553.1333

23 Meridien $$$$ Striking ziggurat-shaped member of an international chain of French-owned luxury hotels. Though its address is Newport Beach, it is located well inland, across from the airport. **Bernard Jacoupy**, formerly of the Biltmore, is the manager. Swimming pool, exercise rooms, and good weekend rates. The hotel has 3 restaurants, including **Café Fleuri**, a sophisticated coffeeshop, and the **Bistrot Terrassel**, which offers exquisite spa cuisine on an outdoor terrace. ♦ 4500 MacArthur Blvd, Newport Beach. 476.2001, 800/543.4300; fax 476.0153

Within the Meridien:

Antoine ★★★$$$$ Serious dining in an opulent setting of silk-covered walls, mirrors, and fine furnishings. The consulting chef is **Gerard Vie** (who follows **Jacques Maximin** of the Hotel Negresco in Nice) and the kitchen has drawn raves for its treatment of silky foie gras, meats, and poultry. Superb wine list and polished service. ♦ French ♦ Tu-Sa 6-10PM. 476.2001

24 Chinatown ★$$ **Alice Fong** did the brightly colored decor that makes **Michael Chiang**'s restaurant such a feast for the eye, despite its uninspiring location. The firecracker lamb, gun-powder scallops, confetti chicken, and aromatic shrimp are as tasty as they sound. ♦ Chinese ♦ M-Th 11:30AM-10PM; F-Sa 11:30AM-11PM. 4139 Campus Dr, Marketplace Mall, Irvine. 856.2211

25 University of California at Irvine Founded in 1965 on 1000 acres donated by the **Irvine Company**. Twenty-five buildings house 5 major schools and a number of interdisciplinary and graduate departments. Full-time enrollment is 16,000. The campus was laid out as an arboretum; over 11,000 trees from all over the world form a green grove in the center of the tan hills of the Irvine Ranch. A self-guided tree tour brochure is available at the Administration Building. A rare exception to the prevailing architectural mediocrity of UC campuses is the **Information Computer Sciences and Engineering Research Facilty**—a splendid complex of buildings by **Frank Gehry** located on the

southeast edge of the inner ring—and new work by **Morphosis** and other cutting-edge California architects. The **Bren Events Center, Fine Art Gallery** sponsors exhibitions of 20th-century art and is open free of charge, Tuesday-Saturday 10AM-5PM. Theatrical performances are held in the **Fine Arts Village Theatre**, the **Concert Hall**, and **Crawford Hall**. ♦ San Diego Fwy (I 405) to Jamboree Rd, W to Campus Dr, So. 856.5011

26 Wild Rivers Family water park with 40 rides and attractions on a lush tropical site formerly occupied by **Lion Country Safari**. You can shoot the rapids on an inner tube, be fired over water on the **Wipeout**, or lie back and improve your tan. Paddling pools for very small children, refreshments, and group picnic sites by advance reservation. ♦ Admission. Daily 10AM-8PM, June-Labor Day; some weekends off season 10AM-6PM. 8800 Irvine Center Dr (off San Diego Fwy, I 405) Irvine. 768.9453

27 Kitayama ★★★$$$ This *kaiseki* restaurant is so authentic that it would help to bring a Japanese friend along to translate the menu—though there is also an excellent and more accessible sushi bar. The fixed-price *omakase kaiseki* (chef's choice) is highly praised, as is the bargain lunch. ♦ Japanese ♦ M-F 11AM-2PM, 6-10PM; Sa 6-10PM. 101 Bayview Pl, Newport Beach. 725.0777

28 Upper Newport Bay A remarkable and idyllic 741-acre preserve for ducks, geese, and other avian users of the Pacific Flyway, surrounded by the bluffs of Newport Bay. Paths along the far reaches of the estuary are wonderful for quiet early morning walks. ♦ Backbay Dr (Jamboree Rd) Newport Beach

31 The Golden Truffle ★★$$$ Friendly neighborhood café and restaurant. Caribbean-influenced California cuisine from chef/owner **Alan Greeley**. ♦ Eclectic ♦ Tu-F 11:30AM-2:30PM, 6-10PM; Sa 6-10PM. 1767 Newport Blvd, Costa Mesa. 645.9858

32 Ho Sum Bistro ★$ In an all-white space you can enjoy light, delicious chicken, dim sum, noodles, and other snacks. ♦ California/Chinese ♦ M-Th 11AM-10PM; F-Sa 11AM-11PM; Su 9PM. 3112 Newport Blvd, Costa Mesa. 675.0896

33 Zeppa ★★$$ Atmospheric decor and a surprisingly innovative menu for a pier-edge restaurant. Beyond the designer pizzas there are wine-glazed rack of lamb and some unusual treatments of vegetables and fish. ♦ California ♦ Daily 6-9:30PM. 2304 Ocean Front, Newport Beach. 640.0600

34 The Rex ★★$$$ Clublike seafood restaurant owned by **Rex Chandler**, who has a restaurant with the same name in Hawaii. The abalone is especially fine. ♦ Seafood ♦ Daily 5:30-10PM. 2100 Oceanfront, Newport Beach. 675.2566

34 Doryman's Inn $$$ A '20s house converted to an opulent small hotel with luxurious appointments and Victorian decor. ♦ 2102 W. Ocean Front, Newport Beach. 675.7300

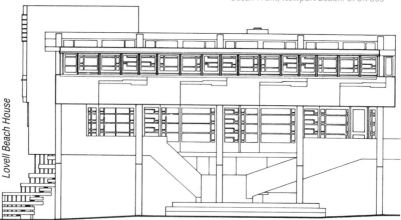

Lovell Beach House

29 Crab Cooker $$$ Well-loved and always crowded. The restaurant does not accept reservations, even, as one story has it, from a president of the United States who wanted to circumvent the line. Mesquite-broiled seafood. ♦ Seafood ♦ Daily 11AM-10PM. 2200 Newport Blvd, Costa Mesa. 673.0100

Orange County South

30 Mandarin Gourmet ★$$ The showcase of **Michael Chiang**, who also owns **Chinatown** in Irvine. Fine Mandarin and Szechuan dishes are served in a contemporary setting. Aromatic shrimp is a standout, but the menu is full of interesting discoveries. ♦ Chinese ♦ M-Th 11:30AM-3PM, 4:30-10PM; F 11:30AM-3PM, 4:30-11PM; Sa 11:30AM-11PM; Su 11:30AM-10PM. 1500 Adams Ave, Costa Mesa. 540.1937

35 Lovell Beach House (1926, **Rudolph Schindler**) One of the great monuments of modern architecture, a beach house for the same progressive doctor who was to commission a house by **Neutra** in Los Feliz a few years later. It is a fine example of Schindler's early constructivist style, combining grace, lightness, and strength in a style far ahead of its time. Private residence. ♦ 13th St at Beach Walk, Balboa

36 Newport Harbor There are 10 yacht clubs and 10,000 boats in this aquatic playground. The exclusive residential area has been a prestige summer resort for many years. The bay includes **Lido Isle, Linda Isle, Harbor Island, Bay Isle**, and **Balboa Island**. Cruises include **Hornblower Yachts** (brunch and dinner/dancing, 548.8700) and the **Cannery Brunch Cruise** (675.5777) ♦ Newport Beach

37 Bubbles Balboa Club ★$$ Exhilarating update of a '30s Art Deco restaurant/lounge, whose stylish interior is enhanced by its trademark bubbles that burst out from a huge Plexiglas tube when the waiters sing *Happy Birthday* (every 15 minutes on a good night). There's a lively jazz group, too. Lamb chops, fresh fish, and wild mushrooms layered between clouds of puff pastry are among the dishes to order. ◆ California ◆ W-Th, Su 5-10PM; F-Sa 5-11PM. 111 Palm St, Balboa. 675.9093

38 Ruby's $ A lovingly re-created streamline diner that helped launch a trend toward white formica, red vinyl, and quilted stainless steel. Cuddle up in a booth to enjoy omelets, mountains of fries, hamburgers, and milk shakes. ◆ American ◆ Daily 7AM-10PM. End of Balboa Pier, Newport Beach. 675.7829

39 Balboa Pavilion (1905) A historical landmark in the heart of the town. It now houses a restaurant, a gift shop, and an ocean-view bar, and is the Newport Terminal for Catalina Island tours, whale-watching expeditions, and harbor cruises aboard the *Pavilion Queen*, which last 45 or 90 minutes and show you the Newport Harbor. ◆ 400 Main St, Balboa. 673.5245, sport fishing and skiff rentals 673.1434

39 Balboa Ferry Three tiny ferries take you between the Balboa Peninsula and Balboa Island. ◆ 24 hours. Palm St on Balboa Peninsula or Agate Ave on Balboa Island

40 Balboa Island Actually 3 islands connected by bridges. They are, in descending size, the **Big Island**, the **Little Island**, and **Collins Island**. A favorite island pastime is an evening stroll among the luxury homes. ◆ Corona del Mar

41 Ruby's Summer House $ Light and airy, with lots of plants—a great place to watch the natives passing by in everything from silk dresses to bikinis. Burgers, chili, sandwiches, and shakes give you an added excuse. ◆ American ◆ Daily 6:30AM-10PM. 203 Marine Ave, Balboa Island. 675.3477

42 Marrakesh ★$$$ Hollywood-Arab decor of tiled fountains and pillows on the floor. A sumptuous setting for elaborate Moroccan dinners that include pigeon pie, couscous, and baklava. ◆ Moroccan ◆ M-F 6-10PM; Sa-Su 5:30-11PM. 1100 W. Pacific Coast Hwy, Newport Beach. 645.8384

43 Newport Dunes Aquatic Park A 15-acre lagoon with sail and paddleboat rentals. There are picnic facilities, campgrounds, dressing rooms, and a launching ramp. ◆ Admission. Daily 8AM-10PM. Pacific Coast Hwy (Jamboree Rd) Newport Beach. 729.3863

44 Newporter Resort $$$ Recently renovated resort comprising 400 rooms and suites on 26 landscaped acres on the Back Bay. Sporting options include golf, tennis, and swimming, and of course, there's a spa with Jacuzzis. The nightclub presents a trip down memory lane. ◆ 1107 Jamboree Rd (Pacific Coast Hwy) Newport Beach. 644.1700, 800/233.1234; fax 644.1552

Within the Newporter Resort:

The Wine Cellar ★★★$$$ Romantic basement restaurant renowned for classic dishes created by chef **John Benson**, formerly of the acclaimed **Le Français** in Wheeling IL. ◆ French ◆ M-Th 6-9PM; F-Sa 6-10PM. 644.1700

45 Newport Harbor Art Museum Changing exhibitions of contemporary art and a permanent collection of 20th-century art emphasizing works by Southern California artists are presented in this internationally famous museum. The **Sculpture Garden Cafe** has light meals and snacks; the gift shop sells catalogs and books. To come, in 1992, is a 25-million-dollar building designed by **Renzo Piano**, who won acclaim for the DeMenille Museum in Houston. ◆ Donation requested. Tu-Su 11AM-5PM. 850 San Clemente Dr, Newport Beach. 759.1122

46 Tutto Mare ★$$ Stylish trattoria serving *vitello tonnato* (veal with tuna sauce), salmon in *cartoccio*, pastas, and grills. ◆ Italian ◆ M-Th 11:30AM-11PM; F-Su 11:30AM-midnight. 545 Newport Center Dr. 640.6333

47 Four Seasons $$$$ Flagship of the luxury hotel chain: a 19-story tower and 4-acre garden located in Fashion Island. The decor is refined, the art of outstanding quality, the views spectacular. ◆ Deluxe ◆ 690 Newport Center Dr. 759.0808, 800/332.3442; fax 759.0568

Within the Four Seasons:

Pavilion ★★★$$$$ Ambitious restaurant offering such specialties as crab fritters, lobster ragout, and tenderloin of lamb with turnip pancakes in a pale, sophisticated decor.

◆ California ◆ M-F 11:30AM-2PM, 6:30-10:30PM; Sa 6:30-10:30PM; Su 10AM-2PM, 6-10:30PM. 760.4920

God Bless the LA police, they were the first Keystone Kops.
Mack Sennet

Restaurants/Clubs: Red	**Hotels:** Blue
Shops/Parks: Green	**Sights/Culture:** Black

193

48 The Ritz ★★★$$$$ Not to be confused with the Ritz-Carlton down the coast, **Hans Prager**'s luxury restaurant draws the same well-heeled crowd. Its bouillabaisse has been acclaimed as the best west of the Mississippi, and the carousel appetizer (with fresh foie gras, sweet smoked trout, and gravlax), the liver with crispy onion sticks, and the classic osso buco have also won devoted fans. Handsome traditional decor. ◆ French ◆ M-Th 11:30AM-3PM, 6:30-10:30PM; F 11:30AM-3PM, 6:30-11:30PM; Sa 5:30-11:30PM. 880 Newport Center Dr. 720.1800

49 Newport Center Fashion Island Classy outdoor shopping center anchored by **Neiman Marcus, Bullock's Wilshire, Buffums, Robinson's,** and **The Broadway.** There are 100 specialty stores, and the **Atrium Court** boasts 3 levels of designer fashions. ◆ M-F 10AM-9PM; Sa 10AM-6PM; Su noon-5PM. Off Pacific Coast Hwy (Jamboree-MacArthur Blvds) Newport Beach. 721.2000

At Newport Center Fashion Island:

Farmers Market at Atrium Court A foodlover's dream of the freshest produce, baked goods, fish, and meat. Clustered around are 17 eateries, from which you can carry food to outdoor tables. Best bets are breads from **Il Fornaio** and the blue-corn tacos from **La Salsa**, a salad, and a glass of wine. ◆ M-Sa 8AM-9PM; Su 8AM-8PM. Lower Level. 760.0403

50 El Torito Grill ★$ From the zingy salsa to the creative tortilla fillings, everything is fresh and served with flair in this casual hot spot. ◆ Mexican ◆ M-Th 11AM-11PM; F-Sa 11AM-midnight; Su 10AM-midnight. 59 Newport Center Dr. 640.2875

51 Hemingway's ★★$$$ Parrot fish with *beurre blanc* and rattlesnake with satay sauce are 2 of the surprises, but there are also good soufflés and salads in this hip, pricey eatery. ◆ Eclectic ◆ M-Th 5:30-10:30PM; F-Sa 5:30-11PM. 2441 E. Coast Hwy, Corona del Mar. 673.0120

51 Oysters ★$$ Attractive modern restaurant with a tiny front patio serving fresh grilled fish, steamed mussels, and clams. ◆ Seafood ◆ M-Sa 11:30AM-10PM; Su 10:30AM-3PM, 4-10PM. 2515 E. Coast Hwy, Corona del Mar. 675.7411

51 Sherman Foundation Center A jewel of a botanical garden and library specializing in the horticulture of the Pacific Southwest. The well-maintained grounds are lush with unusual seasonal flowers and famous hanging baskets. The tea garden serves pastries and coffee. A gift shop sells a variety of horticultural items. ◆ Admis-

sion. Daily 10:30AM-4PM. 2647 E. Coast Hwy, Corona del Mar. 673.2261

52 Trees ★★$$$ Three peach-colored dining rooms, a tree-filled courtyard, and a bar with piano and fireplace create a cozy setting for the eclectic cuisine—which ranges from Maryland crabcakes to Thai fried chicken—of chef/owner **Russell Armstrong.** ◆ Eclectic ◆ M-Th, Su 6-10PM; F-Sa 6-11PM. 440 Heliotrope, Corona del Mar. 673.0910

53 Carmelo's ★★$$ Unpretentious trattoria whose eclectic menu, friendly service, and live piano draw crowds. Specialties include pasta Sorrentina (with fresh porcini mushrooms and zucchini flowers), pumpkin-flavored gnocchi, and Dover sole Milanese. ◆ Italian ◆ Daily 5:30-11PM. 3520 E. Coast Hwy, Corona del Mar. 675.1922

54 Five Crowns ★★$$$ Fine food, professional service, a charming ambiance, and live entertainment account for the popularity of this improved version of England's oldest inn (**Ye Old Bell** at Hurley, AD 1135). Herb-roasted free-range chicken, roast duckling with apple-prune compote, and prime rib are dependable choices. ◆ American ◆ M-Sa 5-10PM; Su 10:30AM-2:30PM, 4-10PM. 3801 E. Coast Hwy, Corona del Mar. 760.0331

Laguna Beach
A Mediterranean climate, a beautiful 3-mile beach, and an artsy atmosphere have made Laguna Beach a popular resort for years. John Steinbeck lived here while writing *Tortilla Flat*, and Bette Davis made her home here during the 1940s. Most of the 20,000 year-round residents commute to industrial areas outside of Laguna Beach; the community supports a primarily cottage industry of small shops, crafts galleries, and tourist services.

55 Hortense Miller Garden Two acres of spectacular native fauna and birds. Reservations required 2 weeks in advance. ◆ Admission. Garden M-F 10AM-4PM; Sa 8AM-noon. 22511 Allview Terrace. 497.3311

55 Festival of Arts/Pageant of the Masters Show biz and technical wizardry combine to simulate great works of art with live models. Using acrylic paints to deflect stage lighting, artists paint backgrounds and create shadows and creases for the wardrobes of models who must hold the pose completely immobile for a minute-and-a-half in sculpture and painting tableaux. For 7 weeks each year, some 400 volunteers and a small staff of professionals draw oohs and aahs from over 100,000 wide-eyed spectators. So critical is the stage lighting that a matinee performance would be unthinkable. Book well ahead for the July-August performances. ◆ Admission. 650 Laguna Canyon Rd. 494.1145

56 Laguna Museum of Art Permanent collection and changing exhibitions of work by California artists. ◆ Tu-Su 11AM-5PM. 307 Cliff Dr. 494.6531

56 242 Cafe ★★$$ Tiny trattoria serving such treats as sautéed eggplant salad, New Mexico fettuccine, and Thai chicken pizza. BYOB. ◆ California ◆ M-F 11AM-9PM; Sa-Su 9AM-9PM. 242 N. Pacific Coast Hwy. 494.2444

57 Vacation Village $$ Resort with a private beach, pools, whirlpool, recreation, and restaurants. Rooms, suites, and studios all reasonably priced. ◆ 647 S. Coast Hwy. 494.8566; 800/843.6895; fax 494.1386

57 Eiler's Inn $$$ Charming bed-and-breakfast with warm personalized service a block from the beach. ◆ 741 S. Coast Hwy. 494.3004

58 The Carriage House $$$ Another charming bed-and-breakfast, with a choice of apartments or a picture-perfect cottage. There's a pretty garden, a friendly dining room, and it's just 3 minutes from the beach. ♦ 1322 Catalina St. 494.8945

59 Surf & Sand Hotel $$$ Modern rooms with ocean views. Two restaurants, entertainment in hotel. Excellent service. ♦ 1555 S. Coast Hwy. 497.4477, 800/LAGUNA1; fax 494.7653

Within the Surf & Sand Hotel:

The Towers ★★$$$ Stunning, mirrored Art Deco restaurant overlooking the ocean. Contemporary French cuisine and elegant atmosphere. ♦ French ♦ M-Th 7AM-2:30PM, 5:30-10PM; F-Sa 7AM-2:30PM, 5:30-11PM; Su 7:30AM-3PM, 5:30-10PM. 497.4477

60 Tavern by the Sea ★$$$ The upstairs dining room offers such creative dishes as stir-fried beef with black-bean sauce, sweetbreads with crisp-fried capers, and grilled prawns in tomatillo sauce in corn crêpes. ♦ Eclectic ♦ M-Th 5:30-10PM; F-Sa 5:30-10:30PM; Su 5:30-9:30PM. 2007 S. Coast Hwy. 497.6568

61 Five Feet ★★★$$ East meets west in this super modern restaurant that is centered on its open kitchen. Chef/owner **Michael Kang** surprises and delights with such dishes as *kung pao* calamari, goat-cheese won tons, and soft-shell crabs with pineapple cilantro salsa. ♦ Chinese ♦ M-Th, Su 5-10:30PM; F 11:30AM-2:30PM, 5-11:30PM; Sa 5-11:30PM. 328 Glenneyre St. 497.4955. Also at: Fashion Island, Newport Beach. 640.5250

62 Dizz's As Is ★$$ A reflection of Laguna's bohemian, laid-back spirit, in which everyone dresses to please him or herself and the plates don't match. Grilled spiced chicken, poached salmon with fresh tomato coulis, and pepper steak are standout dishes.♦ Eclectic ♦ M-Th, Su 6-9:30PM; F-Sa 6-10PM. 2794 S. Coast Hwy. 494.5250

63 The Ritz-Carlton Laguna Niguel $$$$ A luxury resort hotel. It has the style associated with older East Coast establishments, but with a West Coast atmosphere. How could it be otherwise with a setting on a dramatic bluff overlooking the Pacific? Amenities include 2 swimming pools, 4 tennis courts, sailing accommodations at Dana Point, direct access to a 2-mile beach, a restaurant, a café, a club, and a library where high tea is served in the afternoon. Even if you don't stay in a suite that comes with its own Steinway piano, you can still enjoy music. It's the hotel policy to have piano music playing somewhere in the hotel from 6:30AM to 11PM every day of the week. ♦ Deluxe ♦ 33533 Shoreline Dr, Laguna Niguel. 240.2000, 800/241.3333; fax 240.1061

Within the Ritz-Carlton Laguna Niguel:

Ritz Carlton Dining Room ★★★$$$$ Specialties have included pheasant mousse with blueberry vinegar sauce, sweetbreads in port and caper sauce, and saddle of rabbit with basil cream sauce. Outstanding wine list. An ideal place if you want to overindulge in grand surroundings and drop a bundle. ♦ French ♦ Daily 6-10PM. 240.2000

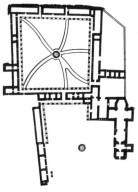

64 Mission San Juan Capistrano Founded in 1776 by **Father Junipero Serra**, this simple adobe is one of the oldest churches in California. In 1796, Indian laborers under the charge of a Mexican stonemason began a grand stone church that was completed in 1806, only to be destroyed by an earthquake 6 years later. Instead of rebuilding the monumental stone structure, services resumed in the older adobe church. In the 1890s, the Landmarks Club saved the adobe from destruction, and in the 1920s it underwent major restoration. The famous swallows that return to Capistrano each 19 March, St Joseph's Day, are cliff swallows that build their gourdlike nests in the broken arches of the ruins of the stone church. ♦ Admission. Daily 7:30AM-5PM. Camino Capistrano at Ortega Hwy, San Juan Capistrano. 493.1111

64 Capistrano Depot $$$ Take Amtrak direct from Union Station to this refurbished train station, where lunches and dinners feature dishes from the best of the old railroad lines, and jazz accompanies drinks in the boxcar bar. ♦ American ♦ M-Th 11:30AM-2:30PM, 5-9PM; F-Sa 11:30AM-2:30PM, 5-10PM; Su 10AM-2:30PM. 26701 Verdugo St, San Juan Capistrano. 496.8181

64 San Juan Capistrano Library (1983, **Michael Graves**) The harmonious but slightly

tongue-in-cheek use of anachronism is a hallmark of this celebrity Postmodern architect. Buildings arranged around an arcaded courtyard, a fountain, gazebos for reading, and the polychrome interior refer to the nearby Spanish Mission. ♦ M-Th 10AM-9PM; F-Sa 10AM-5PM. 31495 El Camino Real, San Juan Capistrano. 493.1752

Desert Areas

Antelope Valley at the north of LA County, is arid high desert, sparsely populated and undeveloped, providing a nearby escape from urban claustrophobia.

1 Vasquez Rocks County Park A surrealistic tumble of lacy sandstone rocks, some several hundred feet high, that are great for climbing. The area is an outcropping of the San Andreas Fault. Named for the famous 19th-century bandit, **Tiburcio Vasquez**, who used it as one of his numerous hideouts. ♦ Free. Escondido Canyon Rd (off Hwy 14)

2 Antelope Valley California Poppy Reserve Two thousand acres set aside for the preservation of the golden poppy, the California state flower. During the spring, the reserve is carpeted with a solid blanket of flowers. Open March-May only. ♦ Free. 17 miles W of Lancaster (off Hwy 138)

Restaurants/Clubs: Red
Shops/Parks: Green
Hotels: Blue
Sights/Culture: Black

3 Willow Springs Raceway One of the best tracks in America for watching top car and motorcycle racing year-round. You can see the entire 1-mile track from almost any point. Light refreshments. Weekend races all day long. ♦ Admission. Take the Rosamond exit off Hwy 14 No of Lancaster. 805.256.2471

4 Edwards Air Force Base This is the place to see the Space Shuttle land, on the dry surface of **Rogers Lake**. ♦ Free. Daily tours 10:15AM, 1:15PM, except on Federal holidays and during Shuttle operation. Rosamond Blvd (off Hwy 14), follow signs. 805/258.3311

5 Saddleback Butte State Park Native chaparral on a sandstone bluff. There is a magnificent stand of Joshua trees, bizarrely shaped plants that are, improbably, members of the lily family. ♦ Admission. 24 hours. 170th St (off California Hwy 138). 805/942.0662

6 Devil's Punchbowl Regional Park A 1310 acre county park located in the high desert area near Pearblossom. The rocky area is rich in native plants and includes a number of hiking trails. The **Punchbowl** is a natural depression in

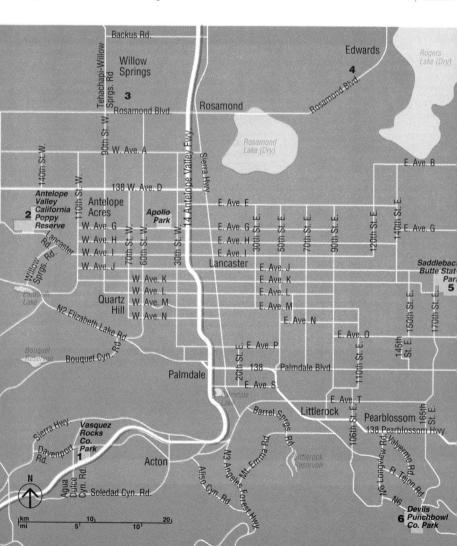

a slope of tumbled boulders. The park also includes a lovely stream, the size of which varies greatly with the season, ringed with willows and other water-loving plants. ◆ Free. Daily sunrise-sunset. 2800 Devil's Punchbowl Rd, Pearblossom. 805/944.2743

San Bernardino/Riverside Counties

To the east of LA is a vast area, part desert, part mountain, into which man has introduced some of the ugliest development and worst smog in America. But there's much to see. Marvelous terrain, year-round sports, and hedonistic pleasures are found in the Colorado Desert, a little more than 100 miles from downtown LA.

7 Mt. Baldy Ski in winter, hike in summer. By lift or on foot, it's over 10,000 feet to the top and worth it for the view. ◆ Turn off San Bernardino Fwy and follow signs to Mt. Baldy Village. 714/982.2829

8 Sycamore Inn $$$ Built on the site of a historic stagecoach stop, the restaurant continues a tradition of warm hospitality. Prime rib on the buffet, a huge stone fireplace, and wingback chairs. ◆ American ◆ M-Th 11AM-2:30PM, 5PM-10PM; F-Sa 11AM-11PM; Su noon-10PM. 8318 Foothill Blvd, Rancho Cucamonga. 982.1104

9 Ontario International Airport A fast-growing alternative to LAX, now served by 13 commercial and 3 commuter airlines. There's one central and 2 satellite parking areas. Public transportation to the surrounding area is limited. Most reasonable is the airport coach that runs directly to LAX 4 times a day (800/772.5299). Other choices, for hotels, LA, and Palm Springs, include **Airport Shuttle** (714/780.2170) and **Super Shuttle** (714/973.1100). The airport is located northwest of Riverside, between the San Bernardino (I 10) and Pomona (I 60) freeways. ◆ 714/983.8282, 714/984.1207

10 San Bernardino There's a City Hall by **Cesar Pelli** (300 N. D St), and to the west on the old Route 66, a marvelous folly: the **Wigwam Village Highway Hotel** (2728 W. Foothill Blvd just off San Bernardino Freeway 10).

10 Bobby Ray's Texas BBQ ★$ Ribs, chicken, and links slowly cooked in a smoky oven and served with a zesty sauce. ◆ American ◆ W-Th 11AM-8PM; F-Sa 11AM-10PM. 1657 W. Baseline St, San Bernardino. 714/885.9177

11 Big Bear Lake At 9000 feet, surrounded by forests, it has a tranquility that **Lake Arrowhead**, walled off by home sites and full of ear-shattering speedboats, now lacks. You can stay at **Gold Mountain Manor** (714/585.6997), where **Clark Gable** and **Carole Lombard** spent their honeymoon, or at the historic **Knickerbocker Mansion** (714/866.8221). Hearty German dinners are served at **George & Sigi's Knusperhauschen** (714/585.8640).

12 Riverside The **Mission Inn** (Main and 7th sts., 714/784.0300), undergoing restoration, scheduled to open early 1991 and there's a splendid Beaux-Arts County Courthouse (4050 Main St)

12 California Museum of Photography (1990, **Stanley Saitowitz**) Newly housed in a remodeled downtown Kress store, this collection rivals those of Eastman House and the Smithsonian. Director **Jonathan Green** presents a lively program of exhibitions and events; researchers may use the study center. ◆ Tu-Sa 10AM-5PM; Su noon-5PM. 3824 Main St, Riverside. 714/784-FOTO (recording) 714/787.4787 (offices)

13 Redlands An architectural gem founded on the affluence of early citrus farming. Notable are the Tuscan-style loggia of the **Santa Fe Railroad Station** (Orange St south of Pearl), the picturebook **Morey House** (a bed-and-breakfast, 140 Terracina Blvd, 714/793.7970) of 1890, which is open for tours, and the Victorian mansions along Olive St.

13 Kimberly Crest House & Gardens (1897) A flamboyant château with Tiffany glass, formal gardens, lily ponds, and citrus groves recalls the city's heyday. ◆ Admission. Th, Su 1-4PM. Alvarado St at Highland Ave, Redlands. 714/792.2111

14 Perris The **Orange Empire Railway Museum** displays 150 steam locomotives and streetcars, including some you can ride. This was once a railroad town and there's a fine surviving station. ◆ Free, except for special events. Daily 9AM-5PM. Train rides 11AM-5PM. 2201 S. A St, Perris. 714/657.2605

More contemporary in spirit is the **Perris Valley Airport,** which features gliders, hot-air balloons, ultralight planes, and parachuting.

Palm Springs

is a smartly casual resort located at the base of **Mt. San Jacinto** that is rapidly building itself into extinction. Avoid the hideously commercialized traffic-clogged route 111, with its succession of lookalike developments. It is the golf capital of the world, sponsoring over 100 tournaments annually, as well as being a mecca for tennis players, sunbathers, shoppers, and diners. Mineral hot springs have been an attraction here for millenia; the **Agua Caliente Indians** utilized natural spas for ritual and medicinal purposes. Soaking and sunning continue today as favorite Palm Springs pastimes, not only in the hot springs, but also in almost 7000 swimming pools. Natural artesian springs in several nearby canyons create oases where the native **Washingtonian Palm** can grow. The region is also known for its beneficial climate. The clean air has a light-as-a-feather quality at an average daytime temperature of 88 degrees (though it can easily reach 120 in summer). Humidity is low, and the yearly rainfall averages 5.39 inches. Around town are

Desert Areas

some remarkable modern desert houses designed by **Richard Neutra** and **John Lautner**. For information on hotels, restaurants, and other attractions in the Palm Springs area, call 619/327.8342; for hotel and condominium reservations in Palm Springs, call 800/472.3788.

15 Dinosaur Gardens Claude Bell designed and built the 150-foot-long brontosaurus and matching *tyrannosaurus rex*, which occupy a garden in the **San Gorgonio Pass**, 18 miles northwest of Palm Springs, on the north side of I 10. ♦ Nominal admission. Children under 10 free. M, W-Su 9AM-5PM. 5800 Seminole Dr, Cabazon. 714/849.8309

16 Whitewater Canyon Interesting scenery and a trout farm. Picnic facilities and grills for freshly caught fish. Rental tackle and bait available.

17 Joshua Tree National Monument A natural wonder that's just 2½ hours' drive from LA, comprising 870 square miles of unearthly mountain and desert flora. The granite monoliths around **Hidden Valley** challenge the skills of rock climbers. ♦ 74485 National Monument Dr, off Rte 62. 619/367.7511

18 Palm Springs Aerial Tramway A spectacular tramride, the largest single-span lift in the world, travels to an altitude of 8516 feet on **Mt. San Jacinto** for a view of the surrounding area that is more than eagle's eye. At the top there is a bar, restaurant, shops, and 54 miles of hiking trails. ♦ M-F 10AM-8PM; Sa-Su 8AM-8PM. N. Palm Canyon and Tramway Rd. 619/325.1391

19 Palm Springs Desert Museum A large cultural facility with permanent collections and changing exhibitions of contemporary and historical art. There is a fine collection of over 1300 American Indian artifacts. ♦ Admission. Tu-Sa 10AM-5PM; Su 1-5PM. 101 Museum Dr. 619/325.0189

20 Indian Canyons Andreas, Murray, and Palm canyons offer large and unusual rock formations, hiking trails, and a stand of majestic **Washingtonian Palms** believed to be almost 2000 years old. ♦ S. Palm Canyon Dr

21 Idyllwild A community nestled in mile-high mountains. There are tall stands of pines, a tumbled rock formation for climbing, trails for hiking in summer, skiing in winter.

22 Anza Borrego Desert This 470,000-acre state park is a well-maintained desert preserve with an unusual number of flora and fauna varieties. The striking geological formations here resemble a miniature Grand Canyon. **Carrizzo Gorge** and **Plain** are particularly beautiful.

Restaurants/Clubs: Red	Hotels: Blue
Shops/Parks: Green	Sights/Culture: Black

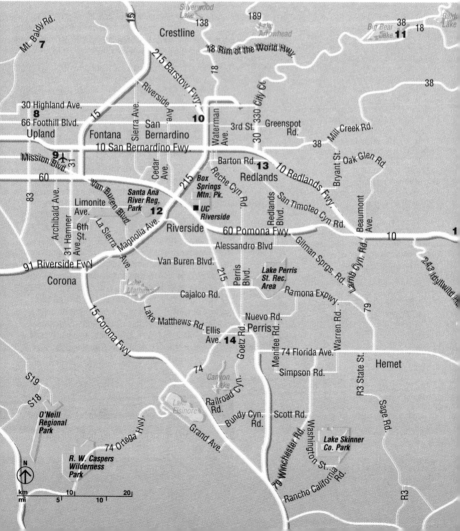

23 Living Desert Reserve A 900-acre desert interpretive center containing nature trails, a botanical garden, a visitors center, and a gift shop/book shop. Information is available from the **Palm Springs Desert Museum**, which administers this reserve.

24 Lake Cahuilla Fishing, swimming, boating, and picnicking. ♦ 25 miles So of Palm Springs in Indio. 619/564.4712

25 Salton Sea Swimming, boating, and water skiing are available at this 38-mile-long inland sea, which lies 235 feet below sea level. A **National Wildlife Refuge** is located at the southern end. The **Visitors Center** has history and wildlife exhibitions.

Bests

Tim Street-Porter
Photographer

The **Temporary Contemporary Museum** by architect Frank Gehry is still the best reason to visit LA's downtown district. Its vast, lofty interior is not only one of the best places to view contemporary art in the USA, but is also one of LA's most exciting interior spaces.

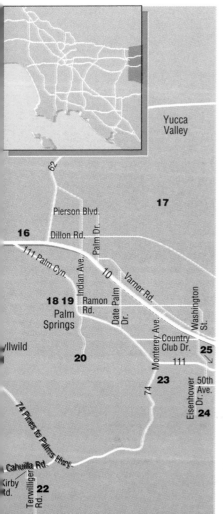

The museum suggests more a working environment for artists than it does the mausoleumlike galleries offered by more conventional museums.

LA exists so resolutely in the present that reminders of how the city lived and looked at the turn of the century are hard to find. Among the most evocative is the **internal courtyard of the Bradbury Building**, another of the city's best spaces. Built in 1893, it seems little changed. Even the small rented offices on each floor seem haunted by Philip Marlowe. The view from the top can't be that high, but it does induce vertigo, and getting there in the glazed Victorian elevator (a forerunner of all those glitzy capsules in John Portman-designed hotels) is fun, too.

On a clear day one of my favorite drives is to Pasadena on the **Pasadena Freeway**. The first of LA's freeways, it features tightly radiused curves and a succession of Art Deco tunnel entrances as the highway cuts through Elysian Park. At one point there are 3 of these visible at once. On toward Pasadena the mountains loom grandly, framed by the steep sides of the arroyo through which the freeway winds. Just east of Pasadena are the **Huntington Gardens**, with the world's largest cactus garden. Wander through these groves of giant convoluted plants and imagine yourself on another planet.

Although not a horse-racing fan, I love to visit the **Santa Anita racetrack**. This is also east of Pasadena. The buildings are a soft green and perfectly maintained, built in a graceful Regency Deco style. The grandstand faces the mountains, which (again, on a clear day) offer a majestic background to the action on the track.

Disneyland is at its best on a hot summer night, preferably when the usual attractions are augmented by live jazz or salsa. Best of all is the Electric Parade, with its mesmerizing electronic music—an endlessly repeated hypnotic theme that emanates simultaneously from the floats, the surrounding bushes, and seemingly from the air itself: 10 minutes of irresistible artifice, kitsch, and pure magic.

Hollywood (the film capital) may be little more than elusive myth these days, and there is little to send the tourist home satisfied, except for 2 venerable institutions. One is **Mann's** (formerly Grauman's) **Chinese Theater**. The other is **Musso & Frank Grill**. The former will satisfy most tourists who penetrate only as far as the famous courtyard, but the theater itself must be seen—well worth the price of a movie admission ticket. As for Musso's, don't expect the latest in cuisine. Instead, there are career waiters (as opposed to actors in between jobs) and an enormous menu of traditional American food, which like the interior rooms, has probably not been altered in over 50 years. The ambiance is what still makes it a favorite among a number of LA's leading artists and a steady selection of movie industry people. There is nowhere else like it.

Finally, for the Hollywood that was, the **Will Rogers State Historic Park**, out near the beach end of Sunset

Boulevard (an excuse for that long, beautiful drive along Sunset itself), offers the restored home of one of American's best-loved characters, with its inspirational Western interior decor, and its extraordinary home-movie footage (seen in an adjoining theater) of the great man doing his rope tricks.

Beaches North

Time:	3-6 hours
Mileage:	53 miles round trip from the intersection of the Santa Monica Freeway (I 10) and the Pacific Coast Highway (1).
Area:	A drive up and down the Pacific Coast Highway past some of the loveliest beaches in Los Angeles County.

Take the Santa Monica Fwy (I 10) to its end at Santa Monica, where it will merge into Pacific Coast Hwy (1). Go north on this road for the tour. Although much of the beachfront is public, you will notice numerous private homes; many are elaborate residences of the rich and famous. Almost all the beaches are free and open to the public. A parking fee is charged in lots adjoining beach areas. On summer weekends, parking may be difficult to find. Getting across Pacific Coast Hwy on foot or turning around in a car is dangerous; extreme caution is advised.

The first major public beach is **(1) Will Rogers Beach State Park**, named for the famous cowboy humorist. This beach stretches for several miles along the Coast Hwy and is well-provided with parking, facilities, and volleyball areas. Surfers congregate along the area opposite Sunset Blvd.

You may detour up Sunset Blvd to visit **(2) Will Rogers State Historic Park** or the **(3) Self Realization Fellowship Lake Shrine**. See pages 93, 94.

At the corner of Coastline Drive is the **(4) J. Paul Getty Museum**. See page 111.

At Topanga Canyon Blvd, a right turn will take you to the semirural community of **(5) Topanga, Topanga State Park** (see page 112), or a drive to the **(6) San Fernando Valley** over a winding and scenic canyon. See page 118.

(7) Malibu is a long stretch of beach with homes pressed against the ocean edge and dotting the chaparral-covered hills. The area on the right side of the Coast Hwy is subject to landslides; you will notice retaining walls holding back the earth. Much of the beach is walled off by the "cottages" of the rich and famous, but there are about 10 public access paths, with minimal parking, that are sign-posted on the Coast Hwy. And you can walk or jog down from the pier. Malibu is one of the most famous of the seaside communities, as much for its residents as for its scenery.

The **(8) Malibu Sportfishing Pier**, located about 10 miles along our route, is a charming spot for surfer-watching and reviving breaths of ocean air.

Surf Riders State Beach, located just east of **(9) Malibu Point,** is a favorite with surfers. About 12 miles out, you may take a detour right on Malibu Canyon Road, which traverses the Santa Monica Mountains to the San Fernando Valley, following the edge of a colorful and rugged canyon with some vista turnouts along the way. **(10) Malibu Creek State Park** is located beside this road. This is also the road to **(11) Pepperdine College**.

(12) Paradise Cove is located just east of **Point Dume**, approximately 16 miles along our route. It is a sheltered beach with white sand, tumbled sandstone cliffs, and fishing and boat launching facilities. Admission is charged.

(13) Zuma Beach is on the west side of Point Dume. This broad, flat beach is one of the most popular, offering volleyball, facilities, easy parking, miles of smooth sand, and good body-and board-surfing.

(14) Leo Carrillo Beach is pretty and secluded, located in a wide cove that is slightly sheltered by rock at either end. The northern portion of the beach is popular with surfers. Swimmers should go to the center of the cove to avoid underwater rock formations.

Across the Coast Hwy, approximately 26 miles from our start, is **(15) Point Mugu State Park**, an expanse of rolling hills and sycamore-shaded canyons that is a perfect spot for an easy hike or a picnic. See page 115.

To return, retrace your route on Pacific Coast Hwy to the Santa Monica Fwy.

Time:	4-6 hours
Mileage:	4 miles round trip from Santa Monica Pier.
Area:	Santa Monica, Ocean Park, Venice, and Marina del Rey, the most popular and colorful of the southland beach areas.

The Santa Monica/Marina del Rey area is a compact neighborhood best seen on foot or on bicycle. We recommend the use of a car only to get from neighborhood to neighborhood. The bike path begins just north of the **Santa Monica Pier** and parallels the beach south to **Palos Verdes**, a distance of some 30 miles. A short ride through the marina to **Playa del Rey** is highly recommended. The best walking and skating sites are on **Oceanfront Walk** between the **Santa Monica** and **Venice piers**, and along Main Street.

Begin at the **(1) Santa Monica Pier** at Colorado and Ocean avenues in Santa Monica. You might want to stop here for a carousel ride to get into the proper playful mood for the tour. Take Ocean Avenue south to the intersection with Pico Blvd where the road forks. Take the right-hand fork that parallels the ocean; this is Barnard Way. Follow Barnard around to the left until it rejoins the former Ocean Avenue, which has been

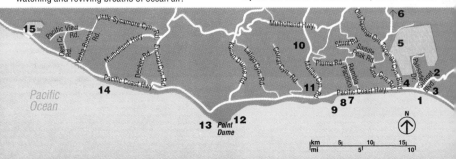

rechristened Neilson Way. Turn right at Neilson and continue. Surprisingly, the street changes names again in the next block as you enter Venice, and becomes Pacific Avenue.

Continue down Pacific past the corner of **(2) Windward Avenue**, the last remnant of old Venice, whose beachfront is now a frenetic mixture of skaters, cyclists, joggers, entertainers, and assorted eccentrics. Bikes and roller skates can be rented.

At Washington Street, a short stroll takes you to the Venice Pier for views, fishing, people watching, and snacks. There are several bicycle-rental shops along this street. Continue down Pacific. You are now entering **(3) Marina del Rey**, about 3 miles from the Santa Monica Pier. The Marina section of Pacific takes you past frayed relics of the old Venice: canals, bridges, and a few disguised oil wells.

At the end of Pacific, where it abuts on Via Marina, is a small promenade area and jetty looking out over the Marina del Rey entrance channel. This is a fine place to stop and watch the sailboats glide by. Via Marina curves around the entrance channel and enters a densely built area of apartments and condominiums until it reaches Admiralty Way.

At the corner of Admiralty Way and Via Marina is a **(4)** public park with facilities and a small protected beach with a children's swimming area.

Turn right onto Admiralty. At 5.5 miles you will pass the **(5) Bird Sanctuary** on the left and the **Marina City Towers** on the right.

Follow Admiralty to Mindanao Way and turn right. Continue to the end of the street where you will find the entrance to **(6) Burton Chace Park**. The well-maintained park has picnic areas, soft grassy knolls, facilities, and a tower to climb from where you can watch the boats in the marina.

Return to Admiralty and turn right to the next peninsula, Fiji Way. Go right again to **(7) Fisherman's Village**, a place for shopping and strolling.

Follow Fiji back to Admiralty and go left. At the corner of Admiralty and Via Marina, go right. Go to Washington Street and turn left. Go a few blocks to Pacific and turn right. At Rose Avenue, turn right, go one block to Main Street, and turn left.

(8) Main Street, beginning near Marine Street and continuing almost to Pico is a delightful small shopping and dining area. Park in the city lots west of Main Street. To return to downtown LA on the Santa Monica Fwy (I

10), follow Main Street to Pico, turn right, and at Lincoln Blvd, turn left. The freeway intersects Lincoln in 2 blocks.

Beaches South

Time:	**6-8 hours**
Mileage:	**115 miles round trip from Civic Center**
Area:	**The *Gold Coast* beaches of Orange County from Newport Beach to Laguna Beach, and the new planned community of Irvine. An alternate route goes down to the Mission San Juan Capistrano.**

Take the Santa Ana Fwy (I 5) south from Civic Center. An alternate route is the San Diego Fwy (I 405). At 34 miles, take the Newport Fwy (I 55) south. Go to the end of the freeway, where it becomes Newport Blvd, a 4- to 6-lane street. Continue straight through Costa Mesa into **(1) Newport Beach**.

At 44 miles, get into the left lane and go over the bridge onto the **(2) Newport Peninsula**. You'll notice the yacht anchorage in the **Lido Channel** on your left as you pass over the bridge. Continue on Newport Blvd, which curves to the left as it follows the penin-sula. Opposite the **(3) Newport Pier**, Newport Blvd becomes Balboa Blvd.

At Palm Street, turn into the parking lot for a visit to the **(4) Balboa Pier** to enjoy the ocean view and a breath of air. You can also rent roller skates here.

Walk across Balboa Blvd into the **Fun Zone** for some snacking and a visit to the **(5) Balboa Pavilion**.

To get to the ferry to **(6) Balboa Island**, follow the signs from the parking lot to the crossing. The 3-minute cruise across the **Main Channel** can be made

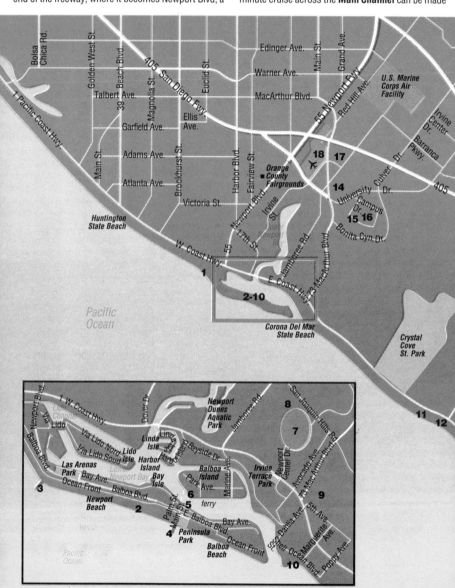

aboard the *Admiral*, *Commodore*, or *Captain*. When you disembark at Agate Avenue, continue straight for 2 blocks to Park Avenue. Go right and travel through a neighborhood of shipshape homes to Marine Avenue. Go left on Marine, through the center of the business district, and over Back Bay Channel on a little bridge. Continue straight a short distance to Bayside Drive, veer left, and continue up the hill to East Coast Hwy. Go right, past the **(7) Fashion Island Shopping Center**.

For a detour to shop or to visit the **(8) Newport Harbor Art Museum**, go left at Newport Center Drive.

Continue straight on East Coast Hwy, past the **(9) Sherman Foundation Gardens**, and turn right on Marguerite Avenue. Go through beautifully manicured residential streets to Ocean Blvd. Turn left and park near the hilly knoll that tops **(10) Corona del Mar State Beach**. This is a beautiful seaside area, rocky on the south, sandy cove on the north, with a superb view. There is excellent swimming in the northern waters that are protected by the east jetty of the Newport Harbor entrance.

Follow Ocean to Poppy Avenue and turn left back to East Coast Hwy. Turn right onto the Coast Hwy and continue south. The stretch between Poppy and Laguna Beach has rolling golden hills coming down to meet the undeveloped beach, giving a last glimpse of what the coast was like prior to the 20th century. **(11) Cameo Cove**, just north of Laguna Beach city limits, is a breathtaking scene of dark rock promontory and emerald-green water.

At approximately 55 miles, you enter **(12) Laguna Beach**, an area known for beautiful scenery and *scenic* artists. Go left at **Forest Avenue**. Park to spend some time strolling down pleasant shop-lined streets, or cross the Coast Hwy to follow the Pacific Ocean along the boardwalk.

To return to LA from this point, go north a short distance on Coast Hwy to Broadway. Go right to Laguna Canyon Road (133), and then to the San Diego Fwy (I 405).

At this point, hardy souls with unflagging energy may wish to continue south to **(13) Mission San Juan Capistrano**. Follow Pacific Coast Hwy down to Del Obispo Street, which is just past Dana Point. Go left to Ortega Hwy (74). Go right to the mission at the intersection of Ortega Hwy and Camino Capistrano. To return to LA from Capistrano, take the San Diego Fwy (I 5) north from its intersection with Ortega Hwy.

To continue back up to **(14) Irvine** from Laguna Beach, return north on Pacific Coast Hwy to MacArthur Blvd (Route 73). Go right.

Lovers of trees, education, and/or architecture may wish to detour to the **(15) University of California at Irvine**. From MacArthur, go right on University Drive to Campus Drive. Go right on Campus to Bridge Road. Go right on Bridge to North Circle View Drive, then turn left. The **(16) Administration Building** and **Visitor Center** are located on the right-hand side of North Circle View Drive.

Meanwhile, the future may be taking shape in the **(17) Irvine Industrial Park**, located on both sides of MacArthur Blvd. The simple, monolithic shapes of these structures contain business concerns whose products are invisible in many cases: computer software, technological systems, and other forms of up-to-the-minute know-how.

(18) John Wayne Airport, located on the left of MacArthur Blvd, is one of the busiest small-craft airports in the nation.

To return to LA, go to the San Diego Fwy (I 405) on MacArthur Blvd and head north.

It was more like Egypt, the suburbs of Cairo, or Alexandria than anything in Europe. We arrived at the Bel Air Hotel—very Egyptian with a hint of Addis Abada
Evelyn Waugh, 1947

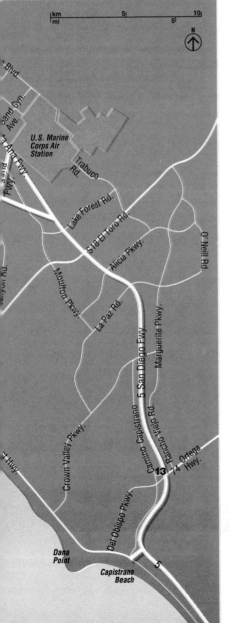

Beaches South

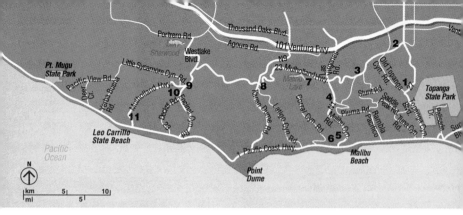

Mountain Areas

Time:	Minimum tour: 2¹/₂ hours
	Maximum tour: 8 hours
Mileage:	Minimum: 47 miles round trip from Ocean Avenue and Pacific Coast High way in Santa Monica.
	Maximum: 100 miles with alternate routes round trip from Ocean Avenue and Pacific Coast Highway.
Area:	Some of the most scenic but easily driven coastal mountain routes, showing rugged mountains and beautiful ocean views.

Begin at Pacific Coast Hwy where the Santa Monica Fwy (I 10) ends near the Santa Monica Pier. Follow Coast Hwy north for 5.5 miles to Topanga Canyon Blvd.

Turn right on Topanga Canyon Blvd. The narrow 2-lane highway winds past a sycamore-shaded creek at the base of chaparral-covered cliffs. As the road ascends into the hills you will see spectacular rock formations and abruptly tilted cliffs.

At about 10 miles is the main part of the rustic community of **(1) Topanga**. The narrowness and sinuous winding of the road sometimes slows traffic—particularly on weekends.

At 15.2 miles the road descends to a panoramic view of the San Fernando Valley, and the **Simi** and **Chatsworth hills**. This is a good place to stop and appreciate the huge expanse of the valley's wide territory.

At 16.9 miles turn left on **(2) Mulholland Drive**. A great deal of housing construction is going on in this once rural area.

At this point, carsick travelers or those who wish to make only a short trip can continue straight on Topanga Canyon Blvd to Woodland Hills and the Ventura Fwy (101), which takes you back to LA.

At 17.5 miles make a left near the Woodland Plaza Shopping Center to continue onto **Mulholland**

Highway. The road widens to 4 lanes near Daguerre Road, but narrows back to 2 soon afterwards.

At about 19 miles the intersection of Old Topanga Canyon Rd and Mulholland Hwy is confusing, but continue straight ahead and soon a sign will appear confirming that you are indeed on Mulholland Hwy.

(3) Steep rock, jagged hills, and abrupt terrain become an interesting backdrop for the road around 23.7 miles.

Breathtakingly beautiful scenery and rock formations with all the drama of an old Western movie—probably because many were filmed out here—begin at around 25.5 miles.

At 27 miles is a stoplight intersection for Las Virgenes Road. Turn left. The 2-lane highway passes rugged wide-open vistas of classic western scenery and horseback-riding trails.

At 28.7 miles is **(4) Tapia Park**, a wilderness park along Malibu Creek with great hiking paths through fields and wooded areas. This is an ideal place for picnicking and relaxing.

At about 30 miles a series of geologically wondrous gorges and steep valley formations begins. Many turnouts provide a chance to stop and examine the intricate stratification of rock layers, all tilted upward in various directions.

At 32.5 miles, several palm trees announce the **(5) Hughes Research Laboratories**, where the first practical laser was built. The lab is at the peak of a hill and just at the other side is a spectacular ocean view.

The road to **(6) Pepperdine College** soon appears. The intersection of Pacific Coast Hwy and Malibu Canyon Rd is at 33.4 miles. Turn left to return to Santa Monica.

Alternate tours:

At the intersection of Las Virgenes and Mulholland Hwy, continue straight on Mulholland and go west past **(7) Malibu Lake**.

At the intersection of N9 or Kanan Road and Mulholland Hwy, a detour can be made through the rugged scenery of Latigo Canyon by going south or left a short while on N9 and then turning left on **(8) Latigo Canyon Road**.

Mulholland Hwy (23) loses its state highway designation to **(9) Decker Road**. You can follow Decker (now state 23) south to the ocean from their **(10)** intersection, or continue west on Mulholland, skirting the Ventura County line until Mulholland takes you onto **(11)** Pacific Coast Hwy (1) at Leo Carrillo State Beach.

Follow Pacific Coast Hwy back south to Santa Monica.

Time:	8 hours
Mileage:	60 miles by car from the intersection of Routes 210 and 2 to the intersection of Routes 14 and 210; 4 miles on foot.
Area:	A vigorous driving and hiking expedition that traverses the San Gabriels from La Canada to the Antelope Valley. The hike visits the Arroyo Seco Cascades.

From the Foothill Fwy (I 210), take the Angeles Crest Hwy (2) north into the mountains for 10.5 miles. At approximately .5 mile past the intersection of Route 2 and the Angeles Forest Highway (N3), turn right off Route 2 at the Switzer Campground sign. Follow the road a winding 1/4 mile and park near the picnic area, following the stream for 1 mile to the **Commodore Switzer Trail Camp**. The trail then crosses the stream, whose waters abruptly drop off into a 50-foot fall. Follow the trail uphill to a fork. Take the left branch of the fork into the gorge beneath the falls. To return, retrace your steps. Drive back to the intersection of Route 2 and Angeles Forest Hwy (N3). Go right for 30 minutes to the intersection with the Antelope Valley Fwy (14). Go west to the Foothill Fwy (I 210), a distance of 20 miles.

Time:	2-8 hours
Mileage:	30 miles by car round trip from the Foothill Freeway (I 210); .5 to 16 miles by foot.
Area:	Hikes within Eaton Canyon, ranging from the 1/8-mile Arroyo Nature Trail, through the natural rock pools of Upper Eaton Canyon, to a 16-mile overnight jaunt to Mt. Wilson.

The starting point may be reached by car or bus.

Bus: Take No. 79 north on Olive Street in downtown LA to the intersection of Huntington Drive and San Marino Avenue. Transfer to No. 264. Get off at New York Avenue and Altadena Drive. Walk one block north on the east side of Altadena to the gate of Eaton Canyon Park.

Car: From the Foothill Freeway (I 210), go left on Altadena Drive to No. 1750, which is the entrance to Eaton Canyon Park. Go through the gates to the **McCurdy Nature Center**, 1/4 mile down the path. The center has brochures for the self-guided **Arroyo Nature Trail**, as well as information on the other trails in the park and canyon. Among the possibilities are a .5-mile hike to **Eaton Falls**; a 3-mile climb to the **Henninger Flat Campground and Ranger Station**; a 3-mile excursion to the natural stone pools in upper **Eaton Canyon**; and for those who bring their pajamas, a 16-mile overnighter to **Mt. Wilson**.

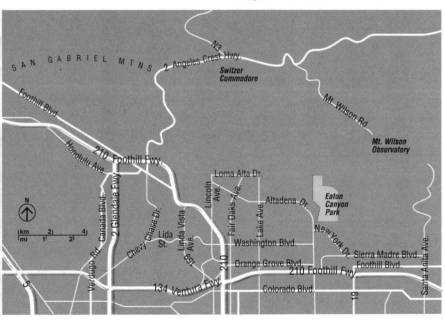

The San Gabriel mountains tower above the city to the north. A century ago, **John Muir** described them as among the *most rigidly inaccessible* he had ever trod. Today, these guardians are laced with trails and roads. The visitor who tours by car will see spectacular vistas from the Angeles Crest and Angeles Forest highways, but the serenity and majesty of the range is revealed only to those who explore on foot. Roads can be blocked by snow in winter. Information and maps are available from the **Ranger Station** in Oak Grove Park off Oak Grove Drive in La Canada (818/790.1151), or from the **U.S. Forest Service Information center**(701 N. Santa Anita Avenue, Arcadia, 818/574.1613). Hikers are no longer required to have entry permits, but

are strongly urged to advise friends of their itinerary in case of accident. All visitors should bring water and take special precautions during the fire season—from June to December.

Don't touch the shiny clusters of trilobed (3) serrated leaves; they are poison oak. The rattlesnakes that live in this wilderness strike only to protect themselves.

The foregoing cautions are given not to frighten, but in the belief that it is easiest to enjoy when you're prepared.

Architecture Tours

LA has always been a mecca for architects with a strong sense of individualism and style. The following 4 driving tours take you by LA's best architecture, from highrises to houses, and from the cultural to the fantastical.

The architectural heritage of Los Angeles is rich and varied. This day-long pilgrimage will take you in a broad sweep of the area to see some of LA's best architectural landmarks.

It is a rewarding journey and one during which—in typical LA fashion—you hardly have to leave your car. The tour is approximately 46 miles long and takes at least 5 hours. **Private residences should be viewed only from the street**. Begin in Pasadena, an area rich in fine turn-of-the-century domestic architecture.

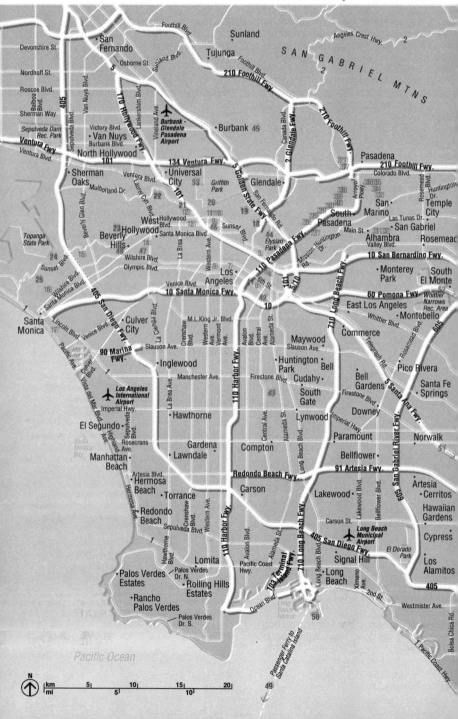

lightly north of the interchange of the Long Beach (710) and the Ventura (134) freeways, or north from the Orange Grove Boulevard exit of the Pasadena Freeway (110) is the (1) **Gamble House** (1908) at 4 Westmoreland Place, a large vacation bungalow by Pasadena Craftsman architects **Charles** and **Henry Greene** (Th-Su noon-3PM). All along (2) **Arroyo Terrace**, the street to the left of the Gamble House, other houses by Greene and Greene can be seen. Take Orange Grove Boulevard south to the Pasadena Freeway (110). Go south on the freeway, stay to the right and connect with the Hollywood Freeway (101) going north. Exit at Echo Park-Glendale Boulevard and turn right at the end of the exit onto Bellevue Avenue. Turn left (north) on Edgeware Road East and turn left again on Carroll Avenue. This is the (3) **Carroll Avenue Historic District**: the 1300 block of Carroll Avenue, lined with late Victorian homes. Take Edgeware south to Temple Street, turn left (east), continue into downtown and turn right on Spring Street. At 3rd Street turn right and park nearby, because the Victorian (4) **Bradbury Building** (1893), at the corner of 3rd and Broadway (304 S. Broadway), must be seen from the inside to appreciate its interior court (M, Th, Sa 10AM-3PM). Continue on 3rd and turn left (south) on Figueroa Street. You will pass the arresting mirror-glass (5) **Westin Bonaventure Hotel** (1977-78) by **John Portman** on the left at 350 S. Figueroa Street. Continue on Figueroa. The (6) **Linder Plaza** (1977), at 888 W 6th Street is a handsome contemporary tower in gray metal by **Honnold, Reibsamen & Rex**. Take Figueroa to Wilshire Boulevard and turn right (west) to see some moderne commercial buildings. Visible at a distance is the tan terra cotta and green copper-trimmed tower of the (7) **Bullocks Wilshire Department Store** (1929) at 3050 Wilshire Boulevard by **John** and **Donald B. Parkinson**. Further west is the (8) **Wiltern Center Building** (1931), 3790 Wilshire Boulevard, a zigzag moderne complex of turquoise terra cotta that includes a theater, shops, and offices. Turn right (north) on Western Avenue and turn right (east) at Hollywood Boulevard. Enter Barnsdall Park on the right, before the intersection with Vermont Avenue. Here is **Frank Lloyd Wright**'s first Los Angeles project, the (9) **Hollyhock House** 1917-20, Tu-Th 10AM-1PM; Sa and 1st 3 Su of every month noon-3PM). Return to Hollywood going right (east) and immediately turn left at Vermont Avenue. Cross Los Feliz Boulevard, and where Vermont forks, go to the left on Glendower Avenue. At 2607 Glendower Avenue is Wright's stunning concrete-block (10) **Ennis-Brown House** (1924) with its spectacular setting in the hills. Return to Vermont and at Franklin Avenue turn right (west). On the right, at 5121 Franklin, is the dramatic (11) **Sowden House** by **Lloyd Wright**, Frank Lloyd Wright's son. Continue on Franklin following the jog to the left at Highland Avenue. Three blocks past Highland Avenue, turn left (south) on Orange Drive and come up the back way to **Meyer and Holler**'s extravagant (12) **Grauman's** (now **Mann's**) **Chinese Theatre** (1927), at 6925 Hollywood Boulevard. Turn left onto Hollywood Boulevard for a better view.

Turn right (south) onto Highland and turn left (east) on Sunset Boulevard. At 6671 Sunset Boulevard is the (13) **Crossroads of the World**—international theme shops designed by **Frank Derrah** in 1936 as a tourist attraction. Turn right (south) on Cahuenga Boulevard and right again (west) on Santa Monica Boulevard.

Continue on to San Vicente Boulevard and turn left (south). The large blue-and-green glass structures at the corner of San Vicente and Melrose Avenue are the (14) **Pacific Design Center** (1975). The building, with an interior court and shops, was designed by **Cesar Pelli** for **Victor Gruen and Associates**. Return to San Vicente going north to Sunset and turn left (west). Continue on Sunset past UCLA and turn left at Veteran Avenue. At the first street, turn right on Cashmere Street and right again on Greenfield Avenue. **Rudolph Schindler's** (15) **Tischler House** (1949), with its angular facade, is at 175 Greenfield Avenue. Take Greenfield to the end of the block and turn left (west) on Sunset. At Bundy Drive turn left (south) and at Montana Avenue turn right. Turn left on 22nd Street. At Washington Avenue and 22nd is the dramatic (16) **Gehry House**, a 1977-78 remodeling of an older house using corrugated steel, wood, and glass, by architect **Frank Gehry**. Go north on Washington Avenue to 26th Street and turn right. At Broadway turn right and at Ocean Avenue (Neilson Way) turn left. In order to enter the one-way street of Hollister Avenue, take a left turn on Strand Street and right turns on Main Street and Hollister. To conclude the tour, view the white cubistic (17) **Horatio West Court Apartments** (1919) at 140 Hollister Avenue, by **Irving Gill**, one of California's leading architects of the modern movement. To get back to the Santa Monica Freeway take Ocean Avenue (Neilson Way) left (west) to Pico Boulevard and turn right. At Fourth Street turn left and you will see signs for the Santa Monica Freeway toward downtown.

LA living has been established in style by trendsetting architects. This tour is a sampling of the finest houses designed by modern architects with the addition of a few excellent Revival-style homes found from Silver Lake west through Hollywood to Santa Monica.

The tour is approximately 37 miles long and takes at least 3 hours. **Private residences should be viewed only from the street**. Begin in Silver Lake. Turn north on Reno Street from Sunset Boulevard onto Silver Lake Boulevard. (Silver Lake cannot be entered directly from Sunset.) Follow Silver Lake to the right around the lake. At 2300 Silver Lake Boulevard is the (18) **Neutra House** (1933; rebuilt 1963), an International Style house by Viennese immigrant **Richard Neutra** (Private residence). Down the street are a number of other houses by Neutra at Nos. 2250, 2242, 2240, 2238, 2226, 2218, 2210, and 2200. (Private residences.) Continue north on Silver Lake and turn left at its end onto Glendale Boulevard. At the fork go left on Rowena Avenue and at Los Feliz Boulevard turn left. Two blocks further, at Commonwealth Avenue, turn right (north). Turn left at the third block on Dundee Drive. At the end of the street is Neutra's (19) **Lovell House** (1929), 4616 Dundee Drive, a classic International Style house cantilevered on a hillside. (Private residence.) Return to Los Feliz and turn right (west). At Vermont Avenue turn right and veer to the left to take Glendower Avenue. Winding up the hill you will reach **Frank Lloyd**

Wright's spectacular concrete-block house, the (10) **Ennis-Brown House** (1924) at 2607 Glendower Avenue. (Private residence.)

Return to Vermont and turn right at Hollywood Boulevard. On the left is Barnsdall Park. See Frank Lloyd Wright's first Los Angeles project, the (9)Hollyhock House (1917-20, Tu-Th 10AM-1PM; Sa and 1st 3 Su of every month noon-3PM).

Return to Hollywood and turn left. At Normandie Avenue turn right (north) and at Franklin Avenue turn left (west). Lloyd Wright's dramatic concrete-and-stucco (11)Sowden House (1926) is at 5121 Franklin Avenue. (Private residence.) Continue on Franklin and turn right (north) on Western Avenue. Take it to its end where it veers right connecting with Los Feliz. Get in the left lane in preparation to turn left at the first street, Fern Dell Drive. Turn left again to Black Oak Drive. Turn left on E. Live Oak Drive and right on Verde Oak Drive. Veer to the left on Valley Oak Drive. At 5699 Valley Oak Drive is Lloyd Wright's spacious copper-trimmed (20) Samuel Novarro House (1922-24). (Private residence.) Retrace back to Los Feliz and Western turn left (south). At Franklin turn right and continue past the jog to the left at Highland Avenue. Three blocks past Highland turn right on Sycamore Avenue and drive up to the (21)Yamashiro Restaurant at 1999 N. Sycamore Avenue. The restaurant, designed as an authentic Chinese palace by Franklin Small in 1913, was formerly the home of art dealers Adolphe and Eugene Bernheimer. Return to Franklin, turn right (west), then left on Sierra Bonita and right on Hollywood. At the end of this street you will automatically enter Laurel Canyon up to Mulholland Drive and turn right (east). At Torreyson Place turn right. From here you can see the (22) Malin House, known as the Chemosphere House, a private residence designed by John Lautner in 1960. Return to Mulholland and turn left (south) on Laurel Canyon. When you reach Sunset, turn right (west). At the intersection of Cory Avenue and Sunset, take the small street to the right on Sunset Boulevard, going straight onto Doheny Road. The (23)Doheny Mansion is located at 501 N. Doheny Road in Greystone Park. Its major entrance is on the right side on Loma Vista. The expansive English Tudor mansion, designed by Charles Kauffman in 1923 for oil millionaire Edward Doheny, is owned by the city of Beverly Hills.

Return to Loma Vista and go south. At Mountain Drive veer left and turn right (west) at Sunset. Continue on Sunset and pass UCLA. Turn left on Veteran Avenue and turn right at the first block, Cashmere Street. Turn right on Greenfield Avenue and see Viennese immigrant architect Rudolph Schindler's ingenious (15) Tischler House (1949) at 175 Greenfield Avenue. (Private residence.) Continue north on the street to return to Sunset and turn left (west). At the Bundy Drive-Kenter Avenue intersection turn right onto Kenter, and at the second block on the right, Skyewiay Road, turn right. Frank Lloyd Wright's redwood-and-stucco (24) Sturgis House (1939) is at 449 Skyewiay Road. Return to Sunset and turn right (west). One block past Mandeville Canyon, turn right at Riviera Ranch Road. Here and on Old Oak Road are architect Cliff May's original "ranch houses" popularized throughout America during the '40s and '50s. Return to Sunset and turn left (east). Turn right at Rockingham Avenue.

Architecture Tours

Across 26th Street and after a slight jog to the right, Rockingham becomes La Mesa Drive. From 26th to 19th Streets, La Mesa is draped by huge Moreton fig trees, and in the 2100 to 1900 block of La Mesa are a number of (25)Spanish revival homes by John Byers from the 1920s-'30s. They can be seen at Nos. 2153, 2101, 2034, and 1923 La Mesa Drive. (Private residences.) At the end of the road is San Vicente Boulevard. Take it to the left one block and continue on 20th Street, jogging left at Montana Avenue. Turn left on Washington Avenue. At 22nd Street you will see a dramatic house on the southwest corner, the (16) Gehry House, 1002 22nd Street, which will conclude the tour. The Dutch Colonial house was remodeled in 1977-78, by architect Frank O. Gehry, using corrugated metal, wood, and glass. (Private residence.) You can return to the Santa Monica Freeway by going south on Washington. At 20th turn right to connect with the freeway.

The strongest cultural influence on Los Angeles architecture has been the Spanish tradition. This tour views a number of Spanish Colonial, Mexican, and Spanish Mission Revival buildings. It also concentrates on the Craftsman Movement from the turn of the century.

The Pasadena area abounds in fine architecture of many styles, but the English-based Arts and Crafts Movement found one of its strongest American outlets here. This tour is approximately 19 miles long and takes at least 4 hours. Private residences should be viewed only from the street. Begin this tour at a location adjacent to the Pasadena Freeway (110). On the west side of the freeway at Avenue 43 exit is the (26) Lummis House (1898-1910), 200 E. Avenue 43. The boulder home was built by Charles F. Lummis, enthusiast of the Spanish, Mexican, and Indian heritage of Southern California (tours W-Su 1-4PM). Across the freeway, (27)Heritage Square is a bright cluster of Victorian mansions in various stages of renovation. Take Avenue 43 left (west) to Figueroa Street and turn right. At 4603 N. Figueroa Street is the (28)Casa de Adobe, a 1917 reconstruction of a Mexican adobe house that is part of the Southwest Museum. Continue on Figueroa going northeast to Arroyo Glen and turn right. At 6211 Arroyo Glen is the (29)San Encino Abbey (1909-1925), a private residence built by Clyde Brown in a combination of Spanish Mission and European Gothic styles. Return to Figueroa and turn right, continuing northeast. At York Boulevard, turn right (south). The (30)Judson Studios are located at 200 S. Avenue 66. These turn-of-the-century studios are famous for their Craftsman glass-and-mosaic-work production. Return to York and turn right. Continue on as the road becomes Pasadena Avenue and then Monterey Road. At Huntington Drive jog left and turn right (south) on San Marino and at a fork in the road go to the right onto Santa Anita Street. At the corner of Santa Anita and Mission Drive is the (31)Mission Playhouse (1927), 320 S. Mission Drive, designed by Arthur Benton to appear similar to the Mission San Antonio in Monterey County. Go east one block to visit the (32)San Gabriel Mission at 537 W. Mission Drive, the fourth mission established by Fr. Serra. The restored mission was originally built between 1791 and 1805 (daily 9:30AM-4PM). Go north on Serra Drive and turn left on San Marino Avenue. Turn left on (33)Lombardy Road and notice the Spanish Revival homes, all private residences, in the 1700 to 2000 blocks, especially No.1750 by architect **Roland Coate, Sr**; No. 1779 by **George Washington Smith**, at the corner of Allen Avenue; 665 Allen Avenue, another Smith house; and 2 **Wallace Neff** houses at Nos. 1861 and 2035. Turn right (north) on Sierra Bonita Avenue and go one block to California Boulevard. Before you is the campus of **(34)California Institute of Technology**. The oldest buildings, from the 1930s, were designed by **Gordon Kauffman** in the Spanish Renaissance and Spanish Baroque styles. Note especially the **(34)Atheneum Club** facing Sierra Bonita and the adjacent dorms seen as you turn left (west) onto California Boulevard. Continue on California to El Molino Avenue and turn right (north).

At 37 S. El Molino Avenue is the Spanish Colonial **(35)Pasadena Playhouse** (1924-25) by architect **Elmer Grey**. Turn left at the corner on Colorado Boulevard and at Raymond Avenue turn left. One block away is Green Street. Turn left and you will be in front of the large turretted Spanish Colonial **(36)Green Hotel** (1890-99) by architect **Frederick Roehrig**. Turn left on Arroyo Parkway and at Colorado Boulevard turn left (west). Turn right on Orange Grove Boulevard. Just past Walnut Street you will see a small street flanking Orange Grove Boulevard on the left. This is Westmoreland Place. At No. 4 is the **(1)Gamble House** (1908) by famous Pasadena Craftsman architects **Charles** and **Henry Greene** (Th-Su noon-3PM). To the left of the house is **(2)Arroyo Terrace**, which has a number of Greene and Greene houses. All are private residences. Especially note Nos. 368, 370, 400, 408, 424, and 440, built between 1902 and 1913. Return to Orange Grove Boulevard and turn right. At Holly Street, one block away, turn right to Linda Vista Avenue then go one block to **(37)El Circulo Drive**; turn left. At Nos. 65 and 95 El Circulo are 2 rural Spanish Revival homes designed by amateur architect **Edward Fowler** in 1927. Backtrack to Linda Vista Avenue. Turn right (north) to Holly Street and turn right (east). At Orange Grove Boulevard turn right (south). Turn right at California Boulevard and see the **(38)Cheesewright House** (1910) at 686 W. California Boulevard, a Craftsman house appearing like an English snuggery with its thatch roof. At Arroyo Boulevard turn left (south). See the **(39)Batchelder House** (1909), 626 S. Arroyo Boulevard, built by **Ernest Batchelder**, Pasadena craftsman and renowned tilemaker. Conclude this tour with the finest example of a Spanish Monterey Revival house, the home at **(40)** 850 S. Arroyo Boulevard (1927), by **Donald McMurray**. (Private residence.) To return to the Pasadena or Ventura freeways, turn left at Grand Avenue and right on Bellefontaine Street to get to Orange Grove. From Orange Grove you can connect with the Pasadena Freeway (110) by turning right, and with the Ventura Freeway (134) by turning left.

This tour is a sampling of some of LA's fantastic architecture that ranges from the serious to the whimsical.

A bit of fantasy abounds on almost every street of LA, so along the way you might note additional constructed visions that have adopted the styles of other areas and other cultures, or present straightforward indulgence and delight in commercialism, futurism, and personal eccentricities. The route is around the city in an extremely broad sweep from downtown to Watts,

and north to Glendale ending in Beverly Hills. The tour is approximately 52 miles long and takes at least 4 hours. **Private residences should be viewed only from the street.** In downtown LA the shimmering futuristic apparition at 350 S. Figueroa Street is the **(5) Westin Bonaventure Hotel** (1977) by architect **John Portman**. Take Figueroa south to Olympic Boulevard and turn left. At Hill Street turn right to see the **(41) Mayan Theater**, now the **Mayan Nightclub** at 1038 S. Hill Street. The pre-Columbian facade was designed by **Morgan, Walls and Clements** in 1927. Continue on Hill to Pico Boulevard and turn left (east). At the end of Pico you will come to Central Avenue and the shiplike **(42)Coca-Cola Building** (1935-37) at 1334 S. Central Avenue with its enormous Coke bottles at the entrance to the plant. Turn right onto Central and follow the signs on the right to enter the Santa Monica Freeway (I 10) going west (to Santa Monica). After a short distance connect with the Harbor Freeway (110) South (headed toward San Pedro).

Turn off at the Manchester Avenue exit and go left (east). (Manchester turns into Firestone Boulevard.) At Elm Street turn right (Elm turns into Wilmington Avenue), and at the intersection of 107th Street, turn right. There you will see the unique monument, the **(43)Watts Towers** (1921-54) at 1765 E 107th Street. These are a personal vision made of broken tile, glass, and debris erected by an Italian immigrant tile-layer, **Sam Rodia**. Retrace back to the Harbor Freeway (110) and go north on the freeway (to LA-Pasadena) and connect with the Hollywood Freeway (101). Take the Hollywood Freeway west and get off after a short distance at the Echo Park-Glendale Boulevard exit. Take Echo Park north to Baxter Street and turn right. At Avon Street turn left (driving the streets around here is like taking a roller coaster ride). You will want to park and walk on the right (east) side of Avon to Avon Park Terrace. There you will see what seems to be an authentic Indian pueblo, the **(44) Atwater Bungalows** at 1431-33 Avon Park Terrace (1931), by **Robert Stacy-Judd**. Return to your car and at Baxter turn right. At Alvarado Street turn left and at Glendale turn right. Take Glendale to San Fernando Road and turn left. At Grandview Avenue turn right and take it to its end.

At the intersection of Mountain Street and Grandview you will enter the **Brand Library**, formerly the **(45) Brand House** (1902), an exotic East Indian and Moorish mansion now a public library. Return to Grandview and at San Fernando turn left. At Los Feliz Boulevard turn right. Turn left at Vermont Avenue and right onto Sunset Boulevard, you will pass the Indian **(46)Self-Realization Temple** at 4860 Sunset Boulevard and the **(13)Crossroads of the World** at 6621 Sunset Boulevard. This 1935 tourist attraction presents a ship sailing into a courtyard of shops representing various European countries. At Highland Avenue turn right and at Hollywood Boulevard turn left. At 6925 Hollywood Boulevard you will see **(12)** **Mann's** (formerly **Grauman's**) **Chinese Theatre**, an extravagant and exotic Chinese design from 1927. Continue west on Hollywood and at La Brea turn left.

At Santa Monica Boulevard turn right and at San Vicente Boulevard turn left (south). On the right, just north of Beverly Boulevard is the **(47) Tail-o-the-Pup** hot-dog stand, 329 San Vicente Boulevard. On the corner of the Beverly Center is the **Hard Rock Cafe**, with a 1959 Cadillac and palm tree on its roof (San Vicente and Beverly Blvds). Turn right on La Cienega Boulevard, right on Wilshire Boulevard, and continue west on it into Beverly Hills. Slightly before the intersection of Wilshire and Santa Monica turn right on Linden Drive. At Carmelita Avenue turn left. At the corner of Walden Drive and Carmelita is the **(48) Spadena House** (1921), 516 Walden Drive, a Hansel and Gretel cottage that was originally a combined movie set and production office, and may soon be moved back to Culver City. From Wilshire going west you can connect with the San Diego Freeway (I 405) to the Santa Monica Freeway (I 10).

This tour by no means covers all the fantasy architecture in Southern California. Interested viewers should also make it a point to see **(49) Avalon Casino, (50) Queen Mary, (50) Spruce Goose, (51) Crystal Cathedral, (51) Disneyland, (52) Drive-thru Donut**, and **(53) Hollywood Sign**,

LA Firsts

1881	1st issue of the *LA Times*.
1888	1st LA swimming pool: the LA Natatorium—a Swimming Bath.
1897	1st LA golf course—9 holes (tin cups) at Pico Blvd and Alvarado Street.
1901	1st discovery of La Brea fossils by Union Oil.
1902	1st movie house in the world: The Electric Theatre.
1903	1st Pacific Coast baseball league formed: Two teams—LA Angels and Hollywood Stars.
1905	1st directional traffic signs in LA erected by Southern California Automobile Club.
1906	1st Rose Bowl football game—declared too dangerous to repeat by Tournament Committee.
1906	1st LA escalator: Bullock's.
1912	1st LA gas station—located at Grand Ave and Washington Blvd: 8 cents/gallon.
1917	1st million-dollar movie contract signed by Mary Pickford.
1922	1st LA shopping center: A.W. Ross buys 18 acres of bean fields on Wilshire Blvd; begins "Miracle Mile."
1922	1st LA radio stations: KFI and KHJ.
1927	1st footprints at Grauman's Chinese Theatre: Norma Talmadge.
1927	1st LA Supermarket: Ralph's.
1928	1st Mickey Mouse.
1932	LA hosts its first Olympic Games
1940	1st LA freeway: Arroyo Seco Parkway.
1944	1st use of the word *smog*.
1945	1st LA Baskin Robbins.
1948	1st Rolls-Royce dealer in the US: Peter Satori.
1949	1st *Emmy* awards.

Architecture Tours

1959	1st Barbie Doll manufactured by Mattel.
1973	1st black LA Mayor: Thomas Bradley.

Books and Periodicals

The Best of Los Angeles by **Gault Millau** (1990, Prentice Hall Press). Authoritative reviews of hotels, restaurants, and shops.

Zagat Los Angeles Restaurant Survey edited by **Merrill Schindler** and **Karen Berk** (1990, Zagat Survey, New York).

California Festivals by **Carl** and **Katie Landau** with **Kathy Kincade** (1989, Landau Communications, San Francisco).

The Movielover's Guide to Hollywood by **Richard Alleman** (1989, Harper & Row). Historic sites and lore of tinseltown.

Raymond Chandler's Los Angeles by **Elizabeth Ward** and **Alain Silver** (1988, Overlook). Quotations from LA's acerbic scribe juxtaposed with photos of real-life locations.

Bargain Hunting in Los Angeles by **Barbara Partridge** (1987, Peregrine Smith Books).

Happy Birthday, Hollywood by **Michael Webb** (1987, Motion Picture and Television Fund, LA). A hundred years of movie history, and the town that became a symbol of the industry.

LA Lost and Found by **Sam Hall Kaplan** (1987, Crown). Outstanding photographs by **Julius Schulman** accompany an architectural history of the city.

The Magic of Neon by **Michael Webb** (1987, Peregrine Smith Books). Follies that have survived and the renaissance of neon on Melrose Avenue.

Architecture in Los Angeles by **David Gebhard** and **Robert Winter** (1985, Peregrine Smith Books). Future editions of this indispensable guide will cover all of Southern California.

Inventing the Dream: California Through the Progressive Era by **Kevin Starr** (1985, Oxford University Press). Chapters on the growth of Southern California, Pasadena, and the movies, plus an excellent bibliography.

The City Observed: Los Angeles a Guide to its Architecture and Landscapes by **Charles Moore, Peter Becker**, and **Regula Campbell** (1984, Vintage Books).

Trails of the Angeles: 100 Hikes in the San Gabriels by **John W. Robinson** (1984, Wilderness Press, Berkeley).

California People by **Carol Dunlap** (1982, Peregrine Smith Books). Short biographies of men and women who made LA and the rest of the state what it is, from **Earl C. Anthony** to **Frank Zappa**.

LA Freeway: an Appreciative Essay by **David Brodsky** (1981, University of California).

California Crazy: Roadside Vernacular Architecture by **Jim Heimann** and **Rip George** (1980, Chronicle). An amazing collection of follies, nearly all of which have now been demolished.

Hollywood: the Pioneers by **Kevin Brownlow** and **John Kobal** (1979, Knopf). A fascinating anthology of pictures and text on the silent movies.

Los Angeles: Biography of a City edited by **John** and **LaRess Caughey** (1977, University of California). Brilliant anthology of writings on LA, grouped by topic.

Southern California: An Island on the Land by **Carey McWilliams** (1973, Peregrine Smith Books). An impassioned exposé of the dark side of the dream.

Los Angeles: the Architecture of Four Ecologies by **Reyner Banham** (1971, Penguin Books). An approving look at LA by a maverick English architectural historian years before it became fashionable.

Walking and driving tours of LA (illustrated fliers published by the LA Conservancy).

Fiction: Writers and journalists flocked to Hollywood with the coming of the talkies and bit the hand that fed them. The classic put-down is **Nathanael West**'s *Day of the Locust* (1939). **Budd Schulberg**'s *What Makes Sammy run?* (1941) is a devastating portrait of greed and chicanery by a movie industry insider. **F. Scott Fitzgerald**'s *The Last Tycoon* (published posthumously in 1941) is a romanticized portrait of **Irving Thalberg**, MGM's boy wonder. **Evelyn Waugh** was invited by MGM to discuss a movie version of *Brideshead Revisited*; the visit yielded the funniest-ever poison-pen letter to LA, *The Loved One*. **Raymond Chandler** and **James M. Cain** created memorable portraits of Depression-era LA, as did **John Fante** (*Dreams from Bunker Hill*). **Joan Didion** (*Play it as it Lays, The White Album*) and screenwriter-husband, **John Gregory Dunne** (*The Studio*) continue the tradition.

Periodicals: *LA Style* carries some of the city's sharpest reviews of restaurants, cutting-edge music and fashion, architecture, and design. *Angeles* takes a gentler approach in its coverage of residential design and the visual arts. *LA Weekly* seems torn between compulsive consumerism and outspoken radicalism, but is valuable for its comprehensive listings of movies, concerts, and theater.

Films on LA

Early moviemakers shot in the streets, making everyday life a part of the action. The **Keystone Kops** comedies, **Harold Lloyd**'s *Safety Last* (1923), and **Laurel and Hardy**'s *Big Business* (1926) document the city as it was. Some of the best later features include:

Miracle Mile (1989) Wilshire Boulevard has never looked so good as in this confused eve-of-Armageddon drama.

Tequilla Sunrise (1989) Seductive images of life in the fast lane in South Bay beach communities enhance **Robert Towne**'s thriller.

The Morning After (1986) New York director **Sidney Lumet** captures the texture of LA's commercial strip and apartment buildings; an aspect of the city that is rarely filmed.

Ruthless People (1986) Designer **Lilly Kilvert** exploits the surreal juxtapositions of LA architecture to comic effect.

Down and Out in Beverly Hills (1984) Feature-length version of the caricature of Beverly Hills in Woody Allen's *Annie Hall*.

Valley Girl (1983) Teenage morality drama that contrasts the white-bread Valley lifestyle with the sleazy energy of Hollywood Boulevard at night.

Blade Runner (1982) **Ridley Scott**'s fantasy of LA in 2019 as a megalopolis of 90 million people choking on smog makes inspired use of the Bradbury Building and **Wright**'s Ennis-Brown House.

E.T. The Extra Terrestrial (1982) TV-perfect suburbia, as exemplified by the San Fernando Valley, is the setting of this and other **Steven Spielberg** movies.

True Confessions (1981) **Robert De Niro** plays a priest and **Robert Duvall** a cop in this inventive re-creation of LA in the '40s.

Annie Hall (1977) For **Woody Allen**, the only cultural advantage of LA is turning right on red—and he can't drive.

Shampoo (1975) Beverly Hills as seen by hip hairdresser **Warren Beatty**, and designed by **Richard Sylbert** as a study in narcissism.

Chinatown (1974) **Robert Towne**'s script and the white-and-burnt-ochre images capture the true look and feeling of LA in the '30s.

The Long Goodbye (1973) The classic **Raymond Chandler** movies used few locations; **Elliott Gould**'s *Philip Marlowe* ranges all over town.

Save the Tiger (1973) **Jack Lemmon**'s finest performance as a man at the end of his tether, set in LA's garment district.

Zabriskie Point (1970) **Michelangelo Antonioni** sees LA as a pop icon, dominated by billboards and Farmer John's pig murals.

The Loved One (1965) **Liberace** plays a funeral director in this uneven adaptation of **Evelyn Waugh**'s satire of Forest Lawn.

Smog (1962) LA through the eyes of a visiting Italian lawyer: an alienating city of cracked stucco, empty vistas, nodding oil wells, and **Pierre Koenig**'s Stahl House in the Hollywood Hills.

Touch of Evil (1958) **Orson Welles** uses the arcades and crumbling canals of Venice at night to conjure a sense of fear and corruption in a Mexican border town.

No Down Payment (1957) The suburban dream turns sour in a new development in the West San Fernando Valley.

Kiss Me Deadly (1955) LA's mean streets, Malibu, and a decaying Bunker Hill are expressive backdrops for **Micky Spillane**'s thriller.

Rebel Without a Cause (1955) The Griffith Park Observatory and a deserted house in the hills are sets for angst-ridden **James Dean**.

Sunset Boulevard (1950) **Gloria Swanson**'s *Norma Desmond* holds court in her crumbling mansion, and **William Holden**'s screenwriter escapes his creditors to end face-down in her pool.

Mildred Pearce (1945) In this adaptation of **James M. Cain**'s novel, Glendale, Pasadena and Malibu chart **Joan Crawford**'s social ascent.

Architecture Tours

A Star is Born (1937, 1954) Time capsules of the vintage movie landmarks, from the Coconut Grove to the Chinese to Malibu.

I

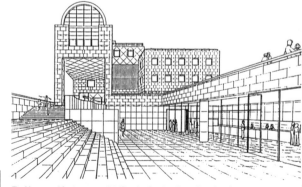

The Museum of Contemporary Art (Drawing Courtesy Gruen Associates)

Granada Building (Drawing Courtesy Carlos Diniz Associates)

LA Restaurant Index

Only restaurants with star ratings are listed below. All restaurants are listed alphabetically in the main index.

LA Hotel Index

LA Bests Index

Index